ECONOMIC CRIME IN RUSSIA

ECONOMIC CRIME IN RUSSIA

Edited by

Alena V. Ledeneva
Lecturer in Russian Politics and Society,
School of Slavonic and East European Studies,
University College London

and

Marina Kurkchiyan
North Fellow in the Sociology of Law,
Centre for Socio-Legal Studies, Oxford
and fellow of Keble College

KLUWER LAW INTERNATIONAL
THE HAGUE / LONDON / BOSTON

Library of Congress Cataloging-in-Publication Data is available.

ISBN 90-411-9782-6

Published by Kluwer Law International,
P.O. Box 85889, 2508 CN The Hague, The Netherlands

Sold and distributed in North, Central and South America
by Kluwer Law International,
675 Massachusetts Avenue, Cambridge, MA 02139, U.S.A.

In all other countries, sold and distributed
by Kluwer Law International, Distribution Centre,
P.O. Box 322, 3300 AH Dordrecht, The Netherlands

Cover illustration:
M. C. Escher's "Smaller and Smaller"
© 1999 Cordon Art B. V. – Baarn – Holland.
All rights reserved

Printed on acid-free paper

Printed and bound in Great Britain by Antony Rowe Limited

Contents

Preface

This volume is distinctive in at least three ways. First, we approach economic crime in Russia without its *a priori* stigmatization as part of the general 'criminalization' of the economy. Rather, we view it as a generic response to and an integral part of post-Soviet transition and analyze the role of economic crime for the functioning/ subverting of state, market and civil society institutions in the new Russia. Second, we reveal the latent constituents of economic crime – the mundane practices which are so widespread that they become commonly accepted or tolerated in society, but at the same time constitute and nurture an environment for economic crime. Third, we offer clues for solving some of Russia's paradoxes: How do people survive if wages are not paid on time or in full, and even when paid, are still inadequate for basic living standards? If the rule of law does not rule, then what does? What are the rules of the alleged Russian disorder? How is it possible to combat corruption in a society where supposedly no agency or institution is free from it?

We are most grateful to our authors who made their original contributions to this volume. It was an honour and a great pleasure for us to work with them.

The idea for this book came from a workshop on *Shadow Economy and Economic Crime in Central and Eastern Europe* that was set up as a regional programme of the 16th Annual Symposium on Economic Crime, held at Jesus College, Cambridge, in September 1998. We would like to thank John Lloyd, Saul Froomkin, David Bickford and Cecile Ringgenberg for chairing the sections of the workshop, and the audience for the contributions that helped to turn the discussion into a book. Some speakers do not appear here as authors but we tried to make sure that the ideas of Andrei Konstantinov, Endre Sik, Paddy Rawlinson, and the others did not get lost. We are grateful to the organizers of the Symposium: Barry Rider, Chizu Nakajima and Tracy Paradise for enabling the East European regional programme to take place.

For the book as a whole we wish to express our gratitude to Rosemary Mellor, Michael Banks and Anthony Giddens, whose support and suggestions on the editing were invaluable. Karen Birdsall put a lot of effort into making this book publishable.

We owe a particular word of thanks to Anne Lonsdale, the President of New Hall, Cambridge. Her understanding and encouragement helped to make this book possible. We also appreciate the company and advice of our colleagues at New Hall, especially Houshang Ardavan, Chris Huang, Alison Wilson, Patrick Baert, Sue Benson, Joan Hinde and Caroline Blyth.

A. V. Ledeneva and M. Kurkchiyan (eds.), Economic Crime in Russia, vii
© 2000 *Kluwer Law International. Printed in Great Britain.*

Notes on the Contributors

Johan Bäckman is researcher at the Criminological unit of the National Research Institute of Legal Policy (Ministry of Justice, Finland). He has undertaken extensive fieldwork in Russia and published several articles and monographs about crime in Russia, including 'The Inflation of Crime in Russia: The Social Danger of the Emerging Markets' (National Research Institute of Legal Policy, Publication Series no. 150, Helsinki, 1998) and ' "The wolf has a hundred paths …": Organized Crime of St. Petersburg in the Framework of Russia's Culture of Criminal Justice' (National Research Institute of Legal Policy, Publication Series no. 166, Helsinki, 1999). At present he is preparing a study on the internationalization of crime around the Baltic Sea, entitled 'Eurobandits'. Mr. Bäckman is preparing his dissertation at the University of Helsinki, Finland.

Eva Busse has undertaken research into the Russian tax system with a focus on local practices and difficulties of taxation in the 1990s. She is currently expanding the scope of her earlier research and preparing PhD on *Tax Evasion in Russia: A Predicament of Practices* at the Faculty of Social and Political Sciences, University of Cambridge. Her main interests lie in the sociological approach to the analysis of institutions and in the field of economic anthropology.

Karen Birdsall became interested in approaches to everyday survival during the years she spent working on civil society initiatives in Russia. Economic crime at the workplace was the focus of her recent study of a Russian steel town, the findings of which were set forth in her thesis on *Practices of Survival: Covert Earning Schemes in the Russian Workplace*, University of Cambridge. Her primary interest is the application and transformation of Soviet-era informal practices in the conditions of the new Russian order.

Vladimir Chorniy divides his professional career between risk-management, working for an international investment bank in the City, and academic research at the University of Cambridge where he is a visiting scholar. He was a business consultant for commercial organizations in St. Petersburg. His expertise covers a range of issues from a specialized area of numerical simulation to the regulation and management of financial institutions and other economic themes.

Frédérique Dahan is Lecturer in Law at the University of Essex and a qualified advocate at the Paris Bar. She developed an expertise in commercial legal developments in the states of Central and Eastern Europe, and published articles in

The Company Lawyer, European Financial Services Law, European Business Law Review, and *Company Financial and Insolvency Law Review*; chapters in books and loose-leaves *International Tracing of Assets* (Sweet & Maxwell, London); *Anti-Money Laundering Guide* (CCH, London).

Leonid Fituni is Director of the Centre for Strategic and Global Studies of the Russian Academy of Sciences and the Dean of the Department of World Economy and International Relations at the International Independent University of Political and Ecological Sciences in Moscow. He is an internationally renowned expert on capital flight and money-laundering control. His publications include 14 books and many articles on finance, economic crime and security issues published in Russian, English and other languages. His latest book *Capital Flight from Transitional and Developing Economies* (Nauka, 1999) is published in Moscow.

Mark Galeotti is Director of the Organized Russian and Eurasian Crime Research Unit at Keele University, and Senior Lecturer in International History. He is an acknowledged expert on post-Soviet security issues, with particular interest in organized crime. He has served on secondment to the British Foreign and Commonwealth Office and advises a wide range of police, government and commercial bodies.

Åse Grødeland was Co-director of the ESRC funded project 'Public Perspectives on Post-communist Governance' in the Politics Department at the University of Glasgow. She has published widely on post-communist Europe in, for example, *Europe–Asia Studies, Public Administration and Development, Journal of Communist Studies* and *Transition Politics*, and *Nations and Nationalism*. Her doctorate (1996) was on the *Emergence and Development of the Green Movement in Ukraine*.

Caroline Humphrey is Fellow of King's College and Professor of Asian Anthropology at the University of Cambridge. She has carried out anthropological research in the USSR/Russia, Mongolia, Nepal, India and Inner Mongolia (China). She is author of books on Inner-Asian pastoralism, collective farms in Russia, theories of ritual, and on Mongolian shamanism. She has also published articles on kinship, economic exchange and barter, bribery and post-socialist transformations.

Tatyana Koshechkina is currently International Director of the market research company GFK-GB. She was formerly Managing Director of USM (Ukrainian Surveys and Market Research), now GFK-USM, and an Honorary Fellow in Politics at Glasgow University. Earlier she worked in the Institute of Sociology of the National Academy of Sciences, Kyiv, and later founded and became the first Managing Director of SOCIS-GALLUP in Ukraine.

Marina Kurkchiyan is North Fellow in the Sociology of Law at the Centre for Socio-Legal Studies, Oxford, and Visiting Fellow of Keble College. Her current research deals with economic culture and attitudes to law in the FSU countries. She is a consultant to the World Bank, and UN Development Programme and the Save the Children Fund, and is the author of a number of official reports. Her publications include papers on the media, social structure, the informal economy, health care, ethnic conflict and national identity.

Alena Ledeneva is Lecturer in Russian Politics and Society at the School of Slavonic and East European Studies, University College London. She is the author of *Russia's Economy of Favours: Blat, Networking and Informal Exchange* (Cambridge University Press, Cambridge, 1998). Her recent publications include *Bribery and Blat in Russia: Negotiating Reciprocity from Middle Ages to the 1990s* (Macmillan, London, 2000), co-edited with Stephen Lovell and Andrei Rogachevskii, and articles on barter and network economy in Russia.

William Miller is Edward Caird Professor of Politics at the University of Glasgow and a Fellow of the British Academy. His recent publications include *Values and Political Change in Post-Communist Europe* (Macmillan Press, London, 1998), co-authored with Stephen White and Paul Heywood. He is currently completing a book, with Grodeland and Koshechkina, entitled, *Bureaucratic Encounters in Post-Communist Europe* (Central European University Press, Budapest, 2000) and another with Malcolm Dickson and Gerry Stoker entitled, *The New Local Governance: Political Theory versus Public Opinion* (Macmillan Press, London, 2000).

Heiko Pleines is a researcher at the German Federal Institute for East European Studies (BIOst, Cologne) and a freelance writer for, amongst others, *NewsBase*, *Financial Times*, and *Business Publishing*. His publications include various articles on organized crime and corruption, capital flight from Russia, and most recently on corruption and crime in the Russian oil industry in *The Political Economy of Russian Oil* (Rowman & Littlefield, Oxford, 1999), edited by David Lane.

Vadim Radaev is Deputy Rector on Research and the Chair of the Department of Economic Sociology of the State University – Higher School of Economics, Moscow. He is also Director of the research centre at the Moscow School of Economics and Social Sciences and Co-Chair of European Research Network on Economic Sociology, European Sociological Association. He has published four books and more than 100 papers in the field of economic sociology.

Bill Tupman is Lecturer in Politics at the University of Exeter. He was Director of the Centre for Police and Criminal Justice Studies from 1985 to 1995, and is a member of the Scientific Advisory Group, Intercentre, University of Messina, Italy. He has published in the *Journal of Information and Communications Technology Law*. His recent publications include a series of articles on cross-border responses to organized and economic crime in the *Journal of Financial Crime* (Henry Stewart, London) and *Policing in Europe: Uniform in Diversity* (Intellect, Exeter, 1999), co-authored with his wife Alison.

Federico Varese is Prize Research Fellow at Nuffield College, Oxford. His doctoral dissertation at Oxford (Nuffield College) was based on a yearlong study of organized crime in the city of Perm, Russia. He is presently working on a book *The Emergence of the Russian Mafia* (Oxford University Press, Oxford). He has published papers on the Russian Mafia and Soviet criminal history in *Archives Européenes de Sociologie*, *Low Intensity Conflict and Law Enforcement*, *Political Studies* and *Cahiers du Monde Russe*.

Vadim Volkov is Associate Professor at the European University at St. Petersburg and a SSRC-MacArthur Foundation Post-Doctoral Fellow, Program on Peace and Security in a Changing World. He founded the Faculty of Social and Political Sciences at the European University at St. Petersburg, and has published widely in the field of social theory and on issues of organized crime, state formation and market building in Russia.

1

Introduction:
Economic Crime in the New Russian Economy

Alena Ledeneva

I.   INTRODUCTION

The post-Soviet order has become known not only for its integration with global capital markets but also for the spread of the informal economy, the rise of corruption and organized crime, enormous wages arrears, tax evasion and barter. To a large extent these phenomena – which derive from the Soviet past but acquire new features in the market context – account for the non-transparency of the Russian economy for the outside world. Unfortunately the market reform policies, aimed at attracting Western investment and encompassing the exchange rate policy, control of the inflation rate and the budget deficit, did not take into account seemingly non-economic factors, such as the specifics of political culture, lack of civil society or inefficiency of the rule of law.

In other words, the difficulties of democratization and marketization in Russia can be explained through the imbalanced nature of macro/micro reforms. Preoccupied with the 'state,' the privatization of its property and the marketization of the command economy, reforms were not oriented to (or did not ensure an adequate transformation of) customary law, civic responsibilities and civil justice, 'which always had been alien concepts in Russia'.[1] It is one thing to introduce sound laws designed to guarantee the rights of Western investors; it is quite another to enforce them if arbitration practices and court procedures are corrupt. As a result, Western investors have chosen mainly to avoid the Russian economy, which – as far as the global business community is concerned – does not operate as an economy should. This chapter intends to integrate the sometimes discrepant arguments presented in the book into a coherent story about why this is the case. It will begin with a brief overview of criminal statistics in Russia in the 1990s and the problems of quantitative methods for assessing economic crime, and then move on to consider the forms in which economic crime is integrated into society by looking at state, market, and civil society institutions.

---

[1]   J. Kampfner, *Inside Yeltsin's Russia*, (Cassell, London, 1994), p. x.

A. V. Ledeneva and M. Kurkchiyan (eds.), *Economic Crime in Russia*, 1–15
© 2000 *Kluwer Law International. Printed in Great Britain.*

II. Criminal statistics and economic crime

As a result of the legalization of certain activities and the criminalization of some new offences in the new 1997 Criminal Code of the Russian Federation, comparing statistical data before and after 1996 has become very difficult. This problem is addressed by Leonid Fituni (Chapter 2) through a detailed periodization of the dynamics of economic crime between 1988 and 1999 and their interpretation in the context of transition to a market economy. He indicates a tendency towards growth in economic crime and its sophistication over the period, even when a decrease in absolute figures has taken place.

General statistical data indicate a stabilization in the criminal situation in Russia in 1994–1996 after the peak reached in 1991–1993: the number of criminal offences in general declined and so did the number of homicide victims.[2] The number of solved cases and the number of individuals prosecuted have risen. It may seem that the state has become more successful in combating crime. The report of the Russian Criminological Association, however, presents arguments against such a conclusion. First, the period of 1990s reforms is radically different in terms of the scale of crime, as one can see in Table 1.[3]

Table 1. Dynamics of Crime Coefficients in Five Year Periods
(Number of registered criminal offences per 100,000 people)

	1961–1965	1981–1985	1986–1990	1991–1995
Coefficient	407	901	983	1770
Increase from 1961–1965 (per cent)	-	+ 123	+ 142	+ 440

Despite the decline in the number of registered criminal offences in 1996, the number of identified criminals went up 1.4 per cent, and the crime coefficient rose from 1047.9 to 1097.2.

Second, the structure of criminal offences has undergone significant change. The 4.7 per cent decline in absolute figures is mainly accounted for by the decline in conventional criminal offences, while criminal offences related to economic crime increased: offences against public order and authority[4] rose by 15.4 per cent; management offences by 18 per cent. Registered drug-related offences increased by as much as 20 per cent.

Third, according to experts and opinion polls, the incidence of unregistered crime is increasing. Assessments vary for different types of offence, from 40 per cent for general criminal offences to 95 per cent for economic crime. Surveys among

---

[2] A. I. Dolgova *et al.*, 'Prestupnost' v Rossii: statistika i realii' in A. I. Dolgova (ed.), *Prestupnost',* *Statistika, Zakon*, (Kriminologicheskaia Assotsiatsiia, Moscow, 1997), pp. 4–62.
[3] For more statistics and analysis see ibid.
[4] Particularly theft and forgery of stamps, documents, headed paper (Arts. 195–196) as indicated in Appendix 1 in Dolgova, n. 2 above, p. 205.

victims indicate an increasing frequency of self-reliant responses to such situations: 'I solved it myself' (*sam razobralsia*). Criminal offence has become psychologically more acceptable, due to poverty and social polarization. Harsh economic conditions (80 per cent of the population lives below the poverty line[5]) and people's frustration over state policies have generated crime reflecting 'relative deprivation'.[6] The impossible challenge of sustaining one's well-being with legal income has produced a wide range of illegal responses, from 'outwitting the system' by inventing covert earning schemes to child prostitution and trade. In an all-Russian opinion poll of 2,500 people from 102 rural and urban settlements, 50 per cent concluded that 'it is easier for swindlers and manipulators to achieve success in their career and to gain recognition'. In response to the question 'who has the best conditions for increasing their incomes and earnings', 53 per cent indicated 'swindlers and manipulators', second only to bankers and financiers (54 per cent) followed by executive managers (33 per cent) and state officials (30 per cent). Only 17 per cent of respondents named small businessmen, 2 per cent – farmers, 0.5 per cent – workers.[7] Interestingly, 'swindlers and manipulators' is offered as a choice in the questionnaire as if it were just another occupational group – a fact which bewilders neither interviewees nor respondents.

Apart from the presence of latent or hidden crime, the generally unsatisfactory demographic situation has had an impact on crime indicators and to some extent, structural change in criminal offences. For example, the overall positive trend in registered criminal offences in 1996 should be viewed in the context of the 475,000 decrease in the population: the death rate was twice as high as the birth rate. The number of dead amounted to 672,000, with every third being of working age. Eighty per cent of these are men, which accounts for some reduction in so-called 'risk groups'.

In a wider sense, statistics are also determined by the efficiency of the legislation and the law enforcement institutions, qualities of control and registration of crime, characteristics of the criminal code, as well as political pressures and influences. Fituni (Chapter 2) suggests that organized crime is increasingly penetrating the political sphere. This takes the form of proposed criminal candidacies to Russia's elected bodies and financial support of political figures whose political ideas and activity comply with the interests of the mafia or criminalized business. The interpenetration of state institutions and criminalized agencies has consequences from top to bottom. The erosion of legitimacy of political and other state institutions facilitates people's distrust of the state and serves as a justification for their own involvement in illegal activities. This highlights not only the issues of corruption in Russia, but also poverty which generates so-called practices of survival and which accounts for their pervasiveness.

---

5 *Vashe pravo*, No. 38, 1996. Quoted from Dolgova, n. 2 above, p. 10.
6 R. V. Ryvkina, 'Social Roots of the Criminalisation of Russian Society' (1998) 37 (2) *Sociological Research*, p. 15.
7 *Rossiiskaia gazeta*, 27 December 1996, p. 27.

[handwritten annotation: Q = this is not a rapid ~ roots in anti state or anti-b'ais movements, there are people who want to be bourgeois]

III.   Definition of Economic Crime

By definition, economic crime focuses mainly on corruption (government and corporate), customs and excise fraud, corporate fraud (theft and false accounting), bank fraud, investment and securities fraud, future and derivatives fraud, insurance fraud, fraud in international trade, tax evasion and the misuse of tax havens, underground banking, and money-laundering.[8]

Economic crime can be distinguished from organized crime. On the one hand, economic crime can be wider than organized crime, as not every economic crime is conducted by identifiable criminal organizations. Economic crime can occur in the form of white-collar crime, pervasive tax evasion or covert earning practices exercised by various groups of the population. On the other hand, organized crime can be wider as it involves violence not necessarily implied in the notion of economic crime. However, if we take the point made by Mark Galeotti (Chapter 3), Vadim Volkov (Chapter 4) and Vadim Radaev (Chapter 5) that violence is convertible into capital and that organized crime is organized business, we can use these terms almost interchangeably. The important distinctions to make, however, are the ones Galeotti emphasizes by the use of the term *mafiya* as opposed to mafia.

First, the Russian *mafiya* is a somewhat disorganized form of organized crime in the sense that it is organized as a series of networks rather than formal structures. Gangs recruit on the basis of common background, friendship, hometown or ethnicity, and form long- and short-term affiliations for performing particular tasks.

Second, the *mafiya* is responsive to the market and is unusually commercial. Unlike the older generation of *vory v zakone*, the *avtoritety* tend to see crime as merely one route to acquiring money and power. As such, they have no particular commitment to crime in and of itself, only when it pays. Most gangs operate across the spectrum, from entirely legitimate enterprises, through 'grey' or paralegal business into overtly criminal ones. As Volkov puts it, it is functionally integrated into emerging markets and should be understood in the context of discontinuity with the old Soviet criminal world.

Third, the *mafiya* not only exploits but also shapes the economic order. Its involvement takes three main forms: 'ownership' (privatization, banks etc.), affiliation (laundering money, contract killing, contracts for debt collection) and protection against attacks from other thugs (a 'roof'). In other words, the *mafiya* actively penetrates informal networks and associations (especially sport clubs, churches and other associations with status providing tax or export–import privileges), thus appropriating the niches of civil society. It becomes a significant player on the market and also creeps into state and political institutions.

---

[8]   See R. Bosworth and G. Saltmarch, 'An International Overview of the Incidence of Economic Crime' in J. Reuvid (ed.) *The Regulation and Prevention of Economic Crime Internationally* (Kagan Page, London 1995), p. 3.

IV. ORGANIZED CRIME AND STATE INSTITUTIONS

The functionality of organized crime should be viewed in terms of enabling the post-Soviet market economy to operate by creating structures the Russian state has failed to create. Volkov suggests that as criminal groups sought to gain control over the Russian economy, they themselves became subjected to some basic laws of economic action that then tended to transform these groups from within. The scale of such 'institutionalization' of contemporary Russian organized crime, however, should not be overstated. He argues that the power of criminal syndicates (especially in protection business) is largely inflated, not least in order to veil the main agents that actually control the transition to the market, namely, private protection companies created by, and linked to, the Interior Ministry (MVD) and the Federal Security Service (FSB).[9]

The fragmentation of the state is central to an understanding of the scale of the phenomenon. Indeed, the loss of the state monopoly of legitimate violence, taxation and law enforcement in the post-Soviet period has enabled uncontrolled sources of organized violence to provide more effective protection for economic subjects and thus claim a significant share of the tribute formerly paid to the state in the form of taxes. Apart from tax collection (tribute), the newly emerged organized groups that command means of violence have also taken over – with great efficiency – the functions of enforcing laws and contract relations in the private sector of the economy, thus undermining another key state task – the enforcement of justice. This is not to say that the 'state' no longer plays a role or that the state is weak. Rather, it suggests that the 'state' is just one of the actors and does not necessarily have unconditional priority in those areas that formally constitute its domain. According to Radaev, when subjected to threats, only 13 per cent of entrepreneurs would normally turn to the police for support. Eight per cent would address a professional security agency, 15 per cent would resort to criminal groupings (*bratva*), 34 per cent would solve the problems themselves and 30 per cent found it difficult to say.[10]

Radaev points out that state protection agencies in Russia have undergone a remarkable evolution in the 1990s. First, they have been strengthened from the viewpoint of their personnel, material resources and organization. Second, they gradually commercialize their activities by selling their protection services both in the formal and shadow economies. Third, state protection agencies are coming to intertwine with criminal groupings. In their interviews entrepreneurs comment that both tend to act in very similar ways. This does not mean that the 'mafia is running the state', as is often announced in the mass media. It means something different: a flexible system of informal links among state-run, semi-state and criminal agencies is being formed.

---

[9] According to official data, 60 per cent of those in charge of the non-state security firms and private protection business are former KGB officers, 30 per cent came out of the militia (mainly departments of economic crime (*OBKhSS*) and criminal investigations (*UR*)), eight per cent are former military officers, and only two per cent were never related to the state coercive structures. See Dolgova, n. 2 above, p. 26.

[10] The data are based on two 1997–1998 surveys of non-state enterprise managers and entrepreneurs: 227 questionnaires of entrepreneurs from 21 regions of Russia, and 96 semi-standardized in-depth interviews with entrepreneurs.

The emergence of a ramified network of control and forced sanctions outside state regulation evolved in tandem with the establishment and certain 'formalization' of informal codes (*ponyatiia*). These informal codes regulate routines and are a substitute for the law in conflict resolution in and between criminal groupings. Relationships between entrepreneurs and protection groups are also built upon a specific ethic based upon a respect for force. The parallel existence of informal codes and legislation (which in turn can be inconsistent at its local-regional-federal levels) is indicative of the gap that has to be bridged in order to establish the rule of law. In other words, informal associations must be persuaded to operate in accordance with the law. So far the opposite has increasingly been taking place.

The dark side of the fragmentation of the state is that the other 'fragments' do not exist without penetration into state institutions, without corruption and without the attraction of state officials (including law enforcement officials) into criminal activities. The so-called 'roofs' offer, among other things, services of 'solving problems' through informal channels in local and regional authorities, tax inspection offices and state coercive institutions. However, it would be naïve to place all the blame on them. Radaev's data in this volume indicate a significant spread in the practices of bureaucratic extortion. 87 per cent of entrepreneurs claim that such pressures do exist in Russian business today, including 38.5 per cent of them who report that extortion occurs frequently. We do not have data on the relationship between state institutions and 'roofs' but as both are involved in 'solving problems', one should think they are quite complex. The formal structures not only restrict but also enable economic crime to occur, while the latter not only subvert but also function to support and sustain formal institutions whose resources criminals are interested in exploiting. By grasping the actual role of organized crime in Russia, we acquire a better understanding of the nature of the formal order and the difficulties of its transition from the Soviet command economy to 'democracy' and the 'market economy'.

Such difficulties reside in the unregulated and largely unreported parts of the economy that operate beyond state control. Marina Kurkchiyan (Chapter 6) argues that apart from the changes in the official economy of post-Soviet society, one should also focus on the transition that has been taking place in the unofficial sector. Despite its hidden character, the unofficial economy is not an alien or separate presence; it is embedded in the integral body of society. On one hand, it depends heavily on formal structures and institutions and makes use of their resources. On the other hand, the unofficial sector is grounded in people's beliefs and expectations, their attitudes towards officialdom and each other, and their shared understandings of how things get done in their society. The former accounts for the fact that reorganization of the official economy brings radical changes to the unofficial economy which is forced to adapt to the new realities. The latter channels the reverse: the reform itself becomes subject to the influences of customary practices and attitudes shaped in the unofficial economy of the past. Kurkchiyan illustrates how all three phenomena – which she defines as second economy, economy of collapse and informal economy – evolved successively from the long-established Soviet tradition of informal practices of bypassing officialdom, mainly opposed to western traditions of the rule of law. Let us consider these customary practices reflecting the relationship between the state and the population in more detail.

V. CUSTOMARY PRACTICES

Although from a juridical perspective each practice can be classified as either legal or illegal, the existence of customary practices often causes controversy, especially when they surface in litigation. In day-to-day life, however, the ambivalence of informal practices towards the formal system is often non-problematic and widely accepted. It is only through their pervasiveness that informal practices develop their subversive potential, transforming from a 'benign aid' to the system into 'corrupting' and potentially 'system-threatening' phases.[11]

Practices which used to dominate the Soviet informal sector (*blat*[12] and *pripiski*,[13] for example) were widespread but well adjusted to the Soviet formal regime. The formal order not only enabled but also efficiently restricted the spread of informal practices. Once the Soviet system collapsed, the transformation of the informal sector became inevitable, both in quantitative and qualitative ways. The course of such transformation can be described as a circuit with accumulative negative feedback, launched by the highly exploitative Soviet state and matched by extreme parasitism on the part of its population,[14] which had to be allowed by the state in exchange for its own legitimacy. This vicious circle has not been broken in the course of post-Soviet reforms. Rather, the reforms induced various mutant forms of parasitism, created new niches for unwritten rules and enhanced the strength of shadow practices.

The grand scale of Russia's shadow economy – its turnover has been estimated at 750 trillion roubles per year (1997 prices), thus making up 45 per cent of the country's overall turnover[15] – raises new concerns about the micro-level economic relationships in the 'shadow' market segments. What makes the shadow economy so prevalent? If shadow practices are so pervasive, should they be viewed as norm or as deviation? What is the nature of customary practices? At which point does the customary become functional, the functional become subversive, the subversive turn corrupt and the corrupt end up being system-threatening? How is it possible to prevent phenomena that are so mundane and so damaging at the same time? What

---

[11] Sampson distinguishes three modes of interaction between informal practices and formal bureaucratic structures: 'benign', 'corrupting' and 'system-threatening'. See S. Sampson, 'The Informal Sector in Eastern Europe' (1985–1986) 66 *Telos*, pp. 44–66.

[12] *Blat* refers to the use of personal networks in order to obtain goods and services in short supply or to influence decision-making. For details see Chapter 11, pp. 163–175 in this volume and A. Ledeneva, *Russia's Economy of Favours: Blat, Networking and Informal Exchange* (Cambridge University Press, Cambridge, 1998).

[13] *Pripiski* is false reporting.

[14] For example, the *blat* system of exchange was grounded in the possibility to extend favours at the expense of state property. The dubious nature of state property and the repressive nature of the Soviet state have contributed to the spread of all-pervasive practices of cheating and outwitting the state: *blat* and other forms of diversion of state property, smuggling out (*vynos*), false reporting (*pripiski*), stealing, etc.

[15] For the source of this figure see Chapter 2, pp. 17–30 by Fittuni in this volume, p.18.

are the loopholes that accommodate customary practices and is it possible to block them?

Customary practices are pervasive. Generally, they are so minor and widespread that they become taken for granted and often escape legal sanction. Some methodological aspects of pervasive practices, where norm and deviation merge, are explored in Federico Varese's analysis of pervasive corruption (Chapter 7). Varese implies that a corrupt practice can be considered widespread when one would expect deviation rather than norm to take place. For example, a society with widespread corruption is characterized by a common assumption that a bribe will be expected and a bribe will be given. People routinely become aware of pervasive corruption and unconsciously promote further corruption by developing a 'culture of justified bribery'. We do not have data for Russia, however, William Miller's data for Eastern Europe (Chapter 8) show that 31 per cent of respondents were willing to excuse or approve corruption in the Czech Republic, 40 per cent in Slovakia, and 42 per cent in Bulgaria and Ukraine.

As corruption becomes widespread, the very concept of corruption loses its meaning for the actors involved. People 'misrecognize' their own involvement with controversial practices, but easily recognize when other people do the same. This type of 'misrecognition game' helps to support one's positive self-image and therefore allows one to be involved in corrupt practices while sincerely negating and criticizing them at the same time. Although the notions of honesty and fairness do not disappear, they certainly diverge from the impartial application of the law. Some evidence for the 'misrecognition' argument comes from the comparative research of Miller *et al.* They show that respondents ordinarily argue for the pervasiveness of corrupt practices without acknowledging personal experience of them.[16] In part, this fact should certainly be related to a tendency on the part of respondents to generalize or to express resentment in such a form, but this gap is also indicative of a universal tendency to forget, misrecognize or reduce one's own experience, unless the experiences were particularly painful or unsuccessful.

Another feature of pervasive practices is their compulsive character. In other words, to get involved in such activities to 'solve problems' is considered more normal than to sacrifice one's self-interest in order to refrain from such involvement. Miller's inquiry into bribery indirectly supports this argument. His findings suggest that where bribery was least common (in the Czech Republic), the relatively small number of people who gave bribes were more likely to be accomplices or even corrupters. Where bribery was most common (in Ukraine), the much larger number of people who gave bribes were much more likely to be victims of extortion.

Pervasive practices are very difficult to combat. As Varese points out, to single out any one case of corruption raises the question: Why him? Why not somebody else? Because punishment is seen as selective, it provokes suspicion towards the

---

[16] See Figure 16.2 in W. Miller, T. Koshechkina, and A. Grodeland, 'Bureaucratic Encounters in Post-communist Regimes: Evidence from 26 Focus Groups in the Former Soviet Union and East-Central Europe' in S. Lovell, A. Ledeneva, A. Rogatchevsky (eds.), *Bribery and Blat in Russia: Negotiating Reciprocity from Middle Ages to the 1990s* (Macmillan, London, 2000), p. 267.

policy itself. Therefore, to enforce the law does not restore faith in the law, but rather confirms the opposite cynical view of it. Many authors in this volume agree that combating pervasive practices is possible only through changing the structural conditions that generate it. To illustrate this point let us turn to the issue that competes with corruption for pervasiveness in Russia.

Tax evasion has been strongly fought in the post-Soviet period, but is still omnipresent. Eva Busse (Chapter 9) argues that systemic and social conditions are responsible for the evasion problem. Practices of tax evasion complement the inefficiency of the formal tax system by adjusting to and blending with given bureaucratic and legal structures, rather than blatantly deviating from them. This also explains why the processes constituting tax evasion are not considered criminal by the taxpayers, tax inspectors and political authorities involved in local taxation. Such attitudes are deeply engrained in the everyday practices of circumventing formal procedures inherited from the Soviet past but are also fuelled by the tax system's lack of legitimacy. First, Russian entrepreneurs are not used to paying direct taxes and do not consider taxes as given costs – the fact that they have not paid taxes from the start undermines the legitimacy of the taxation system. Second, the discrepancy perceived by respondents between paid taxes and received public services weakens the motives for paying. A third problem with the legitimacy of the tax system is the uneven distribution of the tax burden. In comparison to the taxation of individuals, taxation of the corporate sector appears to be excessive. As taxes are so high, people evade; and because people evade, there is no political will to lower the tax rates sufficiently. Busse suggests that this 'vicious circle' creates a relatively stable situation based on the interrelation between institutional constraints and informal ways of circumventing them. Potentially, however, such stability is destructive as it allows an inefficient system to survive.

Customary practices account for the paradoxes of both the Soviet and post-Soviet economy[17] and articulate the logic of the Russian order. Karen Birdsall (Chapter 10) scrutinizes the puzzling ability of Russian people to function and survive despite conditions in which wages are extremely low and employees often fail to receive them at all. She suggests that people rely heavily on informal techniques for coping, such as the surreptitious earning of unofficial money at the official workplace through secretive manipulations – 'covert earning schemes'. Covert earning should be seen as a normal reaction by ordinary people to the constraints of daily life in post-Soviet Russia, rather than being indicative of criminal or deviant behaviour. Those who would label Russia's economy as criminal or chaotic might regard covert earning schemes as simply another manifestation of the larger disorder. On the contrary, we suggest here that Russia's economy, far from

---

[17] Consider the following anecdote about 6 paradoxes of socialism: 'No unemployment but nobody works. Nobody works but productivity increases. Productivity increases but the shops are empty. The shops are empty but fridges are full. Fridges are full but nobody is satisfied. Nobody is satisfied but all vote unanimously'. Each paradox implies or hints at a pervasive practice in the Soviet economy: absenteeism; false reporting; inefficiency of the planned system resulting in shortages and the ways of coping with them; use of perks and privileges; cynicism and anecdotal culture developed by the Soviet regime.

being chaotic, follows its own coherent order which is grounded squarely in customary ways of getting things done. These customary practices – to do with covert earning or 'covert reward systems' (as in the case of Russian hackers which is presented in Chapter 11) and other informal practices – co-exist and make use of formal structures and procedures. Viewed from the outside, these practices are regarded as deviations and criminal infractions that impede the emergence of economic transparency, while for insiders they are a natural component of everyday life and a self-evident way of defending one's interests. For example, hacking is often perceived as routine by the insiders of the computer underworld but would be considered electronic crime by outsiders. This discrepancy in perception is critical for understanding the friction between the ideals of market reform and the realities of the evolving post-Soviet order.

Further exploration of the customary order of doing things is offered by Caroline Humphrey (Chapter 12) who indicates that there is a call for values of 'law', 'fairness', and a 'normal life', and a social group which really means it. Humphrey suggests that Russian entrepreneurs have no nostalgia for 'old ways', if only because they feel trapped by them on all sides. The greater the distance between the 'distorted' practice of law and the ideal of law, the more the entrepreneurs demand for it to be reformed. The problem is that calls for 'good laws' are insufficient without simultaneously addressing customary practices, because it is not simply the law but the practices of its enforcement that matter. As customary practices to some extent compensate for the inefficiency of the formal system, 'the good law' will reduce the number of loopholes in the formal system accommodating them. The good law and an efficient legal system will also make it harder to scapegoat the state and to legitimate informal ways of doing things 'out of necessity'. It is my belief, however, that to find a way of changing pervasive customary practices alongside legal reforms would be the most effective way of transforming formal institutions in Russia.

VI.   MARKET INSTITUTIONS AND ECONOMIC CRIME

Not only state institutions suffer from the pervasiveness of customary practices. Heiko Pleines (Chapter 13) illustrates how damaging they are for market institutions, including their most liquid financial sector. Given that the conditions under which commercial banks would normally lend money for investment – sufficient information to judge the liquidity of the potential debtor and reliable means to enforce payments or to recover collateral in case the debtor is unwilling to meet his obligations – are not fulfilled in Russia, it is more gainful for Russian banks to engage in business with the state rather than in risky and not very profitable credit business. Evidence supplied by Pleines suggests that corruption networks between state officials and business managers are likely to account for the super-profits made on the Russian market, the 1995 loans-for-shares auctions, GKO-pyramids and the role of 'authorized' banks in covering state budget deficits, as well as for large-scale corruption. As a result of such networks in operation, market criteria get diverted: badly managed banks may survive due to good connections with state officials while good banks with few connections are eliminated through bureaucratic arbitrariness. Promising enterprises may not get credits for investment because banks are too busy dealing with state officials. When the bank with the best connections rather than the most attractive offer becomes responsible for the handling of state funds, banking fees are higher, efficiency is lower and the risk of embezzlement increases.

Large banks and the state become dependent on each other. The state is of major importance to large banks as a customer, as a bond issuer and as the regulating and controlling body. In turn, the state needs the large banks to finance its budget deficit and to stabilize financial markets. Also, the banks can help state officials and politicians conceal illegal income and transfer it abroad. Fituni's analysis (Chapter 14) reveals that even officially acknowledged illegal flight of capital from Russia is almost as large as the amount of international aid Russia received during the period 1992–1999.[18] He illustrates that capital flight, money-laundering, and the legalization of illicit gains are not merely issues of law but of politics as well. The Russian authorities realize that any serious and far-reaching investigation may threaten the achievements of capitalist restoration over the last decade. A 'conspiracy of silence' exists, both internationally and in Russia, about the doubtful legal nature of many privatization projects in the country. On one hand, it is an open secret that privatization was carried out with various violations of law and therefore that profits generated from those privatized entities may formally be considered illegal. On the other hand, such acknowledgement would immediately make hundreds of transnational corporations, which purchased stakes or otherwise participated in the activities of privatized businesses, immersed in contexts they can never accept.

Further diversion from market development is caused by the spread of the barter economy in Russia. This argument has become known in the West as the 'virtual economy' – a phrase coined by Pyotr Karpov, the head of the government commission which made an inquiry into the tax arrears issue in 1997:

> An economy is emerging where prices are charged which no one pays in cash; where no one pays anything on time; where huge mutual debts are created that also can't be paid off in reasonable periods of time; where wages are declared and not paid; and so on … [This creates] illusory, or virtual earnings, which in turn lead to unpaid, or virtual fiscal obligations [with business conducted at] non-market, or virtual prices.[19]

Advocates of the virtual economy thesis argue that it is based on the illusion, or pretence, about almost every important parameter of the economy: prices, sales, wages, taxes, and budgets. It is inherited from the Soviet days, when enterprises

---

[18] Allegations that even International Monetary Fund (IMF) loans were 'laundered' appeared in the press during the money-laundering scandal of August 1999. The scandal has become the best illustration that international cooperation on money-laundering diminishes when the interests of politics come into play.

[19] P. A. Karpov, 'Report of the Inter-Agency Balance-Sheet Commission' (Moscow, December 1997). Quoted in C. G. Gaddy and B. W. Ickes, 'Beyond a Bailout: Time to Face Reality about Russia's "Virtual Economy"': See <www.brook.edu>.

could operate without paying their bills and destroy rather than produce value. According to Gaddy and Ickes, the virtual economy is non-market in nature and in many ways accounts for the fact that most of the Russian economy has not been making progress towards the market. Although Russian companies have changed the way they operate over the past years of radical reform, they have not done so in order to join the market but rather to protect themselves against it.[20] According to Yavlinsky, a leading pro-Western advocate of the market system, 75 per cent of the country's domestically produced goods in 1997 were traded in barter.[21] Before it was prohibited in 1997, 40 per cent of all taxes paid to the Russian federal government were in non-monetary form. The degree of non-monetarization of local and regional budgets is even higher. Vladimir Chorniy (Chapter 15) analyses the criminal implications of the multiple financial system resulting from state intervention, distortions of financial institutions and the spread of barter in the economy. He distinguishes two broad categories of criminal activity: acts in which the law is clearly broken and acts that emerge in response to the inadequacy of the law. One would expect that only the first category would remain, while the second category will disappear when the legal system catches up with 'capitalist' development. In fact, Chorniy suggests, it is not so much underdevelopment as over-development of the legislation that causes criminal and near-criminal activities in the financial sector. He also emphasises the danger of political influence in the legislative process and the impact corruption has on state institutions, which undermine the disinterested role the state should be playing in relation to market institutions.

VII. Civil society, the rule of law and prevention of economic crime

Issues of control and prevention of economic crime have been central to state policies in the 1990s, but no significant success can be reported. The legal framework, law enforcement agencies and the development of civil society are the core elements of crime control and prevention. Frédérique Dahan (Chapter 16), Johan Bäckman (Chapter 17) and William Tupman (Chapter 18) consider these themes respectively and diagnose the following problems:

- Criminal, economic and civil laws are not coherent and do not work as a system (including the lack of consistency of local-regional-federal legislation);
- Legislation is not oriented towards the long-term; it is mainly coercive and does not address the structural conditions that create an environment favouring economic crime;
- Law enforcement practices are inadequate, inefficient and corrupt;
- Customary practices are pervasive and impede the development of civil society;
- Civil society does not work as expected if it is not based on working democratic freedoms and human rights.

[20] Gaddy and Ickes, ibid., p. 1.
[21] See J. Steele, 'Blatting Order' *The Guardian*, 8 August 1998, p.16. For 1998, in his speech at the 1999 World Economic Forum in Davos, Yavlinsky quoted a figure of 85 per cent.

Dahan indicates that the Russian legislature is fully aware that money-laundering is not only a criminal law issue and that criminal law and economic regulation should work hand in hand. Moreover, civil law has weapons to use in order to inhibit money-laundering. Generally, civil measures can be taken in areas that are not usually related: administrative law, tax law, banking law, civil and commercial law, competition law, etc. Nonetheless, the draft law 'Countering the Legalization (Laundering) of Illegally Obtained Incomes' gives priority to criminal provisions and criminal sanctions. The legislature is still using law as a coercive tool when addressing the question of money-laundering and economic crime. The approach to the principles of the rule of law in recent Russian practice has been rooted in the Soviet tradition that emphasized law as a tool for social control, making it an effective instrument for the state to impose its policy goals by coercion. As such, the law as an independent entity never really mattered.

What is also characteristic of Russian law is the lack of orientation to remedy the structural conditions that provide fertile ground for money-laundering activities. For example, laws and enforcement policies that are fashioned to address money-laundering through conventional banking systems are at present of little relevance as these systems are, to a large extent, inadequate. Due to the lack of healthy background practices the simple adoption of international instruments into domestic Russian law will not be sufficient. Therefore, the fight against economic crime and money-laundering control must be coordinated with human rights and the protection of individual freedoms.

Bäckman reinforces this point in his analysis of the 'undemocratic' police culture in Russia and its growing influence. Although the Russian police system is modern in terms of its organization, education and the laws regulating its activities, it is strongly influenced by the totalitarian legacy of exceptional powers embedded in the criminal law and informal practices that developed during Soviet rule.

Contemporary Russian criminologists, and often high-ranking police officers, greatly exaggerate the 'social danger' of organized crime. In criminal policy rhetoric, 'organized crime' has assumed an analogous position with 'class enemies,' the previous principal foes of the Russian state. The central idea is that organized crime poses a pronounced social danger for individuals, state and society and should be combatted ruthlessly even if this is not feasible within a legal framework. 'Breaking the law to prevent the law being broken', however, has never been a sensible policy slogan for law enforcers. However, in conditions where customary practices are pervasive and set against the rule of law or democratic values, the predicament of establishing justice by breaking the rule of law, or establishing democratic institutions by undemocratic measures, is especially difficult.

Tupman shows the inadequacy of those strategies for countering organized crime which threaten democracy and the development of a healthy civil society. On the one hand, society is unlikely to permit the state to become strong enough to take the necessary measures against organized crime networks, because such a state could then take measures against any organization within society and presumably move towards a form of totalitarianism. On the other hand, a strategy to counter criminality that does not include provisions for strengthening civil society, essential for the underpinning of a successful transition to democracy, is a short-term strategy doomed to fail. It is citizens, not police officers, who report crime, give evidence and identify offenders. The police cannot deal with all crimes on their own, while customary practices widespread in the economy hardly facilitate cooperation between the population and state institutions, such as the police. The vacuum of civil society is being filled with associations and networks based on the exploitative and parasitic use of somebody else's resources and run by the logic of 'people of the circle' (*svoi lyudi*) inherited from the Soviet order and incompatible with developed civil society.

VII. CONCLUSION

The tendencies in the state, market and civil society institutions that have been described in this chapter are interrelated. The state lost the monopoly of legitimate violence, law enforcement and taxation and therefore its functions became performed by economic agents pursuing private interests. As a result, the legal foundations of the market system (including anti-monopolist regulation) have not been established, and market instruments, such as competition, minority shareholders' rights and property rights, do not work. Economic agents, both big players and the general population, are forced to play by unwritten rules, often introduced and negotiated by the players themselves outside formal (and legal) institutions. The customary practices which facilitate and foster economic crime are easily justified by those who exercise them, since state institutions, including law enforcement agencies, are widely seen as corrupt and unable to establish the rule of law. Allegations of high level corruption and money-laundering involving FIMACO and the Bank of New York in 1999 again highlighted the necessity of measures to strengthen control over budgetary expenditures and the need to adopt anti-corruption and anti-money-laundering legislation. Even with inconclusive evidence, such allegations deprive the state of its legitimacy and produce civic passivity, which together represent deep-rooted obstacles to the development of a fully-fledged democracy in post-Soviet Russia.

In order to counter economic crime and to break this vicious circle the following principles should be followed:

- Different types of legislation should be made coherent and should work as a system;
- Long-term principles enhancing democracy and civil society should be pursued in legislation;
- Legislation will not work without systematic attempts to improve the work of state and market institutions;
- Market institutions should operate according to market criteria;
- State institutions should be disengaged from market institutions (cronyism and nepotism should be watched particularly);
- Police culture should be reflected upon from the standpoint of democratic values;
- An adequate system of filters against the proceeds of economic crime has to be thought through;

- Law enforcement practices, especially court and arbitration practices, should be improved;
- Soviet stereotypes and customary practices should be revealed and acknowledged by those driven by them;
- Future generations should be brought up to exercise a new professionalism rather than customary practices for getting things done.

By revealing the contexts in which economic crime flourishes this book attempts to clarify what makes the Russian economy inefficient and unaccountable.

2

Economic Crime in the Context of Transition to a Market Economy

Leonid L. Fituni

I. INTRODUCTION

Russia's transition to a market economy has created new social and economic conditions in the country. New types of businesses, institutions and relations are emerging. Unfortunately, the process of reforming Russia has not been an orderly one. A logical programme of change never existed in the minds of reformers; nor were the goals of reform clearly defined, the necessary stages determined, or the results foreseen. There were no realistic prognoses of economic performance resulting from the introduction of various social innovations. The legal basis of reforms lagged far behind practical changes. The legality of reformers' actions or behaviours was often sacrificed for the sake of what they believed to be political necessity. All this was conducive to a sharp rise in violent and economic crime. During the years of reform, violent and economic crime grew at such a pace that it soon overshadowed all the other fruits of transition.

The near paralysis of state authorities and the high level of corruption within the bureaucracy and business circles allowed organized crime to expand its influence within the state machine, and to establish control over some civil servants and politicians. This increased both the differentiation and concentration of power within the criminal world. With the help of corrupt elements in the state machine, stronger criminal leaders gained additional means of suppressing their weaker rivals and competitors. The spread of crime and the growth of illegal capital greatly intensified the struggle for spheres of influence and control by organized criminal groups in various sectors of the Russian economy, individual industries and territories. It also exacerbated violent crime, which brought about a wave of criminal terrorism and the general destabilization of social and economic life.

These new trends created a less favourable environment for some criminal leaders in Russia, who preferred to emigrate to other countries in search of better conditions. Currently, it is easier and safer for many Russian criminal leaders to direct the activities of their criminal groups from abroad. They use foreign jurisdictions for legalizing their profits, while receiving the major part of their criminal incomes in Russia. The world has learned about the omnipotent Russian mafia.

A. V. Ledeneva and M. Kurkchiyan (eds.), Economic Crime in Russia, 17–30
© 2000 *Kluwer Law International. Printed in Great Britain.*

However, other criminal leaders found it more convenient to live and conduct their criminal business in Russia, limiting their overseas exposure to opening small offshore firms controlled by home-based parent companies. In such cases, criminal leaders only pay inspection visits abroad, usually disguised as vacations. Such trips, however, are also useful for temporary disappearance from the limelight, especially if a threat of criminal persecution or tax investigation is looming at home.

During the period of market reforms, leaders of the criminal world extended their interests not only to the sectors of economy which were traditionally perceived by Russians as 'attractive' (like the exports sector – oil, gas, non-ferrous and ferrous metals etc.) but also to new emerging sectors. These sectors did not exist as such in Soviet times, but promised to be economically and socially prominent and lucrative under the new economic system (such as sports and show business). In any case, for the ringleaders, there never existed a chasm between crime, business and culture.

For example, according to the Office of the Prosecutor General, the murder of the President of the Russian Ice Hockey Federation in 1998 was a result of an internal struggle in the organization, and of attempts on the part of organized crime to get access to its financial resources. Facts uncovered during the investigation show that the homicide case was closely connected with a number of economic offences and cases under investigation relating to tax evasion, fraud, smuggling, money laundering and capital flight.[1]

Organized crime dictates to individual industries how to behave in markets and also controls whole regions. Underworld godfathers are setting up closed syndicates and have them infiltrate the state's economic institutions. According to the Ministry of Internal Affairs, their actions are well planned and methodical. Such criminal rings are rigidly centralized and disciplined; they have their own intelligence and counter-intelligence and commando units.

According to the Ministry, Russian law enforcement agencies are aware of the existence of over 9,000 organized criminal groups that control 40,000 commercial structures, including 449 banks. First Deputy Interior Minister Pavel Maslov acknowledged, at parliamentary hearings in the Federation Council, that the grey economy turnover in Russia in 1997 amounted to 750 trillion roubles per year (1997 prices), thus accounting for 45 per cent of the country's overall turnover. He underscored that, 'the process of redistribution of state property carried out in the absence of an appropriate legal basis and a high degree of corruption had driven up domestic organized crime, which represented a real threat to the country's national security'. He alleged that about two million people in the country were using narcotic drugs and that the number of drug addicts was rising 10–20 per cent annually. Estimated profit of the narco-mafia exceeded six trillion roubles.[2]

---

[1]   'Organizovannaia Prestupnost', (Kriminologicheskaia Assotsiatsiia, Moscow, 1998).
[2]   'Russian Grey Economy Flourishing', *Interfax Daily Report*, 1 July 1997.

In total, about 3,200 criminal cases were opened against members of organized criminal groups annually. In general, cases on about 20,000 crimes of this category are handed over to the court each year. In 1997 alone, a total of 51.8 billion roubles worth of criminal groups' property was arrested; 102.3 billion roubles worth of property and 47.2 kilograms of precious metals were seized. Twenty 'bandit groups' were neutralized that year and more than 100 members of these groups accused of having committed over 150 contract murders were brought to criminal accountability.[3]

Organized criminal groups are planting their people in official positions, are using the latest technological methods for the collection of information, and are using the media to form the public opinion they need. The capabilities of law enforcement agencies are limited. On average, one investigator has to deal with 47 criminal cases simultaneously. One investigator in charge of urgent investigations has to deal with 37 crimes at the same time, while the feasible standards are about half of that number. However, under the current conditions in which Russia is permanently pressed by international financial institutions to cut government expenditures, one should not count on a considerable increase in the funding of law enforcement agencies in the near future.

Criminal control over the economy suggests that 'around 60 million Russians are involved, against their will, in criminal economic activities,' with most of them at work, 36 million using it as a sideline, and nine million working in 'openly criminal businesses'. Ministry experts believe that up to 75 per cent of shadow capital is used to establish or maintain a lavish life-style. The wellbeing of individual social groups rests on the mass impoverishment of the population. This 'provokes protest actions, including those with anti-government slogans'.[4]

II.   METHODOLOGICAL ISSUES OF THE ANALYSIS

The growth of crime achieved its qualitative peak in 1995–1997. By then, economic crime had reached such a scale that it became the main impediment to economic development in the country. Statistical data from criminological surveys conducted by the Russian Office of the Prosecutor General and the Ministry of Internal Affairs show unfavourable trends in the criminal dynamics of the 1990s. During the four years between dissolution of the Parliament in 1993 and presidential elections in 1996, the growth rate of crime was nearly 150 per cent and the increase in serious crime was 75 per cent. In the following two years (1997–1998), the growth was about 50 per cent.[5]

The following table gives a general idea about the growth of offences in the Russian Federation from 1961–1998.

---

[3]   Ibid.
[4]   A. Galkin, *RIA Novosti Daily Report*, 2 July 1997.
[5]   Centre for Strategic and Global Studies. Unless otherwise indicated, the statistical data in the paper are drawn from current reports of the respective state agencies and processed by the staff of the Centre for Strategic and Global Studies of the Russian Academy of Sciences.

Table 1. Number of Registered Criminal Offences in Russia (per 100,000 inhabitants)

Year	1961–1965	1981–1985	1986–1990	1990–1995	1996	1997	1998[1]
Number of cases	407	907	983	1170	1778	1629	1600
Growth index (1961–1965 =100)	-	+223	+243	+287	+437	+400	+393
Chain index (previous period = 100)	+223	+198	+119	+152	-8	-2	
Increases as percentage of 1961–1965		+121	+142	+187	+337	+300	+293

Source: Ministry of Internal Affairs, Office of the Prosecutor General.
Notes: [1] Preliminary figures

   While general methodological approaches to the analysis of recent trends in economic crime remain unchanged, researchers should bear in mind that a significant part of pre-1997 statistical data is incompatible with later figures due to changes in Russian criminal law. Certain changes occurred in the criminal law even before 1997. The chapter on crimes committed against socialist property, including the article concerning grand and extra grand embezzlements of state and public property, was removed from the Russian Federation Criminal Code, which has led to a reduction in numbers of reported grand and extra grand larcenies. A number of new *corpora delictis* were introduced envisaging legal accountability for encroachment on other persons' or entrusted property, regardless of its forms.

   On 1 January 1997 a new Criminal Code of the Russian Federation came into force.[6] The code criminalized new offences and legalized some of the activities that previously had been penalized as criminal. Due to the change in the socio-economic system, lawmakers had to rework the nation's law fundamentally. Part Eight of the new Penal Code was specially devoted to 'Crime in the Economic Sphere'. This part of the Penal Code now includes new chapters, such as that on 'Crime against Property' (Chapter 21), which covers predominantly offences already present in the Soviet period versions of Penal Codes (e.g. robbery, theft, fraud, etc.). Chapter 22, 'Crime in the Sphere of Economic Activity', includes many new types of violation of the law, e.g. illegal banking activity (Article 177), fraudulent entrepreneurship (Article173), legalization of illicit incomes (Article174), and unlawful acquisition of loans (Article176). This chapter also contains articles penalizing some 'old' types of criminal activity, e.g. manufacturing of counterfeit money and smuggling. Chapter 23, 'Crime against the Interests of the Service in Commercial and Other Organizations', covers, *inter alia*, criminal acts committed by auditors, notaries, etc.

---

[6]   *Ugolovnyi Kodeks Rossiiskoi Federatsii* (Pravo Publishers, Moscow, 1999), p. 34.

The new structure of the Penal Code facilitates analytical work for researchers by offering more precise definitions and by better delimiting similar offences. Though this merit prevents researchers from accurately comparing the data before and after 1977, it cannot hide the fact of the swift criminalization of entrepreneurial activities in Russia. Laws are more and more frequently violated in the field of finance and banking, in deals relating to the agro-industrial sector, and in external economic activities. This phenomenon is connected, first of all, with the economic turmoil.

A recent study of entrepreneurs conducted by experts from the Investigation Committee of Russia's Interior Ministry, and the Ministry's Research Institute in 15 major regions with a developed infrastructure, a large number of commercial enterprises, and a high level of economic crime (the republics of Altai, Bashkortostan, Tatarstan, the Krasnodar and Stavropol territories, the Volgograd, Leningrad, Novgorod, Novosibirsk, Rostov, Saratov, Sverdlovsk and Tyumen regions, and the cities of Moscow and St. Petersburg), provides evidence about the spread of economic crime.[7] The study shows that along with professional crimes, numerous conventional crimes are committed by businessmen. Criminal groupings are boosting their fight for spheres of influence and profit sources; armed clashes continue as a result of deals gone awry. A characteristic feature is that victims almost never ask for the assistance of law enforcement bodies due to mistrust of these bodies and imperfect legislation. There is a high percentage of criminals among businessmen who maintain close contacts with the underworld. Their goal is profit at any price, with complete non-compliance to laws.

One of the peculiar features of Russia's transition to the market economy is the high percentage of entrepreneurs with a criminal past. Research by the Institute of Applied Politics showed striking results – out of nearly 1,000 randomly selected entrepreneurs, 40 per cent had black market experience, 22.5 per cent had previously been charged, and 25 per cent were in contact with the underworld. Apart from that, criminal organizations are stepping up the establishment of their own businesses for committing economic crimes, laundering money, and transferring hard currency to Western banks. According to expert estimates of the Interior Ministry Research Institute, over 50 per cent of businesses are engaged in such activity, and up to 70 per cent of money received unlawfully is laundered through legal businesses.

The dynamics of officially registered economic crime between 1990–1996 (according to the old structure of the Penal Code) is illustrated in Table 2.

Table 2. Investigated Cases of Economic Offence in Russia

Year	1990	1991	1992	1993	1994	1995	1996
Number of cases	70,656	59,742	41,421	37,065	57,987	97,442	114,970
Share in the total number of registered offences	3.8	2.7	1.5	1.3	2.2	3.3	4.4

Source: Office of the Prosecutor General

---

[7] 'Organizovannaia prestupnost', n. 1 above, pp. 74–121.

The official figures above show a curious trend – the number of cases between 1990–1993 was reducing, while it is well-known that this period was characterized by an unprecedented growth in crime. The explanation lies not only in the under-reporting and under-registration of cases, but also in the fact that during the initial free-rein period of reforms the government closed its eyes to economic crime for the sake of 'breeding up a class of owners'. It is not an exaggeration to say that until the financial crisis fiasco in 1998, the government was consistently creating an ideal climate for the growth and spread of economic crime.

III.   CAUSES AND EVOLUTION

Two basic factors were decisive in this respect: the swiftness of change and the lack of preparedness for it on a large part of the population. Russians (no matter whether 'old' or 'new') were unable to get accustomed to the 'capitalist' rules of the game, which they knew only from Marxist textbooks. The market economy was reduced to the formula: 'If one promises a capitalist a 300 per cent profit, there's no crime he won't commit for it'. Russians accepted the change and acted accordingly. They quickly began to construct the only capitalism they knew. To be fair, just as in the 1920s and 1930s while building Socialism, they have achieved their aim in a historically unprecedented timeframe. The problem is that it was made in the image of 'capitalism' as understood in classical Marxist theory. In such capitalism, economic crime is immanent. In fact, it is an in-built rule of the game.

Meanwhile, socio-economic changes required that every member of Russian society abandon old understandings of 'good' and 'evil'. Russians had to accept that they had to play according to new legal rules which were often opposite to what they had been taught throughout the better part of their lives. What had been regarded as criminal in Soviet days (private entrepreneurship, dealing in hard currency, etc.) became a norm of life. The transition became a complex socio-psychological breakthrough, which violated the fundamental behavioural taboos of the old days.

The growth of economic crime correlates with the growth of crime in general, but does not fully coincide in periodization. In Russia, the general criminal situation passed four major stages:

- 1988–1992 – The period of catastrophic increases in crime (at this stage, relative indicators such as the percentage of growth and geographical spread, were especially impressive). Economic crime grows more or less in tandem with common crime.
- 1992–1995 – The period of stabilization of the growth rate. Extremely high absolute figures are characteristic to this period. Continued growth of economic crime – basically straightforward unsophisticated types.
- 1995–1998 – Decrease in the rate of growth and limited decrease in the absolute figures of some of the types of crime in general. Reduction in simple economic crime. Further growth of serious economic crime.
- Post-August 1998 to present day – Oscillating criminal growth rate (on a month to month basis). Increase in the rate of crime resulting from poverty conditions.

Temporary reduction in serious economic crime and increased number of uncovered corruption cases (referring mainly to previous periods).

The division into periods reflects how the current level of criminalization of the economy was reached in Russia. The basic causes of the high criminal rate remained the same over all the periods – the absence of an adequate mechanism of control and protection against criminal offences, plus the participation of a significant part of the establishment in the redistribution of direct or secondary criminal incomes.

The periodisation starts well before the August 1991 coup, which was the end of the old regime in the country and the virtual end of the Soviet Union. During the first stage, the new political elite of the *perestroika* period was pondering perhaps the most important question – how to make the post-coup economic and political changes irreversible. In bringing about the transition, the reformers (since 1985 they were both the top bureaucrats and officials) were unanimous that they must have their own social basis – a class of owners. The latter had to be rather large and capable of supporting their patrons. The problem was to create this class starting from the point where all were roughly equal in terms of income and property. The political elite could not afford the luxury of indulging in selective breeding – they feared that by the time they created a new class, some other party or parties would have come to power. Another reason was that in order to follow this course, it would be necessary to reveal their plans to the public – a sure way to create general resentment.

The major obstacle for the new *nomenklatura* in the Kremlin was the law. What is important is not the Soviet law in particular, but the mere existence of the law. According to presidential aides in 1991, it 'hampered the progress of democracy'. This brought about the first big legal clash of the post-Soviet period – between the President and the Parliament, which was the core event of the second stage. The legal side of the conflict dated back to 1991, when the Russian Parliament, in order to speed up reforms, gave President Yeltsin temporary extraordinary powers to rule by decree in implementing changes. No matter which way relations between President Yeltsin and Khasbulatov, leader of the rival Supreme Soviet (Parliament), developed, the Supreme Soviet was doomed since its very existence was a major threat to the idea of the accelerated breeding of the new rich. The deputies in the Supreme Soviet, though greedy and venal, would never have legalized theft and embezzlement on such a scale as we see now. The conflict between the Kremlin and the Parliament, presented as a struggle between the progressive democratic world against old dying communism, cannot be regarded as a collision of ideologies. Basically, it was a war over property between two parties – a war that was to ultimately decide who would rule Russia.

As a result, the economic crime rate jumped 16 per cent in 1994 compared with 1993. The number of counterfeiters grew by more than 3.5 times; income concealed from taxation increased by some 200 per cent; the number of embezzlements from the state and individuals was also on the rise. A number of commercial banks and pseudo-financial companies went bankrupt with ensuing scandals, including 'Chara', 'Europa', 'LLD', 'Ostbank', 'Tibet', 'Kapital', and a number of other medium-size banks and financial companies such as 'Lenin' and 'Neft-Almaz-Invest'. The sum of their investors' losses exceeds many trillions of roubles. The Podol'sk-based (Moscow region) private enterprise 'Vlastelina' alone robbed 20,000 people of more than USD20 million. Nevertheless, such banks and firms continued to mushroom and subsequently go bankrupt almost every week.[8]

From the point of view of trends in economic crime, this second stage was just plain theft committed by the ruling elite. It out-stripped the 'modest embezzlements' of the pre-reform period that lacked gangsters – the major operators of the present economy. Pre-reform thugs were a modest lot – they worked several levels below, mugging and robbing people in the streets while being careful not to go too far. The initial major capital was established on the streets through trade in alcohol, beverages, cigarettes, household electronics and second-hand cars. This trade was under the control of Russia's criminal community from the very beginning. At that stage, the apogee of economic criminal activity was reached with the introduction by presidential decree of the so-called voucher privatization, instead of the privatization accounts mechanism which had been envisaged in the Law on Privatization, adopted by the Parliament in 1992.

Vouchers (privatization cheques issued by the government for each Russian to represent the person's share of national wealth to be divided; the market worth of this share never exceeded USD10) or government securities, which entitled the owners to purchase a stake in state property, were the most generous presents given by the ruling elite to the criminal community. It was an hour of triumph for the former mobsters; they bought out vouchers by the sack and rapidly became the richest people in the country. Piles of anonymous, unnamed papers confirmed the right to purchase no less anonymous state property. They were the key to many privatized companies that called the tune at sectional and regional levels. The criminal community was almost legalized. The criminal community succeeded in creating a simple and effective mechanism to buy out vouchers. While investment funds and financial companies were still 'in diapers', the street already had much to offer: large packages of privatization vouchers capable of winning any tender. To have them meant an advantage over the rivals. With such common interests, there is hardly a commercial business in Russia at the present time that would not have contacts with the mafia. In simple terms the situation is this: entrepreneurs who have been terrorized by bandits are forced to relinquish part of their earnings to the mafia or the so-called 'roof' (cover). In large and mid-size businesses these relations look like mutually beneficial cooperation.

The second stage gradually grew into the third one with the so-called privatization auctions swindles as its centre-piece. The scale of the swindle is graphically described by Vladimir Polevanov, former chairman of the Russian Property State Committee, in one of his interviews in 1998:

Question: To what extent do you think mistakes in privatization influenced aggravation of the economic crisis in the country?

---

[8]   'Strategicheskie Issledovaniia', *CSGS* (Inafr, Moscow, 1995), p. 34.

Answer: They were a decisive factor. Let me recall what happened in Russia with regard to the so-called vouchers. You and me both got a 1/150,000,000 share of the general state property. Actually, of 50 per cent of that property. If you recall, no names were on the vouchers. Every voucher cost 10,000 roubles in the prices of early 1993. Do you know how much every one of us should have got for his share?

Question: How much?

Answer: Two million roubles. For every voucher [...]. Do you now see the scale of the swindle? These days, they claim that it was the only way. As I see it, it's a lie. All they had to do was take a look at how they implemented privatization in Czechoslovakia or Poland. They all had their names on the vouchers, and the securities signified the real cost of the property, not symbolic. That's how they made them true state securities, which would have been madness to barter for a bottle of vodka or a kilogram of sugar. And in this country that was precisely what the majority did. Actually, two privatizations took place in Russia. One of them for the masses. The other one, in secrecy, for the selected few. And the latter was thoroughly criminal. Huge slabs of state property ended up in the hands of some previously obscure men who had nothing for their country [...]. It's just that they turned up at the right time in the right place. And probably, with the necessary sum of money on them. Not to buy property as such, you know. To buy the state official in charge. Hence the appearance of so called oligarchs [...]

The second phase of privatization followed, so-called investment auctions. They offered considerable enterprises for sale. Nobody thought about issuing vouchers with our names on them, and let those who wanted these enterprises buy the vouchers from the population. No, they began explaining at once that investment auctions were only for the rich. The media did all they could to drag us into the discussion over who will get Svyazinvest – Potanin, Berezovsky, or Khodorkovsky. Why is it that nobody recalled that Svyazinvest had been built by generations of Russians and belonged to them? And that it should be bought from Russians, not from some state bureaucrat? Nobody recalled that Svyazinvest gave us a billion dollars in annual profits, and it was sold for only 1.8 billion. And only 100 million of the sum was directly invested in economy. And that is not all there is. The money our oligarchs paid at the auctions was, more often than not, interest-free credits from the Central Bank, i.e. they were buying expensive enterprises virtually for a song.

Question: Would you care to give facts?

Answer: In April 1995, the governmental commission for financial and credit policy transferred accounts of federal treasury in Moscow and Moscow region to 'Menatep' bank. Soon afterwards Minister of Economy Panskov issued a personal order to place 50 million dollars in 'Menatep' with very little interest. All the money was spent by the bank to repay its obligations for investment competitions. In other words, we ourselves were killing the geese laying the golden eggs. It's hardly surprising that in the long run we got the crisis of 1997 and finally the 1998 default. In mid-1998 we have living standards in the country like we had in 1947. We remain afloat only thanks to the giants like Gazprom. Thank God, they haven't split it yet and sold for a pittance.[9]

The authorities turned a blind eye to what was happening and no attempts were made to prevent criminals from participating in denationalization. Officials seemed to regard the mafia's infiltration as a 'necessary evil' on the way to a market economy. They continued to bet on the elite commercial businesses which they had taken pains to create. That was probably the worst that happened during those years.

At present, a considerable part of the Russian economy is controlled by seemingly respectable commercial businesses thanks to the support of street barons. Sometimes one has an odd feeling that the government did its best to destroy all the healthy 'cells' in the economy. Quotas, licenses, special exporter status etc. stirred up the mafia's interest in such privileged businesses; later it took them under its wing. One of the well-known Russian entrepreneurs admitted that no sooner had his firm won several export incentives than it became the focus of mafia attention. Often criminals do not demand a share in profits, although such things also happen. They are mostly interested in pushing their goods through the border. Large-scale entrepreneurs react differently: they may turn down such proposals, but if an offer comes from big mafia bosses, they readily comply because it's safer and even more profitable.

Large enterprises, the backbone of the economy, outlasted all other businesses but eventually they, too, came under mafia control. Similar situations are mirrored in many sectors of the Russian economy.

IV.   STRUCTURE OF ECONOMIC CRIME

The third and the current fourth stages of development of economic crime in Russia are characterized by a stable structure of offences. From the point of view of a number of cases, different types of larceny are leaving all other kinds of economic crime far behind. However, from the point of view of values, the privatization fraud and offences in the financial and banking sectors are more important. The incompatibility of data does not allow one to compare fully the dynamics of economic crime along the lines of the articles of the Penal Code, but in the table below we can see a general picture of the situation.

The financial sector offers a number of lucrative directions for criminal activity. Emphasis during reforms was placed upon the creation of a strong financial intermediary sector that developed at the expense of the other sectors of the economy. This immediately made financial institutions a favourite object of attention for

---

[9]   'What the Papers Say' (WWTP, London, 15 October 1998), p. 10.

Table 3. Number of Cases of the Most Frequent Types of Economic Crime in Russia

Year	Larceny	Bribery	Consumer Fraud	Speculation
1980	39,394	3,268	16,072	14,569
1985	54,662	5,909	14,798	19,396
1990	43,368	2,691	19,842	24,325
1991	39,070	2,534	18,934	18,988
1992	36,867	3,337	23,131	3,959
1993	33,114	4,511	19,846	843
1994	The norm was changed	4,921	24,012	n.a
1995	-	4,889	31,155	n.a
1996	-	5,453	29,108	n.a
1997	-	5,608	n.a.	n.a
1998*	-	6,000	n.a.	n.a

Source: Ministry of Internal Affairs. *Notes*: * Projection, n.a.: Data not available

organized crime. The sector offered quick returns for comparatively low investments. At the same time, the control over financial institutions allowed organized crime to establish control over the rest of the economy. Later, the newly acquired financial power allowed criminal elements to dictate their conditions to politicians, who needed funds for election campaigns.[10]

The mafia's influence on commercial banks varies. In some banks, the mafia has its people on the board of directors. According to some sources, all the small banks pay off the mafia, i.e. they have a 'cover'. The mafia's part of the bargain is to protect the bank from young racketeers and to supply it with clients who have cash. In this case, the bank has to share profits derived from operations with entrusted resources. This particularly concerns state budget-related assets. Larger banks offer preferential treatment to firms controlled by the mafia, which in turn commits itself to make clients pay their debts. At the present time, only acknowledged leaders of the underworld can cope with this task.

Recent government policy did nothing to prevent mafia bosses from advancing to key positions in the economy. At present, they control not only private retailers and small wholesalers, but also commercial exports of raw materials including products defined as 'strategically important'. In confidential talks, many Russian commercial exporters complain that it is impossible to get even a small amount of non-ferrous metal, oil products or timber outside Russia without coming under the scrutiny of some criminal group – and perhaps more than one group. With a formidable network of informers, the mafia knows virtually all that is happening in the economy – it receives information direct from manufacturers, banks which credit transactions, transport companies, customs officials and even border check-points.

---

[10] The situation with financial crime is described in detail in the chapter on capital flight.

During the third stage of our periodization (between July 1996 and July 1998) according to the Main Department for Economic Crime of the Interior Ministry, the damage to the Russian securities market by fraud was 590 billion pre-1998 roubles. The average monthly number of fraud attempts has snowballed 75 per cent in comparison with the previous period. In one criminal case alone, counterfeit Sberbank notes worth USD320 million and 12,000 blank forms were confiscated. An intricate chain of financial transactions with Energoatom securities worth USD2 billion was discovered in another case. The Ministry quoted experts as saying that the financial crises of the past few years have not simply been controlled but sometimes clearly provoked. The attempts of individual financial and industrial groups, both Russian and international, to redistribute property and exert political pressure are at the core of the crises.[11]

Insider trading, government favouritism and corruption were behind a majority of fraud cases in the Russian securities market, primarily the short-term GKOs (Treasury Bills). Many top government officials were active players in this market, including at least one deputy Prime Minister. Some were working on behalf and/or in the interest of foreign investors with obscure backgrounds. Modern criminal conflicts are fought not for territories but transnational financial, informational and intellectual flows. The ability to influence stock markets or the rates of foreign currencies is regarded as a strategic course of winning economic and financial territory. In this respect, the removal of restrictions on the involvement of non-residents in operations with government securities had a harmful effect on the economy as a whole. Russia became the first victim of the process of globalization of crime. There is evidence that 30 investment companies control almost the entire Russian securities market, or about 70 per cent of its turnover.[12]

Over the period of reform, some USD50–100 billion worth of credits received from the USA, the World Bank, the International Monetary Fund (IMF) and from the Gore-Chernomyrdin Commission have been moved abroad, as Jeffrey Sachs of Harvard University, a former advisor to the Russian government, indicated in an interview with the newspaper *Noviye Izvestia*. This money was mostly transferred to Western banks and invested in property abroad. Commenting on his resignation from the post of Gaidar's government advisor in 1993, Sachs said that while working in Russia he was confronted for the first time with a government that squandered money intended for economic reform. Moreover, if the situation has changed, it has unfortunately changed for the worse, he said. He added that the IMF is responsible for many of the problems facing Russia. The IMF, which has actually become a mediator between Russia and the West, pursued an erroneous policy, injecting billions of dollars into Russia, but not into its economy, Sachs continued. This money was instantly stolen by the upper echelons and by the government's friends. He announced that the IMF's latest credit extended in July, has been almost entirely moved to Western banks.[13] The result of this policy was the catastrophic financial August crisis of 1998.

---

[11] *Interfax Daily Report*, 30 July 1998.
[12] Ibid.
[13] *Noviye Izvestiia*, 1 October 1998, p. 2.

V. Post-august 1998 trends and forecasts for the 21st century

The date of 17 August 1998 became a symbol of the total failure of President Yeltsin's economic policy. It erased all hopes for the successful capitalist development of Russia. It also gave birth to new trends in economic crime in the country. The changed economic environment forced organized crime to discover other means of maintaining an inflow of profits.

For a short period (August–November 1998), there was a decline in economic crime as the main perpetrators tried to salvage their assets in the dwindling banking sector. However, very soon after they turned their attention to look for new ways of ensuring their continued prosperity. The main result was politicization of economic crime. Their strategy was to prove that any measures taken against economic criminals were in fact attempts to reverse the reforms and to restore communism. A number of cases under investigation on charges of economic crime against the so-called oligarchs (fraud, money laundering, tax evasion) were labeled as political persecution.

Another trend is the increase in criminal acts that show the growing disrespect towards representatives of state power, official bodies and public order on the part of the population. In 1996, 263 cases of offence against the lives of law enforcement officers were registered, in 1997 – 321 cases, in 1998 about 400.[14] In the second half of 1998 and the first half of 1999 there was a startling increase in murder and kidnapping of top law enforcement officials, tax inspectors, parliament deputies etc.

The criminal statistics register a close correlation between the growth of crime and the spread of demoralization and criminalization of the population, unemployment and homelessness. The share of previously convicted, homeless, and unemployed individuals increased within the total number of criminals. Curiously, the number of offences committed in a state of drunkenness decreased. At the same time, the share of those who committed crimes under the influence of drugs grew significantly.

Organized crime became an element of life for a significant proportion of the Russian population. It is penetrating the political sphere more and more. The latter takes the form of support of criminal candidacies to Russia's elected bodies. Such support combines financing political figures whose political ideas and activity comply with the interests of the mafia, funding their political campaigns in the mass media, as well as bribing government officials – including members of election commissions. Corruption as a means of securing necessary political decisions now gives way to direct participation of criminals in political decision-making without intermediaries. Corruption itself became omnipresent. It is fully integrated with economic crime.

Organized crime (both Russian and international) concentrated about half of Russia's national wealth in its hands. It continues to amass greater value. According to an informed pro-western Russian weekly *Argumenty i Fakty*, 20 influential Russians smuggled out at least USD40 billion, which they keep in overseas accounts.

---

[14] *Militeiskaia Gazeta*, No. 3, 1999, p. 2.

The sum is equivalent to two annual Russian state budgets.[15] In Russia, economic activity and, in particular, private enterprise are inseparable from a number of economic offences – graft, tax evasion, smuggling and violations of customs regulations, and physical violence against competitors and individuals who are regarded to be stumbling blocks in the way of one's business.

Those trends reflect a grim picture of the situation with economic crime in the country in the 1990s. They also provide little hope for the improvement of the situation. The situation will continue to deteriorate for several years before any improvement may take place. However, in some areas the situation may be reversed relatively soon. Three main groups of offences may show different dynamics in the future.

The first group consists of crimes with high and stable growth rates in the first years of the next century. This includes 15–17 types of offences (false entrepreneurship, fraudulent obtaining of loans, tax offences, gross violation of accounting regulations, limiting competition, hampering legal entrepreneurial activity, violations of regulations on securities, fraudulent bankruptcy etc.). The annual increase will be between 100 and 200 per cent for each type of offence.

The second group is 17–20 economic *corpora delictis* that will demonstrate oscillating growth. Those include, for example, misappropriation of entrusted property, larceny of especially valuable objects, legalization of illicit incomes, consumer fraud, excess of power by security and detective services.

The third group of 12–15 *corpora delictis* will probably recede. Those include thefts, willful destruction or injuring of property, acquisition and selling of stolen goods, violation of competition laws, etc. From 2000, they will decline at a rate of 30–40 per cent per year.

However, against the background of a stable improvement in the uncovering of economic offences in the first two groups, the anticipated reduction in the third group will not significantly influence the grand total figures. The latter will remain within the region of 380,000–420,000 cases annually. Moreover, the quantitative overall growth will be accompanied by an increase in public danger of economic offences because of their better organization and more sophisticated forms, wider corruption, and further fusion with conventional criminal offences.

The undertaken analysis and the forecast data speak about the necessity of an urgent intensification of the struggle against economic crime. However, many doubts remain that this struggle can be successful as long as the issue is viewed as a case of political confrontation between different segments of the society.

---

[15] *Argumenty i Fakty*, No.13, 1999, p. 2.

3

The Russian Mafiya:
Economic Penetration at Home and Abroad

Mark Galeotti

I. INTRODUCTION

Crime pays, and organized crime is organized business as much as a predator on the legal economic system. In Russia and the other post-Soviet states, organized crime has had a particular role, not just in exploiting but even shaping the economic order. After all, as well as the usual staples of organized crime, such as drug smuggling and gun running, the Russian *mafiya* has an especially significant involvement with a vast range of economic crimes. These range from participation in the widespread flight of capital and assets from Russia (the usual estimate is of anything between one to two billion dollars every month)[1] to intellectual piracy (Russia is second only to China as a producer of illegal recordings).[2]

II. MAFIYA IN THEORY: DEFINITIONS AND DIMENSIONS

This is not the place to embark on too long a semiological excursion into just what we should call this criminal phenomenon. Many government agencies prefer a neutral term such as Russian, Russian-speaking or even East-European organized crime.[3] This is understandable for political reasons, as it is uncontroversial, although to call gangs based in Vladivostok 'East-European' is stretching geography a little. 'Russian-speaking' is also awkward, not least as it fails to capture the distinctiveness of these organizations. Diego Gambetta's work on the Sicilian Mafia[4] led him to

---

[1] This figure is remarkably – perhaps suspiciously – stable over time and has been repeated by sources ranging from Western observers to Deputy Interior Minister Kozhevnikov. *Itar-Tass*, 29 November 1998. It may prove to be one of those figures which become authoritative simply because it is impossible to check and is repeated often enough.

[2] According to the International Federation of the Phonographic Industry, *Reuter*, 21 November 1995. This also very much applies to computer software: Microsoft estimates that 98 per cent of 'its' products in use in Russia are counterfeit. See R. Linberg and V. Markovic, 'Organized Crime Outlook in the New Russia' <www.search-international.com/artruss.htm>.

[3] As used, for example, in the British National Criminal Intelligence Service's two 'Project Ivan' assessments, or the reports of the Canadian Criminal Intelligence Service.

[4] D. Gambetta, *The Sicilian Mafia* (Harvard University Press, Cambridge, MA, 1993).

31

A. V. Ledeneva and M. Kurkchiyan (eds.), Economic Crime in Russia, 31–42
© 2000 *Kluwer Law International. Printed in Great Britain.*

redefine 'mafia' specifically as organized crime groupings involved in the provision of non-state protection, and Federico Varese has ably developed this thesis to make a case for all or some of Russia's gangs to be treated in the same way.[5]

However problematic, the transliterated term *mafiya* has certain advantages. It emphasizes that the dominant model for post-Soviet organized crime, while bearing an often striking resemblance to its Sicilian cousin, is distinctive. As a working definition, it is a form of organized crime further displaying certain broad characteristics reflecting its historical roots and the extent to which it evolved in step with the new post-Soviet states.

Like many other organized criminal cultures, from the Sicilian Mafia to the Chinese Triads and Japanese Yakuza, it has a keen – if often mythologized – sense of its own history. The nineteenth-century criminal traditions of the so-called *vorovskoi mir*, 'thieves' world,' were transformed by Stalinism.[6] The mass prison camps not only gathered 'critical masses' of criminals, who could articulate, codify and propagate their own values, hierarchies and even code of tattoos – tellingly, the camps became known as 'academies' in Russian criminal slang – they also presented the authorities with a huge logistical problem. As millions of political prisoners were rounded up and put to forced labour, the state began co-opting criminals as enforcers, to keep the 'politicals' in line. From this emerged a new criminal tradition, built on cooperation between law-breakers and the Communist Party. Emerging as victors in the internecine 'scab wars' which raged across the labour camp system in the late 1940s and early 1950s, the members of this new criminal culture were largely freed in the amnesties which followed Stalin's death, and proceeded to stamp their authority on the wider Soviet underworld. Increasingly, the links between organized crime, the underground economy and corrupt elements within the Party became all but institutionalized. However, the senior role was still played by the Party, which helped keep the other members of this unholy trinity fragmented and forced to work behind the scenes.

As the Soviet Union and the Party's very authority collapsed in the late 1980s, though, the *mafiya* was able to consolidate and emerge. In particular, it used its wealth, contacts and, ultimately, coercive power to redefine its relationship with the new political elite (largely drawn from the old Party) and economic structures (either privatized elements of the Party-controlled economy or legalized aspects of the former underground economy). In 1992, for example, state assets to the value of 92 billion roubles were sold off in privatization campaigns – of which organized crime spent a reported 50 billion. Viktor Ilyukhin, chair of the Russian parliamentary Security Committee, claimed in 1994 that organized crime controlled 55 per cent of capital in the country and 80 per cent of all voting stock, while another estimate had it controlling 15–25 per cent of Russia's banks.[7]

---

[5]   F. Varese, 'Is Sicily the Future of Russia? Private Protection and the Rise of the Russian Mafia' (1994) 35 *Archives europeennes de sociologie*, pp. 224–258; and 'What is the Russian Mafia?' (1996) 5 *Low Intensity Conflict and Law Enforcement*, pp. 129–138.

[6]   On the prehistory of Russian organized crime, see A. Gurov, *Professional'naya prestupnost'* (Iuridicheskaya Literatura, Moscow, 1990); V. Chalidze, *Criminal Russia* (Random House, New York, 1977).

[7]   *ITAR-Tass*, 13 May 1994; *Nezavisimaya gazeta*, 17 January 1997.

Secondly, *mafiya* is defined not by ethnicity, nor even by language, but by style. This is not simply 'Russian-speaking organized crime', in that it includes Georgians, Latvians, Poles and, soon enough, will include Israelis, Germans, Americans, and who knows who else. Instead, just as the Italian Mafia managed to cross-cultural divides in America and incorporate members of other communities prepared to work by their rules and methods, so too the 'Russian mafiya' is defined by its methods of operation and organization. It is, after all, not too tongue-in-cheek to describe it as post-Fordian organized crime. The prevailing models have been either feudal or industrial in pattern, dominated by hierarchies of personal authority or management.

The *mafiya*, though, is a most disorganized form of organized crime. This does not mean that it is not efficient, but that it is best characterized as a series of networks rather than formal structures. Even the 'godfathers' of the *mafiya*, the *vory v zakone* (literally 'thieves-within-the-law', but best translated as 'thieves-within-code') are not necessarily at the head of the largest gangs. Instead, they are figures with authority – and, indeed, the new generation of younger, more entrepreneurial figures are known as *avtoritety*, 'authorities'. When even the largest 'gangs', such as the Moscow-based *Solntsevo* or St Petersburg *Tambovskaya*, are essentially loose alliances of smaller groups and affiliated individuals, it becomes clear that the *mafiya* is a collection of criminal entrepreneurs. They form long- and short-term affiliations on the basis of common backgrounds, friendships, home-town or region or ethnic identity, but they do not fit into formal hierarchies. Instead, the pattern is of individuals and small 'crews' operating largely autonomously, perhaps coming together on a case-by-case basis to exploit a particular opportunity, but then as easily fragmenting. The role of the *vory* and *avtoritety* is thus complex. They are criminal entrepreneurs in their own right, and they will often hire others for particular operations or franchise out opportunities. They are matchmakers facilitating the formation of these customized alliances. They are arbiters settling disputes within the alliance and with other combines. Finally, they are the repositories and distributors of intelligence and what, in business terms, would be termed 'best practice'.

As a result, unlike the relatively disciplined organizations of the *Cosa Nostra* or the Japanese *Yakuza*, which gain in economies of scale and discipline what they may lose in flexibility, the *mafiya* is prone to internal disagreements and bloodletting, but it is also extremely flexible and responsive to its market. After all, the *mafiya* is also unusually commercial. Unlike the older generation of *vory v zakone*, the *avtoritety* tend to see crime as merely one route to acquiring money and power. As such, they have no particular commitment to crime in and of itself, only when it pays.[8] To an extent, this reflects their upbringing in a society where all forms of private enterprise were illegal, eroding any distinction between forms of so-called 'speculation'. As a result, most gangs operate across the spectrum, from entirely

---

[8] 'Traditional' organized crime, after all, tends to become closely involved in legitimate business as a front or to exploit it through criminal methods. For an especially thorough examination of *Cosa Nostra* operations in New York, see J. Jacobs, *Gotham Unbound* (New York University Press, New York, 1999).

legitimate enterprise, through 'grey' or paralegal business into overtly criminal activities.[9] Thus, an *avtoritet* may own a private bank set up with money embezzled from Party funds in 1990 but now operating legitimately, a property company which also launders drugs money and a 'private security firm' which is merely a front for protection racketeering. People and resources can switch back and forth within this diversified portfolio of operations as market opportunities demand. It is thus often difficult to tell a gangster from a *'biznesmen'* – a distinction, indeed, many within the Russian business class themselves see as irrelevant. According to Russian Interior Ministry figures, organized crime controls 40 per cent of the Russian economy.[10] This specific figure may be meaningless – much of the official research is very dubious, and it is hard enough to quantify the notionally legal economy – but it gives a sense of the penetration of the economy by the *mafiya*, its front organizations and its allies.

III.   MAFIYA AT HOME: ORGANIZED CRIME AND THE ECONOMY

Given that the *mafiya* played a major role in the evolution of the post-Soviet Russian economy, it is hardly surprising that it is a major player within it. This involvement takes three main forms: ownership, affiliation and protection.

Ownership, either directly or – more often – through front companies and intermediaries, is the most obvious. While the aforementioned figure of 40 per cent control may be impossible to confirm, this reflects the essentially confused and even lawless beginnings of Russian capitalism. Emerging through systemic collapse, it is built on massive privatizations of often dubious legality and morality, as well as the Party's own efforts to salt away assets for the future. When the Soviet banking system began to be liberalized and compartmentalized, for example, the first creations were the so-called 'pocket banks' serving heavy industry (the name comes from their effective status, 'in the pockets' of enterprise managers) and the Party's 'zero banks', which acted little more than money laundering ventures.[11] This helps explain the widespread Russian police perception that the banking sector is the most crime-ridden element of the economy.[12] Similarly, when Gorbachev began trying to encourage grass-roots economic activity in the form of cooperatives, he did so without creating for them a safe and viable legal and political environment. They proved useful fronts for the *mafiya*, and vulnerable targets. By late 1989, organized

---

[9]   For discussion of the underground economy, see 'Russia: Black Economy' *Oxford Analytica Daily Brief*, 1 August 1997, pp. 1–3.

[10] However, official figures also claim that around 40 per cent of the economy is 'underground'; *RIA-Novosti*, 29 November 1996; *Interfax*, 1 July 1997, cited in *BBC Summary of World Broadcasts: Former USSR*, 4 July 1997), suggesting that there may be a conceptual confusion between underground and *mafiya*-dominated.

[11] T. Burlingame, 'Criminal Activity in the Russian Banking System' (1997) 3 *Transnational Organized Crime*, pp. 46–72.

[12] *Nezavisimaya gazeta*, 10 September 1994. This view has since been repeated to the author by different officers at different times every year since. Furthermore, in 1998 the FBI reportedly estimated that nearly half of Russia's banks were controlled by the *mafiya*. *Washington Times*, 21 October 1998.

crime controlled or was paid off by an estimated 75 per cent of cooperatives.[13] By the time of the privatizations, the *mafiya* had the political and economic capital to corner the market. It is thus often difficult to distinguish between an entrepreneur who took full advantage of the opportunities available because of the nature of the transition and a member of organized crime.

There are, after all, few parts of Russia which do not have some resource open to exploitation. Even in distant and poverty-stricken Kamchatka, for example, there are huge opportunities in the fishing industry, from salmon and caviar to the giant Kamchatka crab, an endangered species which sells from up to USD100 a specimen in Japan. In the early 1990s, criminals and corrupt officials from the region 'privatized' for themselves much of the industry (an estimated 70 per cent – including all the modernized sectors), either directly or through existing agencies such as TINRO (the Pacific Scientific Fisheries and Oceanography Research Institute), which often became little more than front companies. Since then, there has been a degree of 'regularization', with state licenses being granted to many of these operations. Illegal and such 'grey' (untaxed) fishing out of the region nets an estimated 2.1 billion USD per year.[14] This is the general pattern, experienced by industries from aluminium to tourism.[15]

This blurring of the boundaries also points to the way organized crime has an important stake within the economy not just by outright ownership, but affiliation with owners, regulators and shareholders. Even back in 1995, 40 per cent of business-people deemed 'licit', polled by the newspaper *Argumenty i Fakty* admitted that they had been engaged in criminal activities in the past.[16] Even today, organized crime is a frequent partner or service provider, whether in opening up investment opportunities with dirty money or resolving business disputes through force. Contract killing as a business tactic re-emerged with a vengeance following the 1998 crash of the Russian economy: in the first five months of 1999, 567 business-people were assassinated, compared with 232 in the same period in 1998.[17] Less dramatic, but more pervasive, is the use of *mafiya* contacts for debt collection, something of a necessity given the weakness, venality and slowness of the Russian courts.

Perhaps most notorious, though, is the *mafiya*'s relationship with business as the supplier of *krysha*, a 'roof'. This notion of 'protection', is very important, but also complex and sometimes ambiguous. The term is used for a whole range of separate activities, from the simple – and parasitic – extortion of protection money, to rather

---

[13] *Krasnaya zvezda*, 4 October 1989.

[14] The criminal situation in the Russian Far-East has been ably summarized in a series of reports in *Organized Crime Watch – Russia* (later re-named *Organized Crime Watch – NIS*) 1 (1998–1999). See also M. Galeotti, 'The Russian Wild East: A Complex Criminal Threat' (September 1998) *Jane's Intelligence Review*, pp. 3–4.

[15] In the Siberian province of Kemerovo, for example, governor Aman Tuleev estimates that the *mafiya* owns 60 per cent of the coal mines and 30 per cent of its metal and chemical industries, *Washington Post*, 7 January 1999. Elsewhere in Siberia, the so-called 'aluminium wars' for control have led to killings and physical 'invasions' of plants. As for tourism, the murder in 1996 of American hotelier Paul Tatum in a feud over control of the Radisson-Slavyanskii Hotel was just one in a string of assassinations connected with the city's hotels.

[16] *Interfax* News Agency, 12 July 1995.

[17] *St. Petersburg Times*, 25 June 1999; <www.sptimes.ru>.

more positive services. A 'minimal' *krysha* might mean that the criminals themselves would not victimize or rob the client. A more advanced one would probably also extend to protecting the client business from other criminals. The 'best' sort, though, also provides a range of other services absent or unreliable in Russia, from cheap loans (often as money-laundering ventures) to an inside track on whom to bribe within the local authorities to get things done.[18] It is thus the norm to seek a *krysha*, unless either too small-scale to be noticed by the *mafiya*[19] or else sufficiently powerful either to have a substantial private security force or else to be able to rely upon the protection of state authorities. Either way, an estimated 70–80 per cent of businesses pay 10–20 per cent of their profits for a *krysha* – while those which do not have to spend on average 30–40 per cent of profits on other forms of protection. In this respect, turning to the *mafiya* may seem a wise business decision: in the words of one young entrepreneur, 'choosing the right *krysha* is the single most important decision in setting up a new business in Russia'.[20] However, it is more complex than most legal choices of service providers, as the 'protectors' may then often seek to renegotiate the terms of their arrangement, typically requiring services or demanding part-ownership of the enterprise.

However, most foreign firms will not experience a direct 'squeeze' from the *mafiya*. This may represent either high-level political contacts (implicitly bringing the firm under the protector's 'roof') but more often reflects the fact that the pressure is being applied to local partners or suppliers – who then pass on these extra enterprise costs through their fees.

IV. *MAFIYA* AT WORK: CHARACTERISTICS OF *MAFIYA* ECONOMIC CRIME

Reflecting the amorphous, flexible and entrepreneurial nature of the *mafiya* – perhaps best imagined as a shoal of piranhas, as opposed to the *Cosa Nostra*'s great white shark – it can and often will identify and target new opportunities with great speed. Without the need to seek clearance through hierarchies, devoted acolytes of the mobile telephone and, increasingly, email, members of the *mafiya* can assemble a team and launch an operation overnight. While Switzerland was a favoured money-laundering centre – the total amount of Russian criminal money in Swiss banks had topped an estimated USD40 billion by the beginning of 1998[21] – following the trial of the alleged *Solntsevo avtoritet* Sergei Mikhailov ('Mikhas')

---

[18] To take one example, personally known to me, the *krysha* of one Moscow-based firm is provided by a criminal group, largely of ex-KGB and police officers, who operate as a 'private security company'. When the firm ran into difficulties as a result of expansion, the *krysha* were able to find it new, larger offices within a day, get them wired to the telephone network within two and even provided a complimentary pot palm for their new reception! The price? 'You do more business, our cut is worth more'. As of 18 months later, the *krysha* had not tried to exploit this any more. It must be recognized, though, that this is an unusually positive tale – and there are many more nightmare stories of 'protectors' becoming parasites.

[19] Although Federico Varese has demonstrated how even street kiosks are subject to organized provision of such 'protection'. See F. Varese, 'The Emergence of the Russian Mafia' (DPhil Thesis, University of Oxford, 1996).

[20] Conversation, July 1998.

[21] *Reuters*, 23 January 1998; see <insideworld.com>.

in 1998 and the subsequent Swiss decision to tighten their controls on Russian money, alternatives were rapidly found. By the middle of 1999, the tiny Pacific Island of Nauru was reportedly laundering as much *mafiya* money as Switzerland.[22]

Also reflecting this diffuse structure, *mafiya* economic criminal activities tend in the main to be job rather than process or structure based. In other words, the 'team' will be assembled to carry out a particular operation, which could be a single scam or a more lasting project. It will rarely remain the same from operation to operation (structure-based). Similarly, it will be driven by opportunity more than a long-term function, such as laundering a steady stream of drug revenues (process-based).

However, the fluid and often *ad hoc* nature of *mafiya* organization should not be confused with a lack of resources or sophistication. A Russian-related Wall Street securities fraud scheme broken by the FBI in 1997, which cost investors several million dollars, involved a complex web of companies as well as a keen understanding of how to manipulate the stock market.[23] Most criminal networks encompass high-level resources, from control of a bank to access to senior government figures or skilled experts. The post-Soviet underworld contains extremely proficient specialists in a variety of arcane arts, from contract killers trained by the KGB's special forces to computer hackers whose background was as academic mathematicians. They tend to operate as freelance service providers, and their services ensure that *mafiya* operations can be as sophisticated as any. In 1996, for example, hackers penetrated police databases in the Baltic and deleted the records and serial numbers of all cars stolen in the former Soviet Union.[24] After all, organized crime can and does recruit and draw upon many of the most able of post-Soviet citizens. It is also often able to use elements of the Russian state, exploiting its inefficiencies or simply by bribing or suborning key figures within it. The most egregious example was the notorious Chechen *aviso* case, in which criminals were able to use the auspices of its Chechen branch to defraud the Russian State Bank of USD600–700 million between 1987 and 1992, through the use of forged *avisos* (proof of fund documents).[25] However, this is by no means an isolated incident.

V.   *MAFIYA* ABROAD: FORMS OF PENETRATION

The mafiya is also fervently internationalist: according to the Russian authorities, it was active in 26 foreign countries in the middle of 1998.[26] The various types of *mafiya* penetration outside the former Soviet Union can be divided broadly into three categories, which I would rather inelegantly term 'hard', 'soft', and 'service' penetration respectively.

---

[22] *Parlamentskaia gazeta*, 1 June 1999.
[23] *FBI New York Press Release*, 2 April 1997.
[24] *Ekspert*, 23 September 1996.
[25] *Interfax*, 7 July 1992, cited in *BBC Summary of World Broadcasts: Former USSR*, 10 July 1992.
[26] *Itar-TASS*, 21 July 1998. For an especially insightful Russian article of this subject, see (November 1996) 46 *Ogonek*.

'Hard' penetration entails the direct intrusion of Russian organized crime, establishing its criminal networks and authority alongside or generally in competition with indigenous organizations, a process that often involves considerable violence. This has been especially visible in the Baltic States, Central and Northern Europe. Austria, for example, is home to a number of *vory v zakone* and their operations.[27] Neighbouring Hungary is host to the infamous Semen Mogilevich, described in one report as 'the most dangerous mobster in the world' – his financial empire spanned the Channel Islands import-export firm Arbat International, nightclubs in Prague and Riga and the North American firm YBM Magnex, which was raided by police in 1998 and then dropped from the Toronto Stock Exchange index list.[28] Israel has also begun suffering such an intrusion, as Russian criminals make full use of the Law of Return, which permits immigration rights to those able to claim Jewish descent (a suitable passport can be bought for around USD10,000 in Moscow). In 1995 and then again in 1997, the Israeli underworld was torn by gang wars as *mafiya* gangs successfully took on their rivals and since then, gangs linked to the *mafiya* (especially the ubiquitous Solntsevo combine) have acquired powerful financial, narcotic and perhaps even political empires.[29] In 1996 alone, the Israeli police estimated that between three and four billion dollars of *mafiya* money flowed into Israel.[30]

This process can also take place on a sub-regional basis. New York's Brighton Beach Russian émigré community had, for instance, been the focus of small-scale organized crime since the 1970s. In 1992, though, the *vor v zakone* Vyacheslav Ivankov (known as *Yaponchik*) – incidentally, a 25 per cent shareholder in Mogilevich's Arbat International – was dispatched to bring Moscow's writ to Brighton Beach. By 1993, he had accomplished his task, forging strong links between the Brighton Beach *Organizatsiya* and the Russian *mafiya* underworld.[31]

Such countries tend to experience a marked increase in organized economic crime. Greek and Turkish–Cyprus alike, for example, became convenient bases for *mafiya* money-laundering and fraud operations. By 1997, some 3,000 of the 25,000 offshore companies in Greek–Cyprus were formally in Russian or East European hands,[32] although many others were probably indirectly controlled by the *mafiya*. In Germany, which has suffered a generalized increase in crime in general and organized crime in particular, Chechen gangs have, for example, a reputation for extortion and fraud, while Georgians specialize in counterfeit currency.[33]

---

[27] Including, some of the time, at least, Sergei Mikhailov and Viktor Averin of *Solntsevo* and Anatolyi Roksman of the predominantly Georgian, but Moscow-based *Mazutkinskaya* gang.

[28] R. Friedman, 'The Most Dangerous Mobster in the World' *Village Voice*, 20–26 May 1998; *Financial Times*, 22 May 1998; *Reuters*, 11 December 1998; see <insideworld.com>.

[29] *The Guardian*, 29 June 1995; *The Times* (London), 11 September 1995; *The Sunday Times*, 2 March 1997; *Segodnya*, 14 May 1997.

[30] *Associated Press*, 3 April 1997.

[31] R. Friedman, n. 28 above.

[32] According to the State Department's 1997 Financial Action Task Force report.

[33] (March 1995) 41 *La Dépêche Internationale des Drogues*, see; *Die Presse* (Vienna), 28–29 May 1997.

'Soft' penetration, by contrast, sees the *mafiya* showing its more respectable face, establishing legal or para-legal businesses (which can be used for illicit purposes in the future) and also contacts with local criminals. In some cases, this reflects a lack of sufficient opportunities or interest in full-scale involvement. Costa Rica, for example, has become an area of interest to many *mafiya* figures – so much so that Sergei Mikhailov procured for himself the title of Costa Rican honorary consul to Moscow in 1995[34] – but has not yet merited a major incursion. Instead, it is regarded as a convenient place to meet Latin American criminals and a convivial place to acquire a tan. Canada is similarly experiencing only sporadic efforts at serious penetration.[35] In other cases – Italy and Japan are the obvious examples – it can reflect the presence of powerful indigenous criminal organizations: the advantages in cooperation and discretion and the dangers in open conflict deter anything more intrusive. 'Soft' penetration can, however, also be just the first step, to be followed by full-scale 'invasion' once the ground is prepared, new opportunities emerge or are identified or scope for expansion elsewhere is exhausted. This may be the case in Spain, as Russian criminals, who for years have been enjoying the climate of the so-called 'Costa del Crime' – and the company of fellow mobsters from across the world – begin to adopt a more purposeful campaign, buying up properties, establishing front companies and building on their links with local criminals.[36]

This more overtly legal and tentative penetration lends itself to different forms and levels of economic crime. In the Netherlands, for instance, the *Podolskaya* gang from Moscow has allegedly established an operation producing counterfeit food and drink products for sale in Russia, the sort of activity which is illegal but, not having a direct negative impact on Dutch society and economy, is less likely to be detected or treated as a serious threat.[37] In Italy, the *mafiya* has largely confined itself to money-laundering. In 1997, for example, *Solntsevo* member Yurii Esin was arrested by Italian police for his role in a money-laundering venture and import-export scam.[38] Russian penetration has even reached as far as New Zealand, where investigations were opened in 1999 into the activities of two Russians, suspected of laundering possibly millions of dollars, most of which then flowed back to Russia or elsewhere, but some of which was used to buy property.[39]

In these days of economic globalization, it should come as no surprise that this also applies to criminals, and the *mafiya*'s 'service' penetration reflects this. The *mafiya* is increasingly involved in providing 'criminal services' for other groupings

---

[34] *Izvestiya*, 15 November 1995.
[35] The Canadian Criminal Intelligence Service noted in its 1997 report that 'East European-based organized crime' was 'operating in virtually all areas of the country' and was likely to expand; see <www.cisc.gc.ca/1997e/cisc97.html>. In part, though, the *mafiya* has found itself blocked by powerful indigenous groups, including the Hells Angels, who are especially involved in drug trafficking.
[36] *The Daily Telegraph*, 4 March 1996.
[37] P. Williams (ed.), *Russian Organized Crime* (Frank Cass, London, 1996), p. 69.
[38] *Kommersant-daily*, 21 March 1997; *Izvestiya*, 25 March 1997; see also the statement by Giovanni de Gennaro, head of Criminalpol (Italian criminal police) to the US Congressional Committee on International Relations, 1 October 1997.
[39] *Itar-Tass*, 14 April 1999, citing New Zealand TV reports.

across the world, from contract killing to cybercrime. This risks providing a criminal 'force multiplier'[40] as gangs acquire access to higher-order resources than would be expected.

This also has implications for *mafiya* economic crime, but beyond this essentially quite limited form of interaction, it is also clear that the *mafiya* – or, more accurately, criminal entrepreneurs within it – have developed links with many of their counterparts across the global underworld. The most serious and long-lasting connections are with the Sicilian Mafia and other Italian groupings, such as the Neapolitan *Camorra*, Calabrian *'ndrangheta* and Puglian *La Rosa/Sacra Corona Unita* ('The Rose/United Holy Crown') combine. The Italians were, after all, the first criminals actively to seek partners in Russia, with early contacts dating back to Soviet times. Russian criminals based in the Tri-State Area (New York, New Jersey, Pennsylvania) ran fuel-excise tax scams with the US-based *Cosa Nostra*, which netted at their peak up to one billion dollars a year.[41] In the Russian Far-East, gangs have been cooperating both with Chinese gangs in managing cross-border smuggling and also Japanese *yakuza*, especially the *Yamaguchi-gumi*.[42] The more adventurous *mafiya* groups – especially from the *Solntsevo* combine – are also seeking partners in Latin America, trading Central-Asian heroin for Colombian cocaine and laundering money for each other.[43]

Relations within the global underworld are, needless to say, far from always cordial. The image of a global concordat, a *Pax Mafiosa*, as popularized by Claire Sterling, does not hold true.[44] Many of these accords are very loose, little more than temporary alliances of convenience: already, for example, the relationship between Russians and Sicilians appears to be coming under pressure as the former begin to edge into southern Europe. Similarly, the gangs of the Russian Far East will soon have to decide which is the lesser of two evils: encroaching 'Varangian' gangs from European Russia, or their Chinese and Japanese counterparts. In the long term, the seeds are here for continent-spanning crime wars. In the mean time, though, there is a complex and healthy international criminal trade.

VI. PROSPECTS AND PROGNOSES

Little seems to stop the onward march of the *mafiya*. Even Russia's economic crash in 1998 seems to have been a 'good crisis' as regards the major players. It certainly squeezed the lower echelon of the *mafiya*, whose incomes tend to depend on

---

[40] A military term referring to the advantages – better training, communications and the like – which can give a unit the effective capabilities of a rather larger force.

[41] These operations are discussed in A. Block, 'On the Origins of Fuel Racketeering: The Americans and the Russians in New York City' and 'Analysis of Russian Émigré Crime in the Tri-State Region' in P. Williams (ed.), n. 37 above, pp. 156–176 and pp. 177–226, and also J. Finckenauer and E. Waring, *Russian Mafia in America* (Northeastern University Press, Boston, 1998).

[42] M. Galeotti, n. 14 above.

[43] Statement by Drug Enforcement Administration Special Agent Harold D. Wankel to US Congressional Banking and Finance Committee, 28 February 1996.

[44] C. Sterling, *Crime Without Frontiers* (Little Brown, London, 1994).

racketeering and vice, and are thus linked to enterprise profits and disposable incomes. The total effort put into extortion appears to have increased considerably, as each individual *krysha* client could contribute less. However, the major *mafiya* players, whose resources are in foreign currencies or represented by control of lucrative state assets, were able to take full advantage of the opportunities offered. They were able to extend and rationalize their business holdings, snapping up new purchases at bargain-basement prices.[45] Ironically, this led to a reversal of capital flight, assets being repatriated to Russia to take advantage of these opportunities. They were also able to extend their criminal empires, 'buying out' impoverished smaller gangs or more generally simply acquiring new, dependent clients within their networks. In the middle, a number of criminals with protected adequate assets simply took the opportunity to move abroad, further contributing to the *mafiya* diaspora.[46]

The size and growing maturity of the *mafiya* is also giving rise to processes of differentiation and specialization. Some of the richest criminals are putting greater effort into the legal sides of their business portfolios, perhaps motivated by a need to acquire respectability and security, perhaps a concern for their international freedom of travel and investment, or perhaps simply a desire to bequeath legal inheritances to descendants. This process of 'personal laundering' only rarely extends to a complete break with crime, though. Instead, this differentiation generally takes the form of passing or even selling businesses on to offshoot companies or trusted lieutenants, generally on the understanding that the principal will continue to receive tribute. It remains to be seen, then, whether this is anything more than a purely cosmetic exercise and extends to wider business attitudes. After all, most business carried out by the *mafiya* is essentially geared towards substantial short-term profits rather than long-term and sustainable growth.

Finally, as mentioned above, the size of the Russian (and post-Soviet) criminal 'industry' has also created numerous market niches for specialized groupings, typically smaller outfits or individuals working as 'outsourced' specialists. This is not confined to the usual computer hackers and contract killers, but also extends to a variety of specialties, from the obvious to the esoteric: accountants, international lawyers, stock manipulators, producers of synthetic drugs, even skilled linguists able to pass themselves off as foreigners in the course of frauds.[47]

The ways in which organized crime in and from the former Soviet Union represent a challenge to national and international security are many. The pervasiveness of crime is subverting hopes of a transition to genuine participatory democracy and a

---

[45] In one case, an *avtoritet* whose main business holdings were in import-export through St. Petersburg, used the opportunity to buy a haulage firm to distribute his goods, warehousing and a marketing firm.

[46] I discuss this diversity of experiences more fully in my article, 'The Three Faces of Russian Crime' *The Times* (London), 11 September 1998.

[47] In one case, in which I became involved as a consultant to the 'target' firm, an individual purporting to be a South African national emerged as a 'bona fide' in support of a notionally Czech but actually Russian-owned venture looking for foreign 'partners'. His accent, background knowledge and documents all appeared very plausible, and it looks likely that he was a former KGB agent, now turned free-lancer.

working market. Too many Russians equate democracy with *mafiya* and poverty. Nor is organized crime a rough and ready first step towards the market:[48] ultimately it creates and perpetuates uneconomic monopolies, pushes up business costs and has little interest in the creation of a stable and enforceable legal basis for property rights. There is also the subtle danger that concern about the *mafiya* simply demonizes the people of the post-Soviet states in the eyes of the outside world. The unthinking – and inaccurate – assumption that 'all Russians are crooks' will not only create new 'us' and 'them' divides in a world only recently rid of the manichaeism of the Cold War, but also fuel existing fears and resentments of the outside world in Russia.[49]

Estimates both anecdotal and statistical suggest that *mafiya*-led economic crime in Russia and outside its borders can only increase for the foreseeable future.[50] However, there is also a need for some caution and realism. This is not some criminal tidal wave breaking on the outside world, sweeping away democracy and legitimacy. In 1993, for example, the Deputy Assistant Commissioner of the Metropolitan Police was predicting armed *mafiya* mayhem on Britain's streets: 'in five years' time, there is no doubt that the major threat confronting the inner cities of the United Kingdom (UK) will come from central, eastern European and Russian countries.[51] Yet it is clear that the *mafiya* regards the UK as an enviable money-laundering centre (after a suitable 'pre-wash' in, perhaps, Cyprus or Austria), a pleasant place to shop and a secure place to send children to private school in the fond hope that they will learn how to become proper '*dzhentelmeny*'. Given that UK law enforcement still has a strong reputation, and the advantages in maintaining a low profile are still dominant, the threats, such as they are, come from isolated frauds and cybercrimes, or the relentless and possibly irreversible sifting of dirty money into the legitimate economy. It is therefore important to maintain a sense of perspective. The *mafiya* is powerful, deeply rooted within Russia, entrepreneurial and ruthless. It is not, however, richer than the Sicilians; it is not more vicious than the Colombians; it is not more determined than the Yakuza. The *mafiya* is a powerful criminal force, especially within the realms of economic crime, but it is no more ubiquitous than it is all-powerful, and to portray it as such would be to give it more authority and thus power than it deserves.

---

[48] Foremost in expressing this optimistic perspective is Edward Luttwak. See his 'The Good Bad Guys' *The Guardian*, 31 July 1995. For an effective rebuttal to simplistic parallels with the 'robber baron' era in US history, see A. Anderson, 'The Red Mafia: A Legacy of Communism' in E. Lazear (ed.), *Economic Transitions in Eastern Europe and Russia* (Hoover Institution Press, Stanford, 1995). Also available on <andrsn.stanford.edu/Other/redmaf/html>.

[49] I discuss these various dangers in 'The Mafiya and the New Russia' (1998) 44 *Australian Journal of Politics & History*, pp. 415–429.

[50] The Russian Interior Ministry's forecast for the period 1997–2000 anticipated a 150–200 per cent rise, *Rossiiskaia gazeta*, 8 February 1997.

[51] *The Independent*, 25 May 1993.

4

Organized Violence, Market Building, and State Formation in Post-Communist Russia

Vadim Volkov

I. INTRODUCTION

By adopting an analytical viewpoint of economic sociology this paper seeks to question a number of misconceptions shared by many studies of Russia's organized crime.[1] Let me briefly name the major ones and then offer an alternative vision. First, it is commonly held that organized crime in post-communist Russia is an expression of deviant behavior and anomie, that is, a purely dysfunctional element of the social system. Second, the so-called 'Russian mafia' of the 1990s is considered to be the heritage of the powerful Soviet criminal underworld that surfaced and started to grow as economic liberalization began. Third, most analysts agree on the fact that organized crime has attained control of the new market economy and that the task, therefore, is to assess the degree of that control. Fourth, organized criminal groups are seen as the major and most powerful force unleashed by the market reforms threatening to undermine the latter.

This paper advances an alternative set of propositions. First, organized criminal groups and similar agents perform some important institutional functions, creating structures which the Russian state failed to create and without which the new market economy could not work. Second, to understand contemporary Russian organized crime it is vital to stress its discontinuity with the old Soviet criminal world, to see it as a new type of action, a specifically capitalist type of organized crime brought to life by and functionally integrated into the emerging markets. Third, as criminal groups sought to gain control over the Russian economy, they themselves became subjected to some basic laws of economic action that then tended to transform these groups from within. Fourth, the power of criminal syndicates is largely inflated, not least in order to veil the main agents that actually control the transition to the market, namely, private protection companies created by and linked to the Interior Ministry (MVD) and the Federal Security Service (FSB).

---

[1] A shorter version of this paper was published as 'Violent Entrepreneurship in Post-communist Russia' (July 1999) 51 *Europe–Asia Studies*, pp. 741–754.

A. V. Ledeneva and M. Kurkchiyan (eds.), Economic Crime in Russia, 43–61

This paper is about the role of organized violence in the process of market-building and state formation in Russia. Instead of offering yet another review of Russia's notorious organized crime, I will analyze institutions and practices of violent entrepreneurship, criminal as well as legal. Violent entrepreneurship can be defined as a set of organizational solutions and action strategies enabling the conversion of organized force (or organized violence) into money or other market resources on a permanent basis. If consumer goods, for example, constitute the major resource for trade entrepreneurship, money – for financial entrepreneurship, information and knowledge – for informational, and so forth, violent entrepreneurship is constituted by socially organized violence, real or potential. Violent entrepreneurship, however, is different in one important respect: throughout modern history, organized violence, unlike other resources, has been managed and controlled by the state alone, that is by a public rather than private authority and used for public rather than private ends. With the rise of modern centralized states this key resource has been largely excluded from the sphere of private entrepreneurship. In today's Russia it is back again. This paper intends to demonstrate that what from the macro perspective appears as the crisis of the state in everyday practice takes the form of violent entrepreneurship.

The main unit of violent entrepreneurship we shall call 'violence managing agency'. In post-communist Russia such agencies can be provisionally classified into three types: state and illegal (units of state police and security forces acting as private entrepreneurs); non-state (private) and legal (private protection companies); and private and illegal (the so-called organized criminal or 'bandit' groups). These should be seen as ideal types, the boundaries between which in real life are blurred. Despite the differences in their legal status, violence managing agencies perform similar functions and display similar patterns of action on the economic market. This derives from the specificity of their major resource – organized force. Their main function will be defined as 'enforcement partnership' (*silovoe partnerstvo*), the term which was used by one of my respondents to describe the practice of his criminal group and which conveniently lends itself as an analytical category. Enforcement partnership is a business function of an organized group or enterprise deriving from the skilful use of actual or potential force on commercial basis and employed to maintain certain institutional conditions of business activities, such as security, contract enforcement, dispute settlement, and transaction insurance.[2]

II.   THE INSTITUTION OF ENFORCEMENT PARTNERSHIP

The institution of 'enforcement partnership' of the 1990s grew out of the regularized protection racket of the late 1980s which, in turn, goes back to the practice of

---

[2]   In this study the author has relied on the data obtained from different sources: recent journalistic publications and books, interviews with experts, businessmen, representatives of criminal groups, private protection companies, and the state police organs as well as from personal observations. I am grateful to Andrei Konstantinov for his generous help.

extortion in the Soviet-time shadow economy. Nonetheless, the protection racket should be analytically distinguished from mere extortion: the latter lacks regularity, reference to a broader organization in the name of which the money is collected, and the claim to offer real or imaginary services in return. The surfacing of extortion and its conversion into the regular observable pattern of the protection racket occurred in 1988–1989 as the cooperative movement, the first effect of the economic liberalization, gained momentum. Initially, cooperators and petty traders became victims of those extortionists who were formerly engaged in 'gambling debt recovery' and shadow business protection. Soon new groups, composed of former sportsmen, emerged on the scene and began to earn money by selling protection to small entrepreneurs and traders at city markets.[3] Official statistics registered a 30 per cent increase in racketeer offences between 1987 and 1988. The scale of the phenomenon in question was no doubt much wider than its reflection in statistical accounts: according to expert estimates only every fourth victim appealed to the police organs; the police reacted only in 80 per cent of cases; criminal charges were only pressed against every sixth racketeer; and only every eleventh served the sentence in prison, while the prison term for this kind of offence was rather lenient, maximum of three years.[4]

What stimulated the spread of the protection racket? A substantial part of assets of the first private entrepreneurs originated from the shadow economy of the Soviet era, therefore, many were naturally unwilling to have any relations with the state police. The state police, in turn, generally did not regard *kooperatory* as a legitimate object of protection – not least because of the negative Soviet moral attitudes towards private entrepreneurs – thus leaving an empty niche to alternative informal groups forcefully offering protection services.

Apart from the insufficient protection of private business by the state police, another major factor that produced a demand for enforcement partnership was the high entrepreneurial risk caused by frequent non-returns of debts and failures to observe contracts, not to mention the spread of swindling and theft.[5] The state organs were incapable of reducing these risks due to the poor definition of property rights, the inefficiency of the state courts of justice (*gosarbitrazh*) in resolving disputes and their incapacity to enforce decisions.[6] The combination of high risks and the shortage of protection and justice created an institutional demand for

---

3   On the genesis of regular rackets in Moscow, see V. Karyshev, *Zapiski 'banditskogo advokata':
    zakulisnaia zhizn' bratvy glazami 'zashchitnika mafii'* (Tsentrpoligraf, Moscow, 1998), pp.
    30–40; also M. Kleimenov and O. Dmitriev, 'Reket v Sibiri' (1995) 3 *Sotsiologicheskoe
    issledovaniia*, pp. 115–121.

4   S. Diakov and A. Dolgova, (eds), *Organizovannaia prestupnost'* (Iuridicheskaia Literatura,
    Moscow, 1989), p. 98.

5   The perception of entrepreneurial risks and ways of dealing with them are well reflected in a
    recent study of the emerging markets in Russia. See V. Radaev, *Formirovanie novykh rossiiskikh
    rynkov: transaktsionnye izderzhki, formy kontrolia i delovaya etika* (Tsentr Politicheskikh
    Tekhnologii, Moscow, 1998), pp. 116–127.

6   Evidence of this is provided in the dissertation by Federico Varese. See F. Varese, 'The
    Emergence of the Russian Mafia: Dispute Settlement and Protection in a New Market Economy'
    (DPhil thesis, University of Oxford, 1996).

enforcement partners, a kind of business mediators who could ensure the smooth functioning of private business.

In the contemporary Russian business lexicon the functions of the enforcement partnership are referred to by a modest phrase 'to solve questions' (*reshat' voprosy*). What does it involve? The first racketeer groups were mainly engaged in physical protection from other such groups and debt recovery (*smotreli chtoby ne naezzhali i ne kidali*). As private entrepreneurship developed and the intensity of transactions increased, the functions of enforcement partners diversified. They actively participated in business talks, giving informal guarantees of transactions and demanding the same from other enforcement partners involved in the deal. These tasks were performed either by organized criminal groups or state police and security employees acting on an informal basis. Expert and interview sources indicate that even today the majority of high-value business agreements can only be concluded given the participation and mutual guarantees of enforcement partners. Apart from security, risk control, debt recovery, and dispute settlement, enforcement partners also came to mediate relations between the private business and the state bureaucracy, helping to obtain permissions and licenses, registration, tax exemptions, as well as using the state organs (e.g. police, fire inspection and sanitary control services) to close down the companies of their competitors.

The evolution of patterns of enforcement partnership is described, by the participants, by three terms: 'to get' (*poluchat'*), 'to control' (*kontrolirovat'*) and 'to hold a share' (*byt' v dole*). A brigade of racketeers 'gets' (the tribute in cash) from a business in return for protection from other such brigades. A criminal group 'controls' a business enterprise when, in addition to physical protection, it introduces into the enterprise its own book-keeper or regular auditor who supplies information about business transactions and their value, while the group supervises and secures major contacts and transactions for a fixed share of the profits. At this stage the group can be said to turn from racketeering to enforcement partnership. When a group of violent entrepreneurs that 'solves the questions' of a given business enterprise invests its money into this enterprise and introduces its representative on to the board of directors, it becomes a shareholder and increases its share of the income. If at an earlier stage enforcement partners preferred to achieve one-time big gains through active intimidation and violence, the increasing competition between them and their aspiration to control the business produced incentives for creating a more favorable environment for, and sustained relations with, the clients in order to achieve longer-term gains.

The institution of enforcement partnership rests on the power of deterrence – the capacity to use force and cause physical damage to those who inflict financial or other losses on the businessman that the criminal group claims to protect. Thus the value of force is determined in proportion to the value of the potential damage – financial, material or otherwise – that may be caused in the absence of protection. But later, if and when enforcement partners get involved in business transactions on a permanent basis and, consequently, turn from episodic damage and risk control to the broader set of tasks of securing and expanding the field of business activity of a given firm, it is the business skills of, as it were, non-violent use of force that becomes the source of value rather than force as such. No fixed price list for enforcement partners' services ever existed – the price varied depending upon the evaluation of risks, the income of the specific firm, the duration and nature of its relations with the enforcement partner and the latter's reputation. In the retail trade and similar kinds of small businesses, simple protection was normally 'offered' at the initial rate of USD300–500 per month and then increased depending upon the economic performance of the business. The average price of 'question solving' or the full package of security and enforcement services, more relevant to larger scale business activity, was established at a level of 20–30 per cent of the profit of the client enterprise. When the group holds a share, it claims up to 50 per cent of the profit. The price of debt recovery stabilized at the level of 50 per cent of the sum of the debt.[7]

For the client enterprise these payments are part of its transaction costs. Transaction costs are the costs required to transfer and secure property rights, get access to resources, and maintain business relations.[8] They refer to the institutional conditions of business activity in the market economy and include the costs of making an exchange, such as discovering exchange opportunities, negotiating, monitoring, and enforcing exchange relations, and costs of maintaining a judiciary and police apparatus that protects institutional structures of economic exchange. A large number of small and medium sized firms ended up being under control of criminal groups either due to the shadow nature of their own economic activities or because they yielded to the intimidatory tactics of criminal groups. In most cases, however, criminal groups were simply more efficient than the state organs in solving the day-to-day problems of the new Russian entrepreneurs. Due to the predatory tax system and inefficient state protection and arbitrage, transaction costs incurred by private rule-enforcers were lower than the costs of legal economic activity.[9]

III.   THIEVES AND BANDITS

The legendary Soviet criminal underworld, the world of thieves (*vorovskoi mir*) has received a fair amount of scholarly attention.[10] Formed in labour camps and prisons in the early-Soviet times, the world of thieves became a powerful informal organization that survived until the end of the Soviet system. Thieves (*vory*) observe a complex set of mores and prohibitions that regulate their relations with one another, the authorities and with outsiders. Prohibitions are particularly strong with reference

---

[7]   A. Konstantinov, *Banditskii peterburg* (Folio-press, St. Petersburg, 1997), p. 175.

[8]   D. North, *Institutions, Institutional Changes and Economic Performance* (Cambridge University Press, Cambridge, 1990).

[9]   No comparative calculation of transaction costs have been made so far. Theoretical argument of the economic efficiency of informal rule-enforcers was advanced by Svetozar Pejovic. See S. Pejovich, 'The Transition Process in an Arbitrary State: The Case for the Mafia' (1997) 1 *IB Review*, pp. 18–23.

[10]   See V. Chalidze, *Criminal Russia: Essays on Crime in the Soviet Union* (Random House, New York, 1977); D. Likhachev, 'Cherty Pervobytnogo Primitivizma Vorovskoi Rechi' in *Iazyk i myshlenie*, Proceedings of the USSR Academy of Science, Vol. III–IV (Academy of Science, Moscow: 1935); A. Gurov, *Krasnaia Mafia* (Mico, Moscow, 1995); A. Gurov and I. Ryabinin,

to having a legitimate job and a family, the cooperation with prison or any state authorities, the use of violence towards other thieves unless a collective decision is taken, and personal luxury. The central element of the world of thieves is the so-called *obshchak*, the communal fund that accumulates the money acquired by theft and other illegal methods. Having donated the money to the *obshchak*, the thief then receives his share and thus his living. But the bulk of *obshchak* is used to support those who serve their prison term. The elite of this underworld consists of the so-called 'thieves-in-law' (*vory v zakone*), whose main function is *obshchak* management and exercise of criminal justice. Recent journalistic publications claim that the world of thieves has been challenged by a new type of criminal structure – the world of so-called 'bandits' (*bandity*).[11] Due to the restrictions of space, this paper will not reproduce the journalistic descriptions but will turn directly to the interpretation of the differences between thieves and bandits from the standpoint of the sociological view adopted in this paper.

Unlike bandits, thieves are not engaged in violent entrepreneurship. The thief's major task is to steal (in a broad sense) and avoid being caught. They do not produce anything and tend to keep a low profile unless in their own milieu. The bandit, on the contrary, considers himself a producer of certain services or at least makes such claims to his clients. His claim to being productive and his ability to affect business transactions derive from his capacity to apply and manage organized force. This capacity should be conspicuous, since it represents the group's major market resource and the source of its income. Hence the elaborate system of external symbolic attributes (e.g. gold jewelry, sport haircuts and leather jackets) and an easily recognizable assertive style of behavior. One would find it hard to identify thieves in urban public places, while bandits are easily recognizable. The thief's income comes from illegal secondary redistribution of property and consists of the appropriation, by illegal means, of the private property of other citizens or of the property of the state. The bandit aspires to receive a share of income of other entrepreneurs, which, as they claim, has been produced under the patronage or participation of the organized group that he represents. The income, therefore, derives from the redistribution of profit and takes the form of either profit share or tax. Being a type of entrepreneur, bandits seek regular income on the basis of a long-term business relationship and often claim to establish and enforce order, which is why they can sometimes get into direct conflict with thieves, for instance, when forcing them out of city markets and nightclubs.

The ethic of thieves is a projection of values and rules of prison life into civic ('free') life. Prison and labour camp terms are the major source of thieves' authority,

Ispoved' vora v zakone (Rosagropromizdat, Moscow, 1991); V. Radzinkin, *Vory v zakone i prestupnye klany* (Kriminologicheskaia assotsiatsiia, Moscow, 1995); J. Serio and V. Radzinkin, 'Thieves Professing the Code: The Traditional Role of *Vory v Zakone* in Russia's Criminal World and Adaptations to a New Social Reality' (Summer 1995) 4 *Low Intensity Conflict and Law Enforcement*, pp. 72–88; F. Varese, 'The Society of the *Vory-v-zakone, 1930s–1950s*' (October–December 1999) 39 *Cahiers du Monde ruse*, pp. 515–538.
[11]   A. Konstantinov and M. Dikselius, *Banditskaia rossiia* (Bibliopolis, St. Petersburg, 1998), pp. 75–107.

respect and career advancement to the highest title of thief-in-law. The bandits' mores were formed in the domain of civic life, they are more rational and practical, containing fewer prohibitions and constraints. The bandit's reputation and his rise to the elite position of *avtoritet* (authority) is built on precedents of successful and stern use of violence. The combination of adroit use of force and organizational skills is of central importance. Unlike thieves, many bandit groups ban alcohol and drugs. Instead, they cultivate a healthy life-style, strict discipline, and physical fitness maintained in specially rented gyms which serve as one of the permanent meeting grounds of the group. If the system of thieves' values and mores ensures their capacity for group survival in the severe repressive conditions of the Soviet labour camps, the value system of the bandits is functionally subjected to the reproduction of the group's capacity to participate in the economic life of society as violent entrepreneurs. Thus, if the world of thieves is a product of the strong repressive state or state socialism, the world of bandits emerges out of the illegal use of violence in conditions of weak-state capitalism.

The above characteristics are more like ideal types that in real life can display deviations and intermixing. In practice, the traditional values and rules of thieves have been undergoing change, adapting to the new post-socialist realities and adopting some features of economic rationality instead of the somewhat parochial values of the criminal sub-culture. The traditional thieves' subculture has been evolving and losing its authority together with the Soviet system that once shaped it. No doubt the actual practice of both thieves and bandits is irreducible to a finite set of rules and principles. But we needed to sharpen their differences in order to articulate the main structural principle of the so-called 'bandits,' that of being violent entrepreneurs. This brief interpretative exercise also helps us to analytically define this new type of criminal business specifically connected with Russia's transition to the market and to distinguish it from more traditional types of criminality, such as theft and illegal (e.g. drugs and arms) trade.

IV.   THE ORGANIZED CRIMINAL GROUP

What is usually referred to by the Russian police organs as the 'organized criminal group' (*organizovannaia prestupnaia gruppirovka*) can now be seen as an illegal violence managing agency.[12] How did they initially form in Russia? Commonplace assertions about either the territorial or ethnic formation principles of such groups should be treated with caution.[13] One should not infer that the criminal group is tied to the name-giving territory (e.g. *solntsevskaia gruppirovka*, from Solntsevo, a Moscow suburb) or that it recruits its members on a strictly ethnic basis (e.g. the Chechens), although it is generally true that the name of the group originally refers

---

[12] According to MVD data, the number of organized criminal groups increased from 952 in 1991 to 6743 in 1996. Cited in A. Dolgova (ed.), *Prestupnost' i reformy v Rossii* (Kriminologicheskaia Assotsiatsiia, Moscow, 1998), p. 254.

[13] See, for example G. Dunn, 'The Major Mafia Gangs in Russia' in P. Williams (ed.), *Russian Organized Crime: A New Threat* (Frank Cass, London, 1997).

to a territory or to the type of ties that enabled initial trust between members and established their common identity. In Petersburg, the first bandit-like violent entrepreneurial agencies called 'brigades' (*brigady*) grew from two types of primary ties: non-resident students' communes (*zemliachestva*) and sport schools. The most influential *tambovskaia* group was formed in the late 1980s by several students who came to receive higher education in the then Leningrad institutes (including the Institute of Physical Culture) from the town of Tambov. Many of such non-resident communes from other cities (Murmansk, Vorkuta, Perm', Kazan') became centres of gravity for other former sportsmen or violent young people willing to earn their living through the use of force. Thus emerged *murmanskie, vorkutinskie, permskie, kazanskie*, and the like. Groups formed by Leningrad residents recruited local sportsmen (e.g. boxers, weightlifters and wrestlers) whose primary cohesion and trust had formed over the course of their joint sporting careers. Unlike the migrant brigades that used topographical labels, the names of the local ones derived either from the kind of sport (e.g. *bortsovskaia brigada*, the wrestlers' brigade) or from the name of the leader – thus emerged *malyshevskie* (from A. Malyshev), *kudriashevskie* (from P. Kudriashev) or *komarovskie* (from A. Komarov).

Many groups have gradually lost their original direct connection with some obscure suburb, sport club, ethnicity or the founding leader. Actually, the meaning of the criminal group's name consists in its practical usage. In the practice of violent entrepreneurship all such names are used as trade marks. The license to use the trade mark practically means the right to introduce oneself as 'working with' such-and-such criminal group or with *avtoritet* X. Such a license is supplied to a brigade or an individual member by the *avtoritet*, the leader of the group, normally after the candidates have been tested in action. For example, a certain Andrei F., for the killing of the managing director of Petersburg northern airport Rzhevka, received USD500 in cash and the right to introduce himself as *murmanskii* (i.e. belonging to the *murmanskaia* criminal group).[14] The amount of cash may seem surprisingly low, but what really mattered in this particular case was the acquisition by the young bandit of the right to exploit the trademark.

The name of the group has a specific function in the practice of violent entrepreneurship: it guarantees the 'quality' of protection and enforcement services and refers to the particular kind of reputation built from the known precedents of successful application of violence and 'question-solving'. As the functional demand for the institution of enforcement partners derives from high entrepreneurial risks, the media stories about 'brutal' and 'omnipotent' bandit groups only help to sustain high-risk expectations and support the reputation of such groups. Before signing formal business contracts, companies acquire information about each other's enforcement partners ('whom do you work with?'), and set a meeting between enforcement partners (*strelka*). Besides, each of the participating sides would check whether the others really belong to the group they claim to represent and seek additional information about the real power (reputation as well as actual firepower) of that group. The deal with all its formal juridical and business attributes will only

---

[14] *Operativnoe prikrytie*, 2 (1997), p. 10.

be signed after the enforcement partners have recognized each other and given mutual guarantees. Likewise, a *strelka* will be immediately set if one of the sides failed or refused to fulfil its obligations. The outcome may be either a peaceful solution as to how the damage will be repaired or a violent showdown (*razborka*). However, in the long term, *razborka* may be a more costly and less efficient solution, especially if it leads to protracted warfare that causes severe damage – primarily to the business firms controlled by the opponents.

V. ELIMINATION CONTEST

In the early 1990s the number of criminal groups grew dramatically. According to official statistics, their number rose from 952 in 1991 to 4300 in 1992 and to 5691 in 1993. By comparison, this figure was only 50 in 1988.[15] Criminal groups, many of whom were initially formed on and named after particular territories, such as Moscow suburbs (Balashikha, Solntsevo, Podol'sk, Koptevo, Noginsk, and others) or city areas, such as *tsentral'naia* and *uralmashevskaia* groups in Ekaterinburg, expanded rapidly to gain control of other territories, especially in large cities. Moscow suburban groups, as well as groups from Siberian industrial towns of Kourgan and Novokuznetsk, moved into Moscow to seize opportunities in Russia's largest business area. The city of Kazan', notorious for its youth gang wars of the late eighties, also exported its criminal groups to Moscow and Petersburg. Some groups failed to establish permanent domains in large cities. *Kazanskie*, for instance, failed to find a niche in Moscow but succeeded in Petersburg. *Permskie* (from the city of Perm' in the Urals), on the contrary, were unsuccessful in their persistent attempts to obtain a share in Petersburg. Apart from these new violent groups of *bandity*, led by *avtoritety* and guided in their activities by sheer economic rationality, there operated, especially in Moscow, the Urals, and the Far-East a large number of *vory v zakone*, who sought to use the authority of traditional criminal values and the power of the old prison networks to secure their share and oppose the expansion of new bandits. Originally ethnic groups, especially Azerbaijan, Chechen and Georgian, were also active in most major cities. Their *diasporas* were traditionally strong in Moscow; Georgians had the highest ethnic representation in the ranks of *vory v zakone*, while Chechens relied more on their own clan structures.

Thus, instead of a well-coordinated and uniform criminal system where each sub-unit had its own clearly circumscribed territorial or business domain, there was a rather heterogeneous, mosaic-like and diffuse realm where territories and businesses were divided in many different ways between criminal groups of different territorial, ethnic, institutional, and historical origin. Although groups often claimed control over certain territories, the subject of their divisions, rivalry, and cooperation were opportunities rather than territories or spheres of economy as such. So there was no single feature common to all criminal groups, except for the means available to them – organized force. Explanations of the activity of criminal groups, therefore,

---

[15] Y. Gilinsky, *Organizovannia prestupnost' v Rossii: Teoriia i real'nost'* (St. Petersburg, Institute of Sociology, Russian Academy of Sciences, 1996), p. 77.

should be sought not in the groups themselves, their legal status or in people that compose them, but in their practice determined by the opportunities opened by the emerging market and the failing state.

The many groups that formed to seize new opportunities quickly got engaged in open as well as covert struggle with one another. However broad, the opportunities were limited, and those criminal groups that did not grow stronger, became weaker and were gradually either eliminated or subsumed by more powerful rivals. The elimination contest of 1992–1995 periodically erupted into massive armed showdowns, such as the one between *balashikhinskaia* and *podol'skaia* groups in Moscow in May 1992.[16] According to official statistics, there were 144 armed showdowns in 1991 and 305 in 1992.[17] However, since strong leadership is the major factor in a criminal group's consolidation and success, leaders rarely took part in day-to-day violence, and carefully staged assassinations of leaders rather than gang wars became the routine method of violent competition. Of the original founders of criminal groups, only a few survived. These years were marked by numerous wars, such as between Slavic and Caucasian groups in Moscow, between local and migrant groups or between groups led by thieves-in-law and those led by new bandit *avtoritety* in Petersburg and other cities. These conflicts were about opportunities, norms, and leadership. Whatever their causes and stakes, these violent conflicts steadily contributed to one general outcome – the formation of a fewer number of larger groups, better organized and firmly integrated into the structures of the market economy.

There is a good deal of bias and confusion in the statistics reflecting the degree of criminal control of the new Russian market economy. The most widely cited data is that provided by the Ministry of Internal Affairs (MVD) in January 1994 with reference to the estimates of the Russian Government Analytical Center for Social and Economic Policies. It established that criminal gangs controlled or owned (the terms were not specified) 40,000 businesses including 2,000 in the state sector. The majority of businesses in Russia (up to 75 per cent) paid illegal protection money.[18] The Analytic Center of the Academy of Sciences provided even more alarming data stating that 55 per cent of the capital and 80 per cent of the voting shares of private enterprises had been transferred into the hands of criminal capital.[19] These and similar estimates inspired the authors of the US Center for Strategic Studies report on Russian organized crime to claim that 'roughly two-thirds of Russia's economy is under the sway of the crime syndicates'.[20]

Later and more sober analyses, such as the study of privatization in Russia conducted by a group of American scholars, established that these figures were either exaggerations

---

[16] For details see N. Modestov, *Moskva banditskaia* (Tsentrpoligraf, Moscow,1996), pp. 149–160.

[17] S. Diakov and A. Dolgova (eds), *Organizovannaia prestupnost'-2* (Iuridicheskaya Literatura, Moscow, 1993), p. 25.

[18] Cited in: *The Economist*, No. 19 (1994), pp. 57–58.

[19] O. Kryshtanovskaya, 'Mafioznyi peisazh v Rossii' *Nezavisimaya Gazeta*, 21 September 1995, p. 4.

[20] W. Webster *et al.*, *Russian Organized Crime: Global Organized Crime Project* (Washington, Center for Strategic and International Studies, 1997), p. 2.

or in fact related to small business only. Thus, the 40,000 businesses referred to in 1994 were four times the number of mid-sized and large enterprises that were privatized at that time and twice the number of large enterprises in existence.[21] 'Many big privatized firms are unprofitable, and even organized crime wants a risk-adjusted return', wrote the authors of the study. 'It is hard to imagine why organized crime would want to control weak firms that are cutting employees, reducing capacity, confronting serious cash flow problems, and struggling to supply the kindergartens, housing and hospitals their employees need'.[22] Surprisingly, at the end of 1997, the MVD provided the data that almost replicated that of 1994: 40,000 economic subjects, including 1,500 state enterprises, over 500 joint enterprises, and over 500 banks were said to be controlled by criminal groups.[23]

Understandably, any quantitative account of the criminal control of the economy is bound to be rather rough because of the lack of adequate accounting methods and reliable information. Sociological surveys of entrepreneurs can provide some additional, albeit only indirect, indication of the criminalization of the economy. Thus, according to the study conducted in 1996–1997, 11 per cent of the sampled entrepreneurs admitted that they were inclined to use force as a method of problem solving; 42 per cent have experienced the use of such methods; 53 per cent admitted regular payments for protection services, of whom more than a third described the level of such payments as substantial.[24] This of course does not imply that all protection money goes to criminal structures. Rather, as we shall see later, it may indicate the existence of alternative structures that provide the same services.

VI.   THE DIALECTIC OF CONTROL

While the majority of analysts of Russian organized crime are preoccupied with estimating the degree of criminal control over the new market economy, few realize that this relation has been gradually inverted over the last two years. Those criminal groups that survived are increasingly subjected to the logic of economic action.

As was discussed earlier, the reputation of enforcement partner, embodied in the name of the criminal group or its leader, is crucial for averting possible swindles in business and acts of violence, since it carries the message of unavoidable retaliation. The license to use the name to conduct violent entrepreneurship, i.e. to act as a commercial enforcement partner, presupposes an informal contract between the leader and the unit (the brigade) that acts in their name. The contract includes the obligation to pay into the common fund and to follow certain rules. A group that has no license from one of the established *avtoritet* will have little success in its business and will either be exterminated or sent to prison with the help of police. The latter will be glad to use the occasion to its own advantage to report a successful operation against organized crime.

---

[21]   J. Blasi *et al.*, *Kremlin Capitalism: Privatizing the Russian Economy* (Cornell University Press, Ithaca, 1997), p. 116.
[22]   Ibid., p. 119.
[23]   *Zashchita i bezopasnost'* 2 (1998), pp. 4–5.
[24]   Radaev, n. 5 above, p. 129, 174 and 185.

The reputation of the group enables entrepreneurship based on virtual rather than actual violence and thus a more efficient and stable practice of conversion of force into money value. It also allows the leader to collect a kind of rent from franchising his name to brigades for their day-to-day business. A reference to the name is the crucial part of the business and presupposes the introduction ritual: 'we are such-and-such' or 'we work with X'. The biggest name rental *avtoritet* in Petersburg was A. Malyshev who managed to unite, in 1991, many smaller groups and brigades into a powerful *malyshevskaia* 'empire' whose members used his name in exchange for a share of their profits. At this stage, the physical presence of the *avtoritet* becomes unnecessary. He can be abroad or in prison: the signifier of force can function in the absence of its physical bearer.

The older the group and the higher its reputation embodied in its name, the more stable the mechanism of rent received by the leader from franchising their name and the less the amount of actual violence required to perform the functions of enforcement partnership. The use value of the signifier of force consists in its capacity to substitute for actual violence and thereby to increase the efficiency of violent entrepreneurship by reducing its costs and potential combat losses. This, in turn, can free investment resources and enable the transition from external control to shareholding and thus to more legal and 'civilized' entrepreneurship.

At the end of 1998, in an interview with a major weekly magazine, one Moscow criminal *avtoritet* made the following claim: 'Over the last two years we (i.e. criminal groups – V.V.) have been the biggest investors in Russian economy. One cannot imagine the country's economy without our investments'.[25] Although exact figures of investments of this kind are unlikely to be ever established, such claims should not be discarded. As wielders of force become owners of capital, and especially in those cases where they take part in its management, their ability to control their domains becomes conditional upon the logic and rules of economic action. To put this dialectic in a concise form, the more criminal groups strove to control the emerging markets, the more the markets controlled and transformed these groups. The acknowledgement by the wielders of force of the rules of the economic domain, from the simple principle that violence, in the long-term, is costly, and to a more complex dependency upon functionally divided management structures as well as upon the impersonal force of the market, transforms the criminal group into a legal business enterprise. The now strongest in Petersburg and north-western Russia *tambovskaia* group clearly displays this transformation pattern. In 1992–1995 the group went through a series of ruthless wars with *kazanskaia* and other groups in Petersburg, as well as through a bloody internal struggle for leadership. It suffered heavy losses, and its founder and leader V. Kumarin was severely wounded but survived an attempt on his life in June 1995. However, in the end the group emerged stronger, concluded an informal pact with the city authorities and invested in the oil industry and the timber trade in the region. It now owns the major share of the 'Petersburg Fuel Company' (*Peterburgskaia toplivnaia kompaniia*) which dominates the Petersburg and north-western oil and

---

[25] *Itogi*, 8 December 1998, p. 16.

petrol market.[26] Kumarin, who has now taken his mother's maiden name, thus concluded his recent interview: 'In June 1998 I became vice-president of the biggest holding – "Petersburg Fuel Company." We have lots of problems to solve: we have to draw up the budget, create a unified accounting office and consolidated holding management. Big changes have happened in my life'.[27]

The correlating transformation of the bandits' values and behavior patterns requires separate sociological research. However, small details of everyday life and the changing fashion also provide telling evidence. For instance, the upwardly mobile and business-oriented bandits now like to wear gold wire-rimmed glasses with plain glass lenses (*nuliovki*, in their jargon) in an effort to look more intelligent – a tribute *they* now have to pay to the emerging business culture.

VII. THE LEGALIZATION OF PRIVATE PROTECTION

Many scholars of Russia's organized crime share its representation in public consciousness and thus uncritically accept another myth spread by the mass media. The myth assigns to omnipotent criminal groups the role of being the major force in the emerging markets. Inflating the role of criminal groups and placing them under the spotlight of the media, the real leaders of violent entrepreneurship thus manage to remain in the shadow.

With the adoption on 11 March 1992 of the Federal law 'On Private Detective and Protection Activity' and on 14 August of the 'Regulation of the Extra-departmental Protection (*vnevedomstvennaia okhrana*) of the Interior Ministry Organs', the former state security officers legally entered the private market of protection and enforcement services. Before that former KGB and MVD cadres, professionals in the use of violence, had been participating in providing such services illegally, on par with criminal groups. It is with their involvement in the business of illegal private protection and dispute settlement that the term 'roof' (*krysha*) gained currency. Such terms as *komitetovskaia krysha* (KGB-provided roof), *mentovskaia krysha* (MVD-provided roof) and *banditskaia krysha* (roof provided by criminal bandit groups) entered the business vocabulary in 1991 to refer to a standard package of enforcement partnership services depending upon the origin of the supplier. Even today expert sources estimate that up to 20 per cent of FSB (former KGB) cadres are engaged in the informal 'roof' business.[28] A recent study of charitable donations by St. Petersburg private business discovered that the organs of the Interior Ministry are, after the invalids, the second biggest receiver of charity from local business companies: 35 per cent of companies represented in the survey admitted such donations (invalids figured in 45 per cent of cases).[29]

The legalization of protection business introduced a new agent to the Russian market – the private protection company. The policy of setting up private protection

---

[26] *Obshchaia Gazeta*, 20–26 August 1998, p. 4.
[27] A. Konstantinov, *Banditskii Peterburg-98* (Olma-Press, Moscow, 1999), p. 390.
[28] *Novaia Gazeta*, 13–19 July 1998, p. 3.
[29] *Pchela*, 12 (1998), p. 7.

companies was a complex and perhaps well-calculated response to the difficulties of the market transition. On the one hand, the criminal market of protection and enforcement services had by then taken shape, and the demand for such services was increasing due to the rapid privatization campaign and the development of financial institutions. On the other hand, there were a number of factors inside the state coercive institutions that produced such a response. First, the functional crisis of these structures and the moral pressure put on them by democratic public opinion, which accused them of being the foundation of the 'totalitarian' state, stimulated the dismissal of security professionals and their search for alternative employment. Second, the decline of central financial support of state security and police created incentives to search for alternative, extra-budget sources of support. Third, the involvement of the state security services in the business of private protection was initially part of the effort to infiltrate the criminal sphere, the tactic known as 'control from within'. However, later, operative goals conveniently coincided with financial interests, as the legal business of private protection started to grow. Thus, the privatization of the state security forces through their involvement in violent entrepreneurship was a corollary of the state crisis, but it may have also facilitated the discovery of new forms of state control of the private economy, more suited to the free market conditions.

By the end of 1997 Russia had 10,200 registered private protection and detective agencies with 140,600 employees. In the city of Moscow and Moscow region over 30,000 people work in more than 1,500 private security structures.[30] The city of Petersburg and Leningrad region have 765 private protection and detective companies with over 15,000 employed.[31] In fact, large companies are few, less than 20, most of which are Moscow- or Petersburg-based. Private protection companies are grouped according to the personnel numbers, annual turnover, and the number of protected 'objects'. The large ones have over 100 licensed armed guards, over one million USD turnover, and over 15 objects; the medium-sized have 50–100 guards, 500,000 to one million dollars turnover and five to 15 objects; and the small have under 50 guards, less than USD500,000 turnover and less than five objects.[32] No unified statistical survey reflecting the structure and geographical distribution of private protection companies has been published so far. From the scanty data available one may assume that the number of such companies and their size are generally proportionate to the scale of business activity of the region. Thus, the city of Cheliabinsk has 150 private protection companies; the city of Novgorod between 50 and 60.[33] According to expert estimates, the highest growth rates for this type of business were achieved in 1993–1994; by the end of 1996 the market had stabilized and further possibilities of extensive growth were exhausted.[34]

The legalization of the business of private protection also gave additional opportunities to criminal groups. Many of them either created their own protection

---

[30] *Operativnoe prikrytie*, 3 (1997), p. 36.
[31] *Bezopasnost' lichnosti i biznesa. Spravochnik' 98* (Agentstvo AT, St. Petersburg, 1998), p. 4.
[32] *Ekspert*, 2 (1996) p. 22.
[33] *Operativnoe prikrytie*, 4–5 (1997), p. 61.
[34] *Ekspert*, 11 (1997) p. 40.

companies or hired personnel of the companies established by the police to do part of the job – the latter phenomenon is known as 'combined roofs'. In Petersburg, for example, one of the oldest and most prominent protection companies 'Scorpion' was set up and headed by A. Efimov (nickname 'Fima'), one of the *avtoritety* of *tambovskaia* criminal group, and actively used to draw police officers to perform the 'roof' functions. 'Scorpion' was closed down by the authorities at the end of 1996; its director managed to escape but was tracked down in Ukraine and arrested a year later.[35] In Moscow, the guards of the special police unit 'Saturn' protected on the basis of a formal contract the leading *avtoritet* of *koptevskaia* criminal group V. Naumov ('Naum') and his company 'Merando' – until the assassination of Naumov in January 1997.[36]

VIII. PRIVATE PROTECTION COMPANY

The majority of the senior staff of large private protection companies are former officers of the state coercive organs – KGB (FSB), MVD, and the Army Intelligence Department (GRU) in the rough proportion of 50, 25, and 25 per cent respectively.[37] The first private protection company set up in 1991 in Moscow to help to design new regulations for protection business was the detective bureau 'Aleks'. A former colonel of the army intelligence, B. Markarov, was one of its founders. 'Aleks' strengthened its positions after its guards joined the defense force of the White House, Boris Yeltsin's residence during the August 1991 coup. However, its first serious 'object' was the Moscow night club 'Night Flight' in the defence of which (unlike the White House) 'Aleks' guards used their firearms several times. The following year the Petersburg division 'Aleks North-West' was established. It signed contacts with five-star hotels 'Europe' and 'Nevsky Palace' and a number of foreign and joint companies, such as 'Philip Morris' and 'Wrigley'.[38] By the end of 1998 it had over 200 licensed armed guards and 120 'objects' of protection.[39]

Many large protection companies are in fact privatized segments of the state security and intelligence organs. In Petersburg, for instance, the firm 'Protection' (*Zashchita*) was created by the North-Western Anti-Organized Crime Unit and is linked to the MVD, while the protection companies 'Tornado', 'Komkon', and 'Northern Palmira' are headed by former KGB-FSB officers and are, accordingly, the domain of this ministry. Though the companies are financially and organizationally separated from the state organs, they have access to information and operative resources of the latter through personal connections and informal relations. Many directors of private protection companies openly admit the fact of 'mutually beneficial cooperation', 'friendly ties' as well as financial aid to the public security

---

[35] *Operativnoe prikrytie*, 1 (1997), pp. 8–9.
[36] A. Maksimov, *Rossiiskaia prestupnost': kto est' kto* (Eksim-press, Moscow, 1998), pp. 260–266.
[37] O. Kryshtanovskaya, 'Nelegal'nye struktury v Rossii' *Sotsiologicheskoe issledovaniia*, 8 (1995), p. 96.
[38] *Operativnoe prikrytie*, 1 (7) (1997), pp. 32–33.
[39] *Lichnosti Peterburga*, 1 (1998), p. 39.

sector from the private one.[40] The activity of private protection companies is formally supervised by the Department of Licensing and Registration of MVD.

What do private protection companies do? Being a type of violent entrepreneurial agency, the private protection company provides the standard set of 'roof' services to other business agents and 'solves' their 'questions' – the phrase also frequently used by heads of MVD- and KGB-set companies even in published interviews. For instance, in 1992 the protection enterprise 'Komkon' successfully solved the question of a large debt recovery for the Petersburg branch of 'Sberbank Rossii', the biggest state commercial bank, and subsequently became its permanent enforcement partner.[41] The work in this field implies competition as well as cooperation with illegal enforcement partners, i.e. criminal groups. According to its director, 'Alex North-West' had a dispute with a Petersburg criminal group over a 'well-known company' [it was a Swiss company 'Ceptor' – author]. 'On the second day after we settled there they tried to intimidate us by phone. Then set up a meeting (*strelka*). In the end threw a grenade into the company's office [the grenade was not meant to explode – author]. But things worked out well in the end, we did not abandon the object'.[42]

Since criminal groups were the first to discover this entrepreneurial niche, they also laid down the basic rules and terms of the game, which every newcomer to the field had to take into account. As the head of St. Petersburg Department of Licensing and Registration of MVD I. Buriak noted, 'The business of private protection is impossible without relations with criminal structures. I do not mind *strelki*, they were and they will be. But I am strongly against what is called *razborki* (violent showdowns)'.[43] Due to the similarity of their functions private protection companies in many ways resemble their criminal rivals. In the same time, the ex-KGB and MVD structures assert their difference in that their service is more reliable, predictable, and has a more competitive price. The charge for debt recovery varies between 15 and 40 per cent of the sum of the debt.[44]

Managers of large private protection companies claim to provide a better quality of services, due to the professional experience of their personnel. While maintaining a formidable firepower large companies rely on informational and analytic methods acquired during their management's career in state service. The major emphasis is said to lie not on direct physical protection or intimidation but on the preventive neutralization of potential conflicts and threats. The vice-chairman of the security service of the Association of Russian Banks A. Krylov thus described the methods of legal enforcement partners: 'To recover the debt one does not need recourse to violent means – it is sufficient just to demonstrate that you have information that compromises the debtor and the channels for its

---

[40] *Operativnoe prikrytie*, 3 (1997), pp. 34–36.
[41] *Operativnoe prikrytie*, 6 (1996), p. 9.
[42] *Operativnoe prikrytie*, 1 (1997) pp. 32–33. In the interview, when asked how the dispute was settled, Boris Markarov said that his men met the bandits again and battered them (*nabili mordy*).
[43] *Operativnoe prikrytie*, 2 (1997), p. 33.
[44] *Ekspert*, 2 (1996) p. 20.

dissemination'.[45] In a private interview with the author the director of 'Alex North-West' claimed to have a database on all business enterprises in the region, allowing the company to assess the reliability of its clients' potential partners. Economic considerations may affect a company's choice of the provider of protection and enforcement services (in case it has such a choice), which is first of all that between a criminal group and legal protection company. Criminal groups can supply credits and investment money to start or expand legal as well as illegal or shadow business but they will then claim their share and interfere in business activities. An increasing number of legal entrepreneurs prefer private protection companies as they do not interfere with business and normally receive a fixed monthly payment on a formal contract basis. In the formal records protection payments can be written off as 'legal consulting' or 'insurance'. In case there is a need to 'solve a question', especially if this involves risk, an informal deal with the protection company management will be concluded and an additional payment made. Private protection companies, however, will not help their contracted clients with cash to avoid bankruptcy.

The commercial success of the major protection companies derives from the conversion of the reputation of the KGB into a market resource, not only of its technical and information resources. These companies assertively advertise their links with the state security structures, increase the value of their trademarks by siding with the state organs and paying them formal as well as informal fees. In search of new opportunities for the marketing of the professional analytical skills of the intelligence services, private protection companies set up investment and organization consulting divisions. Since both criminal structures and legal protection companies are not only force-managing agencies but also in the long run are subject to the logic of economic action, both undergo a transformation into more civilized business enterprises with complex structures. The staff of both is divided into rank-and-file militant fighters (either former sportsmen or special task force combatants) and upper-layer managers who stylize themselves as a business elite.

IX. VIOLENT ENTREPRENEURSHIP AND THE STATE

Economic historians and sociologists have studied the use of violence and the role of states in the development of capitalism.[46] Against the background of this knowledge Russia's present experience becomes much less exceptional. Historically, before markets started to grow, territorial monopolies of force had been established as a result of continuous warfare. Max Weber's classic definition regards the state as the territorial monopoly of legitimate violence.[47] Elias used this conception in his

---

[45] Ibid.
[46] For example, D. North and R. Thomas, *The Rise of The Western World* (Cambridge University Press, Cambridge, 1973); F. Lane, *Venice and History* (John Hopkins University Press, Baltimore, 1966); C. Tilly 'War Making and State Making as Organized Crime' in P. Evans *et al.* (eds), *Bringing the State Back In* (Cambridge University Press, Cambridge, 1986).
[47] M. Weber, 'Politics as Vocation' in H. Gerth and C. W. Mills (eds), *From Max Weber: Essays in Sociology* (Routledge, London, 1970), pp. 77–78.

study of state formation in western Europe, demonstrating the centrality of internal pacification, i.e. the removal of violence from everyday life, for the development of the peaceful economic activity of civil society.[48] The monopoly of force combined with a fiscal monopoly made possible the central function of the state: the enforcement of universal law and order and the exercise of justice. Exploring the economic side of the use of organized violence, the economic historian Frederick Lane identified early-modern governments with violence-using and violence-controlling enterprises that produced and sold a specific service – protection. He described the political economy of force that assisted the accumulation of capital during the pre-industrial phase. If the governments that commanded organized force received the tribute for protection they sold to the subjects of economy and trade, the latter could also gain from what appeared a mere protection racket: they received protection rent. The customers, for example, Venetian merchants, earned protection rent, which is a kind of differential rent, because of the higher efficiency of their protector as compared to that of their competitors: all merchants had to pay the tribute to avoid damage, but those who paid less for firm protection in a dangerous business environment earned protection rent as a result of more competitive prices reflecting lower costs. Thus the institutionalized protection rackets that offered lower prices to clients grew at the expense of their rivals. Lane's major point is that 'during the Middle Ages and early modern times protection rents were a major source of fortunes made in trade. They were a more important source of profits than superiority in industrial techniques or industrial organization'.[49]

The monopoly management of organized force and the economy of the protection racket, so central to the formation of European states, are of course much more relevant to the distant past than to the immediate present. Theories of state formation hardly envisaged a reverse process, so powerful and stable appeared modern states, the Soviet Union included. But today, when the Russian state is in deep functional crisis, historical sociology of state formation can inform our vision of the processes unfolding in the present. Thus, the booming of violent entrepreneurship in Russia means in fact that the state has lost its monopoly of legitimate violence. The present condition can be defined as the covert fragmentation of the state: the emergence, on the territory under the formal jurisdiction of the state, of competing and uncontrolled sources of organized violence and alternative taxation networks. The Russian state does not have unconditional priority in those very areas that constitute it: protection, taxation, and law enforcement. However, organized criminal groups are not the sole and most powerful agents in the sphere of violent entrepreneurship: there are also various semi-autonomous armed formations, such as the president Yeltsin's personal guard, special police forces of all sorts kept by several state ministries, and numerous private protection companies.

In these circumstances the struggle against organized crime cannot radically change the situation. Would it not be more appropriate to talk about the reconstruction

---

[48] N. Elias, *The Civilizing Process. Vol. 1-2. The History of Manners and State Formation and Civilization* (Basil Blackwell, Oxford, 1993).

[49] F. Lane, 'Economic Consequences of Organized Violence' 18 (1958) *The Journal of Economic History*, p. 410.

of the state or simply of state formation, a process that is much more broad and complex than police measures against organized crime? All measures, political, economic, cultural, juridical, and so on, that work towards the restoration of the monopoly of violence and the establishment of firm public control over it contribute to the reconstruction of the state. The establishment of legal protection companies that force purely criminal groups out of the market is also part of the process. The development of the business of private protection, however, is ambivalent. On the one hand, privatized segments of the state coercive apparatus display a dangerous tendency towards autonomization, they have an intrinsic interest in becoming autonomous market actors. Moreover, since the demand for their services depends upon the general level of business risks, the agents of private protection would harbour a hidden interest in preserving the criminal sector as the source of risk rather than eliminating it. On the other hand, the state origin of many of the cadres of private protection companies, and their close relations with the state organs carry a possibility of a new centralization and establishment of close control over the agencies of organized violence with a parallel transition to their centralized budgetary financing. The logic of the economic market, expressed in a specific political economy of force, has its positive aspect as well: intensive violence is economically inefficient. Legal as well as criminal entrepreneurs of violence are compelled to take into account economic limitations on their action as well as the developing business culture.

State formation, taken in its structural rather than its substantive aspect, entails simply the formation and maintenance of boundaries, such as those between public and private, formal and informal, legal and illegal, impersonal and personal. Again, taken structurally, the existence of the economy and of the state, as well as any relations between them, are possible only when the two spheres are divided. With reference to the processes considered in this paper, state formation, or at least the most important aspect of it, coincides with divergent trajectories of violence-managing agencies: some are integrated into the market economy and get transformed into business firms, some become separated from the economy, become subjected to central control and make up the core of the state. Ideally, both sides should be interested in boundary maintenance. Thus, theoretically, the process of reconstruction of the state and the pacification of society should be seen more as a general outcome of violent struggle and peaceful competition between violence controlling enterprises than as an intentional state-building project of politicians.

5

Corruption and Violence in
Russian Business in the Late 1990s

*Vadim Radaev**

I. INTRODUCTION

Nowadays, it is quite common to speak about the 'transition to the market' in the
case of post-communist societies and to search for the 'best model' of the market to
be implemented. However, the concept of 'market' is not clearly defined and presented
either by a rather abstract universalistic scheme or a set of some idealistic
assumptions. Many widespread elements of economic relations like corruption and
violence in business are viewed as marginal phenomena and left to the criminologists.
It is argued here that despite their negative influences such phenomena constitute a
part of important institutional arrangements in which the actual market activity of
economic agents is carried out. It is therefore crucial to investigate the nature and
the sources of these institutional boundaries to render this theory of markets more
inclusive.

In this paper the formation of some institutional arrangements of Russian markets
in the 1990s is viewed from the standpoint of the economic firm and the entrepreneur.
It will concentrate on the micro-level of economic relationships in the 'shadow'
market segments, which will be presented in three main parts. The first one is devoted
to general methodological assumptions and data sources. In the second part we deal
with corruption issues in relations of the entrepreneurs and state agencies. The third
part is devoted to the use of violence in business relations. This paper will attempt
to answer the following question: how specific codes of business ethics are developed
from the elements of informal relationships, which are normally treated as non-
ethical conduct. Finally, a number of general conclusions will be drawn.

* The author and research team would like to express their gratitude to I. Bunin, R.
Kapelyushnikov and A. Zudin for their important comments on the first draft of this paper.
Special thanks to V. Gubernatorov (Russian Federation Chamber of Commerce and Industry)
for valuable support in the survey organization and to N. Nazarova for the organization of
interviewing.

A. V. Ledeneva and M. Kurkchiyan (eds.), Economic Crime in Russia, 63–82

II. SHADOW ECONOMY, STATE AGENCIES AND CRIMINAL GROUPINGS

When considering markets, the investigator is confronting a complex segmented space structured not only by price mechanisms, monetary flows and economic legislation, but also by the numerous practices occurring in the everyday activity of economic agents at a micro-level. It includes the relationships of entrepreneurs with the state officials as well as with semi-criminal and criminal protection agencies involved in shadow economy dealings. What is meant by the 'shadow economy'?

1. Defining shadow economy

The shadow economy represents a part of a broader economic phenomenon, i.e. the informal economy. The latter is a difficult subject for definitions and classifications.[1] However, it can be broadly defined as follows: the informal economy is the set of economic activities that are not displayed in official reporting and/or formal contracting or displayed in a basically distorted way.

The informal economy covers market segments that are different from the standpoint of legality of actions. These main segments are the following:

a) *Legal (rule-of-law) activities.* These are carried out in accordance with the existing law and do not infringe the interests of the other economic agents. The examples are own-account household economy and informal employment of family members.

b) *Out-of-law economic activities ('rosy markets').* These are not subject to legal regulation but may infringe the interests of the other economic agents. For example, the monopolization of markets in the absence of anti-trust legislation; the activity of financial 'pyramids' ('financial bubble'), such as those experienced in Russia in the mid-1990s.

c) *Semi-legal economic activities ('grey markets').* These are normally carried out in the frame of law but violate the law occasionally. They also include activities which have legal targets but provided without official licensing. For example, concealing part of the profits, non-licensed retailing and other tax avoidance strategies.

d) *Non-legal, criminal economic activities ('black markets').* These are banned by the law and have illegal targets. Such activities would include, smuggling, drug production and sales.

The shadow economy is associated with semi-legal and non-legal economic activities. Although criminal business is attracting much attention in the mass media, in the author's opinion it constitutes a relatively small part of the shadow economy nowadays. The latter is largely composed of intermediate 'grey' markets. These 'grey' economic segments are most important and more subject to policy influence.

---

[1]   H. Lubell, *The Informal Sector in the 1980s and 1990s* (Organization for Economic Co-operation and Development, Paris, 1991), pp. 17–20; S. Glinkina, 'K voprosu o kriminalizatsii rossiiskoi ekonomiki' (1997) *Politekonom*, pp. 56–63.

It is significant that 'non-economic' institutions are woven into shadow activities. Of these, state agencies take the primary position.

2.   State vs. market?

The 'state vs. market' opposition is still a dominant stereotype in economic and social sciences. Traditional economic theory either ignores state influence or treats it as an external boundary. The state is viewed as most influential but at the same time a neutral 'third party' providing control and arbitration of economic conflicts. In any case, it opposes the market.

It is argued here that the 'concepts of control'[2] are not confined to the 'vertical integration' within the firm in its opposition to 'competitive markets'.[3] Specific concepts of vertical (political) control are also developed in the links between the firm and the state.

It was Polanyi who powerfully demonstrated that, historically, the major part of markets emerged under the control and direct support of the state.[4] Modern markets are not autonomous from state influence either. Asymmetric relations of power and authority present an inherent part of market transactions.

> The autonomous market did not 'emerge'; it was constructed through the exercise of political and state power ... . Historically we cannot understand the development and operation of markets without recognising the extent to which they have been shaped by the fiscal interests of states and forms of legitimization of state power.[5]

It would be a naïve liberal dream, especially in case of Russia and Eastern European countries, to expect that one day the state leaves the field of economic regulation after having settled favourable legislation and advanced market infrastructure. There exists in Russia, an arena of continuous negotiation and renegotiation of economic rules among the firms and state agents that is associated with differential benefits and non-zero transaction costs. There are even grounds to consider the formation of markets as part of state-building.[6]

Economists suggest their own way of overcoming the state vs. market opposition, i.e. by extending the logic of the self-regulating market to the field of politics. Various sorts of 'new political economy' do not hesitate to reduce state power and

---

2   N. Fligstein, 'Markets as Politics: A Political-Cultural Approach to Market Institutions' (August 1996) 61 *American Sociological Review*, pp. 656–673.
3   O. E. Williamson, *The Economic Institutions of Capitalism: Firms, Markets, Relational Contracting* (Free Press, New York: 1985); O. E. Williamson, 'The Economics of Governance: Framework and Implications' in R. N. Langlois (ed.), *Economics as a Process: Essays in the New Institutional Economics* (Cambridge University Press, Cambridge, 1986).
4   K. Polanyi, *The Great Transformation* (Farrar and Rinehart, New York, 1944).
5   R. Friedland and A. F. Robertson, 'Beyond the Marketplace' in R. Friedland and A. F. Robertson (eds), *Beyond the Marketplace: Rethinking Economy and Society* (Aldine de Gruyter, New York, 1990), p. 7 and 11.
6   Fligstein, n. 2 above, p. 657.

authority to the instruments of 'normal' economic bargaining. The state is becoming one of the regular economic agents pursuing economic interests along with firms and individuals.

It is the author's view, that the state officials do not normally lose their specific political or administrative advantages when bargaining with firms. First, the rights of officials are more extensive and find additional support in their non-economic status. Second, they tend to move beyond the logic of utility maximization or minimization of costs more often than the entrepreneurs do. From this perspective, market transactions do not present a pure exchange of values but also embody the elements of control in which relations are basically asymmetric. 'Administrative rent' and 'political rent' are extracted separately from economic profits here.

The champions of economic evolutionism tend to think that it is economic efficiency that rules out the formation of institutional frames for the economy. However, a different view is supported here, in that emerging institutions are not necessarily the most efficient. One of the important reasons for this is that the civil servants have a wide range of opportunities to pursue their own interests, which may go far beyond efficiency considerations.

> Institutions are not necessarily or even usually created to be socially efficient; rather they, or at least the formal rules, are created to serve the interests of those with the bargaining power to devise new rules.[7]

In the case of Russia, relations with officials present a painful problem for the entrepreneur. Bureaucratic procedures are numerous, complicated and costly. However, administrative barriers and the lack of key information on the formal rules are not just the outcomes of the 'underdevelopment' of market conditions in Russia and other post-communist countries. They are caused by the determination of the officials to maintain bureaucratic control over enterprises under conditions in which many formal property rights have been transferred from the state to the firms.

3.   Business ethics and violence

Markets can never exist without any trust and commitment among economic agents. However, these relationships present an outcome of specific institutional boundaries in which economic actions are arranged. There are at least three different types of ethical theories explaining the motives of economic agents: egoistic, utilitarian, and deontological.

According to the concept of egoism, the agents pursue their own perceived economic self-interests disregarding both moral codes and future consequences of their actions. In this sense they are not consistently rational and are constrained mainly by external sanctions, including coercive ones.

---

[7]   D. C. North, *Institutions, Institutional Change and Economic Performance* (Cambridge University Press, Cambridge, 1992), p. 16.

Utilitarian logic of action is aimed at maximization of 'all benefits'. At the same time it has regard to future consequences and is respectful to business reputation ('organization capital'). The agents follow the norms for their honesty and their consideration is rewarded accordingly.

Deontological theory presumes that the moral dimension is relatively independent from the economic interest. Moral codes are not necessarily backed by external sanctions for these codes have a capacity of self-enforcement. Actors may be driven by their duties and commitments which, in turn, are based upon customs and values. 'Honesty is, in fact, primarily a moral choice ... We keep promises because we believe it is right to do so, not because it is good business.'[8]

The author tends to support deontological views, though all three analytical frames are applicable in different situations. In contemporary Russia, much attention is paid to egoistic actions. It is claimed that Russia is coming through the age of the 'wild market'. This view seems to be too simplistic. However, it could be conceded that a certain upsurge of egoism in Russian business is evident under conditions in which Soviet-type moral codes have become blurred.

Frequent infringement of business contracts compels entrepreneurs to apply precautionary measures and means of violence in relations with their unreliable business partners. An ethic of business is developed which is not based upon widely shared values or expected remuneration of honesty. It is derived from everyday practices of struggle with the systematic violations in business affairs. As was claimed by a respondent, the head of a fuel supply firm: 'It is the infringement of obligations which should have most probably encouraged the following of contracts more strictly.'

Presently, trust among business partners in Russia is not derived from the further development and additional enforcement of formal contracting but rather from the 'shadow', i.e. from the structure of informal relationships and implicit contracts.[9] As a consequence, this is where violence comes into business relationships.

III.   CORRUPTION IN RUSSIAN BUSINESS

1.   *Spread of bureaucratic extortion*

Now let us introduce data of two surveys undertaken in 1997–1998 which illustrate the level of interference of the state.[10] According to these surveys, the spread of bureaucratic pressures in Russian business is estimated by the entrepreneurs as

---

8   A. Bhide and H. H. Stevenson, 'Why Be Honest If Honesty Doesn't Pay' (1990) 68 *Harvard Business Review*, p. 121 and 128; T. Beauchamp and N. Bowie, 'Ethical Theory and Its Application to Business' in T. Beauchamp and N. Bowie (eds), *Ethical Theory of Business* (Prentice-Hall, Englewood Cliffs, NJ, 1979), pp. 14–22.

9   *Natsional'naya Programma: Rossiiskaya Delovaya Kul'tura* (Chamber for Commerce and Industry of the Russian Federation, Moscow, 1997), pp. 50–51.

10   Our analysis is based on data collected in the course of two main 1997–1998 surveys of non-state enterprise managers and entrepreneurs: standardized survey (227 questionnaires of entrepreneurs from 21 regions of Russia) and semi-standardized survey (96 in-depth interviews with the entrepreneurs). The surveys were conducted by the author and research team of the Centre for Political Technologies (Moscow). The US Centre for International Private Enterprise

follows: 87 per cent of entrepreneurs claim that such pressures do exist in Russian business today, including 38.5 per cent of them who report that extortion occurs frequently (48.5 per cent from time to time). General estimations strongly correlate with the personal experience of confronting extortion by the entrepreneurs though the latter is certainly less frequent. Two thirds (65 per cent) of respondents report that they have been subject to extortion; this includes one-fifth of entrepreneurs who encounter it frequently and 45 per cent of those who have, on occasion, encountered it from time to time (see Table 1).

Although extortion does not necessarily end in bribe-taking we have sufficient evidence to conclude that corruption is a widespread phenomenon in Russian business. For which 'services' do the entrepreneurs have to make payment under the table to the officials? These bureaucratic 'services' are listed below:

- Issuing licenses and permissions   47%
- Providing premises   36%
- Giving access to loans   24%
- Ensuring business protection   14%

What conclusions can be drawn about the dynamics of bureaucratic pressures on the enterprises? The major part of entrepreneurs tends to think that the level of extortion remains unchanged over the last two to three years, whereas 28 per cent of them complain that the frequency has increased. It can be concluded from the results of these two surveys, and comparing them with the results of previous surveys, that at the very least, bureaucratic pressures appear not to be decreasing.[11]

As to the all-important possibility of avoiding bribing in economic activity, only 20 per cent of respondents believe that this is possible, while 38 per cent of entrepreneurs are certain that bribery is unavoidable, and a further 42 per cent consider it difficult to avoid. (See Table 1). Thus, presently, successful economic activity without bribery would appear to be an unrealistic option to a majority of Russian businessmen.

It is useful to refer here to three schemes of corruption suggested by Shleifer and Vishny. In the first monopolist model the supply of public goods is concentrated in the hands of one bureaucratic agency. In the second one (to be called the deregulated model), bureaucratic agencies are acting relatively independently, each in their own field. As for the third competitive model, it presumes that every

(CIPE) funded the research. For other results see V. Radaev, 'Malyi biznes i problemy delovoi etiki: Nadezhdy i realnost' (1996) *Voprosy Ekonomiki*, pp. 72–82; V. Radaev, 'Practicing and Potential Entrepreneurs in Russia' (Fall 1997) 27 *International Journal of Sociology*, pp. 15–50; and V. Radaev, *Formirovanie novykh rossiiskikh rynkov: transaktsionnye izderzhki, formy kontrolia i delovaya etika* (Centre for Political Technologies, Moscow, 1998).

[11] V. Radaev, 'Emerging Russian Entrepreneurship as Viewed by the Experts' *Economic and Industrial Democracy* (Supplement to Vol. 14, No. 4, Sage, London, 1993), pp. 55–77; V. Radaev, 'Maly biznes i Problemy Delovoy Etiki: Nadezhdy i Realnost (Small Business and Business Ethics: Hopes and Reality)' (1996) No. 7 *Voprosy Ekonomiki*, pp. 72–82; V. Radaev, 'Practicing and Potential Entrepreneurs in Russia' (Fall, 1997) Vol. 27, No. 3 *International Journal of Sociology*, pp. 15–50.

Table 1. Bureaucratic Extortion in Russian Business (percentage of total)

	Frequent	From time to time	Absent
In Russian business in general	38.5	48.5	13
	Frequent	*From time to time*	*Absent*
In one's personal experience	20	45	35
	More frequent	*No change*	*Less frequent*
Changes over the last 2–3 years	28	60	12
	Impossible	*Difficult*	*Possible*
Possibility of avoiding bribery	38	42	20

Table 2. Personal Experience of Confronting Bureaucratic Extortion and Expenditures on Informal Business Services (percentage of total)

Expenditures on Informal Business Services	Bureaucratic Extortion		
	Frequent	From time to time	Absent
Significant	33	13	8
Non-significant	48	52	37
Absent	19	35	55
Total	100	100	100

public good is delivered by more than one bureaucratic agency. The authors believe that in the post-communist societies there has been a significant shift from the monopolistic to the deregulated model that is associated with the increasing level of corruption.[12]

Corruption imposes additional transaction costs in these payments for bureaucratic services. The latter vary from 'small presents' of several hundred dollars to 10 per cent of the subsidy or contract provided by the official. One can see the links between bureaucratic extortion and expenditures on informal business services (obviously including bribes) in Table 2.

According to the in-depth interview data, the unprecedented openness of bureaucratic services (both voluntary and compulsory) is striking in Russia today, in comparison with the Soviet era. Even if, within the last half decade, bribery may be encountered less frequently, the scale has obviously increased. Using the words of a respondent, the head of multi-profile firm: 'In recent years many [officials] do not take [bribes] but if they do they usually take them very much.' It should also be mentioned that, in the interviews, the opinions on the spread of corruption appears rather diverse. Some entrepreneurs express their strong belief that there is now no way of avoiding bribery in Russian business. Others adamantly claim that they do

---

[12] A. Shleifer and R. W. Vishny, 'Corruption' (August 1993) 108 *Quarterly Journal of Economics*, pp. 604–607.

not give bribes at all. Personal emotions may certainly intervene here. However, the main explanation is the segmentation of markets in terms of relations of entrepreneurs with the officials. In some segments, informal exchange of bureaucratic services are more active; in the other segments it is less regular or even negligible. This segmentation can be described by the following standard variables:

- Size of the firm (large businesses are normally more involved in dealing with state officials though the burden of their transaction costs is relatively low in comparison with small enterprises);
- Area of activity (areas with fast capital turnover and use of cash in their transactions including finance, wholesale trade, retailing, catering, consumer services attract more attention from the controlling bodies);
- Type of activity (necessity to obtain and renew licenses and permissions);
- Type of entrepreneurial strategy (the extent to which the entrepreneur relies upon their contacts with bureaucrats and attempt to mobilize state-owned resources or obtaining individual privileges).

2. *Corruption and entrepreneurial strategies*

The choice of strategy in relations with the authorities plays an important part in forming the profile of the firm. On one hand, there are 'passive' business strategies when the entrepreneur is paying off the officials, trying to minimize this kind of transaction cost and having no extra benefits. On the other hand, there are 'active' business strategies when bribery is used for getting individual privileges and competitive advantages. In the latter case, transaction costs are higher but they are covered by the additional benefits.

It is noteworthy that only 28 per cent of Russian entrepreneurs accuse officials of being the main party initiating bribery. More than one third (34 per cent) of entrepreneurs consider that both businessmen and officials are equally responsible for these practices while 13 per cent of them even lay responsibility on entrepreneurs alone (difficult to say – 25 per cent). Thus, the spread of corruption is, no doubt, stimulated by certain competitive strategies of entrepreneurs. Nevertheless, it would be a mistake to present the entrepreneur and the official as equal agents in 'bureaucratic markets'. So many administrative barriers surround entrepreneurs. Their dependency on bureaucracy is still very high and their choice is far from voluntary.

> According to my experience, there is no way of doing business without people linking you to the regulatory bodies. It is possible to work without it but impossible to raise big money. (Head of real-estate firm)

One has a relative freedom to choose initially after starting up. After that the path dependency increases. A respondent, the head of a tourist firm, stated: 'If you compromise with the officials once it will never end.' Economic action builds up structural constraints of its own.

Additional difficulties for the entrepreneur have originated from the serious changes in the bureaucratic order during the last decade in Russia. First, there was a large-scale redistribution of functions among different authorities and within bureaucratic hierarchies. Second, Soviet-type bureaucratic conventions defining the rules and methods of 'shadow' remuneration of civil servants became blurred. The lack of these conventions (e.g. to take 'according to rank') leads to uncertainty and voluntarism which may be most painful for the entrepreneur. Now these rules of a bureaucratic code are being established anew though it is not easy to say how fast this process is.

Further evidence from the 1997–1998 survey demonstrates that some other elements of a new bureaucratic code are being resurrected. According to the opinion of some entrepreneurs, at the early reform stages there were many officials seeking their 'administrative rent' without taking much responsibility for the outcomes. However, whilst there would appear to be more officials who may be involved in taking bribes, the evidence would indicate that they are also taking care of the provision of public goods. They are becoming more professional and selective and want to provide positive outcomes from the projects together with their personal revenues. Bribes are considered as a 'commission' and a legitimate way to raise the low official income of civil servants.

> It was pretty simple before: you were supposed to pay for everything. You came to the official, made promises, gave money and got access to a land plot or to some other resources. There were plenty of such examples and many of those firms disappeared long ago. After these years civil servants seem to have learned to treat the entrepreneurs in selective ways. (Head of construction firm)

It can, therefore, be concluded that from the very start of the reforms, emerging Russian entrepreneurship was divided into two distinct groups. One group decided to appeal to the authorities for support, invested in their 'political capital' and pursued their interests through the corridors of power. The other group preferred their independence and contacted bureaucrats only in an emergency, preferring to try and rely more on their human and cultural capital. Therefore, at the end of the decade, at least in the case of large businesses, the first strategy has been more successful in economic terms (whatever one's personal views may be). Additional 'political' transaction costs have brought significant economic revenues. As one head of an investment corporation stated: 'The role of the state is crucial today. Those who benefit from the [state] budget have much better chances to survive.'

3. *From bribery to relational contracting*

Informal relations of entrepreneurs and officials are not confined to mere corruption and the latter comprises something more than just bribe-taking. Bribery is an initial and most primitive form of these informal relationships which mediates short-term relations and single transactions and is applied mainly by low and middle-rank bureaucrats. For the higher ranking officials the scale and scope of these relationships may look very different. Firstly, 'elementary' bribery is developing into the exchange of services which are not confined to cash presents and personal gifts. There are many more sophisticated ways to pay back. For example, the entrepreneur can employ a bureaucrat's relative or sign a contract with a firm, which is under their patronage.

> Officials of high level are not paid back with ordinary bribes but with services like building up a summer house, buying a new car, sending relatives for vacations abroad etc. Cash has stopped being the main instrument for solving the issues. Alternative mechanisms have appeared. (Head of wholesale trade firm)

Second, with the strengthening of mutual trust, the links between entrepreneurs and officials may gradually transfer into relational contracting[13] in which the exchange of services does not necessarily presume an immediate reciprocity.

> There are always some informal relationships between the authorities and the enterprises (especially the large ones). We apply for their support. They also apply for our support and we are trying to meet their requirements. Sometimes, it deals with works which cannot be paid for from the municipal budget (to repair a church etc.). Sometimes you have to install a telephone to an official's *dacha*. (Head of construction firm)

This infers a reciprocal arrangement appears to exist based on mutual long-term support. In this way the mixture of economic interest and coercive pressures is enforced by social norms.

4. *Corruption and entrepreneurial types (Typology I)*

It would be prudent at this point to attempt to determine a typology of entrepreneurial groups based on a number of key indicators reflecting the relations of the entrepreneurs and officials. By means of factor analysis six factors describing 70 per cent of variance have been revealed. The author and the research team took two main factors (34 per cent of variance) for clustering procedures. These factors are:

- Spread of bureaucratic extortion and involvement in informal dealings;
- Type of enterprise by size and ownership status.

With the help of cluster analysis we determined four main groups of entrepreneurs, namely:

- Loyal to officials   15%
- Aiming at parity with officials   36%
- Conflicting with officials   28%
- Paying off the officials   21%

Attention will now be given to a brief description of these four groups.

---

[13] Williamson (1985), n. 3 above.

a) Loyal to officials (Group 1). The entrepreneurs in the first group rarely confront bureaucratic pressures. They also do not have much expenditure on informal economic dealings; 54 per cent of them claim that these expenditures are virtually absent in their case. At the same time, the entrepreneurs do have evident problems with the authorities here. For instance, the average number of administrative controlling visits to the enterprise is among the highest. Besides, one third of the enterprise leaders evaluate their relationships with the officials as having tensions or even conflict (see Table 3).

In sum, this group is defined as loyal to the authorities. Despite the pressure of bureaucratic problems, as many as 43 per cent of entrepreneurs believe that the attitude of authorities towards the entrepreneurs is improving. At least 25 per cent support the active influence of state authorities. They are also loyal to formal rules. Compared to all other groups they have the largest number of those who would obey the law under any conditions, and only 11 per cent of those tend to ignore 'inconvenient' laws. More than a half (54 per cent) of entrepreneurs in this group consider the risk of law violation as high (much more than in all other groups).

Moreover, that 82 per cent of the first group consists of the heads of privatized enterprises with the highest share of large and medium-sized businesses – 46 per cent.

b) Aiming at Parity with Officials (Group 2). Bureaucratic extortion is not widespread here and none of the entrepreneurs appear, personally, to encounter such pressures frequently in their personal experience. The combination of a low level of administrative coercion and loose external control constitutes a specific feature of this group, and the number of inspections of each enterprise is minimal. As a result, the representatives of the second group do not spend much on informal business services, about a half of them (51 per cent) claim that they do not spend anything on these purposes. The risk of law violation is considered as relatively high. All in all, there is a remarkable intention not to break the boundaries of the formal economy.

From the data, a minority of entrepreneurs have obvious problems in their relations with the officials – 21 per cent. The share of those who view their relations with the officials as tense and conflictual ones is at a minimum – 17 per cent. At the same time there is maximum representation of those who estimate these relationships as mutual non-interference – 47 per cent (see Table 3).

By and large, the situation in this group looks most favourable. The entrepreneurs are used to avoiding confrontation with bureaucrats and their frequent controlling inspections. They do not spend much on bureaucratic services but manage to keep the relations of mutual neutrality and parity with the officials.

Nearly all (94 per cent) of this group are the heads of new non-state businesses. Their firms are predominantly small – 91 per cent. There is an even representation of all main areas of activity.

c) Conflicting with Officials (Group 3). The spread of bureaucratic extortion in the third group is estimated as being much higher (66 per cent) than in the previous two groups. There is also the highest number of those who face bureaucratic pressures frequently in their personal experience – 45 per cent. The share of entrepreneurs who consider that bureaucratic extortion is becoming more frequent is also at maximum level. Coercive pressures lead to additional costs: 70 per cent of entrepreneurs have expenditures on informal business services; for 21 per cent of them such expenditures are significant.

Informal dealings, in their turn, are often connected with the infringement of laws, and it is no surprise that the level of obedience to the law in this group is less than that of the first and second groups. A majority (82 per cent) of entrepreneurs would follow the law 'when possible'. Seventeen per cent think that the risk attached to the violation of the law is practically absent (see Table 3).

The third group blames the bureaucrats as, more often than not, the initiators of bribery. This is scarcely surprising given that the number of external controlling visits to each enterprise is at its maximum (an average of four times a month). The main distinction of this group is that 55 per cent of its representatives evaluate the relations of business and authorities as tense and conflictual (see Table 3). Accordingly, aggravated tensions lead to a search for the way out. Thus, this group is relatively active in claiming that it is necessary to influence the authorities – 53 per cent.

The majority of the third group is constituted by small enterprises, though 19 per cent of firms are large and medium-sized. A significant share (56 per cent) of firms were created between 1994–1997. The enterprises are mostly concentrated in the wholesale trade, retailing, catering and consumer services, i.e. in areas most attractive for the controlling bodies, though a group of industrial production enterprises is also represented.

d) Paying Off the Officials (Group 4). The last group is also subject to intensive coercive pressures. Two-thirds of entrepreneurs point to the frequent practices of bureaucratic extortion in Russian business. In their personal experience, 34 per cent are used to encountering it on a regular basis. As many as 29 per cent of entrepreneurs have significant expenditures on informal services and 73 per cent of them pessimistically think that bribery is unavoidable today (see Table 3).

It is worth mentioning that administrative control over enterprises is not very tight, and the number of inspections is fairly small. How is this possible given the reports of hard bureaucratic pressures? Most probably the entrepreneurs of this group manage to pay off the officials. Moreover, they are not too scrupulous about compliance with the law: 21 per cent of them would ignore an 'inconvenient' law; 25 per cent of them claim that in their opinion the risk of systematic violations of the law is virtually absent today.

The data indicate that their relations with the authorities are rather tense (39 per cent) though open conflict is less than in the third group. These entrepreneurs express no optimism concerning the attitudes of the officials. At the same time only 23 per cent of them are attempting to influence the authorities by political means. Rather it is easier for them to pay-off the officials.

The fourth group consists of non-state businesses only. Many of these firms were created in the period 1996–1997 – 39 per cent, thus, it is largely new small business. Apart from wholesale trade, retailing, catering and consumer services, these businesses are predominately concentrated in the fields of finance and market services.

Table 3. Bureaucratic Extortion and the Types of Entrepreneurs (percentage of total)

Types of Entrepreneurs				
	Loyal to Officials	Parity with Officials	Conflict with Officials	Paying off the Officials
Number of enterprises	28	70	53	41
Bureaucratic extortion				
Frequent in Russian business in general	11	11	66	68
Frequent personal experience	4	0	45	34
More frequent over the last 2–3 years	11	12	45	42
Impossible to avoid bribery	7	11	64	73
Incur significant expenditures on informal business services	4	4	21	29
Attitude to the law				
Better to ignore inconvenient law	11	14	12	21
Risk of law violation is high	58	58	35	23
Relations with the officials				
Tensions and conflicts with the officials	32	17	55	39
Receiving financial support from the state authorities	15	4.5	2	3
Necessary to influence the authorities	25	42	53	23
Types of the enterprise				
Privatized state enterprises	82	6	11	0
Small enterprises	54	91	81	98

IV. VIOLENCE IN RUSSIAN BUSINESS

1. *Spread of threats and violence*

Informal means of persuading partners with the help of threats and demonstration of force are reported to play an important part in Russian entrepreneurship at present. It is claimed, in the mass media, that up to 70 per cent of enterprises must pay significant sums for their protection. Data from the 1997–1998 surveys shows that 79 per cent of entrepreneurs in the sample agree that the use of threats and force does occur in Russian business today; and 17 per cent (occasionally – 62 percent) think it is a frequent phenomenon. At the same time, personal experience of this sort is relatively modest. Less than a half of respondents (42 per cent) are personally used to confronting this pressure, and only three per cent experience it often (39 per cent – occasionally) (see Table 4). It can be concluded that the popular statements in the mass media concerning the 'total criminalization' of Russian business are exaggerated.

There is slight optimism in estimating recent trends. Thirty per cent of entrepreneurs believe that the attempts to use force are becoming less frequent. At the same time, the majority (56 per cent) think that the situation of violence in business has not changed during the last two to three years (getting worse – 14 per cent). As to the possibility of eradicating this phenomenon, relative optimism is

Table 4. Use of Threats and Force in Russian Business (percentage of total)

	Frequent	From time to time	Absent
In Russian business in general	17	62	21
	Frequent	*From time to time*	*Absent*
In one's personal experience	3	39	58
	More frequent	*No change*	*Less frequent*
Changes over the last 2–3 years	14	56	30
	Impossible	*Difficult*	*Possible*
Possibility to avoid coercion	8	34	58

more evident. Fifty-eight per cent of entrepreneurs declare that it is possible (difficult to avoid – 34 per cent, impossible to avoid – eight per cent) (see Table 4).

What is the normal way of coping with the situation when the entrepreneur becomes subject to threats? The distribution of answers is as follows:

- Solve the problems themselves   34%
- Apply for support of the police   13%
- Address the professional security agency   8%
- Address the criminal groupings (*'bratva'*)   15%
- Difficult to say   30%

The data lead to some additional conclusions concerning the spread of violence in Russian business at present:

- Violence is attracted to the fields that are advertised and, therefore, open to the public. The data prove a hypothesis linking the expenditures on advertising and personal experience of facing threats and violence.
- There is a certain path dependency evident in the cases under consideration. After getting involved in market segments which are more or less criminalized the firm tends to be attached to this niche.

2.   *Transaction costs and routinization of violence*

Confronting violence leads to additional transaction costs for all parties involved in coercive actions. These include:

- Expenditures on one's own security department;
- Payments to the other security agencies;
- Payments for the additional services associated with use of violence.

The transaction costs of business protection can constitute 10–15 per cent of revenues and may be much more, especially in cases whereby the security agencies invest their capital in business apart over and above their regular protection services.

Security groups (both legal and criminal) are widely used to deal with unreliable and dishonest partners, especially debt reclaiming. Prices for these 'services' are high: attraction of criminal groupings (*'bratva'*) will require half the whole debt, whereas legal security agencies will charge from 15–40 per cent of the sum in question.[14]

There are also some quantitative data on the expenditures of the enterprises on business protection. More than half (53 per cent) of our respondents declared that they do incur such expenditures. Two-thirds considered these costs insignificant for their enterprise, with the remaining third admitting that the costs are significant. The amount of these expenditures, not surprisingly, correlates with the frequency of violence confrontation in business relations.

Returning to relevant trends, the interview data confirm decreasing violence in Russian business, in comparison with the early 1990s. There are several arguments to substantiate this view. Firstly, organized crime is attracted to market segments with 'fast' and 'easy' profits. Recently, many of these segments have been shrinking, And criminal groupings shifted towards the field of 'black' market transactions.

> The period of high risk when big and 'fast' money was made has come to an end. Now it is a field of routine hard work, which is not bringing super-profits. Therefore there is no extortion either. (Head of real estate firm)

Secondly, initial division of zones of influence between legal and non-legal protection agencies has also been finished, as well as that between criminal groupings. The clashes that used to occur, attempting to redefine the boundaries and sanctions against transgressors, could be very harsh; however, they are not a matter of concern for the majority of entrepreneurs.

> All areas of influence have been divided by now. Serious *'kryshi'* (protection groups) have nothing to divide anymore. (Head of firm for trade and services)

Third, criminal groupings have undergone significant changes. They have become more professional and started to establish themselves in 'white' and 'grey' market segments. They are motivated by incentives of 'laundering' their profits extracted in black dealings, and of also getting a new image of 'honest businessman'. Thus, they have to adopt at least some of the rules established in business outside their criminal codes. The former opposition of business and criminality is moving to their mutual accommodation.

A decrease in open violence does not necessarily mean that criminalization of business is vanishing. Rather it is changing. There is a routinization of violence that is transformed into a 'normal' element of economic relations. Much of the spontaneous racketeering has been replaced by more sustainable and more 'civilized' forms of control over enterprises by organized criminal groupings.

---

[14] A. Polianski, 'Vyshe kryshi', *Expert* No. 2, 1996, p. 20.

What are the pillars of order and concepts of control established in this situation? This order is implemented by means of specification and identification of agencies that have their legitimate right to carry out violence in certain market segments and exclude all other 'intruders'. Relationships between entrepreneurs and protection groups are built upon a specific ethics, based upon a respect of force. It is a sort of customary law backed by means of violence. The legitimate right mentioned above is enforced not by the strict following of obligations (which is not an inherent characteristic of criminal groupings) but by the sustainability of their positions. The possibility of controlling the area of influence in the long-term is becoming the basis for the exclusive right of selling protection services.

3.   Evolution of state protection agencies

The state protection agencies in Russia have come through a remarkable evolution in the 1990s. First, they have been strengthened from the viewpoint of their personnel, material resources and organization. Second, they are gradually commercializing the office[15] by selling their protection services both in formal and shadow economies. Third, state protection agencies are starting to interact with the criminal groupings. In their interviews, entrepreneurs commented that both the state protection agencies and the criminal groupings tend to act in very similar ways. This does not mean that the 'mafia is running the state', as is often announced in the mass media. It means something different: a flexible system of informal links among state-run, semi-state and criminal agencies is being formed. This fulfils the following functions:

- Division of areas of influence and solvent clients;
- Providing additional revenues for state protection employees;
- Establishing control over the criminal areas.

State protection agencies are known as providing more safety. Besides, their services are normally cheaper. They have more legal opportunities and run lower risks than their criminal counterparts. Many entrepreneurs would, no doubt, be happy to get protection ('*krysha*') from the police or, more preferably, the Federal Security Service. However, their freedom to choose the protection institutions is structurally limited. To get these services one has to establish personal links in the protection agencies. Maintenance of these links is an important element of the business strategy, and it is certainly easier for state-run and large business to solve these issues. Thus, there is a segmentation of markets in terms of protection methods. The latter depend on the status of the enterprise and, in their turn, to enforce this status.

Those in illegal businesses like non-licensed selling of vodka and beer, drugs, cars and armaments attract bandit groupings. The rest of entrepreneurs try to

---

[15] E. Letowska, *Corruption: Towards Greater Transparency? Ethics in the Public Sector: Challenges and Opportunities for OECD Countries* (Organization for Economic Co-Operation and Development, Paris, 1997), pp. 4–5.

get the state protection provided by taxation police, Federal Security Service, police etc. The latter supply services of higher quality and for reasonable money. Naturally, they are acting in informal ways. (Head of trade and production firm)

4.   Violence and entrepreneurial types (Typology II)

The survey revealed four main factors (72.8 per cent of variance) and took two factors for cluster analysis:

*   Frequency of confronting violence (general estimations and personal experience);
*   Enterprise expenditures on business protection and informal business services.

Three main groups of entrepreneurs are categorized as:

*   Protected   43%
*   Resistant   28%
*   Vulnerable   29%

These groups can be depicted as:

a) Protected entrepreneurs (Group 1). Representatives of the first group face the use of force less often today. Only 43 per cent point to this phenomenon in Russian business, and only five per cent confront it in their personal activity. It is a fairly small number given that more than one third (35 per cent) of respondents in this group has significant expenditures on advertising. This group is more optimistic in evaluating recent trends in this area. As for possibilities of avoiding violence in business relations they are estimated relatively highly (see Table 5).

  This does not mean that these entrepreneurs ignore protection issues. Three-quarters spend money on business security, including 22 per cent who have significant expenditures of this kind. The group is also distinctive in the higher share of transaction costs in informal business services. There are grounds for suggesting that the absence of violence in this market segment is caused by the high extent of business protection, as they seem to have sufficient informal networks and security departments of their own. This is supported by the following data: nearly half (47 per cent) of entrepreneurs would, in case of threats and violence, try to cope themselves. Only minor groups would address either criminal groupings (12 per cent) or the police (7 per cent).

  The characteristics of enterprises are close to average here, though the share of those in industrial production is slightly higher.

b) Resistant entrepreneurs (Group 2). The situation in the second group is more complicated. Eighty-eight per cent of entrepreneurs point to the existence of violence in Russian business. More than one third (37 per cent) of them are used to facing it in their own activity, although none of them stated it was a frequent experience (see Table 5). The estimation of trends in this field is rather pessimistic. One out of nine entrepreneurs do not believe that it is at all possible to avoid violence under present conditions.

Despite the evident problems with their business safety, none of them spent much on protection and informal business services. Moreover, only 29 per cent of entrepreneurs in the second group would rely on their own capacities when faced with threats and the use of force. Many of them do not know how to deal with these issues (one third of respondents have no definite answer). There are three possible explanations: the lack of funds for protection; stressing their own undesirability for protection agencies; resistance in relation to extortion. The minimal share of those advertising their activities (22 per cent) is remarkable in this respect.

The elements of a resistance strategy are illustrated by the following data. Representatives of this group tend to find formal ways of settling their problems. They are the most law-abiding and least involved in informal dealings. Compared to the other groups, they are more likely to contact the police if threatened with violence (19 per cent), and an arbitration court in case of cheating (29 per cent). They are also less likely to try using force (3.5 per cent).

There is a relatively high representation of privatized structures and the firms dealing with science, health care and culture in this group.

c) Vulnerable Entrepreneurs (Group 3). The third group is very different from the previous ones for it is subjected to hard coercive pressures. Everyone highlights the manifestations of violence in Russian business (including frequent use of force – 36 per cent). More importantly, nearly all respondents in this group (95 per cent) have to confront violence in their own economic activity (frequently – 11 per cent). These entrepreneurs are, in the main, pessimistic about the trends and possibilities of avoiding violence. More than a half (55 per cent) claim that the liberation of Russian business from the influence of organized crime should be of primary importance. All these indicators are at a maximum level among all three groups (see Table 5).

The vulnerability of the third group is also reflected in the fact that they have the highest expenditures on business protection and informal business services, some of which can also be associated with safety issues. Nearly half the entrepreneurs spend significant amounts on advertising their activity which makes an additional point of attraction for protection agencies to come and offer (or impose) their services.

The entrepreneurs in the third group are more inclined to informal and criminal activities. Twenty-three per cent of them would call for criminal groupings in case of threats and violence. Nearly one fourth would try to use force to influence an unreliable partner. Representatives of this group are the most skeptical about pursuing the existing legislation.

Not surprisingly, the majority of enterprises are concentrated in wholesale trade and retailing, catering and consumer services, finance and market services. The group of Moscow firms is relatively large – 27 per cent. Moscow City is attracting both big money and the pursuers of this money.

Table 5. Use of Threats and Force and the Types of Entrepreneurs (percentage of total)

	Secured	Resistant	Vulnerable
Number of enterprises	86	56	58
Use of threats and force			
Exists in Russian business in general	43	88	100
including: frequently	0	16	36
Confronted in personal experience	5	37	95
including: frequently	1	0	11
Become more frequent over the last 2–3 years	5	16	20
Impossible to avoid use of force	7	11	5
Reaction to the threats and use of force			
in business relations			
Try to cope themselves	47	29	36
Address the police	7	19	13
Address the security agencies	12	6	11
Address the criminal groupings	12	14	23
Reaction to the attempts at cheating			
by business partners			
Appeal to Arbitration court	22	29	14
Try to use force	10	3.5	23
Have significant expenditures			
On business protection	22	0	43
On informal business services	24	0	30
On advertising	35	22	47
Claim that entrepreneurs have to break free from			
the influence of criminal groupings	32	36	55
Type of enterprises			
Privatized state enterprises	15	21	14
Small enterprises	81	79	84

V.   SOME CONCLUSIONS

It is argued that the 'transition to the market' in the case of Russia and Eastern European countries is a common stereotype based upon a rather abstract universalistic scheme. From the viewpoint of economic sociology it is more fruitful to speak of the continuous transformation of a variety of segmented markets, none of which approximate the model of a free market.

It would also be a mistake to treat the state bureaucracy either as opposing the market or as being equal to the other economic agents. State interventions make inherent elements in markets in which asymmetric power relationships between officials and entrepreneurs are reproduced.

The maintenance of numerous administrative barriers is not merely an outcome of the 'poor performance' of state authorities. It reproduces the principle of overall bureaucratic dependency under conditions when many formal property rights have been transferred to the enterprises. These barriers, therefore, force the entrepreneurs into 'grey' market segments and lead to their subordination in two ways: first, given that it is impossible to follow all the formal rules, and almost everyone is subject to selective bureaucratic control and sanctions; second, many economic agents have to start negotiations with the authorities to obtain individual privileges. As a result, entrepreneurs could not envisage the Russian economy without bribes.

Frequent infringement of business contracts also compels entrepreneurs to protect their property and income by means of violence, and the use of force has now been integrated as a 'normal' element in economic relations. Moreover, the media appears to have sensationalized and exaggerated the spread of threats, the use of violence and criminal protection services in Russian business.

This paper supports the view that the intensity of violence in horizontal business relations is gradually decreasing. However, it does not mean the elimination of criminality in Russian business. There is more likely to be a routinization of violence and development of a new ethics built upon capacities to use force. The initial division of zones of influence has been finished. Business and criminal groupings are now moving from opposition to mutual interdependence.

The data assess the group of enterprises that have a propensity to criminal actions of any sort as approximately 15 per cent. However, at the same time many entrepreneurs are involved in various segments of the informal economy and occasionally break the legal constraints.

6

The Transformation of the Second Economy into the Informal Economy

Marina Kurkchiyan

I. INTRODUCTION

Since the fall of the Soviet Union, it is not only the official economy of post-Soviet societies that has been transformed. In parallel to the mainstream changes, transition has also been taking place in the unofficial sector, altering the economic activities in the unregulated and largely unreported parts of the economy that operate beyond state control. Those activities are the focus of this paper. It will argue that in considering each of three distinct phases – the Soviet period, the first few years of the transition, and the present – we are dealing with three different phenomena that need both to be distinguished from each other, and to be described in different terminology. What was known as 'the second economy' in the Soviet period became after 1990 an economy of collapse. It was their manner of responding to general collapse that enabled people to struggle through the painful early years of the transition, managing lives despite the breakdown of all the official systems and arrangements that in normal times exist to make daily life possible. A decade on from that time, the unofficial sector has come to be known as 'the informal economy', and it has become the core pattern of production and exchange in post-Soviet countries.

Despite its hidden character, the unofficial economy of all three periods is not an alien or separate presence; it is embedded in the integral body of society. It depends heavily on the formal structures and institutions, including the body of legislation, the operational capacity of the formal economy, and the regulatory performance of the state. As a behavioural pattern reproducing itself in everyday life, it has a strong socio-psychological basis that consists of the beliefs and expectations of the people, their attitudes towards officialdom and each other, and their shared understandings of how things get done in their society. For these reasons, any reorganization of the official economy, especially one that is rapid and substantial, inevitably affects the non-official sector as well. If the institutional changes are radical, then the unofficial economy will inevitably undergo transformation as it is forced to adapt to the new realities. In the case of the former USSR, although all three phenomena – the second economy, the economy of collapse and the informal economy – evolved successively

83

A. V. Ledeneva and M. Kurkchiyan (eds.), Economic Crime in Russia, 83–97
© 2000 *Kluwer Law International. Printed in Great Britain.*

from the long-established Soviet tradition of informal relationships, each was transformed from its predecessor. The three models, therefore, differ radically in their social meanings and in their roles within the overall socioeconomic pattern.

This paper intends to examine these differences. In relation to the three historical periods, I will analyze the configuration of the official and unofficial economies, assess the regulative capacity of the state, explore the role and social impact of the unofficial economy, and describe the pattern of people's involvement in those activities. Comparison of the differences will allow this paper to demonstrate that the transformations between each stage have a qualitative character and are not mere extensions of previous characteristics, or a deeper criminalization in general. The new market that has now emerged is officially the product of the legislative reform programme, but its behaviour is wholly dominated by the informal economy and is better understood as the outgrowth of successive transformations in the unofficial sector of Russian economic life.

II. THE SECOND ECONOMY

The phenomenon of a second economy in the Soviet Union developed spontaneously as a self-protective response by ordinary people to the failures of the planned economy. It consisted of a vast network of informal dealing; it was not at all what is usually understood, especially in the West, by the term 'black market'. There are significant differences between a black market and the kind of second economy that was characteristic of the Soviet social-economic model of society. Black markets do of course exist in every society to some extent, and consist of illegal transactions, corruption and bribes.

In contrast to the legitimate market/black market model, the Soviet state operated as an economy that commonly had two kinds of transactions within it: the official dealings, announced and recorded, and those of the second economy, which were not. This meant that the second economy was virtually co-extensive with the whole economy, and involved almost the whole population, to at least some extent. In addition to the legal economy operating by means of controls, plans, directives, quotas and the like, the second economy made quasi-market arrangements available for the whole of society in respect to at least part of the material needs of the people. To analyze the working of this second economy, Katsenelinboigen used six colours to describe its complexity and sophistication[1] – though others might argue that the reality was even more multi-coloured.

Nor was the second economy merely a system of tax evasion, as in the typical 'unofficial economy' in Western countries, where tax evasion is the sole aim of such under-the-counter activities, and where 'the primary difference (between the official and the unofficial economy) is that transactions in the unofficial economy are not reported to or recorded by government.'[2] The second economy was the unintended

---

[1]   A. Katsenelinboigen, 'Coloured Market in the Soviet Union' (1977) 29 *Soviet Studies*, p. 78.
[2]   R. Rose, 'Getting By in Three Economies: The Resources of the Official, Unofficial and Domestic Economies' in J. Lane (ed.) *State and Market* (Sages, London, 1985) p. 106.

consequence of the fundamental principle of Soviet society. As is well known, the communist system was based on the utopian vision of equality – equality not just of opportunity (as in western socialism), but equality of outcomes. Creating equal circumstances for everyone was the most important objective of social policy. The objective, however, was never fully achieved, partly because unlimited state intervention in social and economic life produced uncontrolled processes (of which the second economy may have been the most significant) that intensified over the course of time, and distorted both the society and the economy.

To achieve the maximum possible equality, the Soviet state adopted a multi-pronged strategy. It abolished the institution (though it could not erase the principle) of property ownership in combination with tight economic regulation of wages and prices. This policy assured a more or less decent livelihood (although it was one that was not far above the poverty line) for the overwhelming majority of the population. However, the system lacked both the creative energy generated by financial incentives, and the respect for property that results from private ownership. The policy also made it very difficult for anyone to reach a significantly higher standard of living by increasing their work performance within the official economy.

In manufacturing, for example, executives had no interest in taking overall responsibility for the everyday operation of an enterprise by straightforward management practices such as matching resources to output or raising the quality of the product. The state, the sole property owner under the Soviet system, became little more than a bureaucracy. The employees of this bureaucracy, including those at the very top level, did not receive any direct benefit from the managerial control they were supposed to provide.

Under these circumstances, the centrally-controlled distribution of funds throughout the legal economy turned into a competition for resources between enterprises (and in this competition, a traditional 'black market' was indeed widely practiced). However, only part of the resources thus gained was made available for the legal process of production and distribution. Another part was inserted into the process of production and distribution separately, by means of the second economy.

Just as in the case of the legally-approved sector, this subtracted portion of the nationwide allocation was devoted to the production and distribution of goods and services, and as in the legally-approved sector it exploited state property to do so – but its operations were carried out beyond state control. As Grossman described it, 'Within the state sector itself, … [it was] the violation of the innumerable laws, rules, regulations, norms, directives, plans, etc., pertaining to the everyday activity of managers, technicians, workers, clerks, functionaries.'[3] There was no return benefit to the state. Innumerable ways were devised to cover up the disappearance of the resources that vanished from the official record. For sociologists, one of the most interesting phenomena of the history of the USSR was the time and effort committed to the creation of documents which were absolutely irrelevant to anything real except the official record: as Winiecki put it, a 'loss of non-existent output'.[4]

---

[3] G. Grossman, 'The Second Economy of the USSR' (1977) 26 *Problems of Communism*, p. 27.
[4] J. Winiecki, *The Distorted World of Soviet-Type Economics* (Routledge, London, 1988).

Nevertheless, the fake statistics and reports did satisfy the formal requirements of control and the Soviet system survived for four generations.

The benefits generated by production in the second economy were allocated to all the people involved in it. These included workers, managers and the clerical staff who had to deal with the tidal flow of documents. Even unskilled workers usually had their own share of this benefit. In effect, the Soviet Union developed a significant redistribution mechanism with crude free market characteristics, operating in parallel with the official economy. It was extremely pervasive; everybody had to engage in it. It was not possible to live outside the alternative economy other than at great cost, not only in terms of income, but also in terms of social mobility and integration in society.

This informal tradition of relations in business and direct redistribution by means of 'pay-in-cash' transactions for each performance of work was diffused throughout all areas of society, including the social services. As Rose noted,

> While policymakers puzzle about what to do with the wreckage of a centrally planned economy, the masses of people face an existential problem: how to get enough to keep going from day to day. Everyone living in a non-market economy has lots of experience in getting by without official help, for the pathologies of the planned economy forced people to find ways and means to produce and exchange goods and services through a multiplicity of 'second' economies.[5]

This paper will demonstrate the re-distributive potential of the second economy by reporting the findings of a research project that examined the bus service in one of the Soviet Republics – Armenia.[6] Although there were some differences between the operation of bus services in different Soviet republics, or in some cases between regions and towns, the second economy operated uniformly and the pattern of the re-distributive mechanism revealed in this study was typical for the Soviet model generally.[7]

The results showed that although the official wage of a bus driver was slightly higher than the average for the population, it was considered by him to be only a guarantee of basic security. He received his main income separately – directly from his services. Passengers would pay their fares to the driver for each trip, and he never gave them tickets or receipts. In other words, the fares were collected by the driver without any external control.

5   R. Rose, 'Toward a Civil Economy?' (1992) 3 *Journal of Democracy*, p. 10.
6   The research, carried out in 1990, included all five bus stations in Yerevan, the capital of Armenia. It was both a quantitative study and a qualitative one. The researchers administered a questionnaire to bus drivers in combination with one-week of intensive observation in bus stations. They also conducted a series of in-depth interviews with representatives of each of the different occupations within the bus services. The research was sponsored by the mayor of Yerevan within a few weeks of the transfer of control from the Communists to the Armenian nationalist movement.
7   M. Kurkchiyan, 'Old Patterns, New Markets: Episodes from the Transition in Transportation, Health Care and Education in Armenia' Working Paper, Department of Sociology, London School of Economics, 1995.

On the expenditure side of the process, the driver gave only part of his total receipts to the state. A larger part stayed in his pocket. However, at the same time, he had to dig into that pocket to pay for many of the necessary expenses for his work. He spent his money on cash payments for cleaning and servicing his bus, for obtaining spare parts, and sometimes even for getting a better (i.e. more profitable) route. Every driver was engaged in this (essentially self-employed) activity while at the same time working as a salaried employee of the state. From the driver's perspective, the two roles were so completely intertwined that they were impossible to separate. Any driver who sought to escape from the net of the second economy would not only suffer a reduction in his income, but he would also be deprived of the resources needed to fulfil his official, everyday duties – a roadworthy bus, the fuel to propel it, the spare parts to keep it running, and access to the maintenance facilities necessary to keep it safe to drive.

The net effect of the two layers of economic activity was that a bus driver's total income, after expenses, was about two to three times the size of his official state salary. This did not secure a rich lifestyle for him, merely an average standard of living in real terms – average, that is, when compared to the real standard of living achieved by others who also had unofficial, supplementary incomes.

The wage had lost its function as payment for work done and had come to serve only as a guarantee of social security. The work itself was paid for by private interests, beyond state control. Moreover, these conditions applied not only to the drivers but also to all the other occupational groups within the bus services: the people who cleaned the buses, the repair mechanics, the managers at different levels, the route planners and the clerical staff.

The two levels of the economy had different functions. The official level, operating through the payment of salaries, secured a basic standard of living (low, but nevertheless above the poverty level) for the majority. The second economy complemented this, ensuring a principal source of income and providing a reasonable lifestyle for the population.

The two socio-economic structures were linked and interdependent. It was necessary for everyone to continue to fulfil their duties in the legal economy, as involvement in the legal economy was the essential precondition to obtaining the considerable benefits of the second economy. By the time the USSR collapsed at the end of the 1980s, its social structure had changed profoundly in comparison with the plans of its founders. The second economy had become the dominant force in the allocation of goods and services. As Burrage described it, 'the microstructures of family and kin, of friends, of patrons and clients ... [were] the only effective adversaries the Soviet regime ever had, permanent saboteurs of socialist laws, plans, and normative acts, the last impregnable line of defence of the private sphere against the public order.'[8] On the one hand, the state became increasingly poor as a result of the growing pressure by the second economy on the legal economy; the progressive development of the informal economy had the

---

[8]   M. Burrage, 'Russian Advocates: Before, During and After Perestroika' (Summer 1993) 18 *Law and Social Inquiry*, p. 590.

effect of shifting an ever-expanding proportion of the benefits of economic activity away from the state coffers into private hands. However, on the other hand, the income of the population as a whole gradually rose. There was a striking contradiction between the tangibly increasing standard of living and the official statistical data about the wellbeing of the population. The much-publicized reforms of the Soviet Union's dying years were introduced not as a result of any pressure exerted by a reform-minded mass movement, but as desperate measures by the government of a bankrupt state. The rulers had become painfully aware of the need to act, but their programme of so-called *perestroika* was a top-down reform programme. As such, it was an ill-judged response to the success of the second economy, which was entirely a bottom-up process.

At the same time, the centrally-planned economy had always managed to stay in the core position and overall state control of production and distribution was not completely lost. The second economy operated alongside (or indeed inside) the official economy, squeezing the available resources. Not surprisingly, the first economic step taken under *perestroika* was to legalize, in 1988, part of the second economy. 'Cooperatives', in the form of small businesses offering consumer goods and services, became permissible. This set in motion a gradual extension of the territory occupied by the second economy under the Soviet system. It was abruptly stopped when the rapid political changes of 1988–1989 culminated in the total collapse of the USSR.[9]

Ten years on, in attempting to evaluate the second economy, one could simply view it as a stock of resources stolen from the state and improperly exploited. However, this simplification would misrepresent an important mechanism for redistribution in society, and would neglect its market benefits, despite their crudity. The beneficent role of the second economy in facilitating non-violent transition and in overcoming crises would be missed.

On the negative side, it can now be seen that the second economy helped to extend the life of the moribund Soviet political system beyond its sell-by date; for many years it persisted because the public was apathetic towards state affairs. The lessons that people were forced to learn in order to do business in their alternative networks also cultivated an unfortunate attitude towards law, towards public authority and towards political participation. By taking part in the second economy, people grew accustomed to the practice of informal problem-solving. They cultivated a tradition of bypassing officialdom. The overall effect was that during the closing decades of Soviet history, a psychological condition of general alienation from the state became widespread. As the post-Soviet era began, that malignant attitude provided fertile ground for the growth of illegal acts and violent crime.

---

[9]   It is difficult to identify a single date on which the old era ended and the new one began. It would be prefered to choose a series of turning points, such as the dates of the election of the new national governments in the various republics, and the August 1991 *putsch* in Russia.

III.   THE ECONOMY OF COLLAPSE

When the end of the Soviet saga arrived, its official institutions disintegrated like a row of melting snowmen. In this respect the move to the new system was not gradual, but sudden in its velocity and revolutionary in its impact. Among western theorists of the transition such a speedy rejection of the past combined with an immediate imposition of the new life is commonly known as 'shock therapy'. The term is often used to describe the sweeping reforms that were deliberately imposed at the macro level in particular countries, such as Poland. However, on the micro level, the shock began immediately everywhere and struck like a socio-economic earthquake. It was the therapy, rather than the shock, that was delayed in some of the republics.

The term 'economy of collapse' is used here to describe the conditions encountered by ordinary people when the shock occurred. The system was paralyzed, the state became incapable of providing any regulation, and daily life degenerated to such an extent that people began to question their own basic norms and values. The early years of transition in all the countries of the former Soviet Union were marked by the highest level of uncertainty in all areas of life: uncertainty about income (even for those who were still supposedly in a job), about the operational rules of the economy and of society, about the usefulness or relevance of traditional standards of personal conduct towards others, and above all, uncertainty about what might happen from one day to the next. During this period, each state's economy was effectively reduced to the economic survival of each family – struggling to make ends meet and searching for a new strategy and tactics by which to make life possible.

Russians first lost their savings in 1992 when state price controls were removed. Setting prices free brought years of hyperinflation. Hyperinflation in turn caused the gross devaluation of the salaries and pensions of all state employees – who before 1989 made up virtually 100 per cent of the population. Salaries generally became so small in comparison with prices that they lost their significance, even as a guarantee of social security. The only economy that worked during the worst years of transition was the practice of self-reliance – individual, informal problem-solving. In this period, survival became a despairing search for workable forms of economic enterprise, no matter how crude or demeaning the activity involved or how small the return.

The tactics developed within the economy of collapse took a variety of forms, from simple trading to criminal activity. Initially, the kind of trading varied from asset-stripping – selling off household items or objects of value from their stock of personal possessions – to smuggling by pseudo-tourists, a growth industry in which members of all social groups took part. Even former members of the professional classes, people with high qualifications, resorted to the risky business of carrying goods across borders. By the mid-1990s, the catastrophic decline in the general standard of living had become visible everywhere across the former Soviet Union, signaled by the large number of beggars lining the streets and the pathetic efforts to grow vegetables in the polluted dirt along the edge of railway tracks.

The public transport example illustrates the specifics of the functioning of the economy during the worst years of the transition. To a casual outside observer, it would appear that no bus driver could survive in the job. His salary had only a symbolic meaning. The actual sum of cash that he collected as he drove any given route had a greatly diminished value, while at the same time the expenses necessary to look after the bus had increased steeply. Indeed, in our exemplary case of the bus services, the number of buses running on the official routes did undergo a sharp decline during the early 1990s.

However, there were offsetting trends. Informal relations had evolved in a new way. The official control was completely withdrawn and the portion of turnover that previously sustained the official layer of management came to an end. A bus driver was now free to use his bus (the same bus as ten years before – one that still belonged to the state-run station) as the basis of a private business for which he controlled the entire budget. He could charge an unofficial price, i.e. whatever price he judged to be right for the service. Usually it was about four to five times the official price set in preceding years. Even so, the income remained small. Typically, it would be large enough only to provide food for the family and to buy the most limited servicing that would just keep the bus running. Many bus drivers found that they could not make enough to support a family and were forced to quit the job and seek work doing whatever they were capable of, which often meant becoming a casual labourer.

The early transition threatened the existence of everyone and every organization, at all levels, personal, social and institutional. 'The system', which, throughout the lives of every citizen had made all the major decisions, had suddenly gone out of existence, and with it there also vanished the possibility that institutional and social solutions would be provided from above. If survival was to be achieved, then people would have to take action themselves. The story of the economy of collapse is, therefore, a story of solutions achieved by individuals taking steps at the lowest social level of interpersonal relation.

The following responses taken from an interview with a hospital manager are an example of the strategy adopted in the period of the institutional collapse by leaders in the social services.

Question. How could the hospital cope, when the government was not covering even a small part of its expenses despite the fact that medical care was still supposed to be a part of a free national health service?

Answer. First, we have to make an informal charge to those patients who can pay, and we provide only a basic service to those who cannot. But sometimes we have other sources for things as well. Like last winter a local middleman dealer managed to bring us an essential stock of drugs. He had a contact, an employee of one of the international humanitarian organizations that support hospitals in this country by donating drugs. He needed our hospital to make a legal claim in order to get the organization to provide us with a consignment of drugs, and it succeeded. We then divided what we got, and he sold his part in the market. If I had not agreed to that compromise, this hospital could not have survived. We were completely out of stock.[10]

---

[10] The interview was one of a number conducted by the author between 1990 and 1999 in Armenia, Russia and Ukraine, as part of a series of sociological research projects on the

The period of collapse had a strong psychological impact. On the positive side, there was an explosive growth in self-reliance, a quality much praised by ideologists of the free market. However, the conception of rationality underlying it was quite different from the usual western version. Of necessity, the kind of rational action required in the fires of transition gave total priority to the short-term. The urgency of the need to solve everyday problems was so overwhelming that it closed off any possibility of forward planning or thoughts for the consequences of one's actions. It became routine to assume that any investment had to hold out the prospect of yielding immediate revenue; if it did not, it would be dismissed as not worthwhile. Alongside this inability to think in terms of enlightened self-interest, there was a widespread rejection of authority. Traditionally, the characteristic relationship between a Soviet citizen and any government official had been relatively wholesome: distant, often skeptical or even alienated, but also resigned to the need for government, and occasionally playful. The shock of transition, however, converted this typical attitude into deep distrust and detestation. A wholesale loss of trust, faith and respect became a philosophy of society.

Under the economy of collapse, weak government and the absence of legal regulation combined with an atmosphere of overall permissiveness to provide ideal conditions for criminals. Mafia structures flourished and quickly reached the point where they enveloped top bureaucrats in government who were thereby granted all the advantages of unrestricted power. Consequently, by the mid-1990s, post-Soviet societies had produced well-established groups of people who had lost any interest in promoting further transition towards an adequately regulated market.

In duration and extent, the economy of collapse varied from republic to republic within the former Soviet Union, and from region to region within Russia. Large geographical disparities appeared as the economy of collapse cut off neighbourhoods from external sources of income and forced people to rely solely on whatever their locality could provide. In some regions of Russia, the question of how to survive is still unanswered for the vast majority of the population. However, it is argued here that after a decade of transition, most or all of the post-Soviet countries have settled down into a stable pattern that constitutes a model of society. From a sociological viewpoint it is right to suggest that the period of transition (defined as a phase during which the old rules of society were devalued or destroyed while the new ones have not yet been established) is over. It was a period in which, despite all the difficulties, the society was open to innovation and was capable of being pushed in any of several different directions.

In succession to the economy of collapse, the establishment of a set of rules by which society is structured means that we are now dealing with a new, and quite rigid social model. It is arguable how to date its emergence. Personally, the date of the second presidential election in most of the republics would be chosen. Which, in the majority of cases, occurred close to the middle of the decade and marked the

---

evolving nature of the transition. All subsequent references to interview material in this paper are taken from the records of this series. This quotation is taken from an interview conducted in 1995.

moment at which regimes re-established themselves. If that is the case, then the Russian transition lasted until 1996.

Making an analytical distinction between 'an economy of collapse' and its successor, 'the informal economy' does not mean that the period of economic hardship is over for the entire population. That is clearly not the case. The main distinction between the two stages is the decrease in the amount of uncertainty in people's lives. Society shifts from a condition of intense vertical social mobility, during which the majority are forced into a downward slide and a panicky search for a new strategy of life, to a more settled or even immobile social structure. Today, the bulk of the population lives in poverty,[11] a condition that threatens to be developed into a condition known by sociologists as a 'culture of poverty'.[12] At the other end of the social scale, there is a small group of the super-rich, the 'New Russians'. In between are the rest, who have managed by various means and to different degrees to secure their sources of income.

To sharpen the distinction between an economy of collapse and an informal economy, it may be recalled that in the early years of the transition, sociologists were puzzled as to how to define and measure poverty in the former Soviet Union.[13] Traditional methods of poverty research were inadequate. It was not clear how to deal with the complexity of post-Soviet poverty, such as the classification of people who enjoyed good housing but had no income whatsoever, or of highly educated people with no job and no prospect of a job. The high speed of the changes meant that virtually anyone might find themselves quickly moved to either the top or the bottom of the income scale. Even the fundamental notion of a poverty line lost its meaning when the falling value of money left the overwhelming majority of people well below the bottom of any reasonable measure. As time passed, however, some of those contradictions became less striking: people sold their houses if they did not manage to find a source of income, mobility slowed down, and income became more stable even though it remained very unequal. Recent studies of poverty, based on the traditional method that examines income and expenditure, once again give a better understanding of the socio-economic groupings in Russia.[14]

Since the mid-1990s, a new economy has become progressively more apparent. Its foundation is clearly the institution of ownership – of land, capital, and property in general – and its rules of the game, both political and economic, have become socially established and accepted as normal. Alongside the reviving economy, the distinction between its formal and informal layers has become prominent.

---

[11] By the end of the century, 51million Russians, more than a third of the population, were living below the poverty line, according to the Russian statistics agency. 'Russians Sink Deeper into Poverty' *The Guardian*, 31 July 1999, p. 19.

[12] See O. Lewis, *La Vida: A Puerto Rican Family in the Culture of Poverty* (Random House, New York, 1966).

[13] M. Kurkchiyan, 'Poverty: Various Approaches to Concept and Measurement' in L. Harutuniyan (ed.) *Social Work and Social Policy* (Yerevan State University Press, Yerevan, 1995). (In Russian).

[14] J. Klugman (ed.), *Poverty in Russia: Public Policy and Private Responses* (World Bank, New York, 1997).

IV. THE INFORMAL ECONOMY

The term 'informal economy' was first used in the context of the Third World,[15] and was applied to societies that possessed a specific version of the market economy – one that was clearly different from the Western model. It was through analyses of the informal sector of the economy within the developing countries that observers became aware that markets differ between countries and cultures:

> The differences which exist between the planned economies of state socialism, the bureaucratic liberalism of the social democracies of Western capitalism, and the relatively unregulated economies of the 'undeveloped' or 'developing' nations are not simply differences of degree with respect to formality and state intervention. There are three distinct approaches to the state's intervention. As such they are qualitatively different systems.[16]

The question that now arises is this: Are we dealing with a qualitatively new, post-Soviet model of the market, or only with a variant of the 'developing' market that is already understood as a consequence of Third World studies? The answer to this question will require comparative research on the informal sectors in the countries of the Second, post-Soviet World and the Third World. However, what is quite clear by now is that the Russian transition did not follow the path planned for it by the many western advisors, bankers and technical specialists who exerted such a powerful influence on policy in the transition years. The Russian economy has not become a Western type of market, based on the rule of law. It is instead a market shaped by informal exchange, networking and social know-how.

The table below shows the transformations through which the unofficial sector of the Soviet economy passed on its way to form the new Russian market.

The most significant characteristic of the newly developed economy in Russia, as well as in the other post-Soviet republics, is that the informal sector now occupies most of it. However, the people involved in it prefer to keep it concealed below the surface of officially-recorded Russian life. Most economic activity, therefore, is invisible; only its peak, in the form of the official economy, is allowed to show above the surface. The state, after a substantial period of irrelevance to the economy, is once more trying to reassert its position and take control of the levers of regulation. However, after the history of the past generation, it is not surprising that it is meeting strong resistance. The newly formed economy grew out of the economy of collapse. Each person who has managed to survive, having established a source of income only with the greatest possible difficulty, tends to consider it a private achievement and, therefore, one that the government has very little to do with.

---

[15] J. Bryant, 'An Introductory Bibliography to Work on the Informal Economy in the Third World Literature' in J. Laite (ed.), *Bibliographies on Labor Market and Informal Economies* (SSRC, London, 1982).
[16] P. Harding and R. Jenkins, *The Myth of the Hidden Economy* (Open University Press, Philadelphia, 1989), p. 4.

Table 1.

	The Second Economy	The Economy of Collapse	The Informal Economy
Relation to the official economy	Crude market extension to the core planned economy	The only economy	The main economy with the official economy on the surface
Functions	Re-distribution	Survival	Accumulation
State regulative potential over main economy	Significant control	Lack of any control	Very weak control
Impact on the official existing system	Stabilized the official system	Helped to survive during the intensive restructuring	Distorted the official system
Spread	Within Soviet borders	Locally orientated	Internationalized
Variety of forms (in colours)	Multi-coloured	Colourless	Grey and black
People's involvement in official economy	Full employment	Total collapse of workplaces	High unemployment
People's involvement in unofficial economy	Part-time involvement	Full-time involvement	Full-time involvement
Inclusion	Pervasive		Selective
Social impact	Generally increasing standard of living	Sustaining life	Increasing income inequality

The old instinct of distrust of government helped ordinary people to survive when the Soviet state collapsed, and the painful experience that followed during the transition intensified the distrust. Now there is fierce resistance to any attempts at regulation from above. Demands that the new laws should be respected – by registering a business and applying for licenses, by paying taxes, by reporting purchases and sales – are now regarded by people as orders to withdraw from territory they have already occupied in the life space, at considerable sacrifice. Resistance comes not just from organized crime, which obviously has the most to lose from the restoration of order, but also from small business leaders and the self-employed. For example, the manager of a small advertising company in Moscow stated that only a few contracts are ever formalized; most consist only of informal agreements with payment in cash so as to avoid all forms of control and tax deduction.

Why should I pay taxes, when this government not only did nothing to help me establish my business, but created a lot of obstacles? They cannot pay salary to people, they cannot restore order, they cannot provide a proper education to my children or guarantee my business. They do nothing for me, so why should I give them my money?'[17]

There are strong arguments (some of them expressed in this volume)[18] supporting the view that the informal activity in Russia is an expression of civil society, and, therefore, supportive of the development of the newly-born market. If so, that would mean that the Russian model of the market and the civil society is qualitatively different from the Western one. It would have to operate without the trust in government, responsiveness to regulation, and transparency (not in terms of know-how, but in terms of openness and accuracy of information) that characterize Western economies. It follows, that if the aim of the transition was to convert Russia to a Western type of market, then the informal economy is destructive of that process. It prevents the establishment of political equilibrium by involving politicians and bureaucrats in the fight for private economic interests and by drawing them into corruption at every level.

The legislative changes of the transition, altering the official economy from a centrally-planned model to a market model, did inevitably change the structure of the unofficial economy. With the acceptance of the right to engage in private economic activities, it is now entirely permissible to do many businesslike things that were illegal under communism and, therefore, restricted to the second economy. Currency exchange, provision of private services, speculative trading and entrepreneurship itself have all switched categories, from the forbidden to the encouraged. Such a legalization of normal commercial activity is, of course, essential for free enterprise, but it has had an unanticipated consequence: the distinction between the formal and the informal sectors has been sharpened, and the informal sector has been moved closer to the criminal sector. As Sik described it, 'While the second economy represented a multi-coloured variety of household strategies, the informal economy leads to polarized strategies, i.e. it points towards a black and white economy.'[19]

One respondent, the manager of an enterprise in a Russian province, preferred to use three colours to describe the present condition of the Russian economy:

We do not have a white economy at all. Economic activity is either black, completely hidden, or grey, when only part of what happens is reported. I would say that at the present time most of our economy is grey; businesses have cleaned up on the surface to deal with increasing state control. By saying black I do not necessarily mean that it's criminal. It could be a doctor having a private practice without officially reporting it, or a housewife providing delivery of homemade cookies.

---

[17] The interview was conducted in 1997.
[18] See papers by V. Volkov, (chpt 4) and W. Tupman, (chpt 18)
[19] E. Sik, *From the Second Economy to the Informal Economy* Studies in Public Policy No. 207 (Centre for the Study of Public Policy, Glasgow, 1992), p. 5.

To the question about how he would define criminal activity, he responded: 'It is when big money is involved, obtained by violence and/or stealing. You cannot call a poor woman who works in her scruffy kitchen all day to earn a living a criminal, just because she does not pay taxes.'[20] This interview also demonstrated the widely held understanding of crime, which is that the concept does not apply to the resistance of an economic actor to any form of state regulation.

The informal economy of the new market has a different impact on society from that of the second economy of the Soviet time. Today's economy cannot be described as a re-distributive system. The recognition of the right of private firms to take part in the official economy has changed the social function of the unofficial segment of the economy. If we refer back to the example of the second economy within the bus service before the collapse of the Soviet system, then it is clear that all the transactions involved would be considered perfectly legal under today's rules, so long as the business is registered and taxes are paid. So what happens now? The informal economy has been reduced to activities that cannot be called by any names other than cheating and corruption – activities such as tax evasion, stealing from employers, illegal contracts, bribing politicians and officials, money laundering, and so forth (all these facets of the new market are well-described in other papers in this book).

In this new context, informal activities have an accumulative effect, rather than a re-distributive one. Accumulative incomes built up by means of post-transitional informal activities are distributed unequally, and they have vastly increased the income disparity of the population. In analyzing the social impact of this sector of the economy on post-communist societies as a whole, Sik offers five reasons for the radical inequalities of life that resulted:

- The increasing importance of full-time informal activities and the corresponding loss of the small, but safe and effortless, income that people enjoyed under socialism;
- The involvement of foreign capital, which creates a group with extremely high income;
- The high level of corruption, combined with steep transaction costs and prestige consumption;
- Widespread tax evasion that adds to income disparities;
- The automatic creation of extra profits by inflation.[21]

To this list a further point should be added. The informal economy has a rigorously selective character. Resources that are available in the informal economy have been quickly exhausted in the public sector and they are better protected if they are kept private. Sources of income in the informal economy are limited and most are already allocated to those who proved to be the best-adapted to the transitional changes and who continue to be the most competitive. People who have been left outside the market that has now emerged – a large part of the population – have no access to

---

[20] The interview was conducted in April 1999.
[21] E. Sik, n. 19 above, p. 23.

either the formal or the informal sectors of the economy. Such people have to choose extreme poverty as their way of life. This constitutes another face of the new post-communist Russia.

V.   CONCLUSIONS

To understand post-Soviet transition it is necessary to examine transformation that occurs in all areas of social life and social institutions in order to identify both the roots that are behind the newly-emerged social reality, and the substantial changes of their social meanings and the functions that they undergo. Transformation of the unofficial sector of the economy was an integral part of the post-Soviet transition. It was qualitatively transformed and at the present, constitutes an established pattern of the emerging market in Russia and in the rest of the departed states.

Looking at the new values and practicing pattern of economic behaviour, it is clear that the Russian market is not transforming to the Western type of market and needs to be understood in its own right. In the new market, the informal sector is at the core of the economic order, exposing only a thin official surface that accommodates the need to respond to state regulation. This does not mean that there is no order in the Russian market. However, it is an order in the sense of know-how, opposite to the western tradition of the Rule of Law and the demand for open information. Furthermore, it is already an established order in the Russian market, not a temporary 'transitional' effect. It is rooted in the Soviet psychology developed in the second economy of the Soviet period, was re-enforced and evolved in the transitional period of collapse, and ended as a philosophy of life in the new Russia.

The social impact of the informal economy in Russia is very different from the effect that the Soviet second economy had on people's lives. One could point to the similarities between the informal economy in Russia and its social consequences, and the Third Word type of market in terms of its destructive role for development, very unequal income distribution and the large part of population forced to live in poverty. However, at the same time, the specific character of the Second World – for example, its different human potential with high education, tradition of high expectation and ambition, competition with the West throughout Soviet history – must leave its mark on the new social reality. The question of whether the Russian market is merely a new version of developing markets, or represents a new model, is still open and could be answered by deeper understanding of the Russian way of know-how.

7

Pervasive Corruption

*Federico Varese**

I.   INTRODUCTION

This paper offers a preliminary picture of a society marked by pervasive corruption, drawing upon evidence from Italy and Eastern and Central Europe. A definition and general framework for studying corruption is given in the first section. The second part presents data from the Transparency International index of corruption pointing to the existence of pervasive corruption in a significant number of countries surveyed. The third section considers a pervasively corrupt society. In such a society, the cost of identifying a willing partner to a corrupt exchange is virtually zero, facilitating the illegal transaction. However, such an exchange takes place outside the scope of the law, thereby giving rise to uncertainties over delivery. Will the corrupter pay the money they promised? Will the corrupt official keep their word? As a consequence, the demand for services of private protection and enforcement will increase and, if the purpose of paying a bribe is to speed up the bureaucratic process, individual gains can be annulled by the fact that everybody must pay a bribe.

Section four of the paper discusses the effect of pervasive corruption on society's system of beliefs. Individuals come to hold beliefs that justify corrupt behaviours. They come to consider corruption to be a normal or even acceptable state of affairs, which has been in place since time immemorial. Actors in such a world might even hold extreme beliefs that are too costly to test. As discussed in section five, when norms such as 'return a favour when asked' or 'minimize conflict with fellow members of your community' exist in a pervasively corrupt society, they not only encourage further corruption but also promote social ostracism of those who attempt to fight it. Since everybody is prepared to offer bribes, anti-corruption campaigns are greeted with suspicion: why some are targeted for a behaviour that is general? Anti-corruption campaigns are suspected to foster the immediate interest of its initiators, rather than the interest of society. This paper concludes by arguing

*   I am grateful to Vittorio Bufacchi, Diego Gambetta, Åse Grødeland, Marina Kurkchiyan, Gerry Mackie, Karma Nabulsi, Mark Philp and Marc Stears for their comments on an earlier version of this paper. Also grateful thanks go to Omar Azfar for giving permission to reproduce figure 4. The usual disclaimers apply.

99

A. V. Ledeneva and M. Kurkchiyan (eds.), Economic Crime in Russia, 99–111
© 2000 *Kluwer Law International. Printed in Great Britain.*

that as corruption becomes widespread the very concept of corruption loses its meaning for the actors involved.

II.   CORRUPTION: A FRAMEWORK OF ANALYSIS

A corrupt exchange takes place between two actors, the *corrupter* and an official. Although the exchange appears to involve only two actors, a third one lurks in the background: the *principal*. The official is an *agent* employed by a principal in order to implement rules set out by the principal. Typical examples of agents include bureaucrats who oversee the issuing of permits, policemen who patrol a neighbourhood or laboratory scientists who check the quality of retail food products. The principal is usually thought of as the state administration, which employs individuals to undertake such tasks. The corrupters are members of the public or of another organization who wish to bend, in their favour, the rules laid out by the principal.

Corruption differs from other crimes, such as theft. The following diagrams capture of the essence of these two different crimes.

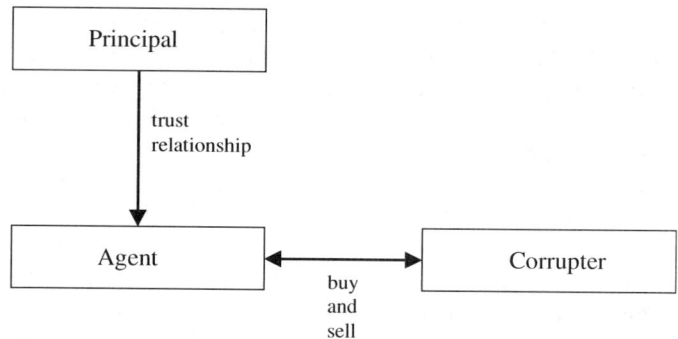

Figure 1. The Corrupt Exchange

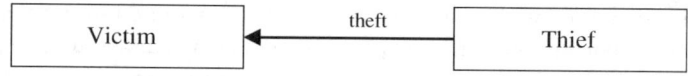

Figure 2. Theft

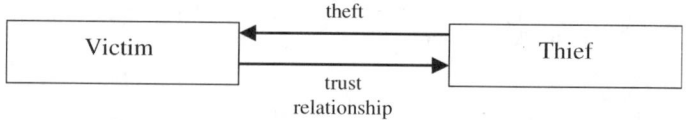

Figure 3. Theft with Trust

Both the thief and the corrupt agent engage in a criminal activity. The act of stealing, however, differs analytically from accepting a bribe and being corrupt. A thief simply takes away property which belongs to their victim. In the purest form, the thief has no previous relationship of trust with the victim: they sneak into the house while the victim is away and takes everything they can find. Theft may also occur in the presence of a trust relationship. One may be robbed by a trusted person. Furthermore, a state employee can steal from their employer. In this case, they break the trust relationship, but they are not engaging in corruption. The picture in the corrupt exchange is more complex. The principal has entrusted the agent with a resource that the latter sells illegally to a third person, the corrupter. The relationship between agent and corrupter is that of an illegal exchange: a price is agreed upon and a resource is transferred from one to another. The corrupter does not steal, but buys a resource that they could not obtain otherwise (alternatively, they obtain the resource at a lower price). The exchange between corrupter and corrupt agent contains all the uncertainties and potential for cheating of any other exchange taking place outside the scope of the law.[1]

What makes an agent decide whether to steal or to accept a bribe? Instead of being corrupt, the official might skim at work. In order to decide which criminal activity to engage in, they will consider a number of variables, such as the risk of being caught, the severity of expected punishment and the 'moral cost' of being dishonest. In this, they are not too different from other rational criminals.[2] A further dimension the agent must take into consideration is the *nature* of the commodity entrusted to them by the principal. Certain commodities cannot be stolen and directly consumed by the agent. For instance, if they oversee the granting of passports, they cannot 'steal' an extra passport for their own use. The official already has their own passport; an extra one would not produce a higher utility. They could only sell a passport to a member of the public illegally, speeding up or delaying the bureaucratic process. Similarly, a corrupt agent cannot grant themselves a public contract, only sell it, for example, to a construction company. (It should be further noted that, once the company obtains the contract, it has a legal right over it, even though obtained illegally. The possessor of a stolen good has no legal right over it, and is forced either to consume or hide the stolen goods in question). In other instances, the agent has a significant scope for choosing whether to steal or to accept a bribe. For instance, if the agent is the guardian of a warehouse, they could either steal the goods directly or turn a blind eye to a party of night thieves, for a cut. When the agent puts their mind to this problematic decision, they will consider the costs of organizing a theft directly, disposing of the loot and so on, as opposed to just accepting a bribe. Certain commodities can only be sold to a third party, while others can either be stolen directly or sold to a corrupter. Legal permissions to obtain goods supplied by the principal can, only rarely, be used directly by the agent, so, if they decide to commit a crime, they can

---

[1]   See D. Gambretta, 'What is corruption?' (University of Oxford, 1998). Unpublished.
[2]   G. S. Becker, *The Economic Approach to Human Behavior* (The University of Chicago Press, Chicago, 1976), pp. 39–85.

only do so by accepting a bribe. Attention to the nature of the commodity helps to identity the realms where corruption – as opposed to stealing – is more likely to occur.[3]

The above characterization of the actors involved in a corrupt exchange covers a variety of cases. For instance, corrupters may have to pay officials in order to obtain what they are supposed to receive anyway. In this case, the official is paid to fulfil the rules laid out by the principal, rather than to bend them in someone's favour. This is a case of extortionate corruption. A typical example is that of the GAI (The State Auto Inspectorate) traffic warden who extracts money from Moscow drivers.[4] The definition may also be applied to the private sector. The principal might be a private corporation that hires people to perform certain functions. A rival firm may wish to bribe those employees in order to obtain confidential information or disrupt the production line of its competitor.[5] Finally, the definition may be applied to politicians or government ministers. A politician can be thought of as the agent of his constituency and government ministers as the agent of the parliament. If either one takes bribes to promote a specific piece of legislation, they might be said to be corrupt.[6]

The exchange of money is not the distinguishing feature of corruption. The 'currency' may vary from cash to sexual services, free plane tickets or employment for relatives. Examples are numerous. Ms. Kutina, the niece of Anatolii Sobchak, former mayor of St. Petersburg, arrived in Petersburg from Tashkent in 1992. Immediately, she received a free flat from the company 'Renaissance'. It later emerged that her uncle has signed a number of illegal degrees that benefited the company. A dozen other officials in the city administration received flats from the same company.[7] The Chief Tax Police inspector in Cheliabinsk had the education of her daughter paid by the company Kaelgamramor. The same company gave her husband a Kamaz truck and a loan.[8] An entrepreneur paid the president of the Italian Highways with

---

[3]   I am greatly indebted to Diego Gambetta for the above discussion of the definition of corruption. In part, I am also drawing on: E. Banfield, 'Corruption as a Feature of Governmental Organization' (1975) 18 *Journal of Law and Economics*, pp. 587–605; and S. Rose-Ackerman, *Corruption: A Study in Political Economy* (Academic Press, New York: 1978).

[4]   For a recent instance, see J. Lloyd, '100 Dollars? That Will Do Nicely' (June 1999) 21 *New Statesman*, pp. 21–22. In fact, paying officials in order to have them perform their duties appears common in four post-communist countries – Ukraine, Bulgaria, Slovakia and the Czech republic. According to a survey of 4,778 citizens: 'over half the public claimed that the officials they had dealt with in recent years had "made unnecessary problems in order to get money or a present to solve them."', Å. Grødeland, W. L. Miller, and T. Y. Koshechkina, *Post-Communist Officials Talk About Bribery* (NISPAcee News, 1999 forthcoming), p. 5.

[5]   See D. Gambetta, 'What is Corruption?' (University of Oxford, 1998). Unpublished.

[6]   In some cases it might not be simple to identify the sense in which politicians are 'agents' of the electorate, or the exact content of the 'contract' the latter have 'signed' with their representatives. Philp points out that corruption in this realm cannot be defined before 'conceptions of the nature of the political and the form of the public interest' are spelled out. See M. Philp, 'Defining Political Corruption' in P. Heywood (ed.), *Political Corruption*, (Blackwell Publishers, Oxford, 1997), p. 30. To the extent that a shared conception of the political exists among citizens of a given polity, it is possible to deduce a conception of corruption for that community. Given that contextual conception, the basic trust relationship between principal and agent can be identified and compared across polities.

[7]   *Izvestiya*, 15 December 1996.

[8]   *Komsomolskaya Pravda*, 30 June 1999.

the free installation of a sink and a gate.[9] According to the chairman of the Christian Democrats (DC) of Lombardy, the Television Company Fininvest paid bribes in airtime, a practice that further reduced the risk of being detected.[10]

III. EVIDENCE OF PERVASIVE CORRUPTION

Some societies are trapped in a high-corruption equilibrium, or, to put it differently, are pervasively corrupt. Figure 4 presents evidence to this. It is based on the Transparency International's 1998 corruption index for 85 countries. This index aggregates several corruption ratings and aims 'to assess the level at which corruption is perceived by people working for multinational firms and institutions as impacting on commercial life.'[11]

Figure 4 plots the score obtained by the countries surveyed on the horizontal axis (10 stands for a country free of corruption) and the number of countries which obtained a given score on the vertical axis. Many countries cluster around 3, including Russia (2.4), Latvia (2.7), Ukraine (2.8), Yugoslavia (3.0) and Romania (3.0). Italy and Poland both obtain a score of 4.6. As noted by Azfar,[12] these data also point to existence of two equilibria, one of high corruption and one of low corruption (19 countries obtain scores between eight and 10), with fewer cases in between.

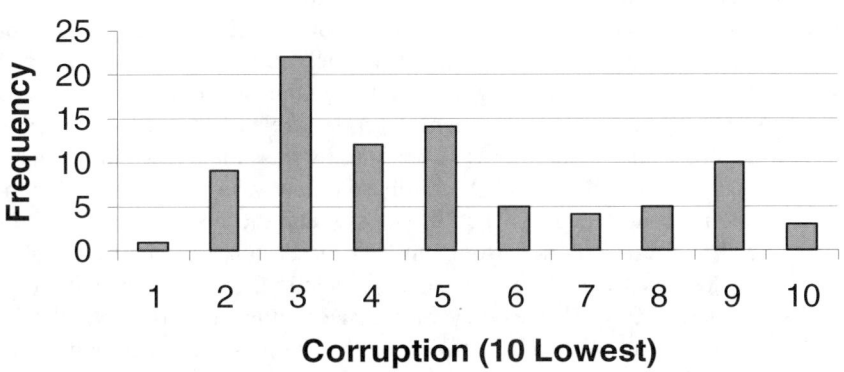

Figure 4. Corruption TI 98 Frequency Table
Source: O. Azfar, 'High and Low Corruption Equilibria: Are there Multiple Equilibria? And How Would We Move to the Good One?' (University of Maryland, 1999). Unpublished. Reprinted with the author's permission.

---

[9] A. Vannucci, *Il mercato della corruzione* (Società Aperta Edizioni, Milan, 1997), p. 44.

[10] L. Ricolfi, *L'ultimo parlamento* (La Nuova Italia, Rome, 1993), p. 137; V. Bufacchi, 'The Success of Mani Pulite: Luck or Skill?' in R. Leonardi and R.Y. Nanetti (eds), *Italy: Politics and Policy* (Dartmouth, Aldershot, 1996), p. 204; Vannucci, n. 8 above, p 44.

[11] Transparency International, 'The Corruption Perceptions Index' (1997): <www.transparency. de/documents/cpi/index.html>.

[12] O. Azfar, 'High and Low Corruption Equilibria: Are There Multiple Equilibria?, and How Would We Move to the Good One?' (University of Maryland, 1999,unpublished).

IV. IDENTIFICATION AND DELIVERY

Identification is a crucial ingredient of a corrupt exchange. In a world where honesty
is the norm, how can the corrupter know who, if offered a bribe, would accept?
Corrupters need to identify potential corruptees, persons willing to accept a bribe
and not to report them to the authorities. The bribe-taker can engage in activities
that signal a willingness to take bribes. For example, joining a political party known
for being more corrupt than other parties, could indicate a disposition to accept
bribes. Other signals might be used, such as physical and vocal cues. Bribe-givers,
however, have to be cautious because they might misinterpret the signal. Bribe-
takers must also be cautious since the member of the public can report the official.
By contrast, an overwhelmingly corrupt setting requires much less caution.
Identification of a willing bribe-taker is not difficult, for the citizen expects the
agent to be one. In other words, once corruption is widespread, the 'identification'
problem is more easily solved. The dominant strategy will be always to offer bribes.
However, a perverse consequence may result. If the purpose of offering a bribe is to
speed up the administrative process (a reason often given by political scientists and
economists who consider bribe-giving as way to cut red tape), pervasive corruption
annuls any gain in efficiency.[13] A parallel example is when the members of an
audience, each of whom wishes to improve their view, all stand on their chairs.
Everybody is twenty centimetres taller, but no one sees better.[14]

Another feature of the exchange between corrupter and agent is uncertainty over
the delivery: once the corrupter has identified a public official willing to accept a
bribe, how can it be ensured that the official will deliver? And how can the official
ensure that the corrupter will not forget or fail to pay the agreed amount?[15] A recent
Russian instance testifies to this problem. Corporal Yelena Troshina, a telephone
operator in an army unit, paid up to USD4,500 to by-pass the queue and get a one-
room flat. The recipient of the money, Vladimir Solomonov, an army general, claimed
he could deliver but in the end pocked the money and did nothing. Eventually he
was sentenced to four years imprisonment.[16] A direct consequence of the above
situation is a demand for private services of protection and enforcement. As the
citizen will always offer a bribe, they might meet either a corrupt but 'honest'
official or a corrupt and 'dishonest' official. In the first case, the corrupt exchange

---

[13] See J. MacRae, 'Underdevelopment and the Economics of Corruption: A Game Theory
     Approach' (1982) 10 *World Development*, p. 679. As MacRae himself notes, one might argue
     that the bureaucracy would be more efficient due to better-paid and more motivated officials
     (MacRae, ibid., p. 687). However, other scenarios may apply, such as a vicious cycle of ever-
     higher bribes. Elster suggests that 'deliberate procrastination and delay for the purpose of
     increasing the size and number of bribes' would occur. J. Elster, *The Cement of Society*
     (Cambridge University Press, Cambridge, 1989), p. 270.
[14] Elster, ibid., p. 270. In this case, the members of the public engage in a prisoners' dilemma
     with each other. The well-known solution of this game is that everybody is worse off.
[15] D. Gambetta, 'Anatomia della tangente' (1988) 4 *Meridiana*, pp. 237–247.
[16] In recent years, 13 army generals have been found guilty of corruption and fraud, mainly
     connected to housing allocation. All of them have been given suspended sentences or granted
     an amnesty by the State Duma. Vladimir Solomonov appears to be only one who will actually
     serve his sentence. *Komsomol'skaya Pravda* 3 December 1998.

takes place smoothly. In the second, the official pockets the money and does not deliver the service, as in the case of general Solomonov. The official who has delivered a service might also not receive the bribe. The mafia is one institution that provides enforcement services that, as a by-product, promote corrupt exchanges and resolve the problem of delivery in illegal markets, at a price.[17] In the aggregate, mafia-like agencies prosper in a highly corrupt environment.[18]

V. BELIEFS

Mackie reports that women living in a world where female genital mutilation (clitoridectomy and infibulation) is widely practiced, over time come to believe that the consequences of this practice are normal. 'The painful surgery, prolonged urination and menstruation, traumatic penetration, and unbearable childbirth accompanying infibulation are all accepted as normal.'[19] People who live in a corrupt environment may come to hold equivalent beliefs regarding corruption. Corruption comes to be considered as the normal state of affairs. The Italian manager Enzo Papi recalls,

> When I was appointed Cogefar managing director I was given a booklet where all the 'obligations' and payment dates of the company were recorded: a list of names and numbers; an obligation that was to be rigorously honoured. Illegal dealings were so common that I did not feel I was perpetrating a criminal act.[20]

Miller *et al.*[21] found that hospital doctors in post-communist countries expect presents from patients ('especially expensive gifts'). If the doctors do not receive gifts, they either delay or refuse to deliver the medical service.[22] Furthermore, 71 per

---

[17] See D. Gambetta, 'Civisme et corruption' in R. Darnton and O. Duhamel (eds), *Démocratie* (Paris, Edition du Rocher, 1998), pp. 221–230; D. Gambetta, 'Comments' to S. Rose-Ackerman, '*Corruption and Development*' in B. Pleskovic and J. E. Stiglitz (eds), *Annual World Bank Conference on Development Economics 1997* 1 (The World Bank, Washington DC, 1998), pp. 58–61.

[18] A demand for mafia services does not explain the emergence of the organization, otherwise one would subscribe to a functionalist argument. A non-functionalist argument is offered for the emergence of the Russian mafia in F. Varese, 'Is Sicily the Future of Russia? Private Protection and the Emergence of the Russian Mafia' (1994) 35 *Archives Européenes de Sociologie*, pp. 224–258.

[19] G. Mackie, 'Ending Foot-binding and Infibulation' (1996) 61 *American Sociological Review*, p. 1009.

[20] Quoted in Vannucci, n. 8 above, p. 29.

[21] W. L. Miller, Å. Grødeland, and T. Y. Koshechkina, 'If You Pay, We'll Operate Immediately' (1998, unpublished), p. 2.

[22] One nurse recalls: 'The surgeon wanted 40,000 – the woman had no money – they delayed the operation but after some time they operated.' Some were not as lucky: 'There are cases when people have died while raising the money ... [One person] was told he had to give 20,000 levs – he said he could afford only 10,000 levs – and two days later his father died.' Miller *et al.*, ibid., p. 6. This survey was carried out in 1998 and is based on 1,307 interviews with a representative sample of officials, including government employees, health care employees (n=292) and hospital doctors (n= 85) in Ukraine, Bulgaria, Slovakia and the Czech Republic. The survey also includes 4,778 interviews with members of the public in the same countries.

cent of the doctors interviewed believe that their government regarded gifts of 'money or expensive presents' as an acceptable, informal way to pay officials.[23] As time passes, the memory of a no-corruption equilibrium fades away.

Similarly, actors come to believe that corruption has been around for a long time and that they had no role in fostering the system of bribes. Sergio Radaelli, a bribe collector in the Milan area, maintains: 'We simply conformed to a system that had been operating since the 1950s.'[24] Bettino Craxi, former Italian Prime Minister, went even further: the system of pervasive bribe-taking 'has been there for a long time, maybe from time immemorial', he declared in a speech delivered in the Italian Parliament.[25] For Maurizio Prada, Milan DC treasurer, 'the system grew by itself, nobody is responsible.'[26]

The two beliefs discussed above emerge as a *consequence* of pervasive corruption. They exist in a pervasively corruption society and are a by-product of it. They do not directly cause further corruption. Other beliefs, on the other hand, promote further corruption. The view that a bribe is necessary for every single transaction leads actors to offer unsolicited bribes.[27] Several politicians and public servants in Italy reported that they received money without asking or knowing exactly for what reason.[28] This belief makes corruption appear as a self-fulfilling prophecy, although it should be stressed that it exists side-by-side with *actual* and widespread corruption. If the belief were truly false, individuals offering bribes would quickly discover it: their bribe would be returned and they would revise their expectations of widespread corruption. Adriano Zampini, a notorious corrupter in the Turin area, recalls:

> As things progressed, I became more and more confident because I realised that nobody refused a bribe. Suffice to say that in my long career as a wheeler and dealer [*faccendiere*], only once did my bribe get refused ... I had sent a box of chocolates with two million lire inside. The person kept the chocolates and returned the money.[29]

When the official accepts the bribe and gets away with it, a vicious cycle is set in motion.

Beliefs can be classified according to different criteria.[30] The criterion adopted here is the test they answer. In the case of the beliefs discussed above, the test is

---

[23] Miller *et al.*, ibid., p. 6. Officials who thought likewise were 54 per cent of the sample. A related belief that could emerge is the view that other countries have a similar level of corruption, implying that nothing is special or abnormal about one's own.

[24] Quoted in Vannucci, n. 8 above, p. 68.

[25] 29 April 1993. Quoted in: S. H. Burnett and L. Mantovani, *The Italian Guillotine: Operation Clean Hands and the Overthrow of Italy's First Republic* (Rowman and Littlefield, Lanham, MD, 1998), p. 111.

[26] Quoted in Vannucci, n. 8 above, p. 68.

[27] J. C. Andvig and K. O. Moene, 'How Corruption May Corrupt' (1990) 13 *Journal of Economic Behavior and Organization*, pp. 63–76.

[28] Vannucci, n. 8 above, p. 73–74.

[29] *Espresso*, 18 December 1984. Quoted in Vannucci, n. 8 above, p. 112.

[30] See for example a classification based on the *object* of the belief in: J. Elster, *Alchemies of the Mind. Rationality and the Emotions* (Cambridge University Press, Cambridge: 1999), p. 49.

Table 1. Corruption Beliefs

Belief	Cause or Consequence of Pervasive Corruption	Nature of the Belief
'Corruption is normal'	Consequence	Fact-based
'Corruption has been around for time immemorial'	Consequence	Fact-based
'Corruption is a lesser evil'	Consequence	Fact-based
'A bribe is always necessary'	Cause	Fact-based
'The postman' scenario	Cause	Fact-based but never tested

empirical and the actors involved are willing to update their beliefs in the light of new evidence. On the contrary, a belief in the existence of God held by a religious believer cannot be tested empirically. Some beliefs are so extreme that the empirical test is thought to be too costly. One may come to think that if no bribe is offered to the postman, the latter will not simply fail to deliver the mail speedily; he will also throw away any letter and instruct his colleagues to do the same for one's near and distant relatives. Although the belief may be implausible, the cost of testing it is too high.[31]

Those who recognize that their country of origin is particularly corrupt and strongly dislike this state of affairs are, *ceteris paribus*, more likely to emigrate. Those who stay behind are, in effect, a self-selected sample.[32] This sample includes two sub-populations: those who still dislike the system but cannot emigrate; and those who benefit from the current system and do not want to emigrate. Not surprisingly, bribe-takers develop an 'easy conscience' and a 'culture of justified bribery'.[33] Officials interviewed by Grødeland *et al.*, 'were remarkably willing to justify accepting gifts from clients.'[34] Radaev also reports that Russian officials consider bribes as a 'commission', a '"shadowy" but morally justified way to increase one's own low income.'[35] The reasons why they hold views that support the system are clear: they are putting forward self-serving notions that help to justify their shady activities.

---

[31] Fiammetta Cucurnia, Moscow correspondent for *La Repubblica*, lists some extreme beliefs that appear in respected, national papers in Russia. See *La Repubblica*, 1 August 1992.

[32] A similar mechanism has been discussed by the public-choice literature on majority voting. After a majority-rule vote is taken and some individuals have the option to 'exit', these individuals might be tempted to exit. In the next vote the majority equilibrium shifts further away from the exit-prone section of the electorate, and provokes further exit and more extreme majority decisions. See D. W. Rae and E. Schickler, 'Majority Rule' in D. C. Muller (ed.), *Perspectives on Public Choice* (Cambridge University Press, Cambridge, 1997), p. 170.

[33] Miller *et al.*, n. 20 above, p. 5.

[34] In Ukraine, '67 per cent of officials said it would be right to at least "accept something if offered" for "extra work" and 18 per cent that it would even be "right to ask for something" for "extra work"'. Grødeland *et al.*, n. 3 above, p. 5.

[35] V. V. Radaev, *Formirovanie novykh rossiiskikh rynkov: transaktsionnye izderzhki, formy kontrolia i delovaya etika* (Tsentr Politicheskikh Teknologii, Moscow: 1998), p. 65.

More interesting, however, is the case of those who dislike the system but cannot emigrate. They will experience a tension between being forced to comply with the system (if they do not, they will be unable to carry out their ordinary existence) and disliking the system and themselves for their behaviour. The result is cognitive dissonance. The psychological difficulty involved in constantly despising one's own country and oneself means that even someone who dislikes the system over time comes to adhere to certain beliefs as a way to reduce cognitive dissonance. 'First you feel uncomfortable, then you get used to it. You also feel satisfaction'[36] said a survey respondent in the Ukraine. Corruption is called by a less pejorative term, the bribe becomes *a token of gratitude*.[37] A Bulgarian respondent readily illustrates this attitude: 'Most clerks are depressed by the constant shortage of money and they tend to .... No, that's not bribing, it is rather an expression of my gratitude and duly expected one'.[38] A supplier of the Milan Bus Company paid bribes by using gold sterling. At the trial, he explained that this practice made him feel better, because the bribe appeared as a gift.[39] Some individuals come to believe that they themselves offered the gift/bribe voluntarily and therefore the situation appears more acceptable, as some Ukrainians maintained.[40] Finally, people trapped in this sub-optimal equilibrium become proud of their extensive networks of favours: 'People would be much happier if they did not need connections to solve their problems, but, on the other hand, they are proud they can use them.'[41] They become experts at networking and wheeling and dealing, an asset that cannot be deployed in a non-corrupt environment.[42]

VI. Social norms

While the beliefs described above serve the rational self-interest of those who benefit from the system, they come to be held by most of the population. Such beliefs will not be held in a vacuum. They will exist side-by-side with other, widely held norms of behaviour. A 'social norm' is usually understood as a socially acceptable behaviour. Deviations from that behaviour are sanctioned by social ostracism or

---

[36] Å. Grødeland, T. Y. Koshechkina and W. L. Miller, '"Foolish to Give and Yet More Foolish Not to Take" – In-depth Interviews with Post-Communist Citizens on Their Everyday Use of Bribes and Contacts' (1998) 50 *Europe–Asia Studies*, p. 669.

[37] This is equivalent to the practice of 'misrecognition' identified by Ledeneva in the case of *blat*. See A. V. Ledeneva, *Russia's Economy of Favours. Blat, Networking and Informal Exchange* (Cambridge University Press, Cambridge, 1998).

[38] Grødeland *et al.*, n. 35 above, p. 664.

[39] Vannucci, n. 8 above, p. 44.

[40] Grødeland *et al.*, n. 35 above, p. 665.

[41] Grødeland *et al.*, n. 35 above, p. 669.

[42] Actors acquire skills that help them survive in such an environment. These skills could be defined as assets specific to a particular setting. Economists have explored asset-specificity in various industries. See for example O. Williamson, *The Mechanisms of Governance* (Oxford University Press, Oxford, 1996), pp. 105–112. For instance, designers of a particular type of aircraft find it difficult to use their skills in a firm that produces a different aircraft. This might explain why actors are resistant to change, even if they do not like the environment in which they find themselves.

even punished physically.[43] In other words, be vengeful, not only against the violators of the norm but also against anyone who refuses to punish a defector.[44]

Norms answer to tests of some general principles, such as fairness, morality or justice. In the case of norms of reciprocity, to return a favour when asked is fair. The underlying situation may be described by a Prisoners' Dilemma: a player would be made better off by receiving a favour and not reciprocating. The norm helps players to reach the equilibrium, where both players reciprocate each other's favours, even if the relationship is not long-term and repeated. (If the relationship is long-term, such equilibrium can be reached through self-interest). Norms differ from social conventions, such as on which side of the road to drive, which colour to wear at funerals or which hand to use to hold a fork. The latter are best described by the various types of coordination games.[45]

In most societies the principle *return a favour when asked* is widely accepted as a proper norm of behaviour. In a country where corruption is the exception, no one would expect the recipient of a favour to reciprocate by breaking the law. By contrast, when such a principle is held in a country where crime and corruption are pervasive, returning a favour might well include breaking the law. 'The debt [of gratitude] is paid back by [whatever] means [are] available', stated a Bulgarian.[46] The relationship between the corrupter and the official evolves into a long-term reciprocal exchange of favours.

> A straightforward bribe evolves into a system of exchange of services, which are not confined to cash and personal gifts. For example, the entrepreneurs can employ a bureaucrat's relative or sign a contract with a firm which is under his or her patronage ... Coercion and self-interest are reinforced by existing social norms.[47]

Andrei Konstantinov, a prominent Russian journalist, describes one such arrangement between a policeman and a boss of a building firm. He concludes by asking: 'Can we regard the mutual "indebtedness" of officials and entrepreneurs as corruption? ... People practicing such mutual debts will be very surprised if they are accused of dishonesty'.[48]

---

[43] It is beyond the scope of this paper to discuss whether social norms are designed intentionally or emerge unintentionally, and whether they serve some rational purpose or not. Furthermore, this paper is not concerned with why people follow a norm, whether or not it serves their interests.

[44] J. Elster, *Nuts and Bolts for the Social Sciences* (Cambridge University Press, Cambridge, 1989), p. 113.

[45] On coordination games, see T. C. Schelling, *The Strategy of Conflict* (Harvard University Press, Cambridge, MA, 1960); and Mackie, n. 18 above.

[46] Grødeland, *et al.*, n. 35 above; p. 669.

[47] Radaev, n. 34 above, pp. 67–68. For the Italian case, see the evidence quoted in Vannucci, n. 8 above, p. 106–107.

[48] A. Konstantinov *et. al.*, *Korrumpirovannyi Peterburg* (Folio-Press, St. Petersburg, 1997), p. 223, as quoted in C. Humphrey, 'Re-thinking Bribery in Contemporary Russia' in S. Lovell, A. V. Ledeneva and A. Rogatchevsky (eds.), *Bribery and Blat in Russia* (Macmillan, London 2000).

Sober and Wilson, after a detailed survey of social norms in a sample of 25 cultures randomly selected, conclude, 'in culture after culture, individuals are expected to avoid conflict and practice benevolence and generosity towards all members of a socially defined group.'[49] Depending on the context, however, this bundle of behaviours might produce the well known and never-enough deplored code of *omertà* of Southern Italy. According to the code, no one should ever report a crime or agree to serve as a witness in a trial.

The interplay between widespread corruption, beliefs and social norms produces behaviours that support norms of reciprocity, 'honesty' and cooperation but discourage public spiritedness. Social ostracism is then not directed towards those who engage in crime and corrupt exchanges but, rather, against those who break the norms. In the case of *omertà*, for instance, those who testify are ostracized by their community. It is not unlikely then that only outcasts enter the witness box, thereby weakening the credibility of their evidence. 'In a society of amoral familists, the claim of any person or institution to be inspired by zeal for public rather private advantage will be regarded as a fraud'.[50]

If everybody engages in corrupt activities (or at least is prepared to do so in case of necessity), to single-out one official or member of the public raises the question: why that person and not somebody else? Bettino Craxi put forward this view forcefully in a 1992 parliamentary speech:

> Parties have relied on, and continue to rely on, the use of funds that come in irregular or illegal forms ... I do not believe that there is anyone in this Chamber, any politician responsible for important organisations, who can stand up and swear the contrary to what I have just said.[51]

Since every single party in Italy has taken bribes, Craxi continued, the Milan prosecutors must have targeted the Socialist Party for political reasons. 'Corrupt' is what political antagonists call each other when one is acting against the interests of the other.

In the above, this paper has presented the worst possible case of a corrupt society. Does such a society have any prospect for change? A distinction must be made between beliefs and norms. The beliefs examined above are fact-based. Beliefs such as 'corruption is normal', 'corruption has been around from time immemorial' and 'corruption is a lesser evil' appeal – at least in principle – to facts. Such facts can be shown to be false. Although fact-based beliefs may be resilient, they might also disappear quickly. Norms, on the contrary, are rules of interaction that do not claim to be true. The norm 'return a favour when asked' answers to a test of fairness. For instance, that there is a connection between the 'character' of the Sicilians and the mafia, and that Sicilians considered the mafia as a legitimate authority, are not

[49] E. Sober and D. S. Wilson, *Unto Others. The Evolution and Psychology of Unselfish Behavior* (Harvard University Press, Cambridge, MA, 1998), p. 172.
[50] E. Banfield, *The Moral Basis of a Backward Society* (Free Press, New York, 1958), p. 98.
[51] *Corriere della Sera*, 9 July 1992. Quoted in Burnett and Mantovani, n. 24 above, p. 87.

norms but beliefs. Moreover, those two beliefs are false, as shown by the fact that consistently, in recent years, Sicilians have voted for anti-mafia political parties and generally supported the anti-mafia movement. The beliefs may be said to have vanished. Whoever will hold them now would have to square them with indisputable facts. Yet their disappearance did not come cheaply. Sicilians changed their political allegiances as a positive response to the effort (that was considered credible) of the central government to sever all links with the mafia. This effort came at the cost of many public officials being killed by the mafia, most notably judges and policemen, and many politicians being charged by the authorities. Only specific actions may elicit a response that in turn will prove certain beliefs to be false. Once these actions are taken, self-serving beliefs disappear quickly.[52]

VII. WHEN CORRUPTION IS EVERYWHERE …

This paper has pointed out that in a world where corruption is widespread, the cost of identification is virtually zero and uncertainty over delivery gives rise to a demand for private enforcement services. A range of corruption beliefs emerge and interact with existing social norms (such as the norm of reciprocity), making corruption an acceptable behaviour even to those who do not benefit from it.

A final alarming conclusion must be drawn, namely that as corruption grows more and more pervasive, 'corruption' itself loses its meaning. The definition adopted in this paper no longer applies. In such a society, formal rules specifying a bureaucrat's duties and sanctions do exist; however, the basic trust relationship between principal and agent is impaired. The GAI traffic warden does not think for a moment that the Russian State has entrusted him with a resource (use of legitimate force) he is supposed to administer according to the rulebook. His mind is not crossed by the thought that, if he fails his duty, he breaks a trust relationship with his employer. He obtained a prerogative and exploits it to the full. In such a world, notions of 'honesty' and 'fairness' do not disappear, but they surely diverge from the impartial application of the law. Punishments against corrupt officials and politicians are passed, but they are often passed in a selective way to serve partisan ends. They do not restore faith in the law but rather confirm the opposite idea. The main lesson to be learnt by the above description of pervasive corruption – especially by Western advisors working in the former Soviet Union – is that anti-corruption programmes will be greeted with suspicion. Any attempt to reduce widespread wrongdoing, crime and corruption must be designed to overcome that suspicion. A consistent and impartial application of general and abstract principles is perhaps the right way to start.

---

[52] D. Gambetta, 'Concatenation of Mechanisms' in P. Hedström and R. Swedberg (eds), *Social Mechanisms* (Cambridge University Press, Cambridge, 1998), pp. 102–124. Under certain conditions, the fight against corruption might become a successful political argument and self-interested politicians embrace it even in a pervasively corrupt society. Such conditions include the nature of electoral and political competition, the number of parties, how easy it is to enter the political arena and to enforce collusion among parties over corrupt practices. These questions cannot be properly addressed in this paper.

8

Victims or Accomplices?
Extortion and Bribery in Eastern Europe

William L. Miller, Åse B. Grødeland and Tatyana Y. Koshechkina

Thank God they're corruptible. They're human and after money like the rest of us. They're not wolves. As long as there's corruption, there's hope. Bribes! They're man's best chance. As long as judges go on taking money, then there's some chance of justice.[1]

I. INTRODUCTION

Mother Courage clearly felt that bribery and corruption had their advantages for ordinary people. However, Brecht's point was that although she seemed so worldly wise in the short-term she was completely and tragically wrong in the longer-term. The purpose of this paper is to explore public attitudes towards low-level corruption in Eastern Europe – to see how many praise it with Mother Courage, and how many condemn it with Bertolt Brecht.

This chapter focuses on the way ordinary citizens use presents and bribes to influence the officials they meet in day-to-day life. Its principal concern is not with high-level corruption involving senior politicians and officials or top businessmen, but with the role of corruption in these everyday interactions between citizens and the state. It will look, in particular, at Ukraine, Bulgaria, Slovakia and the Czech Republic – near neighbours with a common commitment to democratization in the 1990s but very different historical and bureaucratic traditions. The findings are based on 4,778 interviews between November 1997 and February 1998 with representative national samples of the public: 1,003 in the Czech Republic, 1,056 in Slovakia, 1,519 in Bulgaria, and 1,200 in Ukraine. Where appropriate, it has illustrated these findings with verbatim quotations taken from 26 focus-group discussions and 136 in-depth interviews that we commissioned in the summer and autumn of 1996.

---

[1] B. Brecht, *Mother Courage and Her Children* Scene 3, Translated by D. Hare for the National Theatre, (London, Methuen/Random House, 1995), p. 44.

A. V. Ledeneva and M. Kurkchiyan (eds.), Economic Crime in Russia, 113–128
© 2000 *Kluwer Law International. Printed in Great Britain.*

For every bribe-taker there must be a bribe-giver, but the relationship is not necessarily an equal one. If citizens take the initiative, pressing their bribes – and their demands – upon reluctant but, perhaps, badly paid officials, then citizens might be described as the source of corruption. If the opposite happens, and officials abuse their position to extort unofficial payments from weak, powerless and reluctant citizens, citizens might be described as victims. Moreover, if the relationship is more equal, if citizens want to give and the officials are happy to take, than citizens might be describe as accomplices.

II. A CLIMATE OF PETTY CORRUPTION

People in all countries were inclined to the view that even when a person 'asks an official for something to which they are entitled by law' they would probably have to approach the official 'through a contact', or 'offer something' in order 'to get a successful outcome'. Perhaps, in casual gossip, they exaggerated the need to use contacts, presents and bribes. As this paper will illustrate, in their own personal experience, they tended to report rather less need to use presents and bribes.

Nonetheless the figures are very high: between 76 and 90 per cent in different countries said it 'was likely' a person would have to approach the official 'through a contact'. Between 62 and 91 per cent said it 'was likely' that a 'small present' would be necessary, and between 44 and 81 per cent said it 'was likely' that 'money or an expensive present' would be necessary. These were considered most necessary in Ukraine and least necessary in the Czech Republic; and the difference between Ukraine and the Czech Republic grew from 14 per cent on contacts, through 29 per cent on small presents, to 37 per cent on 'money or an expensive present'.

Table 1. Likely that person would have to ... (percentages of total)*

Suppose a person asks an official for something to which they are entitled by law. Q85–7: To get a successful outcome, is it likely or not likely that they would ...	Czech Republic	Slovakia	Bulgaria	Ukraine
Q85: Approach official through a contact	76	87	86	90
Q86: Offer a small present	62	80	84	91
Q87: Offer money or an expensive present	44	62	72	81

* *Note*: 'Don't know', 'mixed/depends' etc. answers were recorded if given spontaneously, but never prompted. They have been excluded from the calculation of percentages.

There was a wide consensus that people would be more likely now to use contacts, presents and bribes than they did under communism. Once again, such claims were most frequent in Ukraine and least frequent in the Czech Republic. Over 80 per cent in Ukraine said people were more likely now to offer officials 'money or an expensive present' than they were during the communist period.

Table 2. More likely now than under communism that a person would ... (percentage of total)*

Q93–5: Compared to the period (under communism) do you think it is now more likely, or now less likely, that people in (country) would ...	*Czech Republic*	*Slovakia*	*Bulgaria*	*Ukraine*
% more likely now:				
Q93: Approach the official through a contact	77	87	79	88
Q94: Offer a small present?	64	83	82	88
Q95: Offer money or an expensive present?	50	69	76	80

* *Note*: 'Don't know', 'mixed/depends' etc. answers were recorded if given spontaneously, but never prompted. They have been excluded from the calculation of percentages.

In gossip at least, there was a climate, an atmosphere, of petty corruption. In the Czech Republic at one extreme, there were limits to allegations of official corruption; however, in Ukraine at the other extreme, perceptions of official corruption were pervasive and unqualified.

III. ATTITUDES TOWARDS CORRUPTION

People were asked whether they considered 'the use of money, presents, favours or contacts to influence officials':

• 'Bad for (the country), and for those involved?'
• 'Bad for (the country), but unavoidable for people who have to live here?'; or
• Did they 'prefer it that way because, when you need a favour from an official, you can get it?'

The first answer corresponds to simple and unqualified condemnation of corruption, whether on moral, egalitarian, economic or other grounds. 'Corruption ... causes a distinction ... [but] every citizen is equal before any administrative official ... that is what equality should mean.' [2] [3] The second answer combines condemnation of corruption with some excuse for those who practice it. 'You can't do anything another way in this situation'.[4] The third expresses a positive preference or approval: 'Someone needs a passport in two months and someone else in two days. For the first person it's not so important as to have to give a gift, but for someone else it may be crucial if they need it immediately'.[5] That makes citizens at least accomplices and often corrupting agents.

Faced with these three options however, relatively few expressed a positive preference for a corrupt system, but a large minority was willing to excuse it. Taken

[2]   Sofia-1, FG-6
[3]   Sofia-1 was the first focus-group discussion held in Sofia. Two focus-group discussions were held in each capital city. FG-6 indicates the sixth participant.
[4]   Horodok, FG-2
[5]   Hradec Kralove, FG-3

together, 31 per cent were willing to excuse or approve corruption in the Czech Republic, 40 per cent in Slovakia, and 42 per cent in Bulgaria or Ukraine.

Table 3. Attitude to the use of money, presents, favours or contacts to influence officials (percentage of total)*

Q153: Which comes closest to your view about the use of money, presents, favours and contacts to influence officials? (i) it is bad for (country) and for those involved; (ii) it is bad for (country), but unavoidable for people who have to live here; or (iii) I prefer it that way because when you need a favour from an official you can get it?	*Czech Republic*	*Slovakia*	*Bulgaria*	*Ukraine*
Bad for (country) and those involved	69	60	58	58
Bad for (country), but unavoidable for citizens	25	28	34	31
Prefer it that way	7	12	8	11

* *Note*: 'Don't know', 'mixed/depends' etc. answers were recorded if given spontaneously, but never prompted. They have been excluded from the calculation of percentages.

At one level, people may feel that the use of money, presents and favours is part of their national tradition, part of their culture. Surprisingly, we found that it was the people in the Czech and Slovak Republics who were by far the most willing to accept that corruption was a 'permanent part of their country's culture'. By contrast, in Ukraine, only 16 per cent saw it as 'a permanent part of Ukraine's culture' and most people blamed the use of presents, bribes and favours on a 'moral crisis in a period of transition'.

People in Ukraine were far more critical than those in the Czech Republic of falling standards in public life: 89 per cent said that 'most officials' now behaved worse than under communism. 'During the Communist regime [we got] better assistance. There was more order ... [officials] were afraid of something.'[6] Such a very recent fall in the standards of behaviour of officials could not be attributed to a 'permanent national culture'; and it was explicitly attributed to the post-communist 'transition'.

Table 4. 'A product of the crisis of transition, or a permanent part of our culture?'*

Q187: Which comes closest to your view? The use of money, presents, favours and contacts to influence officials in (country) is ...	*Czech Republic*	*Slovakia*	*Bulgaria*	*Ukraine*
A product of the communist past	23	23	17	23
Or of moral crisis in a period of transition	31	30	49	62
Or a permanent part of (country's) culture	46	47	34	16

* *Note*: 'Don't know', 'mixed/depends' etc. answers were recorded if given spontaneously, but never prompted. They have been excluded from the calculation of percentages.

---

6   Sholomia, IDI-2

IV. ATTEMPTS AT EXTORTION

We asked, what was 'the main reason why officials take money or presents': was it:

* Because 'the officials are greedy',
* Because 'the government does not pay officials properly,' or
* Because 'people are desperate to buy favours from officials?'

In the Czech and Slovak Republics the respondents most frequently blamed the people themselves for seeking to buy favours. In Bulgaria, they most frequently blamed the government for not paying officials enough. However, in Ukraine they most frequently blamed the extent of low-level bribery and corruption on extortion by greedy officials. If those who blamed governments for paying officials badly are excluded, the balance of public opinion between blaming bribe-giving citizens and bribe-taking officials was firmly on blaming corrupt citizens in the Czech and Slovak Republics, but on blaming corrupt officials in Bulgaria and Ukraine.

Table 5. Greedy Officials (percentage of total)*

Q177: Which comes closest to your view? The main reason why officials take money or presents are ...	Czech Republic	Slovakia	Bulgaria	Ukraine
The officials are greedy	37	30	39	48
The government does not pay officials properly	12	19	47	23
People are desperate to buy favours	51	50	14	30
Difference: % 'officials' – % 'people'	-14	-20	+25	+18

* *Note*: 'Don't know', 'mixed/depends' etc. answers were recorded if given spontaneously, but never prompted. They have been excluded from the calculation of percentages.

Similarly, when asked for the most important reason 'why people might be more willing to give money or a present to an official now than under communism?' People in the Czech Republic were most likely to complain that 'people push harder for special favours now' while a large majority in Bulgaria and Ukraine, along with a narrow majority in Slovakia, complained that 'officials expect more now'.

Table 6. Why people are now more willing to give (percentage of total)*

Q107: Here are some reasons why ordinary people might be more willing to give money or a present to an official now than (under communism). Which do you feel is the most important?	Czech Republic	Slovakia	Bulgaria	Ukraine
People are more able to pay now	12	10	7	5
People push harder for special favours now	50	38	21	31
Officials expect more now	38	52	72	63

* *Note*: 'Don't know', 'mixed/depends' etc. answers were recorded if given spontaneously, but never prompted. They have been excluded from the calculation of percentages.

Officials may extort presents and bribes by making direct and explicit demands. 'They say what is the price of each thing.'[7] More subtly – and more safely for them – officials can convey their expectations or demands by hints, by complaints about their workload, or by comments about the special efforts they are making. 'In the case involving the militia it was their hints that made me do it'.[8]

According to our respondents, officials made direct demands relatively infrequently, though 11 per cent in Ukraine as compared with only two per cent in the Czech Republic reported that they had been 'asked directly' for 'money or a present.' However, one way or another officials often managed to convey the impression that they expected a special gift for their trouble. Almost half in the Czech Republic and Bulgaria, and two-thirds in Slovakia and Ukraine had either been asked directly or made to feel that some gift was 'expected'.

Table 7. Did an official ever ask you or your family directly? (percentage of total)[*]

Q144: In these last few years, did an official ever ask you or your family directly for money or a present, or not ask directly but seem to expect something?	Czech Republic	Slovakia	Bulgaria	Ukraine
Asked directly	2	4	7	11
Seemed to expect	44	64	39	56
Neither	54	32	54	33

[*] *Note*: Don't know', 'mixed/depends' etc. answers were recorded if given spontaneously, but never prompted. They have been excluded from the calculation of percentages.

Moreover, this is not referring to mere 'body-language' here: almost half in the Czech Republic and Bulgaria, over half in Slovakia and two-thirds in Ukraine reported that officials had 'made unnecessary problems in order to get money or a present for solving them.' 'Bureaucrats propose to do it "unofficially" – mentioning the difficulties of solving the problem.'[9]

Table 8. Unnecessary Problems (percentage of total) [*]

Q132: How often did these officials make unnecessary problems for you or your family in order to get money or a present for solving them ...	Czech Republic	Slovakia	Bulgaria	Ukraine
Usually	3	8	4	14
Sometimes	16	22	20	28
Rarely	25	27	25	25
Never	56	44	52	33

[*] *Note*: 'Don't know', 'mixed/depends' etc. answers were recorded if given spontaneously, but never prompted. They have been excluded from the calculation of percentages.

[7]   Sevastopol, FG-1
[8]   Horodok, IDI-4
[9]   Kyiv, IDI-9

V.   ACTUAL EXPERIENCE OF GIVING PRESENTS AND BRIBES

A majority in every country suggested that it was 'likely' that a citizen would have to give at least a small present to get something they were legally entitled to, from an official. However, what had they actually done? We asked a battery of questions about their actual experience of using eight different strategies for dealing with officials 'in the last few years – let's say approximately the last four or five years.' This time span was designed to focus attention on the mid to late 1990s, well after the fall of the communist system. Two of these strategies are relevant here: had they actually offered an official 'a small present?', and 'money or an expensive present?'.

Many who admitted offering a 'small present' claimed they had done no more than that and denied ever giving 'money or an expensive present'. However, almost all those who had offered 'money or an expensive present' had also offered 'small presents'.[10] Therefore, these respondents can be usefully divided up into those who had offered an official:

- Nothing, not even 'a small present';
- 'A small present', but nothing more than that;
- 'Money or an expensive present'.

A majority in Bulgaria and the Czech Republic claimed to have offered nothing, but a majority in Slovakia and Ukraine admitted they had offered at least 'a small present' and perhaps more. The numbers admitting that they had offered 'money or an expensive present' ranged from 11 per cent in the Czech Republic, through 19 per cent in Bulgaria, to 31 per cent in Slovakia and 36 per cent in Ukraine.

Table 9. Giving Presents and Bribes (percentage of total, i.e. usually, sometimes or rarely)*

In dealing with officials in the last few years did you or your family usually, sometimes, rarely or never have to ... Q141: Offer a small present? Q142: Offer money or an expensive present?	*Czech Republic*	*Slovakia*	*Bulgaria*	*Ukraine*
Q141 and Q142: Nothing	76	42	66	43
Q141 and Q142: Small present only	13	27	15	21
Q142: Money or expensive present	11	31	19	36

Note: 'Don't know', 'mixed/depends' etc. answers were recorded if given spontaneously, but never prompted. They have been excluded from the calculation of percentages.

---

[10]   A negligible one per cent said they had offered 'money or an expensive present' but not 'a small present'.

VI.   DOES CONDEMNATION MATTER?

It was found that a majority in every country condemned 'the use of money, presents, contacts, or favours to influence officials' as 'bad for (the country), and bad for those involved'. Whatever their grounds for condemning corruption, did condemnation really matter? Did people really mean it? Were their answers merely ritual condemnation without much thought or much relationship to their actual behaviour?

There was some consistency in their answers. People who condemned the use of presents and bribes were much more likely to opt for an austere, rigid, Weberian system in which 'officials never accepted presents and never did favours for people', rather than one in which 'officials sometimes accepted presents and in return did favours for people'. In Ukraine for example, the austere option was chosen by 64 per cent of those who condemned the use of presents to influence officials, by 46 per cent of those who excused it, and by only 27 per cent of those who preferred it that way. The degree of consistency was far less than perfect but it was significant nonetheless.

Table 10. Prefer rigid system (without presents and favours) – by condemnation (percentage of total)*

Q156: Prefer rigid system (without presents and favours) By Q153. Q153: Amongst those who say the use of money, presents and favours to influence officials is ...	*Czech Republic*	*Slovakia*	*Bulgaria*	*Ukraine*
Bad for (country) and for those involved	95	85	71	64
Bad for (country) but unavoidable for people	85	79	53	46
Preferable, because you can get favours	(68)[1]	(52)[1]	23	27

* *Note*: 'Don't know', 'mixed/depends' etc. answers were recorded if given spontaneously, but never prompted. [1] Based on less than 100, but at least 50, respondents.

Moreover, those who condemned the use of presents and bribes to influence officials were much more inclined to refuse to pay them, and much less tempted to accept them.

Although some of the percentages are based upon fairly small numbers of respondents, they suggest that condemnation increased resistance to paying bribes by 36 per cent in the Czech Republic, by 30 per cent in Slovakia, and by 29 per cent in Bulgaria, though by a mere three per cent in Ukraine. Amongst those who condemned the use of bribes, two-thirds in the Czech Republic, and half in Slovakia and Bulgaria but only a quarter in Ukraine said they would refuse to pay even 'if asked directly' and even 'if they could afford to pay'.

Table 11. Would refuse to pay if asked − by condemnation (percentage of total)*

Q145: Would refuse to pay if asked By Q153Q153: Amongst those who say the use of money, presents and favours to influence officials is ...	Czech Republic	Slovakia	Bulgaria	Ukraine
Bad for (country) and for those involved	67	48	51	27
Bad for (country) but unavoidable for people	53	38	31	23
Preferable, because you can get favours	(31)[1]	(18)[1]	(22)[1]	(24)[1]

* *Note*: Don't know', 'mixed/depends' etc. answers were recorded if given spontaneously, but never prompted. They have been excluded from the calculations. [1] Based on less than 100, but at least 50, respondents.

These questions about willingness to pay bribes were hypothetical. However, condemnation also correlated with actual behaviour over the past five years. In practice, condemnation increased the numbers who never gave even a *small present* to an official by 37 per cent in the Czech Republic, by 18 per cent in Slovakia, and by 29 per cent in Bulgaria, but by only 10 per cent in Ukraine. Furthermore, condemnation increased the numbers who had never given money or an expensive present to an official by 23 per cent in the Czech Republic, by 20 per cent in Slovakia, and by 26 per cent in Bulgaria, but by only seven per cent in Ukraine.

Condemnation, whether motivated by moral, ideological or economic considerations, did matter. It mattered in terms of actual reported behaviour, as well as in terms of what people 'would do' in hypothetical situations. Moreover, it mattered in every country, though it mattered less in Ukraine than in the other countries. If they condemned the use of presents and bribes to influence officials, people in Ukraine were somewhat less likely to have actually given presents or bribes. However, they were scarcely any less willing to submit to extortion if an official 'asked directly'.

Table 12. Never gave presents or bribes − by condemnation (percentage of total)*

Q141−2: Never gave presents or bribes By Q153	Czech Republic	Slovakia	Bulgaria	Ukraine
Never gave anything Q153: Amongst those who say the use of money, presents and favours to influence officials is ...				
Bad for (country) and for those involved	81	45	74	46
Bad for (country) but unavoidable for people	64	33	60	35
Preferable, because you can get favours	(44)[1]	27	45	36

Table 12. (continued)

Never gave money or expensive present Q153: Amongst those who say the use of money, presents and favours to influence officials is ...				
Bad for (country) and for those involved	91	73	87	66
Bad for (country) but unavoidable for people	84	60	77	60
Preferable, because you can get favours	(68)[1]	53	61	59

* *Note*: 'Don't know', 'mixed/depends' etc. answers were recorded if given spontaneously, but never prompted. They have been excluded from the calculations.
[1] Based on less than 100, but at least 50, respondents.

VII. DID ATTEMPTS AT EXTORTION SUCCEED?

Between 37 per cent (in the Czech Republic) and 74 per cent (in Ukraine) said they would pay a bribe 'if asked directly' and 'if they could afford it'. However, what happened in practice? How many of those who had real experience of attempted extortion did actually submit to it?

There was a remarkable similarity between the numbers who said they had actually given something when an official either 'asked directly or seemed to expect something', and the numbers who said they would do so if asked. Some people had given voluntarily without pressure of course, but the effect of this pressure was to increase the numbers who had actually given something by 27 per cent in the Czech and Slovak Republics, by 42 per cent in Bulgaria, and by 38 per cent in Ukraine. Such pressure also increased the (smaller) numbers who had actually given 'money or an expensive present' by 18 per cent in the Czech Republic, by 21 per cent in Slovakia, by 29 per cent in Bulgaria, and by 34 per cent in Ukraine.

Similarly, those who felt officials had made unnecessary problems in order to extort presents and bribes were much more likely to have given them. 'Unnecessary problems' increased the numbers who had given something to an official by 28 per cent in the Czech Republic, by 34 per cent in Slovakia, by 33 per cent in Bulgaria, and by 35 per cent in Ukraine. Moreover, 'unnecessary problems' increased the (smaller) numbers who had given 'money or an expensive present' to an official by 17 per cent in the Czech Republic, by 31 per cent in Slovakia, by 26 per cent in Bulgaria, and by 26 per cent also in Ukraine.

So although citizens' condemnation of bribery had relatively little, if any, effect on their actual behaviour in Ukraine, officials' attempts at extortion clearly had as much effect in Ukraine as anywhere else. People in Ukraine were responsive to pressure from officials, and frequently found themselves under such pressure.

Table 13. Gave presents or bribes – by whether officials asked for, or seemed to expect, a bribe (percentage of total)*

Q141-2: Gave presents or bribes By Q144	Czech Republic	Slovakia	Bulgaria	Ukraine
Gave something Q144: Amongst those who say officials ...				
Asked directly, or seemed to expect something	39	68	58	74
Neither asked nor seemed to expect	12	41	16	36
Gave money or expensive present Q144: Amongst those who say officials ...				
Asked directly, or seemed to expect something	21	39	35	50
Neither asked nor seemed to expect	3	18	6	16
Q145: If you had an important problem, and an official asked you directly for money to solve it, would you: (i) pay if you could afford it or (ii) refuse to pay even if you could afford it?				
Would pay if asked	37	57	58	74

* *Note*: 'Don't know', 'mixed/depends' etc. answers were recorded if given spontaneously, but never prompted. They have been excluded from the calculations.

Table 14. Gave presents or bribes – by whether officials caused unnecessary problems (percentage of total)*

Gave presents or bribes – whether officials caused unnecessary problems	Czech Republic	Slovakia	Bulgaria	Ukraine
Gave something Q132: Amongst those who say officials caused unnecessary problems in order to extort a bribe ...				
Usually, sometimes, or rarely	40	73	51	70
Never	12	39	18	35
Gave money or expensive present Q132: Amongst those who say officials caused unnecessary problems in order to extort a bribe ...				
Usually, sometimes, or rarely	21	45	32	46
Never	4	14	6	20

* *Note*: 'Don't know', 'mixed/depends' etc. answers were recorded if given spontaneously, but never prompted. They have been excluded from the calculations.

VIII. DID OFFICIAL PRESSURE OUTWEIGH CONDEMNATION?

Clearly, both condemnation and extortion seem to have influenced actual behaviour though to varying degrees in different countries. We can usefully summarize these findings by calculating (Pearson) correlation coefficients between giving presents and bribes on the one hand, and condemnation or extortion on the other.

In a highly compressed way these correlation coefficients illustrate what was already discovered from the more detailed tables: condemnation sharply reduced bribe-giving in the Czech and Slovak Republics, and in Bulgaria, but had much less influence in Ukraine. The correlation declined in power from minus 0.25 in the Czech Republic to minus 0.09 in Ukraine. Correlations with preferences for a rigid Weberian system (no presents, no special help) showed a broadly similar pattern – significant in every country except Ukraine.[11] In contrast, the correlation between giving presents and bribes on the one hand and our indicators of extortion by officials on the other, was strong in all four countries. It ranged from a minimum of 0.26 up to a maximum of 0.43.

Table 15. Correlations between Giving, Condemnation and Extortion (percentage of total)

	Czech Republic	Slovakia	Bulgaria	Ukraine
Correlation between Q141-2: 'gave bribes', and ...	$r \times 100^{1}$	$r \times 100^{1}$	$r \times 100^{1}$	$r \times 100^{1}$
Q153: 'Bribes are bad'	-25	-17	-21	-9
Q156: Prefer rigid system	-16	-17	-21	-5
Q144: 'Official asked for, or expected, bribe'	33	26	43	39
Q132: 'Official made unnecessary problem'	36	40	36	33

Notes: [1] (Pearson) correlation coefficient times 100. Variables coded as follows: 'Gave bribes': 0 = did not, 1 = gave only small present, 2 = gave money or expensive present. 'Prefer rigid system': 0 = prefer reciprocal presents and favours, 1 = prefer no presents and no favours. 'Bribes bad': 0 = prefer flexible system, 1 = unavoidable, 2 = bad for country and those involved. 'Officials asked for, or expected, bribes': 0 = neither, 1 = did not ask but expected, 2 = asked directly. 'Officials made unnecessary problem to extort bribe': 0 = never, 1 = rarely, 2 = usually or sometimes.

Indeed these correlations with attempts at extortion are so strong that they raise the question whether anything else mattered. However, tabulating the numbers giving bribes by a combination of condemnation and pressure from officials demonstrate that both condemnation and pressure had an independent influence on behaviour. The effect of condemnation (visible in the columns of the table) was clearly less than that of pressure (visible in the rows of the table) but significant nonetheless.

---

[11] In the Czech Republic, the negative correlation between bribe giving and preference for a rigid system was weaker than between bribe giving and condemnation. However, in the Czech Republic 91 per cent expressed a preference for a rigid system. Such a degree of consensus tends to limit the size of correlations.

Amongst those who had been put under pressure by officials seeking gifts, condemnation reduced overall giving by at least 16 per cent in the Czech Republic, by 13 per cent in Slovakia, and by 17 per cent in Bulgaria, though by only seven per cent in Ukraine. Typically, one Czech IDI respondent[12] felt '50 per cent of officials expected to be given' something but their 'salaries were adequate' and she 'did not feel she should give them anything.' Condemnation also reduced the (smaller) numbers giving 'money or expensive presents' by at least seven per cent in the Czech Republic, by 17 per cent in Slovakia, by 23 per cent in Bulgaria, and by 11 per cent in Ukraine.[13]

Table 16. Gave bribes – by condemnation and pressure to give (percentage of total)*

Q141–2: By Q153 by Q144	*Czech Republic*		*Slovakia*		*Bulgaria*		*Ukraine*	
Q144	If official sought gift		If official sought gift		If official sought gift		If official sought gift	
	did	did not	did	did not	did	did not	did	did not
Who gave anything								
Q153: If say bribes are...								
Bad	32	10	65	36	51	12	71	32
Unavoidable	48	(16)[1]	75	(45)[1]	61	19	75	(42)[1]
Preferable	na	na	(78)[1]	na	(68)[1]	na	(78)[1]	na

	Czech Republic		*Slovakia*		*Bulgaria*		*Ukraine*	
Q144	If official sought gift		If official sought gift		If official sought gift		If official sought gift	
	did	did not	did	did not	did	did not	did	did not
Who gave money or an expensive present								
Q153: If say bribes are ...								
Bad	17	3	35	14	28	4	47	17
Unavoidable	24	(3)[1]	46	(23)[1]	36	7	51	(15)[1]
Preferable	na	na	(52)[1]	na	(51)[1]	na	(58)[1]	na

* *Note:* 'Don't know', 'mixed/depends' etc. answers were recorded if given spontaneously, but never prompted; They have been excluded from the calculations.
[1] Based on less than 100, but at least 50, respondents.
na: less than 50.

[12] Prague IDI-15
[13] Amongst those who had been put under pressure by officials seeking gifts, a preference for a rigid Weberian system (Q156) reduced overall giving by 12 per cent in Slovakia, and by 20 per cent in Bulgaria, though by only one per cent in Ukraine. Moreover, the (smaller) numbers giving 'money or expensive presents' were reduced by 13 per cent in Slovakia, by 25 per cent in Bulgaria, but by only two per cent in Ukraine. The consensus in favour of a rigid system in the Czech Republic makes it impossible to gauge the effect of such preferences there.

Similarly, amongst those who had experienced officials making 'unnecessary problems' in order to get a present or bribe, condemnation reduced overall giving by at least 22 per cent in the Czech Republic, by nine per cent in Slovakia, and by 33 per cent in Bulgaria, though by less than four per cent in Ukraine. And it reduced the (smaller) numbers giving 'money or expensive presents' by at least 11 per cent in the Czech Republic, by 16 per cent in Slovakia, and by 30 per cent in Bulgaria, though by less than four per cent in Ukraine.[14]

Amongst those who condemned the use of bribes, and who had not experienced attempted extortion by an official making unnecessary problems, only three per cent in the Czech Republic, four per cent in Bulgaria, nine per cent in Slovakia, and 14 per cent in Ukraine had given 'money or an expensive present' to an official in the last five years.[15]

IX. DISCUSSION

There were very widespread allegations that ordinary people offer presents and bribes to the officials they meet in day-to-day life in Eastern Europe, and that the officials accept them. Using presents and bribes to influence officials was widely condemned but widely practiced. Yet, a majority in every country condemned the practice as 'bad for their country, and for those involved', and most of the rest said it was 'bad for the country, but unavoidable for people who have to live here'.

The evidence does not support the view that the people were the source of corruption, pressing their bribes – and their demands for favours – upon reluctant officials. However, there remains the question whether the people were victims of the officials or accomplices. Did officials abuse their position to extort unofficial payments from weak, powerless and reluctant citizens, or were citizens as happy to give as officials were happy to accept?

It is a question of some practical as well as theoretical importance. If ordinary people are the victims of extortion by officials then it may be possible to reduce public sector corruption by reforming the administration in one way or another.[16]

---

[14] Amongst those who had experienced officials making 'unnecessary problems' in order to get a present or bribe, a preference for a rigid Weberian system (Q156) reduced overall giving by nine per cent in Slovakia, and by 29 per cent in Bulgaria, though by only four per cent in Ukraine. Moreover, it reduced the (smaller) numbers giving 'money or expensive presents' by 11 per cent in Slovakia, and by 31 per cent in Bulgaria, but not at all in Ukraine. As before, the consensus in favour of a rigid system in the Czech Republic makes it impossible to gauge the effect of such preferences there.

[15] Amongst those who expressed a preference for a rigid Weberian system (Q156: no presents, no special help), and had not experienced attempted extortion an official making unnecessary problems, only three per cent in the Czech Republic, four per cent in Bulgaria, 10 per cent in Slovakia, and 19 per cent in Ukraine had given 'money or an expensive present' to an official in the last five years.

[16] For a discussion of possible reforms and the degree of public support for them, see W. L. Miller, Å. B. Grødeland and T. Y. Koshechkina, 'What Is To Be Done About Corrupt Officials? Public Opinion and Reform Strategies in Post-communist Europe' (June 1999) 65 *International Review of Administrative Sciences*, pp. 235–249 – a revised and shortened version of a paper given at the NISPAcee (Networks of Institutes and Schools of Public Administration in Central and Eastern Europe) 6th Annual Conference, March 1998, Prague.

Reform would then 'go with the grain' of public opinion and, if well planned, should win public support. However, if the public are in essence accomplices in petty corruption then reform is likely to be more difficult and less effective: it would be necessary to reform the people as well as reform the administration.

People in the Czech and Slovak Republics were most likely to blame their fellow citizens 'desperate to buy favours' rather than 'greedy officials'. Conversely, people in Bulgaria and Ukraine were more likely to blame 'greedy officials' than their fellow citizens (though people in Bulgaria were even more likely to blame their government for failing to pay officials properly). Similarly, when asked why people might be more willing to give things to officials now than under communism, people in the Czech Republic were most likely to blame their fellow citizens, but in Bulgaria and Ukraine they were most likely, by far, to blame 'officials who expect more now'. Opinion in Slovakia fell between these two extremes.

Taken at face value, these findings suggest that people who gave bribes to officials in the Czech Republic and, to a lesser extent in Slovakia also, were not victims but accomplices or worse. Reforms in those countries might, therefore, aim as much at bribe-givers as bribe-takers.[17]

In Bulgaria and Ukraine however, people were inclined to place the burden of guilt on the shoulders of their officials rather than on their fellow citizens. To a greater or lesser extent they claimed to be victims of the administration though many in Bulgaria felt that junior officials were also victims – victims of a government that did not pay them properly. However, in Ukraine, people pictured themselves unambiguously as the victims of officials high and low. In their own view, the people of Ukraine were the passive and guiltless victims of rapacious officials. Reforms targeted at bribe-givers in Bulgaria, and more especially in Ukraine, might only make people feel that they were the 'victims twice over' – victims of the low-level officials who extorted bribes from them, and of high officials who then punished them for their submission to extortion.

In the absence of pressure from officials, behaviour did not contradict principle to a very large extent. It was the frequency and effectiveness of extortion – the combination of officials' greed and citizens' submissiveness – that produced high levels of bribery despite opposition to it in principle. In the Czech Republic only 19 per cent had experienced attempts at extortion 'more than rarely' and, amongst those who condemned bribery, only 16 per cent submitted to it. In Ukraine at the other extreme, 42 per cent had experienced attempts at extortion 'more than rarely' and, amongst those who condemned bribery, 44 per cent submitted to it – twice the frequency of extortion by officials, and three times as much submission by citizens, as we found in the Czech Republic.

---

[17] When asked explicitly, a majority in all countries said bribe-givers should be punished less severely than bribe-takers, but this ranged from a bare majority of 53 per cent in the Czech Republic to a massive 80 per cent in Ukraine. See Miller *et al*.., ibid., p. 240.

Finally, the counter-intuitive nature of our findings must be stressed. It is natural to imagine that where bribery is most common, citizens are most likely to be willing accomplices rather than victims. Our findings suggest the exact opposite. They suggest that where bribery was least common (in the Czech Republic), the relatively small number of people who gave bribes were more likely to be accomplices or even corrupters. And where bribery was most common (in Ukraine), the much larger numbers of people who gave bribes were much more likely to be victims of extortion.

9

The Embeddedness of Tax Evasion in Russia

Eva Busse

I. INTRODUCTION

Judging from the public relations effort of the Russian government, tax evasion appears to be the category of economic crime that is battled most fervently in the post-Soviet period. Posters, radio and television clips, and a carefully-designed *nalogi* website[1] condemn tax evaders as treacherous, impotent (!) and criminal. The stylized combat image of the tax police with its masks and machine guns equally seeks to fuel the criminalization of tax evasion.

At the same time as it is forcefully constructed by the government's campaign as a major new category of economic crime, tax evasion in practice does not seem to be losing any of its pervasiveness. Russian tax in reality is characterized by a peculiar contrast between the public condemnation of evasion on the one hand, and the simultaneous inertia to boost efficacy and to increase compliance rates on the other hand. The lack of revenues has become a vital threat to the young Russian Federation, causing Sergei Kiriyenko, the then Prime Minister, to warn: 'If the state does not learn to collect taxes it will cease to exist'.[2] During its first five years, the Russian Federation suffered a drop in tax revenues of almost two thirds. At the end of the 1990s the Russian Tax and Duty Ministry[3] estimates that only 16 per cent of companies and organizations comply with their tax obligations fully and on time. The compliance rate for individual income tax is even more desperate at just over five per cent.[4]

It is argued here that the apparent paradox of the overt condemnation and simultaneous covert pervasiveness of tax evasion is resolved in the Russian context by a selective and superficial criminalization of the problem. The political anti-evasion campaign merely creates a new and abstract category of economic crime whose destructive outcomes, like the instrumentalized plight of Russia's *babushki*,[5]

---

[1] See: <www.nalog.ru>.
[2] Quoted in D. Treisman, 'Russia's Taxing Problem' (1998) 112 *Foreign Policy*, p. 56.
[3] Quoted in V. Virkunen, 'You Don't Have to Pay Taxes in Russia' (February 1999) 5 *Prism*.
[4] According to statistics of the Russian Ministry of Finance. (February 1999) 5 *Prism*.
[5] For months, a shortsighted old woman was staring down from Russian poster fronts, begging: 'Nikto ne pomozhet Rossii krome nas samikh – pozhaluista, zaplatite nalogi!'('No one will help Russia except we ourselves. Please, pay your taxes').

A. V. Ledeneva and M. Kurkchiyan (eds.), Economic Crime in Russia, 129–143

can easily be portrayed and acknowledged as criminal. The underlying practices, however, which result in the condemned phenomenon of tax evasion, are neither addressed nor recognized. Thus, the criminalization is limited to the obvious manifestations of tax evasion, while its actual genesis escapes public recognition. The present paper attempts to close this gap in understanding the Russian tax crisis by empirically tracing some of the systemic and social factors that undermine the efficacy of tax collection. It is argued here that the actual roots of the evasion problem elude the criminalization campaign, first, because they tacitly complement the formal tax system, adjusting to and blending with the given bureaucratic and legal structures, rather than blatantly deviating from them. Second, the roots of evasion can hardly be depicted as criminal because they are deeply engrained in unreflective everyday practices inherited from the Soviet past.

Based on a 1997 study of local taxation practices among small businesses in Peterhof, a town of 88,000 citizens on the outskirts of St. Petersburg, this paper examines the legal and political context of local taxation in order to illustrate that tax evasion is not caused by deviant behaviour outside the legally-prescribed mechanisms that could be labeled criminal. It is instead rooted in a rather coherent unity of the formal framework and informal and personalized practices that close the gaps left by the official system. The local actors use the opportunities indirectly offered within the tax system to pursue their personal interests. The paper then goes on to argue that the informal ways of instrumentalizing the cracks in the tax legislation are socially supported by aspects of the Soviet legacy and by the tax system's fundamental lack of legitimacy. The systemic and social conditions responsible for the pervasiveness of tax evasion can in turn explain why the processes constituting tax evasion are not considered criminal by the taxpayers, tax inspectors and political authorities who are involved in local taxation.

II.   SYSTEMIC FACTORS FACILITATING TAX EVASION

1.   *Local disincentives inherent in the bureaucratic structures of taxation*

The following will discuss an idiosyncrasy of the bureaucratic organization of taxation that is apt to trigger local practices that oppose federal interests and decrease revenues. In scrutinizing the bureaucratic distribution of tax collecting and tax spending responsibilities, it turns out that the bureaucratic structures in fact entail a systemic disincentive for local authorities to increase tax revenues. The system causes a destructive opposition between local interests on the one hand, and regional and federal interests on the other. This is due to the regional government in cooperation with the regional tax service in St. Petersburg submitting two crucial norms to the local authorities every budgetary year. First, the Peterhof tax office is assigned its annual 'target', i.e. the amount of revenue that it is supposed to collect. Second, the administration is presented with its budget that consists partly of local tax revenues and partly of regional subsidies. The exact amount of these subsidies is redefined every year and depends on the target for local tax collection. If the target is high, the regional government transfers proportionally fewer subsidies. If it is low, it transfers more subsidies.

As a result, there is a fundamental divergence of interest between the regional authorities and the local authorities. The St. Petersburg government seeks to pay as little subsidy as possible, and therefore seeks to set the target for local tax collection as high as possible. The Peterhof administration, as the recipient, is on the contrary interested in getting as much subsidy as possible, and informally attempts to underestimate its own tax base so as to keep the target low. The same objective is pursued by the local tax office which seeks to work under as little pressure as possible. So the system of subsidy effectively subverts the tax office's and the administration's motivation to boost tax collection. As the head of the Peterhof tax office puts it:

> It does not make sense for us: if we collect a lot of taxes, we will get less money from St. Petersburg. But if we collect less, they give us more. So even if we work better, we gain nothing.

The head of the financial department of the local administration explains that the political authorities equally prefer to rely on subsidies, rather than on local revenues:

> We are not interested in relying on local taxes, because they are always unstable. We have to fight for them. The bigger part of the budget that is filled by St. Petersburg, the better it is for us. They simply transfer the money to us, and we don't have to care about it.

This situation of centrally imposed plans undermining local initiatives strikingly resembles the problems of the Soviet planning system. For, under Soviet production plans, the local actors, in this case the tax collectors, deliberately understate their real potentials so as to avoid troublesome pressure to collect taxes more efficiently. Once the collection target has been defined, neither the administration nor the tax office has a real interest in exceeding the target. Thus the tax authority appears to be too centrally organized. Spending responsibilities are too remote from tax collection. If taxes could be spent where they are collected, rather than being redistributed along centralized structures, the localities themselves would be interested in a more effective practice of tax collection. The failure of the tax system to gear the interests of centre and periphery appears to result in a fundamental lack of incentives for the primary tax collectors to increase tax turnouts.

2. *Legislative roots of the personalization of taxation*

The previous section has illustrated the crack in the bureaucratic structure of taxation which encourages local authorities to informally negotiate lower collection targets and discourages them from increasing desperately needed tax revenues. Neither reaction to the system's informal opportunities is considered criminal, as the local authorities are simply following the line of least resistance paved by the federal structures themselves. The following part illustrates three characteristics of the legal basis of taxation that facilitate informal interactions between local taxpayers and tax inspectors which result in tax evasion. It is argued that a) the tax legislation's extortionate tax burden, b) its legal leniency, and c) its loose legal restrictions of sanctions encourage and even necessitate the development of personalized relations between the primary actors which penetrate and deform supposedly impersonal routines. As depicted below, the actual rules of taxation are, as a result, not only contingent upon the official legal guidelines, but also upon personal interests and interpersonal factors such as gender and personal sympathies.

3.   The extortionate tax burden

The first aspect of Russian tax legislation that almost inevitably triggers tax evasion on the part of taxpayers, and personal abuse of their position on the part of tax officials, is the unrealistically high level of legally-prescribed taxes. Although the nominal rates are not especially high, with a maximum profit rate of just 35 per cent, there are several structural features that greatly inflate the formal tax burden. First, corporations are faced with a multitude of types of taxes, raised by federal, regional and local authorities, which often overlap. Second, the effect of high taxes is aggravated by the fact that most taxes are not deduced from profit, but from turnover or running costs.[6] Third, the Russian tax system allows only a very limited range of tax deductions which in the West decrease the nominal tax burden considerably. Fourth, the tax sums have been artificially increased as a result of the government-ordered re-evaluations of enterprises' fixed capital in the course of their privatization. Fifth, the tax bill of enterprises that engage in barter trade is inflated because the federal government tries to collect in 'live money', while tax bills are based on prices and balance-sheet information expressed in 'offset roubles' of lower value.[7] Sixth, the nominal tax rates are effectively multiplied by the economy's structural shortage of money. The 1998 report of the Inter-departmental Balance-Sheet Commission (MBK) found that the average company's tax bill amounted to 79.5 per cent of its monetary income.

As a result of these aggravating features, the Russian corporate tax burden is extraordinarily high, with taxation not infrequently imposed even on enterprises' capital assets. Thus the legal tax demands amount to a vital threat to corporate survival and put enterprises into a position where they somehow have to escape from their official fiscal duties. All respondents, including the head of the local tax office, admit that it is impossible to run a business and to pay all required taxes. A private dentist puts it bluntly:

> Do you seriously think that we pay all taxes? Seriously? Of course not. Everyone knows it, our patients, the tax officers, the administration. You cannot live otherwise, no one would do any business otherwise. It simply would not make sense ... I am sure that we pay less than a third of what we are supposed to pay.

---

[6]   The Institut der Deutschen Wirtschaft estimates that about 85 per cent of Russian corporate taxes are not based on profit.

[7]   B. Tompson, 'The Price of Everything and the Value of Nothing' (May 1999) 28 *Economy and Society*, pp. 256–80.

At the same time as the legal structure of backbreaking taxes forces taxpayers to find an informal way out, it also puts tax inspectors under pressure to exceed their formal decision-making competencies. Not uncommonly, the individual tax officer is faced with the decision either to stick to the law and ruin the concerned enterprise, or to find an alternative informal solution. The head of the Peterhof tax office explains:

> At the moment, enterprises have billions of debts with us. It is impossible to collect everything. If we do collect them, we set into motion a vicious circle: Next time, those enterprises won't be able to pay their taxes again, then we will have to sanction them again, the interests will rise and so on. With these taxes the enterprises stand on their knees, and they can never stand up.

So the legislation itself appears to force local tax officers into ad hoc decisions which lack a sound legal basis. This compulsory assumption of responsibilities on the local level is another parallel to the old Soviet system. As many centrally-devised tax norms can only be fulfilled at the cost of destroying the economic base and thus at the cost of long-term budgetary losses, local authorities have to take the autonomous responsibility of weighing short-term revenues versus long-term development. From here it is only a small step to assuming this self-responsibility also in personally-motivated cases, and to make use of discretionary powers on a routine basis.

The legal exaggerations and the semi-legal, informal ways of bailing them out appear to sustain each other. As taxes are so high, people evade; and because people evade, there is no political will to lower the tax rates sufficiently. This relative stability of the Russian tax system, based on the interrelation between institutional constraints and informal ways of circumventing them, is, however, a destructive one as it appears to allow an utterly inefficient system to survive. In the following, this paper will illustrate the strategies used by the local actors in order to adjust to the structural constraints and to accommodate their personal interests within them.

4. The legal leniency

The second characteristic of the Russian tax code apt to trigger informal evasion practices is its general leniency. The tax legislation does not succeed in defining universal guidelines on the basis of which local taxation could be conducted in a predictable, consistent and transparent fashion. Rather, it is so vague, and riddled by so many confusing amendments, that even Western observers have realized that 'the only thing predictable about taxes in Russia is their unpredictability'.[8] The effects of this unreliability of the formal rules on the local level are revealed by one respondent, who complains about the tax office's informal interpretation of the legislation:

---

[8] *The Financial Times*, 23 August 1995.

> The interpretation of the law is a dark game in which they use all the different information they have to their advantage. They are always cleverer than us. We don't know the law because the law is decided in the tax office ... The law should be unambiguous: the traffic light is either red or green. But in our system it can have any colour, depending entirely on the inspectors' mood. That is bad. The law is such a gamble.

Due to the legal vacuum left by the federal legislation, unofficial decision-making assumes a vital role in the local practice of taxation. As taxes and their rates are not bindingly determined by law due to the lack of procedural specificity, frequent amendments and the confusing amount of paperwork, decisions can be taken by local tax inspectors with considerable flexibility. One respondent elaborates on the decisive role of tax inspectors for his enterprise's tax bill which is facilitated by the leniency of the official legal guidelines:

> I have never seen a norm about how much they can take in taxes. It is impossible to know how much to pay. This quarter year I pay a certain sum, and next quarter year I pay a different one. Every time we begin to quarrel again over it with the tax office. They spend their entire time deciding how much an enterprise, which they have known for years, must pay ... A tax inspector has the possibility not to collect some taxes, because the system is such chaos. If there are 1,000 documents to consider, then he can afford to ignore one, and to take a bribe instead of a tax. So of course we can persuade any inspector to ignore some things – only thanks to the stupid paper work.

However, the weakness of tax legislation not only influences the personal relations between tax officers and taxpayers to the effect that the position of power of the former is enhanced. At the same time, the legal instability also deprives local officers of a solid base that would legitimate their authority *vis-à-vis* the taxpayers. The head of the Peterhof tax police points to the dilemma that occurs when common sense tells the tax officer that the constant legal changes are unfair:

> If the state wants the people to pay taxes it should explain the rules of the game in advance. But here new decisions about new taxes appear out of nowhere. A businessman expected a certain profit, but he absolutely did not take into account a new tax on selling or on something else. Therefore, he considers himself right in saying 'I will not pay this tax'. And he is right, in a way. What are we supposed to tell him?

This quote indicates that personal negotiations between taxpayers and tax officers seem to be the norm in the local routine of taxation. To put it bluntly, the legal leniency of the Russian tax system renders the personal confrontation between taxpayers and tax inspectors inevitable. Due to its inherent dynamic, the system's structural conditions trigger individual action on the basis of personal relations that essentially supplement the formal system and redirect its functions according to the individual interests involved.

Therefore, instead of being determined by universal and transparent laws, the local system works to a great extent through informal agreements. It is based, then, on a modern variation of a familiar Soviet phenomenon: the personalization of bureaucratic structures. This means that the individuals carrying out official tasks dominate their supposedly impersonal positions within the tax bureaucracy. From the taxpayers' point of view, the real obstacle in escaping the tax burden becomes the official representing the law, rather than the law itself. As a result of these structural conditions, the obvious strategy for businesses to defend their interests is to cultivate personal, often corrupt, relations with those people who possess decisive discretionary powers within the legal framework. The importance of good relations with the tax inspectors, which often are casually maintained with presents, services and favours, is explained by the owner of a family restaurant:

> It is important that they know me. They even warn me. They call to tell me that I have not paid in time or that I have filled in a document incorrectly. So that they don't have to sanction me much, or so that I don't have to pay enormous interest.

In the case of businessmen who have not mastered the art of networking, the personalization of taxation triggers personal animosity against officials who deny them informal ways out of their taxation problems. These entrepreneurs do not moan about the tax legislation, but about the tax officers. They do not complain primarily about taxes being too high, but about tax officers being too greedy. For example:

> The tax officers are our enemies. They are all bastards. In the administration as well. The people there spit at us. They only want to eat in our restaurants for free. I have understood it. They are the enemies against whom we have to fight. At the beginning I fought openly against them. Against their greed and nastiness. But now I know that they never forgive and I fight in secret.

Thus, due to the personalization of the taxation routine, informal factors like personal sympathies have an important impact upon local tax collection. Another significant informal factor is gender. This is because the sex of the respondents almost invariably corresponds to their profession. Entrepreneurs are predominantly male, tax officers female.[9] This reflects the sexual distribution of labour in Russia – the poorly paid public sector is run by female employees while the private sector is dominated by men. Based on the premise that Russian women generally have a lower social status than men, this gender division may be assumed to have a considerable impact on the personalized practice of taxation. As a result, the female tax officers' position of power is weakened, first, because they enjoy less

---

[9] In 1997, 82 out of 107 inspectors in the Peterhof tax office were female.

recognition and authority than male officers do, and second, because decision-making tends to shift away from the female-dominated tax bureaucracy to the male dominated political bureaucracy of the local administration. The first hypothesis is supported by the condescending and disrespectful way in which male respondents spoke about tax officers, intuitively using the female pronoun. It is unlikely that they would talk like this about men:

> Somehow I can always persuade the girls (*devushki*) to ignore some documents. And then I need to check their calculations, because they always make mistakes ... Their job does not even have to do with maths. Only on a very low level. Girls are good at that, they do what they are told to do.

The second hypothesis is inferred from the informal rule that taxpayers always seek access to those officials whom they regard to have greatest influence. The tendency inherited from the Soviet past to regard the political administration as more influential than the tax office is likely to be reinforced by the fact that the former is run by men and the latter by women. As a result, the tax office is marginalized from informal decision-making processes between male entrepreneurs and male politicians. Female tax officers cannot participate in informal negotiations taking place, crudely speaking, during intoxicated banquets and sauna sessions. Thus, for example, one respondent who used his influence as head of the local Soviet to help another businessman out of his tax problems approached the male mayor rather than the female head of the tax office. To summarize, it is suggested that in the personalized and gendered practice of taxation the tax office is deprived of some of the formal authority and influence it institutionally possesses.

5.   *The loose legal restrictions of sanctions*

Therefore, in practice, informal agreements between the tax collectors and the taxpayers are often found at the expense of the federal budget. From the point of view of the taxpayers, this solution is obvious: They seek to pay as little as possible and to be as safe as possible from unpleasant surprises such as sudden legal changes and increased taxes. As the greatest menace to these two vital interests is the law itself, the obvious way to defend their interests is to cultivate personal relations with the tax inspectors. They prefer to spend a lot of time, effort and money to win over the local office, rather than to face the detrimental legal position of private business. The situation of the tax officers as their negotiation partners, however, is more complex. They seek to profit as much as possible from their position as intermediaries between the tax law and the taxpayers. This position, in fact, appears to be the only asset that their job provides, as their state salaries are low and unreliable. On the other hand, however, they also have to consider the interests of the budget which limit their freedom to tolerate tax evasion for the sake of their personal profit. Therefore, they have to mediate between the pressure to collect sufficient sums and their own interest to receive presents and bribes during inspection.

The idiosyncratic function of fines in Russian tax legislation appears to provide them with a suitable tool to balance these opposing pressures. This is because the legal system entitles local tax officers to impose on-the-spot fines, so-called 'sanctions', without having to instigate legal proceedings. Sanctions are imposed for any kind of offence, from deliberate evasion to minor flaws in bookkeeping. The law does not distinguish between intentional and non-intentional offences. In 1997, any offence was punished by a fine twice the amount of the missing sum plus 0.3 per cent interest on every day in retrospect. Considering the above-depicted ambiguities of tax legislation, this wide-ranging power of sanctioning provides tax officers with an effective means of compensating the loss of any taxes which they have chosen not to collect in one business by sanctioning another. As the confusing stacks of paperwork are apt to trigger careless omissions, it is very easy for tax inspectors to discover mistakes and to impose sanctions. The head of the tax office readily agrees that there are opportunities to sanction during every inspection: 'This year we sanctioned more. Because we inspected more enterprises. And as a matter of fact every inspection uncovers offences. We have to sanction in every case'.

The owner of a construction company describes the informal routines of sanctioning from the taxpayers' point of view:

> Of course, every enterprise constantly has to pay sanctions. With this fact the inspection begins. They almost always sanction you for about 10 per cent of your turnover. Everyone knows it, it is OK, so you have to hide the taxes on another occasion. But this time it was almost 20 per cent, one fifth – then I started fighting. And the fight went on for several months. The result varies – and this is most interesting thing about our system. The inspection begins, let's say you have to pay 100 million. After three months it is 10. Why? Because we became friends with the inspector. After further months it became less. More friendship. Or, on the contrary, it doubled. This kind of numbers game is ridiculous.

This 'game of numbers', however, appears to be of immense importance for the perpetuation of the personalized system of local taxation. After several seemingly deliberate misunderstandings, the head of the tax office revealed that in 1997 sanctions contributed 'at least 40 per cent' to locally-collected tax revenues. This means that almost half of the taxes do not stem from the creation of economic value, but from tax offences, mistakes of accountants, lacking qualification and unfavourable relations with the tax office.

For the practice of tax evasion, the significance of the informal institutionalization of sanctions is threefold. First, sanctions serve as a convenient valve to relieve the local tax office of the pressure from the regional authorities to collect taxes. The sums which inspectors can collect through sanctioning provide them with the flexibility to tolerate tax evasion in other cases. Thus, the tax officers' power of sanctioning creates a semi-legal sphere within which they can autonomously, and according to their own interests, decide how and where to collect the federal revenues. Second, the arbitrary practice of sanctioning results in a further personalization and 'informalization' of taxation. Sanctions are even less predictable and incalculable for businesses than taxes that create more room for informal negotiations and render entrepreneurs at the mercy of individual tax officers. Third, the excessive imposition of sanctions decreases the risk of tax evasion. Although in the short run sanctions may boost revenues, in the long run their inevitability undermines tax discipline and decreases tax turnouts. As entrepreneurs know that they will be sanctioned anyway, it does not make much difference whether they evade taxes or not. Sanctions need not so much be feared by those who evade taxes, as by those who have not mastered the art of friendship with relevant officials. The amount of sanctions, and thereby the amount of revenue lost or gained by the Federation, is subsequently decided by the quality of personal relations.

6. *Limits to the personalization*

It has been argued above that the flawed legal framework of taxation encourages and even necessitates personalized and interested practices of evasion by the primary actors on the local level. Formal constraints and informal dispositions to rework them on the basis of personal relations form a rather coherent and relatively stable local tax system. Its continuous inefficiency may not make sense in the abstract logic of the federal budget, but it does in the personal logic of the various actors involved. Similarly, informal local practices appear deviant and criminal from the federal perspective, but in the local context they are self-evident ways to defend one's interests. This coherence of local tax practices, however, should also not be overestimated. Those involved have to pay a considerable price for the discrepancy between formal law and informal practice. That is, they live under the threat of 'suspended punishment'.[10] This mechanism leaves taxpayers in a constant position of legal uncertainty and correspondingly in fear of potential legal prosecution. Their systemic insecurity is fueled by three sources: first, the inevitability to take recourse in unlawful practices; second, the dependence on the cooperation of officials; and third, the lack of a clear dividing line between what is legal and what is illegal. Thus, the lenient and often hazy legislation on the one hand creates a certain freedom and flexibility for taxpayers, but on the other enables the authorities to intervene whenever they consider this to be desirable. This keeps the taxpayers in a permanent position of uncertainty. As many of their practices lack any legal basis, they are well aware that the current state of suspended punishment could, at any time, turn into actual punishment when the sword of Damocles falls upon them.

This feeling of being at the mercy of informal personal relations on the one hand, and some remote state power on the other, seems to trigger a tacit trend of formalization of local taxation. The evidence suggests that legal qualification

---

[10] This phrase was introduced by A. V. Ledeneva, *Russia's Economy of Favours: Blat, Networking and Informal Exchange* (Cambridge University Press, Cambridge, 1998), p. 77.

is beginning to play a considerable role in the power relations of taxation. Although the local practice of taxation is still determined by informal practices rather than by formal procedures between equally well-qualified actors, qualification is an ascending asset which is increasingly sought after by entrepreneurs to improve their positions of power. This is because the personalized practices illustrated above mainly boost the power of tax officers, but for taxpayers they entail insecurity and dependence. Being at the mercy of individual tax officers still seems to be the lesser evil in comparison to being at the mercy of the law, but the relative merit of personal dependence appears to be shrinking. With political pressure for tax revenues rising nation-wide, and tax laws becoming more comprehensive, the times when everything was possible for all have passed. Local entrepreneurs can no longer rely blindly on the support of tax inspectors. As a result, corporate taxpayers begin to change their strategies and struggle for their interests formal ways by gaining the relevant legal qualification. Taxpayers appear to be interested, crudely speaking, in substituting objective knowledge for subjective relations.

> In 1993, when we started working, everything was possible. Then we could always come to an agreement with the tax office. But by now the whole thing has become more civilized. Today friendship with the tax office has its limits. Only inexperienced businessmen think that a good present solves everything. But experienced entrepreneurs understand that you have to give more and more presents and then you get totally dependent. No, it is better to have a faultless accountancy and to know your own way through the system. This is why juridical firms have begun to flourish.

If legal qualifications indeed become a valuable asset in the daily practice of taxation, they may develop into a considerable counterpoise to the personalization of the system. The notable fact that both parties, the tax collectors and the taxpayers, accused each other of lacking qualification in interviews may be an indication that the value of qualification is becoming commonly recognized. This would be a significant emancipation from the Soviet legacy of a traditionally-low regard for qualification in comparison to personal networking. For this tacit tendency to develop, however, the future development of tax legislation is of great importance. Legislation can triumph over personalization only if it is comprehensible, reliable and comprehensive. Therefore, for the time being, it still seems to be the norm that informal arrangements substitute for the widespread lack of qualification.

III. SOCIAL DISPOSITIONS UNDERMINING FORMAL TAXATION

It has been illustrated above that systemic shortcomings of Russian taxation provide opportunities to engage in informal evasion practices. It is important to note, however, that the incentive function of these opportunities is greatly enhanced in the Russian context by people's dispositions to act in corresponding ways. This social disposition is rooted in a) people's expectations and skills inherited from the Soviet past, and b) their willingness to evade due to the tax system's fundamental lack of legitimacy. Thus the system of inefficient tax collection, which the criminalization campaign appears to be unable to sever, is supported on the one hand by structural shortcomings, and on the other hand by the actors' pre-existing readiness to use these shortcomings. In the following, this observed readiness to circumvent official proceedings in the routine of taxation and to substitute them with personalized ones will be traced back to the Soviet experience of bureaucratic relations. Subsequently, the tax system's lack of legitimacy will be depicted as an additional impetus for informal negotiation and evasion practices.

1.   The Soviet legacy of personalization

The evidence collected in Peterhof seems to suggest that even under conditions of a more comprehensive and reliable legal structure, both taxpayers and tax officers would personalize the system through their behavior. There appears to be a strong disposition to base the practice of taxation on the personalization of official relations, the roots of which are most likely to be found in the actors' Soviet experience, when interactions with any member of the privileged bureaucracy tended to be matters of personal interaction rather than legal guidelines. This notion is supported by comments like the following by the owner of Peterhof's biggest department store:

> People that work for the state have not changed. They never change. They know that we need them, and so they exploit us. Ten years ago I had to bribe them for a new telephone, now I bribe them so as not to pay taxes for a new employee. Or maybe I don't bribe them, maybe I just have to maintain friendship with them, that's all. I have learned to live like this a long time ago, it's OK.

This habitual disposition to personalize legal proceedings is based on coinciding expectations from both sides, and on the corresponding skills to accommodate the informal processes effortlessly in official routines. Thus, the businessmen's art of networking is complemented by the tax officers' skill to receive favours inconspicuously, as expressed by this female tax inspector:

> I know that in my department no one ever accepts anything from entrepreneurs. But when someone brings a box of chocolates, or perfume, or flowers, or offers you coffee during the inspection, I don't regard it as corruption, but simply as attention. After all we are people, aren't we?

These informal expectations, skills and procedures are inherent in the Soviet legacy of relying upon personal trust rather than legality. Combined with the unreliability of the formal legal basis of taxation, they effectively serve to stabilize the inefficient system of local taxation. Below is depicted a third factor of the systemic and social basis of the pervasiveness of tax evasion.

2. The lack of legitimacy

The tax system's fundamental lack of legitimacy is another crucial aspect that fuels people's readiness to disregard their fiscal duties, and which contributes to sustaining pervasive tax evasion practices. It may be traced back in particular to three sources. First, taxes are an almost totally new phenomenon, with which taxpayers are very reluctant to reconcile themselves. In contrast to other market economies, Russian entrepreneurs are not used to paying direct taxes and do not consider taxes as given costs. Before 1992, Russians had virtually no experience of direct taxation, as indirect, price-increasing taxes used to account for, on average, more than 60 per cent of Soviet revenue.[11] As a result, paying taxes never became an established and accepted part of being a Russian citizen or entrepreneur.[12] Therefore, despite the fact that the Soviet indirect tax burden was among the highest in the world,[13] Russia lacks a legitimizing tradition of taxation. This problem is particularly stressed by the tax collectors, as, for example, by the head of the Peterhof tax office:

> There is no such tradition that the duty of paying taxes has already been accepted by generations. The history of our tax system is only five years old … You probably watched it on television, when the Finance Minister met with Agutin and the other pop-stars and explained to them that they have to pay taxes from their income. Do you understand what kind of situation we are in, when we have to meet, explain and persuade our taxpayers to comply with the law? In your country there is no need for that.

Moreover, the tax attitudes of the interviewed entrepreneurs still seem to stem from the late *perestroika* years, when an entrepreneur's duty was fulfilled by showing some self-initiative and by working into his or her own pocket. Ten years ago, young private entrepreneurialism was hardly constrained by the then very lax tax regulations. The head of the tax police alludes to the problem that the recent history of the tax system undermines its current legitimacy.

> People think that once they opened a private enterprise, they can work only for themselves, and don't have to pay the community. Four, five years ago, you probably noticed those masses of kiosks. When entrepreneurialism and the free market were only just beginning, everything was allowed.

---

[11] With the exception of the war years. See F. D. Holzman and P. J. Pettibone, 'Steuern' in C. D. Kerning (ed.), *Sowjetsystem und Demokratische Gesellschaft: Eine Vergleichende Enzyklopaedie* (Herder, Freiburg, 1972), p. 255.

[12] The ignorance about the *de facto* heavy indirect tax burden seems to have been actively promoted by the government: Soviet economic textbooks avoided using the word 'tax', replacing it with phrases like 'the state's centralized net income'. It was then claimed that in contrast to capitalist states, the Soviet government raised nearly all its revenues without recourse to taxation. A. Nove, *The Soviet Economy: An Introduction*, rev. 3rd edtn. (George Allen & Unwin, London, 1968), p. 114.

[13] Under the Soviet regime, taxes used to amount to about half of Gross Domestic Product (GDP), which is twice as much as, for example, in the USA. See Holzman and Pettibone, n. 11 above, p. 258.

A second reason for the tax system's lack of legitimacy is the discrepancy perceived by the respondents between paid taxes and received public services. In Russia's deteriorating welfare state, it is becoming less and less convincing to legitimize the government's tax demands by reference to the public services it provides in return. The government finds itself locked in the vicious circle of decreasing revenues, deteriorating public services and people's growing unwillingness to pay as a result of it. One respondent expresses his perception of having to pay for nothing: 'Maybe I would pay taxes if I knew that in return we would get good hospitals and good pensions. But when I am old they will give me hardly enough for bread and water'.

Moreover, using the provision of public services as an effective source of legitimacy is also problematic in view of the Soviet experience when people hardly paid any direct taxes, but were provided superior services. As a result there was no awareness, as the one carefully fostered in the West, that taxes are necessary to finance public service.[14]

A third problem undermining the legitimacy of the tax system is the uneven distribution of the tax burden. In comparison with the taxation of individuals, taxation of the corporate sector appears to be excessive. According to Goskomstat, individual income tax in 1996 accounted for only 2.1 per cent of government revenues. In the Organization for Economic Cooperation and Deveolpment (OECD) countries income tax accounts for about 30 per cent of revenues on average. Accordingly, the respondents claim to be 'squeezed' as the weakest link in the economic chain. This feeling of being unfairly exploited is expressed by this respondent who complains about the allegedly one-sided financing of the public infrastructure: 'Why should I as an entrepreneur be the only one who pays for streets and transport? No one else does, and they use them as much as I do'.

Another justifies tax evasion by hinting at privileged big and state enterprises:

> The big companies don't pay, it's OK with them, but the small ones they squeeze. Only yesterday they said on television that state enterprises owe USD900 million to the state. So when we as entrepreneurs realize that at the state level they simply delete huge sums of debt, then we try to do the same: somehow escape from taxes.

This is an example of how the disregard for the law, practiced by the government by granting unlawful privileges to major corporations, perpetuates itself. In response, non-privileged enterprises feel unfairly exploited and consider themselves justified in disrespecting the law and evading taxes themselves. This perpetuation of unofficial practices continues to erode the tax system's legitimacy and thus people's impediment to look for cracks in the official system, to instrumentalize them and to circumscribe their fiscal duties. Given that Russian taxpayers and officials have no

---

[14] In mid-1999 the Tax and Duty Ministry introduced a new poster campaign showing run-down hospitals and schools, and asking the onlooker to pay his taxes. By emphasizing the dependence of the social sector upon tax compliance, the campaign seeks to fill the detrimental gap in public awareness created by the Soviet legacy of indirect taxation.

severe social disincentive to ignore the imperatives of the law, they employ their informal skills inherited from the Soviet past and exploit the opportunities offered by the formal system. As it thus synthesizes past experience with present constraints, the personalization of local taxation is carried out in a self-evident and unreflective fashion. It is natural to people rather than abnormal or deviant.

IV. CONCLUSION

This paper has sought to illustrate that tax evasion practices in Russia are based on the solid foundation of, first, shortcomings in the institutional and legal structure, second, the social disposition of personalizing bureaucratic relations, and third, the fundamental lack of legitimacy suffered by the government's tax claims. This threefold support for disregarding official procedures explains both the pervasiveness of tax evasion and the futility of portraying its constituent processes as criminal. The practices that cause the phenomenon of tax evasion are facilitated, and sometimes necessitated, by the structural constraints, and they correspond with people's pre-existing expectations and skills. Thus they are not deviant, but obvious ways of acting according to one's interests, along the line of least resistance under the given conditions. For example, the practices of informally dodging local tax collection targets, or of personally approaching tax officials appear to be too easy and self-evident to the local actors to be considered illegal or criminal.

The conceptualization of tax evasion as consisting of mundane and everyday practices within the given structural constraints thus overcomes the dichotomy between legal compliance on the one hand, and illegal, criminal evasion on the other hand. The self-evidence of the informal strategies, supported both by systemic and social conditions, explains why the processes constituting the phenomenon of tax evasion elude criminalization in the Russian context. Neither the formal system nor people's practical dispositions are directly opposed to the informal practices. People's self-interested and self-defensive strategies do not deviate from the official system, but blend with it. Under these circumstances the actual roots of tax evasion seem to be too deeply engrained in the normality of public routines to be recognized as criminal. As a result, the government's criminalization campaign is doomed only to enter superficially the public's awareness. It may conceptualize and condemn the outcome of the above-depicted fragmented practices as an economic crime, but the constituent practices themselves remain unquestioned aspects of routine local processes. That way the inefficient tax system continues to be reproduced amidst the moralizing posters and television clips.

10

'Everyday Crime' at the Workplace: Covert Earning Schemes in Russia's New Commercial Sector

Karen Birdsall

I. INTRODUCTION

At first glance, Russia's small-scale commercial sector appears riddled with idiosyncrasies. The bewildering paradox surrounding wages highlights some of the most glaring 'irrationalities' – not only are workers' salaries inadequate to meet the escalating cost of living, but even in private firms, employees often do not receive their wages on time or in full. When compared with the transparent regularity of Western commercial sectors, it is difficult to comprehend how Russian workers can survive in their daily lives under such conditions. Equally puzzling is how the system itself manages to endure and to carry on functioning in a surprisingly stable fashion. Russia's abiding 'disorder' has evolved into a natural equilibrium that stands in stark contrast to the anticipated outcomes of market reforms.

As the observable macro reality alone cannot adequately reveal the basis of this paradox, it is necessary to identify the micro-level processes which allow the prevailing order to be sustained in its imperfect state. In contexts in which everyday life is severely constrained and the formal framework is incapable of meeting basic needs, people rely upon informal techniques for coping with the challenges of everyday life. In contemporary Russia, where changes to the formal structures have been hopelessly eclipsed by the runaway pace of economic and societal transformation, recourse to informal practices is the most efficient way to bridge the cracks in the formal system and to solve day to day problems. In the case of the above-mentioned 'wage paradox', one such informal technique for 'closing the gaps' is the surreptitious earning of unrecorded, unofficial money by employees at the official workplace. These financial 'extras' are made, cautiously, through practised manipulations that are carefully concealed in the shadows and carried out alongside workers' official responsibilities. Described by their practitioners through a rich assortment of Russian colloquialisms, this paper refers collectively to these systematic, secretive distortions as 'covert earning schemes'. Money made by overcharging customers, pocketing fees for official services, or diverting clientele from the firm – all examples of covert earning – represent informal sources of income

145

A. V. Ledeneva and M. Kurkchiyan (eds.), Economic Crime in Russia, 145–162
© 2000 Kluwer Law International. Printed in Great Britain.

for employees. While these earnings are based upon isolated, small-scale transactions, they can constitute a fundamental part of workers' overall reward packages when taken as a whole. In the prevailing conditions of economic scarcity, covert earnings can be as vital to livelihood as official wages.

This paper, based upon ethnographic material on contemporary covert earning practices in the commercial sector,[1] highlights the critical role played by the dynamic, but largely invisible 'underside' of the workplace in sustaining its precarious functioning and in contributing to the maintenance of 'civil peace' in Russia.[2] It is argued that covert earning should be seen as a reaction by ordinary people to the constraints of daily life in post-Soviet Russia, rather than being indicative of criminal or deviant behaviour. While covert earning practices may not have a place in the market reform trajectory envisioned by the architects of Russian reform, they play a vital stabilizing role in the turbulent post-Soviet milieu. Those who would label Russia's economy as 'chaotic' might regard earning schemes as simply one more manifestation of the larger disorder; however, it is suggested here that Russia's economy, far from being chaotic, follows its own coherent order which is grounded squarely in customary ways of getting things done.[3] These customary practices, such as covert earning schemes, operate outside the reach of formal structures and procedures. They evince their own logic – one which appears entirely consistent with both historically-conditioned and currently-evolving popular attitudes towards the respective roles of the individual, state and society, and which is based upon shared understandings about the unwritten 'rules of the game'. If, from without, these earning practices are regarded as deviations and criminal infractions that impede the emergence of economic transparency, from within they are a natural component of everyday life and a self-evident way of defending one's interests. This discrepancy in perception is critical for understanding the friction between the ideals of market reform and the realities of the evolving post-Soviet order.

This paper will examine the phenomenon of contemporary earning practices and reveal them as central to the everyday workings of the Russian economy. In the first part of the paper, a conceptualisation of covert earning schemes will be suggested and the operational basis of the practice will be illustrated through a series of examples.

---

[1]   This paper is based upon original ethnographic material collected in Russia in December 1998 and March–April 1999. Fifteen semi-structured interviews were conducted with workers and managers in small commercial firms of less than 50 employees (primarily retail trade, service, and hospitality/catering firms). Interviews with workers were conducted in an industrial community of 150,000 people in the Moscow Region; interviews with managers were arranged separately in Moscow and St. Petersburg. The limited scope of this study means that the conclusions drawn from the material can be taken only as possible indications of larger trends. It is anticipated that more comprehensive research into covert earning schemes would corroborate these initial findings and contribute to their generalizability. For a longer version of this paper, see K. Birdsall, 'Practices of Survival: Covert Earning Schemes at the Russian Workplace' (MPhil diss., University of Cambridge, June 1999).

[2]   A. V. Ledeneva ('Virtual Crime', chapter 11 of this volume) suggests that the notion of 'civil peace' has once again taken precedence over the development of a vibrant civil society, carrying on an established tradition of 'deals' between the population and leadership.

[3]   See C. Humphrey, chapter 12 of this volume.

The second part of the paper will address the practice's internal order by presenting the ways in which covert earning is perceived, understood and reconciled by its practitioners in a benign, not criminal context. In highlighting the systemic and popular forces that underpin covert earning, it is argued that such schemes represent an utterly natural facet of the post-Soviet landscape and a logical response on the part of their practitioners to the constraints of the prevailing structural framework.

II.   WHAT ARE COVERT EARNING SCHEMES?

Covert earning schemes belong to the repertoire of shadowy workplace-based 'tactics' that are employed fluidly in daily life to cope with the pressures of market reform. They represent subterfuges of varying degrees of complexity – from minor deceptions of customers to the systematic undercutting of the firm – which allow workers to garner unofficial income above and beyond their official wages. Money made on the side combines with official income to compose an employee's overall reward package – in some cases they merely supplement low or overdue wages, while in others they form a substantial part of earnings.[4] Earning schemes are a technique by which workers reconcile themselves to the chronic deficiencies of the new market order through short-termist micro-level exploitations aimed at immediate personal gain. Rather than acting collectively to replace the inefficient structures altogether, practitioners instead individually compensate for the flaws in the system on an on-going basis.

Covert earning takes a variety of forms, but can be distinguished by four salient characteristics. First, covert earning schemes are unofficial, unsanctioned tactics for earning money through an official workplace. The Russian workplace, like its Soviet-era predecessor, is rife with opportunities for non-monetary gain.[5] Yet earning schemes are notable for their overt focus upon monetized reward – a fact which is in keeping with the overall monetization of Russian society. Contacts, connections, and access to goods – all vital 'survival' assets during the Soviet era[6] – have been downgraded in the new hyper-monetized atmosphere of capitalist Russia. Instead, money has become the new 'deficit good' as it takes on increasing significance in the daily lives of the Russian population.

---

4   This 'layering' of formal and informal is vital to workers' overall livelihood, as seen in the following account from a parking lot attendant: 'In reality, I have three different wages: there's my official wage as far as the government's concerned, my official wage from the firm, and my own personal 'official' wage! Officially, as far as the state knows, I earn 184 roubles and 26 kopecks. The firm actually pays me 5,000 roubles. At the end of it all, I take home 8,000 roubles ... And that's what I live on'.

5   The Soviet-era practice of *vynos* (the 'carrying-away' of socialist property for personal use or reappropriation) remains alive and well, but was not the focus of this research. On *vynos*, see G. Grossman, 'The "Second Economy" of the USSR' (1977) 26 *Problems of Communism*, pp. 25–40; F. J. M. Feldbrugge, 'The Soviet Second Economy in a Political and Legal Perspective' in E. L. Feige (ed.), *The Underground Economies: Tax Evasion and Information Distortion* (Cambridge University Press, Cambridge, 1989), pp. 318–320.

6   See A. V. Ledeneva, *Russia's Economy of Favours: Blat, Networking and Informal Exchange* (Cambridge University Press, Cambridge, 1998).

Second, covert earning schemes operate in the shadows. Unlike tips, which are usually tolerated by company management, covert earnings are made at the expense of the firm or its client base. This makes covert earning a risky endeavour – practitioners must be vigilant against detection of their unsanctioned activity by management. In contrast to the Soviet workplace where property and assets were 'everyone's and no one's' simultaneously, the privatized workplace is overseen by an owner who is invested in the firm's success and overall solvency.[7]

Third, while covert earnings can supplement a worker's wages, they are not usually done at a scale adequate to clear a serious profit. Earning schemes flourish where there are cracks in the system which are ripe for exploitation; they often depend upon systematic distortions of regular transactions. Thus, their small-scale application allows practitioners to 'tread water', but they do not form a basis for getting ahead. Elaborate manipulations are employed in order to 'break even'.

Finally, covert earning schemes are flexible and situation dependent. They respond dynamically to changing conditions and demand a degree of ingenuity. One respondent, a parking lot attendant, put it this way:

> That there was room to make money here – I knew the very first day on the job. But how to make it – that's a skill that's taken time to perfect. A person can't work all of this out in a day or two. The longer we work, the more the whole thing develops … It's really impossible to explain all the nuances. It all depends upon the concrete situation. You really need to see it and feel it.

For this respondent, covert earnings are the wages he can make 'with his head'. In this sense, the making of unofficial income is a satisfying and cunning game – a departure from official obligations and an unspoken challenge to authority and official structures.

Covert earning schemes should be seen as inheritors of the legacy of the Soviet informal economy, in which a 'mentality of survival' linked together a constellation of everyday informal techniques oriented towards resolving mundane needs. Survival was a continuous, unconscious process guided by a type of circumstantial thinking that allowed changing conditions to be addressed fluidly and automatically by operating on the margins and exploiting grey zones. Given that such habits are engrained, they stubbornly resist the attempts at rational reorganization promulgated as part of the market reform agenda. Thus, for Russians well-schooled in navigating the constraints of the Soviet system, the challenges of the post-Soviet era represent unfamiliar obstacles that can be circumvented in familiar ways. 'How do people here live and get by?' a young mechanic asked rhetorically – 'The same as we always have – through native wit and ingenuity'. Earning practices are viewed as

---

[7] Although not the focus of this study, it became clear during interviews with managers that covert earning is actively 'battled' through a variety of techniques aimed at detection and suppression. While Western-trained managers spoke about motivating employees and regularly rotating them through different positions as a way of minimizing unofficial earning routines, other managers relied upon the use of friends and 'spies' to monitor transactions occurring at the workplace.

part of an unbroken tradition of embedded habits and skills that have been transferred from the past. A manager of a bakery made the following comment:

> I think it's practically a post-Soviet mentality. People were placed into such conditions that they were forced to survive – to think up some way to increase their income. And since people aren't stupid, it follows that they've always come up with lots of different ways to do that ... I've noticed that many workers have retained this style of work and style of life. Although the old way of life may have changed, it certainly hasn't changed for the better for many people.

Covert earning is pervasive and is widely regarded as an unremarkable, self-evident aspect of the Russian occupational experience. 'Each job has its own "specific" ... its own "principle" for unsanctioned business', said one respondent. Another put it this way: 'You have to understand that people never think about it – it's just done automatically'. Covert earning is 'here, there, and everywhere', bearing almost an instinctive, reflexive character. One respondent reflected upon his earnings this way:

> It's like this – I walk by, stop, have a few berries, and keep on going. All the same, I still want to eat. But if there's the chance to help myself to berries on the way, well ...

Yet at the same time that covert earning is seen as universal, it is shrouded in a hushed quasi-secrecy. While its prevalence is not denied, the topic is treated with caution:

> We don't usually discuss these things, to be honest. Maybe if we're sitting around with a group of close friends, drinking and exchanging stories, it might possibly come up. But usually, no ... If you ask me how a friend of mine works the system at his job, I couldn't tell you the details. I know that he does, but I couldn't tell you how. It's just not something you talk about.

This ambiguity is reflected in its diffuse discursive treatment. Practitioners rely upon an assortment of opaque, morally-neutral terms such as *levye den'gi* ('left money'), *levyi zarabotok* ('left earnings'), *kalym* ('gray money'), *svoi biznes* ('my own business'), and *prirabotok* ('extra earnings') to reference unofficial money made at the workplace. These earnings can be realized through the use of *smekalka* ('native wit') or by 'mischievous' actions such as 'playing' (*poigrat'*), 'twisting' (*krutit'*), 'getting around' (*obkhodit'*), 'thinking up' (*pridumat'*) and 'outsmarting' (*obkhitrit'/obvesti*). A much more value-laden, pejorative terminology is utilized by those who view covert earning in a 'criminal' light. Unofficial earnings are equated with *vorovstvo* (theft), *obman* (deception), *khishchenie* (pilfering), and *nezakonnyi dokhod* (illegal income); its practitioners were dishonest (*nechestnye*) or disloyal (*nevernye*) individuals who steal (*vorovat'*), deceive (*obmanut'*) and 'grab' (*urvat'*).

This discursive dichotomy embodies the friction surrounding the realm of earning practices. Those individuals who unreflectively carry out earning schemes understand their actions in benign terms, while those in official or external positions of control label and categorize them unambiguously using the language of criminality. This perceptual schism at the micro level is paralleled, but magnified at the macro level: misperceptions about 'everyday crime' and 'disorder' at the Russian workplace block a comprehensive understanding about the way the Russian economy actually 'works' and the internal logic which guides it.

III.   EXAMPLES OF COVERT EARNING SCHEMES

Interviews with respondents revealed dozens of examples of earning schemes; these have been divided roughly into two groups and will be examined more closely below. The first group of earning schemes involves manipulations of official business transactions to realize monetary earnings. As these distorted transactions utilize standard forms, they *appear* identical to routine interactions. Their success lies in the fact that they are, at a glance, indistinguishable from undistorted transactions. Such practices co-opt established mechanisms that are fundamental to legitimate business and operate squarely within official frameworks. Workers introduce deviations into a set of established, 'official' procedures, but remain strictly within the confines of the existing system. Two types of practices within this group will be examined: 1) substitution of unofficial goods; and 2) distortions of sales transactions.

The second group of earning practices, instead of operating from within official transactions, is located closer to the margins of the workplace. These techniques draw parasitically upon the occupational context, but are not intrinsic to the business itself; they represent external 'add-ons'. Where the first family of practices involves distortions of routine operations, the second set represents exploitations of the 'grey zones' at the fringes of the workplace. Three practices will be considered in detail: 1) diverting customers for a private client base; 2) using the firm's assets for earning purposes; and 3) pocketing fees for services rendered through the firm.

1.   Substitution of unofficial goods

The most frequently-mentioned earning scheme involves employees substituting 'outside' goods for officially-sanctioned ones and profiting off the price differential. Most commonly encountered in trade settings, the substitution of goods was cited by respondents as the simplest and most pervasive technique for profiting off the workplace. The following account of a former salesperson at a 24-hour shop outlines the basis of this practice:

> At the time that I was working, there were a few commercial kiosks in town which opened at eight in the morning and where it was possible to buy goods, including cartons of cigarettes, really cheaply – at wholesale prices. At night-time, we sold a lot of cigarettes. We would probably sell eight cartons of each brand of cigarettes – at 20 packs a carton, that's a lot of cigarettes. We would

write in the inventory log that we sold one or two cartons of each brand. Right at 8 AM when the kiosks with the wholesale goods would open, one of us would run over there, buy up the exact same cigarettes at a lower cost, come back and put them out. No one knew – it was if nothing had been sold. But the difference – that was big money! Over the course of a night, we would sell such a volume of cigarettes that one person couldn't even carry back all the replacements … When I would leave the shop every day after my shift, in addition to my salary, I'd always have in my pocket at least 200 to 300 roubles.

While this example of substitution involved the complicity of a team of employees, individual examples of the practice were also cited:

For example, I have a husband. While I'm standing at the market, selling [coffee], he can quickly dash to the wholesale market and bring back a few cans of coffee. I sell 'my' coffee – the boss's coffee can get sold tomorrow.

Two further examples illustrate a similar principle at work in different settings. The first involves the manipulation of tickets and documentation, while the second is tied to the market in counterfeit vodka:

The system of bookkeeping for selling tickets is absurd, because you are only required to account for the quantity of tickets which you've sold … There are always ways not to give out tickets – or to give out other tickets … I knew a guy who worked at a night club. He did the following. Say that 700 people were admitted into the night club. Well they [the employees] came up with their own ridiculous tickets – a stamp on a piece of paper or something. Not real tickets. The people going in didn't pay any attention – what difference does it make to them what piece of paper they're handed? So they [the employees] would take the money and would give out real tickets to only 300 people. That's a lot of money that they pocketed.

You used to be able to find the fake stuff (*levoe*) everywhere. By quality it was alright, but it was produced somewhere other than at the factory. It was so profitable for me. I could make 200 per cent on a bottle of vodka … Somewhere or other, people collected bottles, bought pure alcohol, brought the bottles home, cleaned them up, bought labels and corks, dumped the alcohol into a washing machine and mixed it up with water. The whole thing was poured into the bottles and sealed up with corks … Of course it's forbidden. But it generated an unbelievable amount of money … People managed to survive as a result of this alone.

A related process occurs when employees surreptitiously introduce products that are not designated for sale through the shop and sell them parallel to the official inventory. In this case, standard commercial mechanisms provide the channels for salespeople to integrate outside goods into an already-functioning framework:

Selling unofficial goods happens in much the same way. The salesperson doesn't enter the products in the inventory, he sets them out on display and sells them alongside the other goods. That way, the salesperson is able to move his own goods through the framework of the shop. Like that. He's right there at work, like he should be, but is able to sell his own things.

The replacement of cheaper, counterfeit or unofficial goods for ones priced by management for retail profit works directly to the detriment of the business by eroding turnover and profit. At the same time, it allows employees to realize monetary earnings from commonplace transactions. As the practice is enacted through routine transactions and the use of seemingly official products, it is a system easy to execute and difficult to detect.

2.   *Distortions of sales transactions*

A second commonly-mentioned earning practice involves the distortion of standard sales transactions. Salespeople, bartenders, and service personnel can 'underserve' or overcharge customers and keep the difference for themselves. Again relying upon a familiar format for official interactions, these practices can be extremely difficult to detect while resulting in meaningful profits when performed repeatedly. The following examples illustrate how these distortions occur:

> For example, a salesperson measures out lengths of fabric for customers – three meters for one, four for another, 10 for someone else, and so forth. And each time, they undermeasure by five centimetres. From that particular roll, a whole meter's left! The money for that meter goes right into their pocket.

> So many people go through a bar ... and you never check how much they pour in your glass. I know that lots of people make money like that ... For instance, in a keg of beer, you know that there are 99 glasses. You sell 99 glasses, but you didn't pour them fully, so now you have more. Every extra glass you sell goes into your pocket.

> You take a weight, make a hole in the bottom, and fill it with a lighter metal. That way you end up with 800 grams instead of a kilogram. So I can underweigh you by 200 grams. And if I underweigh you by 200 grams, I put the difference for those 200 grams in my pocket ... There are so many nuances to this, so many ways that people get cheated.

Many such examples were cited in interviews; in each case the operating principle was the same. Employees use their control over commercial resources and their constant interaction with customers to skim small, undetectable amounts of money off routine transactions. Monetary earnings can, therefore, be realized through the continuous, yet imperceptible under-fulfilment of official responsibilities.

A slightly different application of this technique occurs through the conscious 'undoing' or 'untwisting' of a customer (*raskruchivanie klienta*) on a more significant scale. Employees can use their position, knowledge and authority from the workplace to exploit customers in the market for goods or services:

> Another process that we frequently used was the *raskruchivanie* of customers. If a client would come who didn't know the first thing [about car alarms], we would name a higher price. So if it was supposed to cost USD100 to install a system, we'd quote him USD120. He'd agree and we'd put the extra USD20 in our pockets ... If a customer was willing to pay – just like that – we'd surely take it. There was no reason whatsoever to refuse.

The authority conferred on employees by affiliation with an official workplace aids them in overcharging customers for standardly-priced services. Channeled through a legitimate service framework, the practice blends easily into the prevailing business context.

3.   Diverting customers

Employees in the service and commercial sector continuously meet and interact with potential customers. While the official role that they can fulfil is constrained by the structure of the workplace, informal options exist for transacting business outside the channels of the firm. Respondents' comments indicate that the official workplace can serve as a valuable forum for building a personal clientele that is serviced separate from the firm itself:

> A client comes to a store to buy furniture, for example. The salesperson tells him that the particular furniture he's interested in is no longer stocked. While he could suggest a different option, instead he agrees to find the customer's preferred furniture himself and arranges with another company to have the furniture delivered. So in that way he earns his money separately with the help of another firm.

> There are visiting nurses, like me, who have a way of making additional money. Though our work, we come across clients who will pay money to have their injections done. So besides our scheduled visits for the polyclinic, these clients can call up personally and ask us to stop by when we're near their homes.

> We work out of a garage. A person will stop in to inquire about installing a car alarm. We'll tell him – if it's through the firm, it will cost you such and such. Say USD200. If you don't go through the firm, we'll give you a home telephone number in case anything goes wrong, and will only charge you USD170. Of course he'll agree to USD170.

While in some cases, these are 'one-off' transactions that develop spontaneously to the benefit of both parties, there are other cases in which on-going relationships are established and a personal client base is built. The diversion of clientele from the firm to a personal network provides the worker with an independent base of activity and source of income while eroding the foundation of the firm's business.

4.   *Using the firm's assets for personal earning*

The Soviet era phenomenon of the 'gatekeeper'[8] finds its contemporary parallel in cases where assets belonging to the firm are utilized by employees for private gain. While the employees are not at liberty to dispose of firm assets freely, their occupational role and physical access creates a grey zone in which to play.

The following example from a parking lot attendant at a busy hotel/casino illustrates the way in which official workplace rules are mediated in order to carve out earning opportunities. Responsible for a limited number of parking spaces reserved for free use by employees, management and regular customers, the employee and his co-workers glean hefty earnings by manipulating the official rules and allowing access to parking for non-designated individuals:

> The rules? Well, I don't have the right to park any outside (*chuzhie*) cars in the lot, except for regular customers … Taxi drivers, for example – I don't have the right to let them wait here. [Smiles][9] And I don't have the right to accept any money for parking.

> What happens is that we have official clients who come to the casino, and we have unofficial clients – our own 'personal' clients, who are known only by the six of us who work here. We know them by sight – some come regularly, some come irregularly. Sometimes they come to the casino or just stop by on their own business (*po svoim delam*) … And they know that they can park their car with us, that we're always friendly, we'll take care of everything for them. First of all, it's nice for them. And the money which we get for it – it doesn't matter to them in the slightest. It's not a problem for them whatsoever. They're just pleased to have someone who says hello, goodbye, asks them how things are going … It's not just that we take money from them – it's also a kind of friendly relationship (*druzheskie otnosheniia*) … There are people who have been coming to us for two years now. We know them well and they know us well.

---

[8]   During the Soviet era, public resources were often interpreted as quasi-private; physical or administrative control over goods was a crucial asset. 'Gatekeepers' were individuals through whom goods or resources in short supply could be accessed. This misappropriation of socialist property occurred with the help of a variety of informal techniques, including the use of *blat* and favours. For more on gatekeepers, see Ledeneva, n. 6 above, p. 125.

[9]   At the time of the interview, four taxis were waiting in the restricted parking area. The respondent knew each of the drivers by name.

A similar process occurs among official drivers for state agencies and taxi drivers at private firms, as one respondent explained:

> How can taxi drivers get around official requirements? They have a radio and are summoned by the dispatcher to pick up passengers at a certain location. They pick up the customer and are driving with him when they come across someone on the side of the road signalling for a car. 'Do we take him?' they'll ask the passenger. 'Of course – go ahead'. People have to earn money somehow. So the taxi driver gets 15 roubles from the first client, and 15 for the second. One fare is official, the other goes into his pocket.

In both cases, separate earning opportunities are built up using the time, space and professional context of the workplace. These practices, which constitute a separate strand of informal activity within the same occupational context, are braided together seamlessly with employees' official responsibilities.

5.   Pocketing fees

Respondents frequently mentioned the practice of employees pocketing fees for services rendered through the firm. This form of covert earning depends upon the ability to hide part of the income flow; it appears most effective in contexts where numerous repeated transactions provide a cover for keeping some of the fees.

The following two examples require a degree of collusion between the employee and customer:

> Take an overnight car park, for example. A car comes and the driver wants to leave the car overnight. The driver should get a receipt and the attendant should hand over the money to the boss. But instead, he doesn't log in the car, and keeps the money for himself.

> My wife gets weekly massages. She can pay the full amount of 50 roubles directly to the firm. Or, she can pay a reduced rate of 30 roubles if it goes · directly to the masseuse. Either way, it happens through the firm and during the masseuse's official workday.

In other instances, it may be imperceptible to the client that the transaction is not entirely 'official':

> When a client shows up, we always look at him closely. He could be an inspector from the Tax Police ... So we try never to talk openly about what's happening – for example, this is official, this isn't, and so forth ... We just don't say anything about the firm – that it's supposed to cost such and such to do this job. We tell him that it'll cost USD170, and then we do the job. Even if the client 'wakes up', we can quickly write out papers, like it's all official, and share the money with the firm like we're supposed to.

This practice works directly to the detriment of the firm by diverting part of its income flow. Exploiting the firm's client base, employees who divert income take advantage of lenient accounting and documentation procedures to realize private earnings. The pocketed earnings go undetected among the official flow of business.

The five types of earning practices described above convey the banality of covert earning schemes, while revealing the significant ways in which they contradict transparent commercial activity and undermine the efficiency of small business. In order to understand how these economic distortions can occur regularly over time and changing conditions, it is necessary to examine the systemic and attitudinal underpinnings of covert earning practices.

IV.   THE INTERNAL LOGIC OF COVERT EARNING SCHEMES

While covert earning schemes can be labeled as criminalized distortions of official structures and procedures, it is argued here that they are guided by an inherent logic that is fluid and benign. It would contradict this logic to classify a Russian employee who 'twists' at the workplace as criminal, deviant or corrupt. Instead, he or she is acting in accordance with an unarticulated order that is internally coherent and consistent with both the systemic constraints that provoke it and the popular attitudes that sustain it. Attention now turns to the process by which earning practices are taken as a natural and justifiable component of everyday life.

It is necessary for individuals who earn covertly to integrate their practices into everyday life in a way that immunizes them from the need for conscious reflection.[10] Earning practices are sustained because they do not hold sway over their practitioners; instead, they occupy a peripheral role in individuals' self-perception. Covert earning is not regarded as criminal by its many practitioners. Rather, it represents a comfortable, familiar component of daily life that is rarely reflected upon and is easily 'explained away' when raised as a topic of conversation.

This suggests that practitioners undergo a process of 'reconciliation' to align their earning practices with their self-perception as normal, conscientious people whose actions are unobjectionable and justifiable. Maintaining psychological equilibrium demands that practitioners weave together their objective actions with societally-patterned attitudes towards work, the state, and citizenship. In this process, two main 'pillars' of support for covert earning play crucial roles. First, the material constraints of everyday life (e.g. low wages, inflation, wage non-payment) and the larger macroeconomic volatility compel Russians to resort to informal techniques in order to survive. Covert earning should, therefore, be seen as a systemic informality – the insufficiencies of the formal system prompt economic actors to exploit everyday opportunities to pursue their personal interests, and the practice itself develops and flourishes with the implicit tolerance of official institutions. Second, widespread

---

[10] Other studies on 'workplace crime' have emphasized the way in which employees understand their actions in ways which are compatible with their self-perception as honest, upstanding citizens and workers. See J. Ditton, *Part-Time Crime: An Ethnography of Fiddling and Pilferage* (London, Macmillan, 1977); G. Mars, *Cheats at Work: An Anthropology of Workplace Crime* (George Allen & Unwin, London, 1982).

popular support for covert earning allows the practice to be perpetuated. Society's tacit support for informal earnings and its muted reaction to petty economic infractions assist in this by providing a comfortable social cushion. These two forces which fuel covert earning's stubborn pervasiveness are evident in the various 'techniques for reconciliation' which are used by practitioners to neutralize the friction surrounding their earning practices. Interviews with respondents indicated that these techniques take four primary forms.

The first technique for reconciliation is based on the assumption that covert earning practices are an unobjectionable, matter of fact aspect of everyday life. As such, ethical dilemmas are notably absent and actions are written off as 'just the way things are'. Individuals are absolved of accountability for their behaviour by displacing responsibility onto engrained habits over which they have no control:

> Russians are always thinking up something. It's not because we're so clever, or anything. It's because life forces us to do it.

> Maybe it sounds funny, but it's a skill. Compare Russia with other countries – you don't have this skill. You just don't need it. We have it because we had to work and live in a different way. That's why it happened – it just developed. And we know how to use it. For instance, a Russian person can always find a way to do something – and 99 per cent faster than the foreigner who never deals with it.

The conviction that one's behaviour is no different from the norm is a powerful tool of reconciliation. Moral discomfort with earning practices is assuaged by the knowledge that one is merely conforming to a pervasive way of being. 'When I was working, I simply understood that all around me, people were doing the same thing', declared a shop attendant. The 'norm of life' approach to reconciling earning schemes is woven tightly with automatic, unreflective relationships towards informal economic practices and broader societal acceptance of them. This explains how respondents could regularly engage in earning schemes without consciously acknowledging them as such. It also reveals how prevailing notions about 'ways of being' – such as the eternal and uniquely Russian propensity for ingenuity – serve to buttress earning behaviours.

A second means of reconciling one's earnings is by denying them in their objective form – that is, by 'misrecognizing' them as other behaviours. Similar to Ledeneva's argument on the misrecognition of *blat* practices, denial of covert earnings entails a contradiction between one's self-perception and the perception of others.[11] The most notable use of such a technique came from a car alarm installer, who reconciled his informal income by re-casting it as legitimately earned money:

> I don't consider that what we did was deceptive. We earned that money – we didn't take it from [the director of the firm], we didn't steal it. We earned it

---

[11] Ledeneva, n. 6 above, p. 60.

through our own labour, you see? That is, we simply kept the money for ourselves. We didn't share it with the firm ... I have to make that clear – we didn't steal that money or take it from the firm in some deceptive way. We simply never mentioned it.

The fact that the money was kept for themselves is granted a sense of respectability by invoking the language of 'earning' and 'our own labour', implying a degree of entitlement. While acknowledging a certain deviance from established procedures, and hence an implicit recognition of impropriety, the respondent stops well short of admitting any blame or wrongdoing.

Other examples of reconciliation through denial can be seen in the cases of employees whose marginal 'tack-on' earning schemes are tangled with notions of 'individual service' and 'going the extra mile'. The parking lot attendant who accepts money from his 'personal clients' to park in restricted areas frames his actions in terms of service and friendship:

Yes, we take money from them, but at the same time, there's a friend-like relationship there (*druzheskie otnosheniia*). It's always – hello, goodbye, how are you today, how are things with your son and daughter ... It's about service.

The money that is received is not seen as central to the transaction. Rather, the emphasis is upon the social relationship in which the practice is grounded.[12]

A third technique could be described as 'righteous indignation' – while acknowledging the ethical discomfort involved in covert earning, respondents justify it as a legitimate response to similar behaviours perpetrated 'above'. Such explanations hinge upon the notion that 'they do it, why shouldn't I?' and point to examples of impropriety at the level of the firm or the state as grounds for individual infractions. In this respect, explanations grounded in righteous indignation illustrate the systemic roots of earning practices as they highlight the pervasiveness of informalities within contemporary structures.

'The firm itself steals – look at the kind of taxes it actually pays!' angrily declared one respondent. Accusations levied against the workplace form the basis for a cycle of informal infractions that perpetuate and justify one another. Employees' own sense of suffering and exploitation at the hands of the firm further heightens perceived injustice and fuels reciprocal exploitative practices:

I wouldn't do it if I could be sure that my own bosses weren't robbing me – that they get 1000 bucks and pay me all of 10. Of course I'm bitter (*mne obidno*) – I do the same work, the exact same amount of work – and my labour isn't rewarded.

---

[12] The absence of an engrained 'service mentality' in Russia means that 'going the extra mile' is not considered an inherent part of the customer-employee relationship, but something additional which occurs only in certain instances.

Covert earning can, therefore, be seen as an everyday act of resistance aimed against the transformed post-Soviet order and its constituent elements. By challenging authority (here, workplace authority) and 'beating the system', employees enhance their own sense of control over an uncontrollable situation.

The most intensive resentment is reserved for the state, however. A highly-developed sense of 'us vs. them' is drawn upon heavily in reconciling earning behaviours. Consider the following from the auto mechanic:

> Those guys who are up at the top just line their own pockets without doing a thing. Money straight into their pockets – that's how it is. They don't have any problems. But me? I have a constant headache. Somehow I have to provide for my family, my mother and father ... If I see, anywhere, the chance to earn a rouble, I run towards it. I simply run. Those who are sitting up there at the top – they don't have such problems. They don't need to run anywhere ... Europe and America simply hand it to them.

The salesperson at the local market expressed similar indignation:

> All of this isn't considered theft. It's considered an adaptive ability! And anyway, how is it possible to call it theft, if our own government robbed us through and through ages ago?

The conviction that Russians have been thoroughly defrauded by their state was a frequently-encountered sentiment. The loss of lifetime savings coupled with currency devaluations, rampant inflation, bank closings, and the non-payment of wages create a palpable sense that the state has not only turned its back on the population, but has robbed it blind in the process. Legal nihilism prevails; the state's loss of legitimacy in the eyes of the population is felt acutely. Against this backdrop, individual efforts to shortcut the system for personal gain seem not only justifiable, but utterly logical. While respondents might concede that their actions represent transgressions of certain ethical boundaries, any moral discomfort accompanying this acknowledgement is easily overshadowed by a sense of righteous indignation and entitlement in the face of systemic abuses.

This antagonism towards the state makes the final technique for reconciliation – 'survival' arguments – easier and more convincing. While tacitly conceding the moral ambiguity of informal earnings, responsibility for the practice is deflected onto circumstances far beyond practitioners' control. Variations on the survival argument convey a sense of passive victimization on the part of the population as a whole, expressed in the sentiment: 'We've been forced into this position – it's not of our own doing'.

The first strand of survival arguments emphasizes the role of covert earning as fundamental to everyday survival. No sophisticated explanations or 'excuses' are offered; rather, emphasis is placed upon minimum standards for survival and the day to day process of getting by. 'A person who is simply existing (*sushchestvuet*) thinks only about where he can make money ... People are just focused on how to survive in this world (*kak vyzhit' v etom mire*)'. The respondent continued:

> It [unofficial earning] is explained by the fact that we have to provide for our families. We have to feed them with something. If I were to share all my money with the firm, I don't think I'd have enough money for a lot of things … I have to take care of my family, my parents. That's the only way to explain all of this.

The bakery manager who works to suppress covert earning in his own workplace had no difficulty viewing the practice from the employees' angle:

> It doesn't mean that someone's a kleptomaniac – that he has some sort of obsession with stealing. Not at all. It's a means of survival (*sposob vyzhivaniia*). Unfortunately, that's just the way it is … All the same, this practice will continue, because people receive very little and they have to do something in order to maintain their living standards … No one can survive on 300 roubles[13] a month.

The glaring instability of the current order was frequently cited in connection with this argument and used as justification for earning covertly:

> It's all these leaps (*skachka*) – people more or less settle down, calm themselves and get used to it – and then again! They knock you upside the head (*na tebe po golove*). Just as soon as people began to understand something – aha! You've forgotten your place – get back there into that swamp! (*nazad, opiat v eto boloto*) So, of course people once again start to think – it's impossible to live on this money. Again it's necessary to take something, to steal.

As people are unable to plan for the future, it becomes necessary to seize opportunities as they present themselves; abrupt changes demand a form of fluid, ad-hoc decision-making on the part of economic actors. 'I'm happy for any sum that I can make. Even 20 or 30 roubles a day – for me, that's pure joy (*eto prosto radost'*). I'd agree to making that, because I know that tomorrow I might not have the chance. Or that the day after tomorrow I'll be sitting at home all day with no work'. Concentration on everyday survival means exploiting all available chances for personal gain.

The second strand in the repertoire of survival arguments accuses the system of failing and forcing people into a position where they are obliged to provide for themselves. The notion 'I wouldn't have to do this *if* …' is a prominent theme – while respondents tacitly acknowledge that they may be committing transgressions, they dismiss these thoughts out of hand by blaming the system for letting them down. Faced with a situation in which they cannot cope, 'good people' are compelled to compromise their own values and behavioural standards.

The absence of incentive to work and excel traps people in an endless cycle of short-term opportunistic behaviours. Low levels of investment in the workplace are perpetuated by the sense that one's work is not valued or rewarded, as seen in the following comment from a salesperson at a local market:

---

[13] Three hundred roubles was equivalent to approximately USD12 at the time of the interview.

Every person needs an incentive (*stimul*). If I have an incentive to work for something, naturally I'll work rather than steal. If I know that my child will be provided for, that he'll have a chance to study further – what possible reason is there for me to steal, since stealing in any case – somehow, somewhere – is punishable. Why would I search for some kind of short-cut? Obviously, if my labour is properly compensated, it's better for me to live quietly and to do my work (*delat' svoe delo*) than to search constantly for where and how I can get ahead.

The thing is, everyone aspires to something better (*stremitsia k luchemu*). But we're discussing survival, and what people are living on these days … For example, if I have a good job and receive a normal wage for it, if I know that everything with my family is secure, then if I want to earn additional money somewhere, I would never think about ways to grab something from my workplace (*u menia ne voznikayut mysli gde by na moei rabote urvat'*). I would want to move ahead (*prodvinut'sia*) somewhere, somehow. I wouldn't steal something here – I'd go on in search of a better opportunity. But because we're stuck here, we can't reach something better. Instead we try to snatch up what we can from the place where we are right now.

Humphrey's argument about the desire of entrepreneurs to renounce personalized, informal economic arrangements in favour of more transparent ones[14] appears relevant to this point. Ordinary employees who rely heavily upon informal economic activities such as earning schemes might well prefer to abandon them and to live 'cleanly' on official wages alone – yet the relentless material constraints of the prevailing order demand recourse to unofficial means of getting by.

The absence of social guarantees, personal security, and stability are perceived acutely by respondents who feel betrayed by the system and abandoned to their own devices. Many of them lashed out angrily at the abstract, dissociated remainder of the Soviet state or at their present place of work. 'The firm was absolutely horrible', said the former shop attendant. 'It left its employees no choice but to earn on the side'. Even if they do little to mitigate the unwavering sense of injustice, such indictments appear a logical response by individuals who are experiencing a sharp sense of relative deprivation. By invoking concepts of 'survival,' covert earnings are immunized against morally-based judgements. The imperative of providing for one's own justifies recourse to ethically-questionable activities.

V. CONCLUSION

Covert earning practices provide crucial insights into the distorted trajectory of Russia's market reform program. While earning schemes are indicative of what is 'not working' in the reconstituted Russian order (e.g. low productivity, inefficiency,

---

[14] See C. Humphrey, chapter 12 of this volume.

lack of transparency), they are also essential to understanding the surprising endurance of the chaotic milieu (e.g. chronic non-payment of wages, survival in the face of inflation). Thus, rather than regarding covert earning schemes as simply another manifestation of the overall criminalization of Russia, it is more useful to consider their role in stabilizing systemic inefficiency as a lubricant in the day-to-day functioning of the economy.

Covert earning is much more than an economic practice – it is informed by social, cultural and political factors which reflect people's expectations of the state, society, and themselves. In the current context in which familiar expectations of the state are going unmet, the resulting tension is being channelled into practices that sustain a precarious equilibrium, but distort attempts to build functional, transparent economic and political structures. Here it is important to emphasize the crime-engendering role of the state itself in facilitating this process. By supporting, protecting and deliberately promoting illegal activities within official structures, the state has lost its ability to serve as a 'dependable barrier against criminalization' for society as a whole.[15] Economic actors at all levels regularly evade the law – even the tacit acceptance of corruption and distortions within formal structures directly affects the informal practices that naturally accompany and mediate them. Earning schemes reveal how broad conceptions of legality and standards of permissiveness at the societal level are acted out in concrete ways on the micro level.

Viewed from without, covert earning practices can appear irrational. Petty, small-scale, and oriented on immediate short-term gain, earning schemes seem risky and lacking in any meaningful potential. Underserving customers and pocketing occasional fees for services will not 'lead' anywhere. The short-termist logic underpinning covert earning schemes contradicts that of Western economic policymakers who maintain that the market should engender incentive, investment in the workplace, and a spirit of entrepreneurialism that orients individuals towards profit, productivity and future goals and away from trivial practices like covert earning.

It has been argued here, however, that covert earning schemes evince a coherent logic of their own. Explanations that centre on criminality, corruption or laziness ignore the complex multi-layered nature of Russian informal practices and the 'mentality of survival' in which its practitioners are schooled. Small-scale tactics aimed at personal gain are proven techniques for making ends meet. When there is no faith in the mechanisms of democracy or the market, it is preferable to rely upon familiar 'know-how'. The instinctive orientation on survival reflected in earning practices is a direct carryover from the Soviet era and a self-evident response to the constraining context of post-Soviet Russia. Covert earning is a natural aspect of the post-Soviet employment landscape, prompted by the exigencies of the structural framework and sustained by a set of popular attitudes that sanction small-scale economic transgressions as benign and unobjectionable. The stubborn persistence of such everyday routines is fueling the formation of an alternative post-Soviet order in which informal, ad-hoc economic practices compensate for the striking deficiencies of the formal system.

---

[15] R. V. Ryvkina, 'Social Roots of the Criminalization of Russian Society' (March–April 1998) 37 *Sociological Research*, p. 17.

11

Russian Hackers and Virtual Crime

Alena V. Ledeneva

I.   INTRODUCTION

The Russian people's ingenuity is inexhaustible. Almost everybody in one way or another contributes to Russia's shadow economy, which is estimated to account for just under half of Russia's GDP.[1] The continued existence of the shadow economy in Russia in the 1990s is not surprising. The niches of shadow economy have been sustained by interests in super-profits 'at the top' and the need for income 'at the bottom', which taken together produce a formula: the shadow economy helps to keep civil peace in Russia by providing opportunities for extra earnings and creating jobs. The convenient substitution of the logic of civil society by the logic of 'civil peace' seems to be well in the tradition of Russian, including Soviet,[2] society responsible for creating niches for shadow practices. This paper is an endeavour to delve into the practices of Russian 'hackers' and to consider their links to the shadow economy and criminal underworld.

Shadow practices – sometimes seen as 'forms of everyday resistance' – are practices that circumvent formal rules but escape legal punishment. They are pervasive and banal, often interwoven with everyday routines. In a Soviet society, one of the most widespread shadow practices was referred to as *blat*, understood as the use of personal networks for obtaining goods and services under conditions of rationing.

In a socialist economy which produced constant shortages, *blat* developed into an 'economy of favours' which shadowed an over-controlling centre and represented the reaction of ordinary people to the social constraints they faced. In a social and economic sense, *blat* exchanges became vital to the population. Related to the matters of personal consumption, *blat* was routinely practiced by almost everybody, often being confused with obligations of friendship.[3] It was a customary way of

---

[1]   *Interfax-AiF*, 11 May 1998; see<wwww.interfax.ru>.
[2]   'Big' and 'Little' deals between the Soviet regime and the population were conceptualized by Vera Dunham and James Millar respectively. See V. Dunham, *In Stalin's Time* (Cambridge University Press, Cambridge, 1976), and J. R. Millar, 'The Little Deal: Brezhnev's Contribution to Acquisitive Socialism' in T. L. Thompson and R. Sheldon (eds), *Soviet Society and Culture: Essays in Honour of Vera S. Dunham* (Westview, Boulder, CO, 1988).
[3]   A. V. Ledeneva, *Russia's Economy of Favours: Blat, Networking and Informal Exchange* (Cambridge University Press, Cambridge, 1998), p. 35.

A. V. Ledeneva and M. Kurkchiyan (eds.), Economic Crime in Russia, 163–175

breaking the formal order of 'socialist' distribution and sharing access to the rationing systems pervading the so-called 'administrative' or 'plan' economy.

Similarly, in order to meet the demands of the command economy enterprises had to obtain the resources to fulfill plan tasks through informal channels of *tolkachi* ('pushers' responsible for procuring supplies, obtaining a reduction in the targets and speeding up or even increasing essential supplies to ensure that the plan targets were achieved). Their 'professional' role was to support the Soviet 'command' economy, to enable it to work, which paradoxically could only be done by violation of its declared principles of allocation. In this sense the acceptance of *blat* and other informal practices was a forced choice for people.

Such practices became vital to the functioning of the Soviet system and developed into an economically and culturally grounded *blat* code, which left a significant imprint on the workings of institutions and their transformation in post-Soviet conditions.[4] In a way, old informal rules outlived the formal ones and still operate in post-Soviet conditions. At the same time, they modified under the pressure of new market economic and social arrangements. Informal rules have not simply transferred to new contexts. Following the economic necessities and demands of the reforms, they have also undergone a certain 'marketization'. Some of pervasive and habitual practices became 'monetarized', spread well beyond the limits of personal consumption, and thereby slipped into the domain of corruption. According to Kulikov, a deputy Prime Minister of Russia in 1997, nearly half of private firms' undeclared profits are spent on bribing officials. Accounts are opened in foreign banks in the name of public servants, and they are provided with free trips to the best foreign resorts. What used to be a matter of morals and ethics based on modest norms of Soviet society and notions of kinship, friendship and other social ties, now – in the transitional stage of 'wild capitalism' – involves material and financial capital. The *blat* skills and informal codes in the Soviet era are to a large extent responsible for the scale of present-day corruption and organized crime and account for a great deal in the post-Soviet order.

Blat practices are at the core of the computer underground in Russia today. Not simply because computer software and other items are obtained through friends and connections or in a black market. In a much wider sense, the networks that make up Russian cyberspace serve to circumvent the formal institutional rules and hierarchies. Rafal Rohozinski argues that while Russia's virtual community is small, probably numbering less than one million individuals, this virtual world binds its adherents into a conspiracy of sorts where formal rules and laws are replaced by an unwritten code of practice.[5] Moreover, the informal codes inherent in Russian cyberspace follow the pattern and reproduce the logic of informal practices in social life. So far, Russian cyberspace is a domain where, according to experts, the informal spirit of the Soviet era is still alive. Rohozinski describes it as '*cyberblat*', as the codes and ethics are similar to those of Soviet *blat* where both demands and damages were quite moderate.

---

[4]   Ibid., Chapter 6, pp. 175–214.
[5]   R. Rohozinski, 'Behind the Looking Glass: The Origins, Practices and Daily Life of Russian Cyberspace' (PhD dissertation, University of Cambridge, 2000).

It is possible to argue that the conventions of the shadow economy in Soviet Russia have implications for the nature and scale of activity in a virtual world, while the post-Soviet trends of the transformation of informal codes indicate the direction of its future development. The question is, therefore, whether or to what extent the tendencies of monetarization and criminalization of a post-Soviet shadow economy will be shadowed in cyberspace?

II. RUSSIAN HACKERS VS. WESTERN HACKERS

Before I attempt to answer this question, let us outline a framework encompassing the people referred to as hackers in the West. There are two poles in the computer underground. The unstructured underground consists largely of ego-oriented and attention-seeking adolescents. The structured threat comes from profit-oriented and highly secretive professionals. As stated by Icove *et al.*:

> at one extreme there are the teenage "joyriders", playing around with their computers and modems. At the other extreme are criminals who break into classified military systems or corporate databases, for reasons of terrorism or military or corporate espionage. In the middle are disgruntled or dismissed employees looking to wreak revenge on an employer, as well as hired hackers who break into systems under contract.[6]

The New York State Police's Senior Investigator reported that the angry or dishonest employee contributed 75–80 per cent of computer crime in 1997. Some consultants have engaged in extortion, demanding more money than contracted for and threatening damage to systems.[7]

Howard identifies attackers by their motivations and divides them into six categories:[8]

- Hackers – Break into computers primarily for the challenge and status of obtaining access to the system.
- Spies – Break into computers for political gain.
- Terrorists – Break into computers primarily to cause fear which will aid in achieving political gain.
- Corporate Raiders – Employees of one company break into computers of competitors for financial gain.
- Professional Criminals – Break into computers for personal financial gain (not as a corporate raider).
- Vandals – Break into computers primarily to cause damage.

---

[6] D. Icove, K. Seger and W. VonStorch, *Computer Crime: A Crimefighter's Handbook* (O'Reilly & Associates, Inc., Sebastopol, CA, 1995), p. 61.

[7] Oslo Computer Security Conference '98. See <www.icsa.net/library/research/oslo98.shtml>, pp. 4–5.

[8] J. D. Howard, 'An Analysis of Security Incidents on the Internet, 1989–1995' (PhD thesis, Carnegie Mellon University, 1997), Section 6.2. See <www.cert.org/research/JHThesis/Start.html>.

Attackers	Objectives
Hackers	Challenge, Status
Spies	Political Gain
Terrorists	Political Gain
Corporate Raiders	Financial Gain
Professional Criminals	Financial Gain
Vandals	Damage

Hacking is often perceived as routine by the insiders of the computer underworld but would be considered as electronic crime by outsiders. Much depends on the definition of the term. In *The Economist IT Pocket Guide 1998*, a hacker is defined as a 'skilled and professional programmist, ... to be distinguished from cracker or phreaker'. More often, hackers are associated with breaking the computer security systems.[9] As the computer underground participants freely share information and are often involved collectively in a single incident, media definitions invoke the generalized metaphors of 'conspiracies' and 'high-tech street gangs' etc.[10] The popular image of hacking is stigmatized and normally refers to a criminal whose malicious attacks could bring widespread disorders. The media fail to distinguish underground 'hobbyists', who may infringe legal norms but have no intention of pillaging, from predators, who use technology to loot, and are even less inclined to see the nuances of the 'hobbyists'.

From a legal perspective, hackers' activities are tied up with issues of security. This is a sensitive matter. There is a certain pressure from organizations to keep matters of corporate insecurity and computer crime out of the news. Law-enforcement officials and other intelligence agencies meet a wall of silence when trying to investigate the crimes. The director of information technology for one of the largest British banks stated that the issue is too embarrassing for the industry to discuss. Meanwhile, according to a recent survey of 800 international firms by Ernst & Young, the accountancy firm, computer security lapses cost nearly USD700 million a year.[11]

From a sociological perspective, the difference between criminal hacking and 'hacking' as a shadow practice widespread in the computer underground is important. In the latter sense, hacking is not simply a deviant, but also a cultural phenomenon.

---

[9] The term 'hackers' first came into use in the early 1960s when it was applied to a group of pioneering computer aficionados at Massachusetts Institute of Technology (MIT). See S. Levy, *Hackers: Heroes of the Computer Revolution* (Doubleday, Garden City, 1984). Throughout the 1970s, a hacker was viewed as someone obsessed with understanding and mastering computer systems. However, in the early 1980s, stimulated by the release of the movie 'War Games' and the much publicized arrest of a 'hacker gang' known as 'The 414s', hackers were seen as young whiz-kids capable of breaking into corporate and government computer systems. B. Landreth, *Out of the Inner Circle: A Hacker's Guide to Computer Security.* (Microsoft Press, Belleview, WA, 1985), p. 34.

[10] Ibid., p. 2. For counterimages see Hackers Hall of Fame at <www.discovery.co/area/technology/hackers/hackers.html>.

[11] S. Reeve, 'Corporate Insecurity: Cyber Thieves Step Up Raids' *The European*, 12–18 October 1998, p. 18.

Meyer and Thomas define the computer underground as an invisible community with a complex and interconnected culture, dependent for survival on information sharing, norms of reciprocity, sophisticated socialization rituals, and an explicit value system.[12] Within the computer underworld, hackers are distinguished as being more interested in the challenge of defeating a system's security rather than in the potential for personal gain. Although skirting the law, hackers possess an explicit ethic and their primary goal is knowledge acquisition. Levy identifies six 'planks' of the original hacker ethic; these continue to guide modern hackers:

- First, access to computers should be unlimited and total;
- Second, all information should be free;
- Third, mistrust authorities and promote decentralization;
- Fourth, hackers should be judged by their prowess as hackers rather than by formal organizational or other irrelevant criteria;
- Fifth, one can create art and beauty on a computer;
- Finally, computers can change lives for the better.[13]

Hackers freely acknowledge that their activities may occasionally be illegal, but they insist on limiting violations only to those required to obtain access and learn a system, and display hostility towards those who transgress beyond these limits, including 'criminal' or 'hired' hackers. Although hackers emphasize the learning aspect of their activities, unauthorized access may also result in a variety of offences: corruption of information (any unauthorized alteration of files stored on a host computer or data in transit across a network);[14] disclosure of information (the dissemination of information to anyone who is not authorized to access that information);[15] theft of service (the unauthorized use of computer or network services without degrading the service to other users);[16] or denial-of-service (the intentional degradation or blocking of computer or network resources).[17] Most of these offences, however, are never reported.

Apart from discriminating between 'criminal hacking' and 'hacking', it is also crucial to remember that 'hacking' also connotes a range of activities, such as pirating, anarchy, and phreaking.[18] Both elite hackers and *lamerz*, for example, are often simply called 'hackers', while the distinctions between them are striking. For elite

---

[12] G. Meyer and J. Thomas, 'The Bawdy World of the Byte Bandit: A Postmodernist Interpretation of the Computer Underground'. Article presented at the American Society of Criminology Annual Meeting, 9 November 1989.

[13] Levy, n. 9 above, pp. 26–36.

[14] E. G. Amoroso, *Fundamentals of Computer Security Technology* (Prentice-Hall PTR, Upper Saddle River, NJ, 1994), p. 4.

[15] D. Russell and G. T. Gangemi Sr., *Computer Security Basics* (O'Reilly & Associates, Inc., Sebastopol, CA, 1991), p. 9.

[16] Amoroso, n. 14 above, p. 31.

[17] F. B. Cohen, *Protection and Security on the Information Superhighway* (John Wiley & Sons, New York, 1995), p. 55.

[18] See Meyer and Thomas, n. 12 above. The article retains the computer underground spelling conventions. For example, words beginning with 'f' are customarily spelled with a 'ph', 's' endings appear as 'codez', '*lamerz*'.

hackers, the mere act of gaining entry is not enough to warrant the 'hacker' label; there must be a desire and the skill to use the system after access has been achieved. Elite hacking requires highly sophisticated technical skills to enter the maze of protective barriers, recognize the computer type, and move about at the highest system levels. Not all hackers, however, retain interest in a system once the challenge of gaining entry has been surmounted and not all trespassers are necessarily skilled at hacking out passwords. It is often the case that passwords and accounts are traded, allowing even an unskilled intruder erroneously to claim the title of 'hacker'. Such 'consumers' of the hackers' network are called '*lamerz*' (lame ducks).

These aspects should be taken into account in analysis of any hacking community. There is a fundamental difference, however, between Western and Russian hackers. According to Rohozinski, most Russian hackers[19] tend to be professionals with formal education or work experience involving information technology. Few individuals possess the leisure time or resources to learn hacking as a 'hobby' as is the case in the West. He also suggests that whereas the western computer hackers make up a very small percentage of the computing profession and are members of a subculture by choice, the vast majority of Russian computer professionals live in a semi-legal world out of necessity with roots reaching back to the Soviet period:

> The Soviet computer industry was notoriously ineffective in developing and distributing software … It was up to an institution's software engineers to 'obtain' such goods, which generally meant trading with, or stealing home-grown software from other institutions. So pervasive was the semi-legal exchange of software (which at times involved highly illegal 'deals' between secret Military Industrial institutions and civilian ones) that anecdotes appeared concerning how to distinguish whether a particular institution could be considered '*krutoi*' ('cool'). 'Bardin's Law' (named after the author) states that if a box of computer software is left at an institution clearly labelled 'Duplication Forbidden' and remains un-copied when collected the next day, then the institution cannot possibly possess a '*krutoi*' team of programmers. While humorous in nature, the clear implication of 'Bardin's Law' is that engaging in illegal (and potentially dangerous) activities is an essential part of being a 'professional' programmer.

> The shortage and relative expense of personal computers, components and software perpetuated the spirit of 'Bardin's Law' even as social conditions began to change during the early 1990s. To 'survive' professionally, the young programmers and computer specialists who came of age in 1990–91 openly acknowledge that they relied on stolen components in order to assemble or upgrade home built computers. Even today few 'professionals' legally buy software, most is obtained either through friends, or bought at specialized street markets such as Moscow's infamous *Mitingo* market. As in *blat* practices,

---

[19] The term 'hacker' was largely unknown in Russia until 1990–1991. Since then it gained usage to designate able programmers, as well as hackers in a western sense.

ethical concerns are deliberately misrecognized and obtaining 'stolen' components or 'pirated' software is not considered 'theft' but 'borrowing' for a 'good cause'.[20]

In other words, Russian hackers are involved not just in typical hacking activities of obtaining unauthorized access or using a system in an unauthorized way in a virtual world, but also in activities that constitute a sector of the real shadow economy. They obtain access to information and software through informal channels and provide access to computer resources. The fact that the informal codes dominating their activities developed under the Soviet regime also adds some specifics to Russian 'hackers'.

It can be argued that every person in a Soviet context, in one way or another, was bound to go beyond the prescriptions of the regime to escape into the domain of alternative values and practices. The Soviet regime was known for generating the most skilful, sophisticated and spiritual dissent in every field, normally achieved without opposing the regime in an open way. It is not, therefore, surprising that computer officers (*komp'iutershchiki*) could combine their occupation with hacking and achieve exceptional skills which made them in great demand in Russia and abroad.

The Soviet roots of Russian hacking can also account for the specific attitude to material matters as well as matters of status and prestige. If employed, hackers often work as computer officers and make use of the hidden benefits normally obtainable through their position. The rewards that derive from hacking thus constitute a so-called 'covert reward system'. It involves a higher degree of social satisfaction than that derived from the activities carried out for formal rewards. The economic component of this reward is almost non-existent. Rather, it is likely to involve an element of reciprocity – providing favours, exchange of services, cooperation, etc. Hacking is usually a pleasurable departure from routine and an implicit challenge to authority. When hackers feel that they are beating the system, and are in control of their own fate, the rewards are much more than monetary.

Another non-material reward enjoyed by hackers is status in the eyes of the hackers' community and friends. By passing information and passwords, a hacker can demonstrate that they belongs to a group of people 'in the know' who have the skill and the ability to 'penetrate walls'. Their status is further enhanced by the reputation one acquires in communication, through expertise and skilful use of symbolic means, jargon, and other forms of symbolic capital. Such communication or exchange, in fact, constitutes the hackers' community and dominates the existence of the 'people who inhabit the network',[21] that is, inveterate users who are not able to live without it.

Exchange and sharing practices are deeply rooted in both the Russian and Soviet past. Given that most hackers are formally employed, these practices are potentially dangerous. They create not only a problem of unauthorized access acquired by

---

[20] Quoted from Rohozinski's interviews with Moscow hackers. See Rohozinski, n. 5 above.
[21] E. Lornet, 'Keep Out! Censorship has not yet been Introduced to the Computer Network, but Criminal Punishment has Already been Foreseen' *Novoye Vremya*, 16 March 1997, pp. 36–37.

outsiders, but also a problem of abusing authorized access by the insiders. The procedures of acquiring access from authorized sources in the computer security field are called 'social engineering', that is, talking your way into information that you should not have. It is considered to be one of the most effective methods. In Russia, conventions of sharing access within personal networks are so prevalent and widely accepted that 'social engineering' works even more effectively. Hackers act through networks and electronic contacts, routinely expecting the favours of access. They use certain identifying techniques and jargon in electronic contacts to create trust and establish a kind of fraternity (the existence of *lamerz* strongly suggests that even those who have nothing much to offer can receive favours of access).[22]

An exchange of access in a virtual world is similar to that already mentioned – the 'economy of favours'. In the economy of favours, only certain favours get exchanged – favours of access to the centralized distribution systems. This means that a person exchanges something that does not belong to them; strictly speaking, not even something, but only access to it, and gets a different access in return. Similar to *blat* favours of access to the distribution of state property, *cyberblat* is about exchange of favours of access to the network resources, to the software or sites protected by protocols.

Blat was coupled with the Soviet system of property rights and distribution. Due to the nature of the Soviet order *blat* can be seen as parasitic on the Soviet economy, but at the same time as a natural reaction of ordinary people to the rigidities of the regime. According to Rohozinski, Russian cyberspace is, to a large extent, a technical manifestation of the same reaction. FIDO – an unofficial computer network – was created by computer specialists and enthusiasts, and Russian cyberspace therefore is seen as '*nasha set*'' ('our network') by Russian 'hackers' – a forum for interaction and 'fraternity'.[23] In this sense, *cyberblat* is endemic to the Russian native cyberspace and reproduced within the community of 'hackers', who want to see it 'free' of borders or property rights. The question is, however, whether such values represent a potential danger to the wider fabric of cyberspace, for example, to the Internet-centred cyberspace, if the 'sharing access and other *cyberblat* practices penetrate it? One Russian hacker, who happened to break into the Pentagon, said:

---

[22] Consider the following typical offers:
Sub -> Credit Cards for Codez
From -> (#134)
To -> All
Date ->01/26/xx 07:43:00 AM
Tell ya what. I will exchange any amount of credit cards for a code of two. You name the credit limit you want on the credit card and I will get it to you. I do this cause I do janitorial work at night INSIDE the bank when no one is there ... hehehehehehe
Sub ->phun
From -> (#138)
To -> All
Date -> 02/22/xx 12:31:00 AM
Anyone out there got some good 800 dial ups that are fairly safe to hack? If so could ya leave me em in e-mail or post em with the formats ... any help would be appreciated ... thanx
[23] R. Rohozinski, 'Mapping Russian Cyberspace: A Perspective on Democracy and the Net'. (1998 Unpublished). Quoted with the kind permission of the author.

The Russian part of the Internet is still underdeveloped. As for the official networks in our Ministry of Defence and Central Bank, they simply do not have any access to the Internet, or that access is tightly blocked. So far, Russian commercial banks can also sleep calmly – for a time. Worldwide computer credit card fraud is so far practically impossible in our country. Not because computer systems that operate with credit cards are better protected. It is simply that in Russia there are practically no systems of this kind. But in the near future things will not be so sweet for firms offering Internet-services. As soon as something worthy of attention appears on our territory, there will almost certainly be break-ins. Especially if it concerns money and payment for goods. It is much easier to break into these systems than into the Pentagon. For the time being, however, most of our hackers make do with the fact that they can stroll through the Internet free of charge and behave like hooligans there from time to time ... For now, all that remains is to thank God that our ministries and banks are not rushing into the 'new life' – switching into the worldwide information superhighway.[24]

III.   THE CRIMINAL POTENTIAL OF RUSSIAN HACKERS

On a global scale, the emergence of computer technology has created dramatic changes in social communication, economic transactions, and information processing and sharing, while simultaneously introducing new forms of surveillance, social control, and intrusions on privacy.[25] Chris Goggans of Security Design International pointed out that the nature of electronic crime and types of criminal offence have changed in the last 25 years. There was a time when high-tech crime centred on telephones and supported a free flow of information. Hackers were usually hobbyists who had an exploratory and educational orientation. Today, systems and therefore crime are Internet-centric. Computer criminals are more professional now. Toll fraud is more systematic and managed by organized crime. Cell-phone cloning is widespread. Credit-card fraud is a problem. Where computer network abuse once focused on access, with information stolen as trophies, today information is stolen for sale[26].

The transformation described above will not take 25 years in Russia. The recent boom of electronic crime in Russia started four to five years ago with so-called 'telephone piracy' – cell-phone cloning and phreaking:[27]

---

[24] A. Munipov, ' "Our" People in the Pentagon' *Obshchaya Gazeta*, 6–13 November 1996, p. 7.
[25] G. T. Marx, *Undercover: Police Surveillance in America* (University of California Press, Berkeley, 1988), pp. 208–211; G. T. Marx and N. Teichman, 'Routinising the Discovery of Secrets: Computers as Informants' (Fall 1985) 1 *Software Law Journal*, pp. 95–121.
[26] Oslo Computer Security Conference '98. See <www.icsa.net/library/research/oslo98.shtml>
[27] 'Phreaking broadly refers to the practice of using either technology or telephone credit card numbers (called "codez") to avoid long distance charges widespread in the US. Although phreaking and hacking require different skills, phreaks and hackers tend to associate on the same boards. Unlike hackers, who attempt to master a computer system and its command and security structure, phreaks struggle to master telecommunications technology. "Carding", or the use of fraudulent credit cards, is anathema to phreaks, and not only violates the phreaking ethic, but is simply not the goal of phreaking.' See Meyer and Thomas, n. 12 above, p. 24.

With the appearance of cell-phones in Russia it became possible and extremely fashionable to ring the Bahamas for an erotic chat. High-frequency radio-scanners allowed one to use a 'neighbour's' radiophone for such calls thus avoiding charges. It was profitable to serve clients for international calls in a car, equipped with a radio-scanner, parked next to the 'neighbour's' place (the Bahamas and Israel were the most popular destinations).[28]

Credit-card fraud in Russia is developing, often as an organized group activity. The good news in this context is that electronic crime has not yet reached priority status for Russian organized crime[29] and is restricted by the technological backwardness of Russian institutions. There were, however, some serious offences.

In 1995, Citibank of New York reluctantly admitted that Russian hackers had accessed its computer system and 'withdrawn' an estimated USD10 million in cash. Since then the so-called Vladimir Levin case[30] has become an international brand name for Russian hackers. There is still much speculation about what actually happened. Here are some versions of the story:

*   According to the Citibank official version, it was a group operation, a series of consecutive attacks from different computers, which made a security system vulnerable. Allegedly, hackers had almost transferred USD10 million into the fake accounts when their activities were registered by the administrator, who managed to retrieve USD9.6 million. USD400,000 has gone missing.
*   The Russian official version was that there were no transfers at all. There were hackers trying to break the Citibank server, but they were registered and chased away. Levin's arrest was staged and used according to the traditional 'Soviet threat' scenario. Therefore, Levin should be seen as another victim of the Cold War in its virtual version.
*   People who knew Levin argued that he was unable to do anything like this due to his character and mentality.

What does the St. Petersburg hackers' community think about these accounts? A hacker who was at the centre of all this commented:

Long before the events of 1995, a few hackers broke the Citibank BBS. One of them was Megazoid, who started a dialogue with the Administrator. He asked

---

[28] From an interview with Lev Godovannik, Agency of Journalistic Investigations, St. Petersburg, August 1998. Quoted from scripts of Rohozinski's interviews, with his kind permission, n. 23 above.

[29] A. V. Ledeneva, 'Organised Crime in Russia Today' (17 April 1998) 8 *Prism: A Bi-Weekly on the Post-Soviet States*, p. 3 and 7.

[30] Vladimir Levin, 29.03.67. Degree in chemistry, late interest in computers. His teacher was Leonid Gluzman, known as computer magician. In 1989, Levin organized a cooperative 'Stelit', specializing in computer software and creating accountancy software. In 1991, Levin became a vice-president and a shareholder of AOZT 'Saturn', which grew out of 'Stelit'. Levin was known as a computer specialist of high class with an expertise in computer technology. His colleagues say he could put together a computer with his hands.

not to kick him out of the system in exchange for help with identifying its vulnerabilities. But as in the old fairy-tale, once he told his secret, the administrator knocked him out. He wouldn't be a hacker if he knew just one 'hole', so he reappeared through another one.

Once he needed some money urgently and he sold the secret of penetrating the Citibank BBS to Levin for 100 dollars. What happened then? One of the 3 options. After the scandal most known hackers were cornered by MVD. There is still a strong department combating electronic crime in STP.[31]

The latter interpretation illustrates the difference between hackers (Megazoid) and criminal hackers (Levin), but also – the potential dangers of hackers' activities. Although most of the hackers' competition in breaking the computer security systems is motivated by so-called 'sporting' interest, their skills can be used – with or without their knowledge – for criminal purposes.

Concerning the scale of Russian computer crime, we need to know who is attacking which systems, how often and by what methods. Unfortunately, it is impossible to give any conclusive answers. First of all, an unknown number of crimes of all kinds are undetected. Second, even if attackers are detected, for the reasons mentioned above they are rarely reported (according to some estimates about 10 per cent of attacks get reported,[32] and in Russia this figure is probably even less). Computer crime statistics should thus be treated with skepticism. It is useful, however, to have at least some estimates about damage from computer crime.

According to the Interior Ministry of Russian Federation,[33] in 1993 68 billion roubles were stolen through the manipulation of the Central Bank computer networks. 40 billion and 375 billion of losses were prevented in 1996 by the arrest of two groups of hackers. Unofficial sources report that there are about 250 hackers in Russia today.[34] The number of criminal hackers is much smaller. As indicated by one of the 'hired' hackers, there were about 15 to 20 people like him in Moscow and about 10 in St. Petersburg in 1996.[35]

There have been attempts to update the laws in correlation with the technological processes of the computer world. Three articles were introduced into the new Criminal Code of the Russian Federation, which went into effect as of 1 January 1997, with an attempt to regulate computer networks[36]; there exist special departments of

---

[31] Quoted from Pavel Alashkin, 'Stranichki istorii, ili kak deistvitel'no byl vzloman Citi-Bank', Internet source.
[32] M. E. Kabay, *ICSA White Papers on Computer Crime Statistics*, 1998. See <www.icsa.net/library/research/comp_crime.shtml>.
[33] Ia. Kostyukovsky and V. Bovykin, 'Khakery – prestupniki XXI veka' (1997) 12 *Operativnoe prikrytie*, pp. 22–23.
[34] Ibid.
[35] Aleksei Munipov reports on two nights spent with computer hackers in his article ' "Our" People in the Pentagon' *Obshchaya Gazeta*, 6–13 November 1996, p. 7.
[36] 'Art. 272. Unlawful Access to Computer Information'; 'Art. 273. Creation, Use, and Distribution of Destructive Computer Programmes'; 'Art. 274. Violation of the Rules of Operating the Computer, a System of Computers, or Their Network'. See also Lornet, n. 21 above, pp. 36–37.

'cyberpolice'. The real problem is not the criminal hackers, given their limited numbers and the fact that their efforts are similar to hackers' criminal activities in other countries. In comparison with other forms of financial crime, the scale of computer crime is probably quite insignificant. For the eight months of 1997, about 400 'attempts' to break into Centrobank computer networks were registered, whereas according to General Prosecutor's Office data, there were more than 13,000 recorded crimes in banks and other finance and credit institutions in 1997[37]. The crimes most frequently encountered are theft of money through the use of forged documents, counterfeit bank guarantees and bills, abuses by bank chiefs and employees, and tax evasion. It is thus a problem relevant for the whole of Russian economy and society, not just its cyberspace – illegality having become a norm.

There is another serious obstacle to computer crime control – the lack of mutual consistency between terms from the legal and network systems. It follows from the fact that the Net is worldwide, while legislation is limited to the framework of a particular state. Consequently, the first gesture on the part of the state is to confine the Net to a state framework by one means or another, for example by introducing censorship in communication with the outside world.

In order to control computer networks and catch criminals in electronic nets, the Russian Internal Intelligence Service (FSB) and the State Committee on Communications (*Goskomsviaz'*) have elaborated a project codenamed SORM ('system of ensuring investigative activity' (*sistema tekhnicheskikh sredstv dlia effektivnogo provedeniia operativno-rozysknykh meropriyatii*)).[38] SORM would let the FSB boost its monitoring of electronic mail messages by digitally linking its offices with all Internet service providers throughout Russia.

Certain parts of the document are almost Orwellian. In relation to every individual user the SORM-system should guarantee – apparently in an on-line regime – the following: monitoring of statistical information, incoming and outgoing information belonging to particular users, time of using the Net, Net addresses and/or telephone numbers from which the Net is accessed, and also the possibility of 'disconnecting particular users'. All of this is to take place through a special channel allocated to special agencies without letting the provider know, and ironically, at the users' expense.

The computer underground has accepted the project as a real threat of total monitoring of computer users by the FSB and other agencies. 'The Internet is a virtual land of freedom', said Levenchuk, a founder of Russia's Libertarium's site on the World Wide Web. However, it is something to worry about not just for individuals, but also for serious business organizations, which use the Internet for business negotiations and financial payments. Electronic commerce could be seriously damaged by SORM.

---

[37] A. Yelizarov, 'The Hunt for Fugitive Capital' (Interview with Vladimir Sergeyev, deputy chief of the Federal Security Service Economic Counterintelligence Directorate.) *Rossiyskaya Gazeta*, 19 December 1997, p. 13.

[38] See for example, <www.ice.ru/libertarium/sorm/> and <www.fe.msk.ru/libertarium/sorm/press/spbt.html>.

Russia's looming battle over Internet privacy is part of a wider international struggle between governments and Internet users. In the USA, the federal government has provoked opposition with a plan to keep copies of all commercial encryption keys in secure depositories, available when required by the Federal Bureau of Investigation (FBI), the Central Intelligence Agency (CIA) or the Communications Intelligence Agency, the NSA, to crack codes used by criminals or terrorists. Unlike SORM, however, the US government is not demanding that Internet providers install a direct data link to CIA headquarters.

The natural reaction for many Internet users would be to respond to this surveillance technique by encrypting their e-mail with widely available software. However, the Federal Government Communications and Information Agency (FAPSI),[39] which issues all licenses for encryption technology in Russia, also has the codes to break such encryption. In theory, under Russian law, FAPSI would be restrained by the same legal requirement as those covering phone taps or letter-opening, for which it must make a formal application to the courts. However, FAPSI and its officials have been circumventing Russian law since FAPSI was founded. In recent years, numerous high-ranking FAPSI functionaries have been forced to leave the agency due to financial scandals.[40] Despite the fact that government agencies are not supposed to market products, FAPSI announced in May 1998 that it was entering the wireless communication business with an untappable phone at USD12,000. They claim that this phone – which handles voice and data transmission – 'would be equipped with encryption that would take a hundred years to break'.[41] Except for FAPSI, that is.

It is an old Russian tradition not to follow the law. Government agencies are no exception, which justifies a widely spread distrust of the state. Levenchuk emphasized that the FSB threat will be much more real than the threat of hackers for both business and individual Internet users. He said, 'They can trust the Internet with mythical hackers but they will not trust the Internet with the legendary FSB'. In other words, one has to be beware of both.

---

[39] FAPSI is a Russia's counterpart to the US National Security Agency (NSA).
[40] The list of disgraced former FAPSI officials include its financial director, chief of the military-medical service and the former deputy director. For details, see G. Borisov and Y. Shuvalov, 'FAPSI: Link With Mafia' *Novaya Gazeta,* 15–21 September 1997, pp. 2–3.
[41] 'Electronic Eavesdropping' *The St. Petersburg Times,* 24 July 1998; See <www.times.spb.ru>.

12

Dirty Business, 'Normal Life', and the Dream of Law

Caroline Humphrey

I. INTRODUCTION

This paper explores the idea of law, that is the expressed wish for a fair and universal law, among entrepreneurs in Russia. It will be argued that this call is not just a reaction to current problems but reveals a desire for a particular kind of future for the country.

In Russia in the 1990s the law has both marched before economic practice, aiming to transform it according to market principles, and it has chased behind, attempting to catch up and stop activities considered harmful or wrong. The transformative role of law was most prominent under Gaidar[1] in 1992, when the government realized that privatization in the Soviet aftermath was not creating a 'rational, healthy market' but what Yegor Gaidar called '*nomenklatura* capitalism'.[2] By this he was referring not so much to the presence of former Soviet officials in the privatized industries, as pointing to the persistence of characteristic practices or rules of the game. In *nomenklatura* capitalism the aim was simply to 'add property to power', that is to add a legalized money income to the directors' existing *de facto* control of both resources and the workforce. The old habits resisted rational reorganization, not to mention hard-budget constraints, and the directors propped up ailing firms by accumulating arrears both to the state and to one another in Soviet-like crony arrangements.

What were the rules in this market – open, written, economic, market, subject to the law of free competition, or, as before, secret, conducted by telephone, administrative, constrained by power relations, and oriented to the state-bureaucratic machine?[3]

---

[1] Yegor Gaidar (b. 1956) has a doctorate in economics from Moscow University. From November 1991 he was Vice-Premier of Russia and led the Russian government during 1992 when he started the radical economic reforms often known as 'shock therapy'. He left the government in December 1992. He has been president of the Democratic Choice party and now is prominent in the Right Cause movement along with Anatoly Chubais.

[2] By '*nomenklatura*' Gaidar refers to industrial directors, ministerial officials, Generals of the KGB, the secretaries of province and district Party committees, etc. Y. Gaidar, *Gosudarstvo i Evolyutsiia* (Izdatel'stvo Evraziia, Moscow, 1995), pp. 103–40.

[3] Ibid., pp. 163–164.

177

A. V. Ledeneva and M. Kurkchiyan (eds.), Economic Crime in Russia, 177–190
© 2000 *Kluwer Law International. Printed in Great Britain.*

Gaidar tried to reform this situation by economic measures (limiting inflation, liberalizing prices) but he also aimed to use the law to transform mentalities among Russians in general so that millions of new owners of small businesses could emerge and penetrate the monolithic enterprises. His goal was to separate property from power, to create the conditions for 'normal life',[4] and the issuing of share vouchers, new licensing and tax laws, and changing the law on private international trade were all aimed in this direction.

Now Gaidar's attempt to create small business and thus transform Russian mentalities was seemingly paradoxical, because the existing entrepreneurs in the early 1990s were renowned in Russia for their lawlessness, and indeed ordinary workers still thought of them in Soviet terms as 'speculators' and generators of crime. Today, in the late 1990s, Gaidar is widely assumed to have failed: *nomenklatura* capitalism is still in place and economic actors of all kinds regularly evade the law. Furthermore, there are notorious cases of government officials and delegates to the State Duma engaging in illegal activities,[5] and big business dominates the economy while remaining largely outside the law. Yet this article will argue that Gaidar's Quixotic attempt was not altogether misplaced, for it is precisely among small businesses that we see expressed a real need for a generally applicable law that will be observed. Sachs and Pistor have suggested that the existence of these new demands[6] for law and order cannot be equated with a constituency for the rule of law, since all the entrepreneurs want is protection of their *own* property rights and it would be 'quite a different matter to subscribe to the rule of law which vests others with similar rights.'[7] This paper will suggest to the contrary that the demand of small businessmen is for a universally applicable law and that this is integrally tied to the desire for a 'normal life'. The insistence on the idea of a normal life shows that the issue is not just a matter of protection of economic interests. If, as some argue,[8] a moral consensus is necessary before the rule of law can function, we should investigate what are the normative ideals that might form its basis (a question to which I shall return at the end of the paper).

II.   THE STATUS AND IDEA OF LAW

The situation facing Gaidar demonstrates the dilemma of the status of law during a radical transformation of the political-economic direction of a society. After 1991, activities that had been criminal only a few years ago, such as speculation, were

---

[4]   See n. 2 above, p. 117.

[5]   Under the Constitution of 1993, State Duma delegates were exempted from prosecution with the result that a number of individuals subject to criminal investigation have stood for election to the State Duma. M. Newcity 'Russian Legal Tradition and the Rule of Law' in J. Sachs and K. Pistor (eds), *The Rule of Law and Economic Reform in Russia* (Westview Press, Boulder, 1997), p. 42.

[6]   Commercial banks and 'stake holders in Russia's priced assets' are mentioned as other constituencies demanding law and order, Sachs and Pistor, 'Introduction' ibid., p 19.

[7]   Ibid.

[8]   T. C. Owen, 'Autocracy and the Rule of Law' in Sachs and K. Pistor (eds), *The Rule of Law and Economic Reform in Russia* (Westview Press, Boulder, 1997), p. 37.

suddenly not only made legal but supported by the government, while practices that had been commonplace and ideologically approved, such as dismissal of workers for political reasons, became illegal. (This reminds us that despite their best efforts to come up with an objective and absolute definition of 'crime' valid for all times and places, criminologists have been unable to do so.[9]) It is, however, not so easy for people to change their values quickly, even if the government decides on a new course. Furthermore, Gaidar was faced with a particular impasse that blunted the best weapons of reform from the top: the people of Russia were accustomed to differentiating their own moral values from those embodied in laws. In other words, the state law as such lacked legitimacy.[10] Put crudely:

> In relation to law the Soviet system was built entirely on the arbitrariness of power, and it actively opposed itself to the basic principle of western law-based society, universal equality before the law. It is from this that legal nihilism appeared among ordinary people. Stealing from the state became the norm, although formally this was a serious crime; lying to officials became normal, insofar as the officials themselves were interested in neither the truth nor the law; suspicion of those in power became a means of survival, since the powers could always remove life without warning and without understandable reasons. Despite all this, the majority of ordinary Soviet citizens accepted the system and tried to survive in it. But there also existed a significant category of people – both the most honest and the absolutely dishonest – who placed themselves outside this system.[11]

For Soviet times, it could be argued that a 'nihilist' attitude to the law did not necessarily imply a rejection of the Russian state socialist system, since the law was in practice always subordinate to other political operations. It is not just that Soviet law-making was tactical and instrumental in practice; Bolshevik thinking categorized law as less pure in a socially transformative sense than the direct exercise of morally-justified power. This varied at different historical periods and contexts but included leader's decrees, workers' tribunals, the use of terror (as distinct from law[12]), administrative measures of the Party, and forced participation in great projects of the state. Repressive and punitive as this was, we know nevertheless that millions of people were inspired by, and responded to, the stark grandeur of the exercise of Communist state power.

---

[9] F. Sack, 'Conflicts and Convergences of Theoretical and Methodological Perspectives in Criminology' in E. Ewald (ed.), *New Definitions of Crime in Societies in Transition to Democracy* (Forum Verlag Godesberg, Bonn, 1994), pp. 7–34.

[10] Michael Newcity has argued that popular attitudes of mistrust and cynicism towards the law have deep roots in Russian culture going back long before the Soviet period. See Newcity, n. 5 above, pp. 41–53.

[11] M. Dikselius and A. Konstantinov, *Prestupnyi Mir Rossii* (Bibliopolis, St. Petersburg, 1995), p. 227.

[12] P. H. Solomon, *Soviet Criminal Justice under Stalin* (Cambridge University Press, Cambridge, 1996), pp. 447–459.

Soviet inspirationalism is relevant to the present article if we follow the argument of an interesting paper by Kharkhordin.[13] Kharkhordin maintains that the quasi-religious notion of the Bolshevik vocation assigned a role model for Soviet civilization. In this, the effective functioning of the inspired individual depended on initiative and self-reliance (*samostyatelnost'*) in order to bring to reality the mystical Communist truths. Holding a view similar to Gaidar of the post-Soviet economic landscape (divided between the great industrialists, with their corporatism, and small entrepreneurs), Kharkhordin argues that the cultural value of *samostoyatelnost'*, taking new forms, could transform the scene. Small entrepreneurs are already imbued with the desire for independence, but the religious, almost Lutheran, notion of *samostoyatelnost'* could also come to inspire 'converts' to market capitalism among the older generation:

> In contradistinction to the younger entrepreneurs, who grew up as individualists, the majority of these older entrepreneurs initially adhered to Communist beliefs to a greater or lesser extent. Thus, they experienced the change to a modern notion of *samostoyatelnost'* as a deep personal drama. I would further hold that among these converts the former strongly motivated Communist ascetics are the ones needed for core positions in the state bureaucracy and new economic structures. ... *Samostoyatelnost'* is still predicated on a quasi-religious faith in revealed truth. This new truth now frequently is some kind of grassroots Hayek-style doctrine of the inherent value of capitalism as a civilization promoting human freedom and *samostoyatelnost'*.

Kharkhordin is inspired by Weber's *Protestant Ethic and the Spirit of Capitalism*. His paper shares with Gaidar the idea that there are characteristic economic cultures in Russia, but it adds the more anthropological insight that while these are differentiated, people involved in them hold alternative perspectives on what are at some level *shared* values, like self-reliance.

These are valuable contributions, but they operate through the binarism (the 'old' corporatism to be transformed by the 'new' spirit of the market) which is intrinsic to programmatic national political argument.[14] Since 1993–1994 when these authors were writing, it will be shall suggested here that it has become evident first, that a binary logic can no longer do justice to the economic landscape, and second, that new 'shared values' have come to dominate public discourse, in particular the idea (or ideal) of law. In brief, that we can better understand current economic culture by proposing six, not two, categories of actors:

- State administrations themselves as economic players
- Resource-rich utilities (electricity, oil, gas, transport, etc.)

---

[13] O. Kharkhordin, 'The Corporate Ethic, the Spirit of *Samostoyatelnost'* and the Spirit of Capitalism: Reflections on Market Building in Post-Soviet Russia' (1993) 9 *International Sociology*, pp. 405–429.

[14] M. Hertzfeld, *Cultural Intimacy: Social Poetics in the Nation-State* (Routledge, New York and London, 1997), p. 15.

- State and recently privatized large industries
- Small entrepreneurial businesses
- Private enforcement agencies and rent-seekers ('the mafia')
- Workers

Each of these has characteristic practices and has evolved their own 'rules of the game'. The Russian economy is not in fact chaotic, even though it is often described this way by both Russian and foreign observers, for there is a kind of order – that is, the order of customary ways of doing things – in each of the collectivities of people that are the real, localized manifestations of the six categories outlined. These days, to judge from an investigation of a wide range of economic actors carried out in summer 1998,[15] the call is no longer to 'self-reliance' and 'the free market', but to different values, to 'law', 'fairness', and a 'normal life'.

However, why should anyone call for law (*zakon, zakonodatel'stvo*) if customary and usual ways of operating are already in place? The rest of this article will attempt to explain why, although the need for law is invoked by almost everyone, it is the small business people who really mean it. In the present situation, the actual practice of law is still tangled with government; it is fragmented, confused, over-elaborate, and almost impossible to conform to with the best will in the world. It is still rightly seen as instrumental, as it was all through Soviet times, and it has become an element in the regional barter economies, i.e. a barterable thing with a different value for different actors. The demand for a universally observed law, before which all citizens would be equal, is thus – if not quite utopian – certainly an appeal referring to the future. Thus the call by the 'lawless' Russian entrepreneurs is like a reverse mirror-image of the rhetoric of the 'lawless' Cretan sheep-thieves described by Herzfeld,[16] who bemoan the current necessity of using legal processes to decide matters where once the traditional word of honour sufficed. My materials suggest that Russian entrepreneurs have no nostalgia for 'old ways', if only because they feel trapped by them on all sides. Instead, as many Russian writers have observed, it is the future that has glamour, which is an old, old cultural move in Russia.[17] The greater the distance between the 'distorted' (*urodlivyi*) practise of law[18] and the ideal of law, the more the entrepreneurs call for it to be reformed. This is not only because it is they above all who count the price of the difference, but also because they see how capricious attitudes to law engender a dysfunctional, 'abnormal' way of life.

---

[15] Surveys of business people's attitudes were carried out in summer 1998 in Moscow Oblast and the Buryat Republic. Interviews were conducted with directors, lower managers and workers in a variety of enterprises, including a large former-state-owned rubber goods factory, a decorating materials firm, a computer retail business, a heating-oil provider, a pork producer, several entrepreneurs trading a variety of goods (wood, metals, food), a bakery, a food trader, and several agricultural firms. Administrators in district bureaus and the pensions fund were also interviewed. The author is very grateful to Galina Manzanova and Helen Kopnina for their essential help in providing these rich materials.

[16] Hertzfeld, n. 14 above, p. 8.

[17] Y. Basina, 'Krivoe zerkalo Evropy' (1997) 2 *Pro et Contra*, pp. 92–112.

[18] This expression was used by several business people about the present situation.

III.   BUSINESS LIFE AND ITS EVERYDAY ENCOUNTERS WITH LAW

Much of the customary order of small business works entirely beyond the law, being not even mentioned in any legislation. Notably, this refers to the intense negotiations between firms about who will pay what, when will they pay, and which discounts will apply, most of which is done orally and in person. Even if contracts have a written legal appearance, everyone knows that they can be overturned without effective sanction from the judiciary. Defaults, deception, selling faulty products, and cheating (e.g. watering products such as rice or sugar to make them heavier) go unpunished by the law. However, what the traders complain about most is not that inter-enterprise law remains ineffective, bur rather that tax and customs law is unreasonably extortionate: this forces businessmen to act illegally and places them in a potentially 'criminalized' position in relation to the state.

This situation arouses a kind of existential anxiety. Although the Soviet experience gave rise to deep cynicism towards the government and Communist Party, there are few people who reject the notion of the patriarchal state in principle – that is, the idea of how a state 'should be' as a repository of probity and the arbiter of right action. The corollary of this attitude to the state is that private conscience is not generally seen as sufficient to generate public morality by itself. Indeed for many businessmen it could not do so. They imagine a binary opposition between 'the state' and 'capitalism' in which the latter is identified with the private, the selfish and the amoral. One manager said, 'I understand that capitalism differs from our socialism in one main thing, the brutality (*zhestokost'*) of relations.' [19]

Creating a tax income for the state is not seen as problematic in principle by entrepreneurs in Russia. What arouses anger is that the state does not respond as it should: state pensions contributions do not arrive in time, promised 'transfers' seem to disappear, hospitals are drastically underfunded, and so forth. It is significant that ordinary people like pensioners often say that they feel 'cheated (*obmanutymi*) by the state',[20] which reveals how the state is reified and the relation with it is indeed seen as a bargain. Business people share these views but they seem more likely to deconstruct 'the state' and blame particular parts of it for corruption:

> Look at export licenses. It all began in Soviet times when you had to pay a bribe. Now all licenses are given to friends. The coal mine for example [this mine is a state enterprise, C.H.], they have a license and salt money away abroad for themselves and their bureaucrat friends. A bit of that money is exchanged for food, Dutch butter, full of harmful chemicals, and that food is brought back to Russia and used to pay the miners. It's shameful. And they justify this by saying it is all the fault of the economic reformers.[21]

---

[19] Trading manager of NIIRP factory, Moscow Oblast, 1998.
[20] For example, pensioners of a former state timber trading company said that, having worked twenty years in the company, they were now cheated (meaning they did not receive pensions), Nikolaev 1998.
[21] Director of a computer trading firm in Ulan-Ude, Buryatia, 1998.

Entrepreneurs of course primarily consider of the costs to themselves of such a situation,[22] but their statements almost always extend to the wider economic scene:

> It's absurd. For a private entrepreneur to set up business, he has to go through 11 structures, and each one has to be paid for their licenses (*patenty*). But if he is not yet working, he does not have the money. For the simplest application form or stamp he asked for money. Last year in our Republic 6,000 firms were set up, but only 1,500 of them can work. The government gives no help, though it is constantly pushing everyone to set up business. That's why we have chaos (*bardak*) everywhere. But we have to live by these laws the government dictates.[23]

The same trader said:

> There is money, but it is held back. I personally think that all this barter is a result of corruption. This is ultimately the fault of the state, which instead of paying for the goods it needs from us with money, operates by credits (*zachety*) against tax.[24] If the state paid us in money, we would use money too. As it is, this situation only gives rise to the criminalization of all society.

It is not that law has entirely ceased to be practised. There are court cases, people pay fines and some go to jail. However, court decisions frequently cannot be implemented and therefore there exists an extended imbroglio of dubious transactions that might, or might not, be prosecuted. Here, in effect, the implementation of the law becomes a thing to be bartered. This is particularly the case with tax law. A firm in the provinces which owes taxes is generally not prosecuted but ordered to pay its tax debt by means of transferring goods to some other firm to which the administration owes a debt.

How does tax law affect small entrepreneurs? The extraordinarily high rate of taxation in Russia is widely held by business people to be counterproductive. One Buryat dealer in computers described the vicious circle: 'Costs are increased, products become noncompetitive, profits lessened, and therefore less tax is paid; the whole economy suffers, so the government hikes up taxes further ... and it becomes an endless circle.' [25] The burden is impossible:

> In fact, we should pay more than one ruble of tax for one ruble's worth of production – the firm could not survive. In other countries I believe they pay 12 to 15 different taxes. But here in the last year or two, we counted up, we

---

[22] For business people bribery is unavoidable and a serious cost (it has been estimated that small businesses in Russia paid a minimum of USD500 million per month in bribes during 1998). A significant aspect of this is that respondents say nevertheless that the money on bribes is well spent: the costs of lack of access, having to pay the real customs duties, and so forth, would be far higher. *Argumenty i Fakty*, Sept 1998, No. 36, p. 9.

[23] Director of a general trading firm in Ulan-Ude, Buryatia, 1998.

[24] A typical example of how this works in provinces where the 1998 decree forbidding such deals is not applied is: Firm A does some work for the government, such as rebuilding a school, and receives a tax credit which is greater than its own tax owed. Firm A then goes to Firm B and offers, 'We'll cover your tax and you give us X amount of food in return'. The workers of Firm A thus receive food in lieu of wages, and Firm B has its tax paid.

[25] Director of general trading firm 'Bat-Les', Ulan-Ude, 1998.

were due to pay over 100 different taxes! This year there are a few less, but all the same we cannot do it.

As a result, firms choose which taxes to pay, and in the case of payment, whether to pay directly or to 'cover' the tax by a credit (*zachet*). The decision to pay or not depends partly on the cost to the trader of making the arrangements,[26] partly on personal relations with tax officers (see Chapter 9),[27] and partly on how seriously the tax office pursues a given tax. A trader said:

> The pension fund is very complicated to get round, because it functions as social insurance and it is forbidden not to have insurance – taxes that are for the maintenance (*soderzhaniye*) of an institution, well ... they are more severely implemented. It's very easy to have your property confiscated and there are big fines (*peni*), so we try not to hold back on payments because that would come out more expensive. But other local taxes, like the tax on profit ... well, no one pays that. Ha, ha. Usually people don't have profits anyway, since all profits are hidden.[28]

The distinction made here between pension and profit taxes suggests, it would appear, the existence of certain shared values in Russia. In the negotiation between the tax office and the businesses it is agreed by both sides that pensions, or more generally provision for the old and weak, should be taken seriously and if possible paid in money rather than credits. As Herzfeld points out,[29] however, such 'common ground' is always negotiated from different points of view, and in any case it is not solid enough to prevent traders from feeling unease (even while they make use of it) with the utter 'bargainability' of the tax law.

Given that tax offices in Russia have the right to sequester bank accounts directly, small firms concoct elaborate subterfuges, it seems, just to break even. For individual deals they register falsely low profits in their books and give the appearance of transferring smaller amounts of goods than they actually do. Barter is wonderfully suited to such ploys, since 'prices' (exchange ratios) can be shifted up or down and are less visible and public than cash market prices. Large companies also make use of each other's money substitutes (*veksels*, promissory notes, and scrip) for payment, thus avoiding various taxes due on money held and transferred. The use of such instruments is legal, even though they can be a means of tax avoidance and deception (the illusory nominal value attached to them is often 'realized' by means of shell firms). Small firms usually avoid the use of *veksels* and find themselves in the situation that they are constantly waiting for one or another debt to be paid.

---

[26] Decisions on substitutions by credits, for example, take into account the costs of such operations for traders. In the distant provinces arranging credits for federal taxes is only worth it for large sums because of the expense of the journey to Moscow to set up the deal.

[27] 'Usually no-one can get round income tax (*podokhodyi nalog*)', said one Buryat trader in 1998, 'But I have a friend in the tax office who allows this'.

[28] Director of office equipment trading centre, Ulan-Ude, 1998.

[29] Hertzfeld, n. 14 above, pp. 3–4.

So the general situation is that small entrepreneurs are not only in debt to one another and to the tax office, but also hide several illicit deals that would incur yet further tax were they to be discovered. This is a cost, because it makes it unlikely a firm would turn to legal means for redressing wrongs done to it. To recover debts, especially those involving money, businesses have recourse to 'criminal elements' (the mafia). 'Of course this is wrong', said one trader. 'And it is expensive. But since the law does not work, what can we do?' [30]

This is one aspect of what the businessman quoted above meant by 'criminalization of all society', though he was more directly referring not to himself but to the effect of the whole system on manual workers. Ultimately, the workers are the ones to suffer most (though indirectly) from the system of tax credits and barter, since, in regions like Buryatia, they are paid money only as a last resort and, therefore, they are 'forced' in the opinion of local businessmen to steal from their factories and farms. If *direct* confrontation with the tax system is found most among those running firms, since the corporate sector is proportionally much more heavily taxed than individuals, nevertheless business respondents made several unsolicited diatribes about the wider social decay seen in the spread of extortion and expropriation.

An example is the accusation that even tax officers take part in such acts. 'There are some firms which are not in debt to the tax office!' exclaimed the trader who had earlier talked about workers thieving. 'Which ones? They are the ones where the tax officials simply come and grab goods in lieu. Sometimes they take more than the tax due. And what do you call that? So those firms then get prepared – they even stock up on things the officials want, things like tights or toiletries.' Note the gender aspect of this situation. As Busse (Chapter 9) points out, the tax offices are normally staffed by low-paid women. A local government administrator acknowledged that this practice went on, and she added that the tax inspectors expropriate, for example, food at wholesale prices but they redistribute it to their own staff at higher retail prices. All this is noted down and the food received is deducted from the tax officials' wages (but the administrator did not say where the value that is the difference between the wholesale and retail prices, a ratio of some 3:4, ends up).[31]

Thus, business firms are not the only economic actors to suffer from the battle over taxation. Administrations can end up in dire straits when they themselves 'trade' in taxes. This happened, for example, when the Buryat government in the mid-1990s tried the experiment of allowing agricultural enterprises to pay tax in products rather than money. The administration set up a corporation to receive the tax-products, realize them as money, and pay in the tax. Superficially this was a success – the farms' rate of tax returns suddenly went up from 43 per cent to 88 per cent of their dues – but the administration found itself unable to dispose of mountains of low-quality vegetables, fodder grains, etc.[32] Government departments extricate themselves from such situations by changing the law forthwith.

---

[30] Buryatia, 1998. The lack of effective legal protection for witnesses to crime is another factor increasing the hold of racketeers and gangs. A. Aslakhanov, *Demokratiia prestupnoi ne byvaet* (Institut Massovykh Kommunikatsii, Moscow, 1994), p. 125.

[31] Buryatia, 1998.

[32] Interview with agricultural administrator, Selenga District, Buryatia, 1998.

However, such abrupt changes have a wider socio-economic cost. A time delay is attached to these changes, such that even the government administrators may know that the old law has gone but not be sure about what new one has replaced it. Frequent changes in the law affect the way of life of business people perhaps more than most. The great energy conglomerates are so powerful that they operate in effect beyond the law. The large production industries and farmers are tied to their resources and techniques whatever happens in the law, whereas entrepreneurs, at least in part, have to use the law to make profits. Moreover, taxation law is, of course, by no means the only type around which they have to navigate; traders are directly affected by changing export controls, laws on alcohol production and sales, or laws reflecting ethno-political fears, such as those limiting the registration of Caucasian traders in the Russian Federation, or laws restricting Chinese or Turkish 'infiltration', which end by affecting business more generally.[33] Abrupt legal changes make it impossible for business people to plan ahead; this drives them into habits of *ad hoc* decision-making, and at least some entrepreneurs say that this uncertainty is the most serious cost of all for them in developing their business.

To summarize, this section has suggested that the law, as it is practised directly and pervasively, affects how small business is conducted and encourages activities that the entrepreneurs themselves see as dysfunctional and corrupting. How does this relate to their call for a 'normal life' and a universally observed law?

It should be recalled who the entrepreneurs are from the social point of view. Some are doubtless survivors of the black-marketeers of Soviet times and the dubious cooperatives of the *perestroika* era, but a large number are young educated people who took to business in the early 1990s because they could not find employment. They are (or were) engineers, mechanics, lecturers in political economy, or doctors specializing in neurology.[34] If these people desire a 'normal life,' what does that mean? Clearly a normal life is an ideal, and not the same as the habits and norms that have emerged in actual business activity. The demand for a new kind of law reflects a desire for something far off, holistic, coherent and perhaps unrealizable. Nevertheless, its sources, this paper suggests, are grounded enough. To discover them we should look primarily to entrepreneurs' self-interest, that is to the understanding of the functionality of a disinterested law for realizing the profit of individuals, and secondly to the cultural notions of a 'normal life', that is to the demand, which in the end must be a political demand, for the creation of conditions that would allow normal life to come about.

IV. A 'NORMAL' LAW: A DREAM OR A STRUGGLE?

These two sources are connected, and to see how, this paper returns again to Kharkhordin's article. The theory that zealous administrators would convert from

---

[33] C. Humphrey, 'Traders, "Disorder", and Citizenship Regimes in Provincial Russia' in M. Burawoy and K. Verdery (eds), *Uncertain Transition: Ethnographies of Change in the Postsocialist World* (Rowman and Littlefield, Lanham, Boulder, New York and Oxford, 1999), pp. 405–429.

[34] These are real examples from amongst the traders in the Buryat survey.

quasi-religious belief in Soviet ideals to equally devoted implementation of monetarism now seems far-fetched, but Kharkhordin pointed to another, more promising vector of change. He was the first to note the ubiquity of appeals for a normal life among entrepreneurs. It was difficult to clarify what the expression meant (his respondents frequently took the idea as self-evident), but the best approximation was simply getting the fruits of one's labour in a reasonable activity. Kharkhordin remarks that the idea of life for individual reward sounds banal. 'However, attributing banality to it is profoundly mistaken. In so doing, one takes for granted the values of Western civilization and fails to compare these statements of entrepreneurs with the values of the Soviet civilization.'[35] Kharkhordin sees this as a shift from charismatic sacrifice for a higher cause, the Soviet model, to a mundane individual achievement. My sources suggest, rather, a shift from an alienated subjectification in late Soviet times to the ideal of honest work for oneself, but in either case we are talking of a paradigmatic transformation. For example, a factory manager considering entering entrepreneurial business ruminated as follows:

I consider Communism brought harm to our country. It made our country destitute, a kind of freak, it spoiled the people, brought about alienation, passivity, everything. No, I don't approve of the past at all. So when *perestroika* started I was very positive about it. But seeing what is happening now, I wholly disapprove of it. I don't support the reforms that are going on now in any way. Because, these are not reforms, these are not transformations of society. They are some kind incomprehensible drifting, you don't know where to, you don't know why. And I particularly don't like it that an honest person in Russia now lives badly.

Well, I don't take bribes, I don't use my position to get personal advantages, I am a normal, law-abiding person. I try to carry out my work, I try to do my thing honestly (*chestno*), so there should be a result. I don't want to be a rich person, I don't want to be poor. I just want to be a normal (*normal'nym*) person. I just would like to work ... at my own work ... so ... [long pause] ... put it like this, so I could be my own person (*samim soboi*).[36]

A 'normal life' is thus linked to a sense of selfhood, and at the same time to ethical values such as honesty, reward for merit, and working to good effect. The notion of a 'normal life' seems to be one of those ideas that are shared by Russians of all conditions, but it is significant that there are variations on this idea, variations that could be called different aesthetics of normality. For those still engaged in work for former state enterprises, to become an independent entrepreneur is a radical step and such an existence appears to them incompatible with the notion of 'normal life'. Here can be seen a certain ethic, a passivity and an asceticism that seems derived from Soviet values:

---

[35] Kharkhordin, n. 13 above, p. 19.
[36] Manager in rubber goods factory, Moscow Oblast, 1998.

We don't have the conditions for the honest conducting of business. Therefore, I don't ... well, I don't want to go private. I don't want to own anything. I don't want to be rich. Wealth is connected with criminality. Well, you could be rich, but not for long, you'd be dead. Or, you could be rich and live, but then you'd need to make a huge constant pay out for protection. They [entrepreneurs] have their own world, their own system. And honestly, I used to live in Moscow, and when I visit Moscow now I often feel a kind of ... shame, awkwardness, for all that is going on. ... I think that if I were a rich person, I wouldn't be comfortable. If I am going in a Mercedes and you are still going by bus, I would not feel good. I don't want to be a rich person – that is not real wealth, that is a lack of comfortableness. So I prefer to go on foot, and my car ... that one out there in the yard, well, it is the very cheapest you can get ... I wouldn't even have a car, but to go by bus all the time really is difficult.[37]

Such hesitation contrasts with the responses from people who have taken the step and become entrepreneurs. The concept of what the ideal law might look like also differs. People in state employment, who also call for legal reform, tend to oppose law to spontaneity (*stikhiinost'*),[38] and express hopes that the heavy hand of a responsible central government will reassert law as a means to impose order and control. For entrepreneurs, on the other hand, the possibility of a normal life is associated with economic reorganization and the enabling of spontaneous activity. Legal reform is linked to rational assessment of its advantages to business.

There should be a group of laws, clear laws about exactly how much we should pay. And those laws should not keep changing. Now we have so many duplicated laws; there are federal laws and then local laws. Some sort of local laws. They are completely unjustified. There are so many, you couldn't understand. At the level of the Buryat Republic, the city level, the district level. And so on. There are so many limitations. Nothing will work till the whole system is changed and they establish precise (*chetkie*) laws. Everything will follow from that. If the entrepreneur knows exactly how much percent of his turnover or his profit he should pay – even if it is 50 per cent – and he knows that during the next two or three years this will not change, then on that basis he will be able to work out some kind of policy.[39]

It is important to take into account the aesthetic of active entrepreneurial life. This is unabashed by wealth ('If you ask any businessman does he want goods or money, of course he'll say money. I want money, [laughs], and quickly!').[40] It is also not afraid to talk straight ('In Russia, the economy is absolutely not a market economy and it is also absolutely not democratic')[41] and insists on the necessity of individual effort:

[37] Ibid.
[38] The head engineer of the Bichur Administration of Agriculture, for example, said that an organization set up to control barter in the district should be 'lawful, not spontaneous', by which he meant that it should be set up by the state, not independently. Buryatia, 1998.
[39] Entrepreneur, aged 36, a historian by training, in the firm 'Bat-Les', Buryatia 1998.
[40] Trader in small timber and foods firm, Buryatia 1998.
[41] Director of computer trading firm, n. 21 above.

The economy should be organized in a normal way. Now the government has to try to maintain half the population that doesn't want to work, and still they expect to receive ... In Russian there is still the concept of *poluchka* (receivings), not a wage but specifically a *poluchka*. He visits the workplace, sits a little, receives his bit, and all is quiet. Yes, he doesn't get much, but then he didn't do any work. There is just the idea to do as little as possible and get as much as possible. That must change.[42]

Entrepreneurs have clear ideas about the need for *systematic, universal* change, at the top as well as the bottom.

Why do our banks keep failing? It is because they suffer from bad debts, and what can they do when it is the great firms and the political leaders themselves who do not pay back? Those people just say, 'What can you do with me?' If a leader knew he would sit behind bars, then, I'm sorry, but he would start thinking about whether to take a credit or not. Why don't they make such laws on debt? I think it is because it is the lawmakers themselves who don't pay their debts. So they would be making a law against themselves. From this, we traders suffer.[43]

To conclude, this chapter has attempted to show how small entrepreneurs in Russia maintain ideas of a 'normal economic life'. Such a life is clearly distinguished from the 'distorted' practices they actually engage in. Yet these practices have not extinguished various moral values, not least those new ones grounded in the idea of justifiable self-interest. The law is seen as the key to attaining a normal life, and this means not just reform of laws, but a change in the status of law in society such that it is becomes respected and universally observed. Thus the call for law and order is not limited to self-interested protection of business people's property rights, as Sachs and Pistor argued, but indeed extends to the implementation of the rule of (a new) law. To understand why traders think this way it is essential to expand analysis from a dualistic opposition between '*nomenklatura* capitalism' and entrepreneurism to the full range of economic actors, including government agencies. This is because trading activity, and hence the experience of entrepreneurs, consists in operating through the links and gaps in the whole economic field. The small businessmen want radical reform not because they think they suffer disproportionately from the existing tax system – in fact, they know they suffer far less than workers – but because they perceive the interlocking nature of the economy with politics and power. Yet there is little evidence of resignation among them. Rather, the audacious quality of the aesthetic of entrepeneurship suggests that perhaps the idea of fair law and a normal life could turn from being a dream into a struggle for its realisation.

Therefore, this paper is suggesting that the call for a 'normal life' is to make a commitment to the possibility of a future new society. The evidence is that

---

[42] Vice-manager in computer trading firm, Buryatia 1998.
[43] Trader in food products, Buryatia 1998.

entrepreneurs believe in an order of society that could be lived in decently and believe that they personally could take part in it. However, this is also an issue of agency. On the one hand, there is the legacy of the Russian (and particularly the Soviet) habit of dissimulation,[44] one form of which is the practice of declaring high moral goals while all the time actually living – and making no effort to change – a quite different life. On the other hand, it is because questions of the social good are bridged with their own active interests and a bold sense of knowing what is right that one might speculate that entrepreneurs may move to a more active and hence more political stance.[45]

---

[44] For an extended discussion of this idea see Kharkhordin, n. 13 above.
[45] Grateful thanks to Alena Ledeneva, Oleg Kharkhordia and Frances Pine for their comments on a draft of this chapter.

13

Large-scale Corruption and Rent-seeking in the Russian Banking Sector

Heiko Pleines[*]

I. INTRODUCTION

Corruption can generally be defined as the misuse of public power and/or public resources for personal gains. In a narrow interpretation corruption is directly linked to the payment of bribe money to a state official in return for a specific favour. However, in the case of societies with widespread corruption this definition hardly does justice to the full phenomenon. The following analyses will, therefore, employ a wider definition according to which corruption includes networks between state officials and entrepreneurs. These networks are not necessarily based on direct transactions (bribe payment against favours) but on mutual trust, on the knowledge that granting a favour will offer the right to demand a favour in return.[1]

Large parts of the Russian economy are dominated by such corruption networks between state officials and managers. Svetlana Glinkina claims that:

> today we have an economy which is to a certain degree regulated by the rivalry between corporate-bureaucratic structures (clans), by their fight for power and their regulative activities. One of the main consequences of the new mechanisms for the allocation of resources is the division of the national economy into a sector where these structures are dominant and a sector where they are not really influential. The first sector is characterized by a high level of 1) companies, which are monopolists on technological, market and institutional criteria; 2) liquid monetary resources; 3) bureaucratic-corporate power. The

---

[*] This text is based on research financed by the Volkswagen Foundation as part of a project on 'Russia's Economic Elites' at the German Federal Institute for Russian, East European and International Studies (BIOst), Cologne.

[1] For a brief overview of different definitions of corruption see: N. Kogan, 'Thinking About Corruption' (March 1998) 5 *Transitions*, pp. 40–45; M. Johnston, 'T he Search for Definitions. The Vitality of Politics and the Issue of Corruption' (September 1996) 149 *International Social Science Journal*, pp. 321–335.

A. V. Ledeneva and M. Kurkchiyan (eds.), Economic Crime in Russia, 191–207

fuel energy industry, the finance and trade complex and some industrial branches belong to this sector of the national economy.[2]

II. Rent-seeking and the role of corruption

According to economic theory:

> financial institutions transfer funds from lenders to borrowers. In doing this, they create financial instruments (like checking and savings accounts). However, from a macroeconomic vantage point, the most important instrument is bank money (or checking accounts) primarily provided today by commercial banks.[3]

Thus, commercial banks are an important source of finance for investment and consumption in a national economy. However, commercial banks are only willing to provide this finance, i.e. credits, if they are likely to make a profit in the form of interest payments by the debtor. That means, banks need (1) sufficient information to judge about the liquidity of the potential debtor and (2) reliable means to enforce payments in case the debtor is unwilling to meet their obligations.

Both conditions, by and large, are not fulfilled in Russia.[4] As a result, the share of enterprise loans granted by Russia's commercial banks is very limited, and until 1996 did not exceeded five per cent of Gross Domestic Product (GDP). Moreover, the large majority of these loans were granted for a period of less than a year. In 1997, the number of enterprise loans rose considerably, but interest payments were still responsible for only about a third of the income of Russia's commercial banks.[5]

Whereas the credit business with enterprises was risky and not very profitable, business with the Russian state offered promising opportunities, first of all with regard to the allocation of credits by the Russian Central Bank and the issue of state bonds on extremely good conditions, but also as far as the 'authorization' to manage state funds and the privatization auctions are concerned. In many cases, the fact that major banks have been authorized to manage state funds has led to embezzlement and the accumulation of arrears. Certain large banks were privileged at the privatization auctions 1995–1997 to such a degree that they were able to take over key industries in the Russian economy at 'dumping prices'.

As a result, Russian banks did not so much engage in market-oriented business activities, but rather, concentrated on the development of good relations with the

---

[2]   Abridged quote from: S. P. Glinkina, 'Prichiny usileniia i spetsifika tenevoi ekonomiki na etape perekhoda Rossii k rynku' in American-Russian Center for the Study of Organized Crime (ed.), *Izuchenie organizovannoi prestupnosti*, (Olimp, Moscow, 1997), pp. 251–252.

[3]   P. A. Samuelson and W. D. Nordhaus, *Economics*, 14th edtn. (McGraw Hill, New York, 1992), pp. 506–507.

[4]   For a brief but rather comprehensive elaboration of this point see W. Tompson, 'Old Habits Die Hard. Fiscal Imperatives, State Regulation and the Role of Russia's Banks' (1997) 49 *Europe–Asia Studies*, pp. 1176–1178.

[5]   For an overview of the economic situation and activities of banks until the financial crisis of 1998, see N. Kirichenko and A. Ivanter, 'Rossiiskie banki. Rozhdenie imperii. Chast I' *Ekspert*, 23 March 1998, pp. 20–24.

state in order to receive preferential treatment. This behaviour is defined as 'rent-seeking'. It has a negative impact on the country's overall economic performance. First, the allocative efficiency of the market is weakened. Badly managed banks may survive due to good connections with state officials while good banks with few connections are eliminated through bureaucratic arbitrariness. Promising enterprises may not get credits for investment because banks are too busy dealing with state officials. As a result innovation and growth processes are slowed down.

Second, rent-seeking puts a heavy financial strain on the state budget. When the state pays more interest than necessary on treasury bills or privatizes enterprises on the cheap, the situation of the state budget is worsened. When the bank with the best connections and not the one with the most attractive offer becomes responsible for the handling of state funds, banking fees are higher, efficiency is lower and the risk of embezzlement increases.

Nevertheless, a government can decide to accept rent-seeking as a lesser evil in cases where the market is thought to be unable to provide a desired product.[6] This is, for example, quite often the case with autarky from food imports. The resulting protection of domestic agriculture through regulations and subsidies leads to rent-seeking behaviour on part of the farmers and the food industry. However, in such cases the responsible government clearly defines the areas for rent-seeking and tries to apply strict rules intended to minimize distorting effects. In such cases, rent-seeking is mainly based on lobbying and not on corruption.

In societies with wide-spread corruption, however, a different situation arises. Not only the political decision of the government but also the arbitrariness of a bureaucrat can lay the ground for rent-seeking. Especially when laws and regulations leave considerable discretion to bureaucrats, they can on their own create the conditions for rent-seeking. Rent-seeking activities increase and privileges are more often granted to individual enterprises than to certain branches of the economy. In the resulting rent-seeking society every enterprise with good connections has a chance to obtain privileges from the state.[7] That means, whereas rent-seeking is not necessarily based on corruption, the existence of corruption networks allows for the uncontrolled spread of rent-seeking activities.

Russia's commercial banks adapted to such a situation by developing rather influential corruption networks. Accordingly, Anders Aslund has claimed that:

the main concern with respect to the Russian bank sector is hardly related to fears that the banks are being squeezed by the state. Rather, the concern is linked to worries that the large banks are taking over the state and using it to maximize their benefits, while continuing to ignore the basic business of banking – of granting loans to enterprises and attracting deposits from the public.[8]

---

[6] It is another question of how convincing are the arguments in favour of such a decision.
[7] A standard work on this topic is J. Buchanan *et al.* (eds), *Toward a Theory of the Rent-seeking Society* (Texas A& M University, College Station, 1980).
[8] A. Aslund, 'Russian Banking. Crisis or Rent-seeking?' (1996) 37 *Post-Soviet Geography*, p. 501.

III. Corruption networks of the banking elite

One of the major roots of post-Soviet corruption networks in the Russian banking sector lies in the Soviet banking system. The monobank system of the Soviet Union was regulated by Gosbank, which was under the direct control of the Council of Ministers. Sberbank was the single savings bank for the population and Vneshekonombank/Vneshtorgbank were responsible for the financial side of foreign trade operations. In the wake of economic reforms under Gorbachev a number of 'special banks' were created to finance investment in different branches of the economy. Promstroibank became responsible for industry and construction, Agroprombank for agriculture and Zhilsotsbank for municipal housing and infrastructure.

With the end of the Soviet Union, Russian organizations replaced the Soviet ones in the banking sector of the newly created Russian Federation. Already in 1990 the Russian branch of Gosbank had been renamed into Central Bank of Russia and had started to operate independently. Sberbank was transformed into a limited company with the state as majority shareholder. The state also kept a majority stake in Vneshekonombank and Vneshtorgbank. On the basis of its regional branches Promstroibank was transformed into a number of private banks, with Promstroibank Rossiya and Promstroibank St. Petersburg being the biggest. Agroprombank became a limited company, and in 1996 it merged with the private Bank Stolichnii into Bank SBS-Agro. Most assets of Zhilsotsbank were taken over by Mosbiznesbank.

Additional banks were created from state structures by transforming the financial departments of branch ministries into private banks. The management of such banks was, to a large degree, made up of former employees of the respective ministry. These banks continued to service the financial needs of a specific branch of industry and they maintained close connections with state structures. Important examples are: Neftekhimbank (petrochemical industry), Bank Imperial (oil and gas industry), Avtovazbank (automobile industry) or Aviabank (aviation industry).[9]

Some regions created their own banks for handling the regional state budgets. The most important examples are Bank Moskvy, responsible for the finances of the Russian capital and the bank of the Moscow region, Moskovskii Mezhregional'nii Kommercheskii Bank.[10] In Kemerovo oblast' the regional Kuzbassprombank is at the core of a Financial-Industrial Group which unites industrial enterprises controlled by the regional administration.[11]

Another group of Russia's big banks, including Menatep, Inkombank, Oneksimbank (Uneximbank), Rossiiskii Kredit, Alfa Bank, Mostbank and Tokobank,[12] was created more or less independently from state structures. Due to

---

[9]   For a good overview of the development of the state banking sector, see J. E. Johnson, 'The Russian Banking System. Institutional Responses to the Market Transition' (1994) 46 *Europe–Asia Studies*, pp. 971–995.

[10] On the situation in these and further regions, see Kirichenko and Ivanter, n. 5 above, pp. 26–40.

[11] A. Starozhilov, 'V kraiu nesostoiatel'nosti' *Ekspert*, 2 November 1998, pp. 20–22; *Segodnya*, 23 December 1998, p. 5 and 25 December 1998, p. 1 and 4.

[12] Until December 1996, when it merged with Agroprombank into SBS-Agro, Stolichny Bank also belonged to this group.

private entrepreneurship, a considerable number of smaller private banks also emerged. Until 1995 the number of registered Russian banks rose above 2,500. However, most of these banks had negligible assets and already in 1995 a quarter of them operated at a loss.[13] The 50 biggest banks, on the other hand, accounted for nearly half of all assets of the Russian banking sector.[14]

To sum up one may say that the Russian banking elite consisted of two groups up to the financial crisis of 1998. The first group emerged out of the Soviet *nomenklatura* and held leading positions in banks run (or previously run) by the state. The second group of Russia's banking elite was formed by the owners and managers of the big private banks.

The relevance of the first group is revealed by the fact that many post-Soviet bankers were holding influential party posts in Soviet times. On a scale from one (party secretary at the local level) to ten (party secretary in the Central Committee) the banking elite gets an average of eight.[15] Many members of the post-Soviet banking elite were earlier working in the Soviet economic administration, a quarter employed by Gosbank.

The leadership of the big private banks, on the other hand, comprises hardly any members of the former Soviet *nomenklatura*. The main reason for that is the low age of this part of the banking elite. They account for the nearly 30 per cent of leading bankers, who are less than 40 years old and, accordingly, they were still at university in the 1980s and started their career only at the time of Gorbachev's economic reforms.[16]

However, this new group of private bankers was smoothly integrated into networks between the banking sector and state officials. Large banks and the state were dependent on each other. The state as a customer, as an emitter of bonds and as the regulating and controlling body is of major importance to large banks. In turn, the state needed large banks to finance its budget deficit and to stabilize financial markets.[17] It has also been argued, though no proof has been provided, that the government has used commercial banks to channel additional subsidies to the economy. Jerry F. Hough has claimed that banks were forced to transfer large parts of their income from rent-seeking activities to branches of the economy. This way the government could give the impression that it was meeting the International Monetary Fund (IMF) key condition of reducing state subsidies without actually doing so. The banks, in their turn, kept only a minor, though still considerable, part of the money as payment for their services. Hough suggests 'that the bureaucracy

---

[13]   *Kommersant Daily*, 14 July 1995, p. 5.

[14]   The share of the 10 biggest banks stood at 30 per cent. Calculations are based on the *Interfax-rating of Russian Banks* (as of 1 September 1996).

[15]   For comparison, the corresponding rating for the leading representatives of the oil industry is 4.

[16]   All data according to D. Lane, 'The Russian Oil Elite' in D. Lane (ed.), *The Political Economy of Russian Oil* (Rowman and Littlefield, Oxford, forthcoming). The data are based on a survey of 118 leading business people in the Russian banking and finance sector, who were identified with the help of expert rankings of 'most influential businesspeople' in 1996 and 1997.

[17]   For an elaboration of this point, see K. F. Moors, *Russian Banking. An Overview and Assessment* (Donald W. Treadgold Papers, Washington, 1996).

was very patrimonial and the bank was attached to a high official as part of his responsibility for a sector in society'.[18]

In the Russian context contacts between bankers and state officials were in many cases transformed into corruption networks. When making decisions on licenses, credits, the sale of government bonds or the authorization of banks to deal with state funds, state employees had considerable latitude that allowed them to get into 'negotiations' with individual banks in order to get bribes. In turn, the banks could help state officials and politicians to conceal illegal income and transfer it abroad. Due to their control over important mass media and because of their ability to provide funding for election campaigns, banks were also valued by politicians as contributing to their ability to stay in power.[19]

IV.   CENTRAL BANK CREDITS AND GOVERNMENT BONDS

During the period of hyperinflation, 1992–1994, the most profitable activity of banks was the accumulation of deposits for which they had to pay little or no interest. By investing these deposits in an inflation-proof way, normally by buying hard currency, the banks could make profits as long as interest rates were lower than the inflation rate. Low interest rates were ensured by cheap credits from the Russian Central Bank and, to a certain degree, by big industrial enterprises depositing money in the bank that had been formed out of the related branch ministry. Russian banks also used deposits to engage in large-scale foreign exchange manipulations. An activity that was very profitable as long as turnover at foreign exchange markets in Russia was low and exchange rates highly volatile.[20]

Though the general situation was a consequence of the expansive monetary policy pursued by the Russian Central Bank, some banks were allowed to profit much more from the situation than others. This was due to the fact that there were no fixed criteria regulating the distribution of Central Bank credits. Instead, the relevant employees could decide on their own which banks were to be considered. Thus the classic conditions for the development of corruption networks were created. Accordingly, it is surely no coincidence that many of the leading managers of commercial banks had earlier been employed by Gosbank, the predecessor to the Central Bank.

In 1995, bank revenues were drying up as a result of macroeconomic stabilization. The Russian government now helped the banks out by offering short-term treasury bills (GKOs) with extremely high interest payments. In 1995 and 1996 the average real interest rate of GKOs exceeded 100 per cent per annum. Such extraordinary yields were not simply a risk premium in the emerging Russian market, but they

---

[18]   Letter from J. F. Hough to *Johnson's Russia List* (a free subscription news service) #3313 (30 May 1999), Part 6.

[19]   A. Fadin, 'The Oligarchs in Charge of "Russia Inc."' *Transition (OMRI)*, 4 April 1997, pp. 28–30; J. Johnson, 'Russia's Emerging Financial-Industrial Groups' (1997) 13 *Post-Soviet Affairs*, pp. 348–354; N. Lapina, *Die Wirtschaftseliten im Kräftefeld der russländischen Politik* (BIOst, Köln, 1997), pp. 12–13.

[20]   Aslund, n. 8 above, p. 497; J. Johnson, 'Banking in Russia. Shadows of the Past' (1996) 3 *Problems of Post-Communism*, pp. 49–59.

were a result of the fact that only a limited number of banks were allowed to take part in GKO auctions. The state thus limited the demand for its treasury bills deliberately and accepted the resulting higher interest it had to pay. In summer 1996 the annual yield of GKOs after inflation rose above 150 per cent. This has been interpreted as a sort of compensation payment to those banks that had helped to finance the election campaign of President Yeltsin. Later that summer, when all restrictions for foreign banks had been lifted, GKO yields fell sharply.[21] In 1997, GKO yields after inflation never exceeded 30 per cent. In July 1998, shortly before the Russian government defaulted on GKO payments, GKOs with a face value of USD70 billion were in circulation, issued to cover in total[22] a primary budget deficit of only USD15 billion. Accordingly, the buyers of GKOs received USD55 billion in interest payments in the period from 1994 to summer 1998.[23]

As a result of the default on 17 August 1998 together with the sharp devaluation of the rouble (which increased the rouble value of hard currency debts by more than 300 per cent by the end of 1998) most of Russia's commercial banks became insolvent.[24]

V. MANAGING STATE FUNDS

From 1994–1997 the Russian government annually authorized about 50 to 100 banks to manage state funds. In mid-1997 more than 40 per cent of state budget funds were managed by commercial banks. The remaining funds were handled by the Central Bank and by the treasury system of the Ministry of Finance.[25] The system of 'authorized banks' became a main source of corruption in the banking sector, because it offered attractive possibilities for rent-seeking. Instead of demanding interest payments for the money deposited the state often paid a fee for banking services. By delaying payments the banks, in fact, got interest free short-term credits from the state. Especially during hyperinflation the banks could make considerable profits by investing these state funds in GKOs or by speculating at currency markets.[26] It has also been speculated that only access to state funds allowed the big commercial banks to finance their bids in the privatization auctions from 1995–1997. Moreover, about USD300 million earned by the state during the 1995 auctions were directly reinvested in the banks that had won the auctions.[27]

In addition, the very limited control over the handling of state funds by private banks offered these banks and collaborating state officials opportunities for embezzlement. The first big scandal in this context was the 'grain affair' in the

---

[21] Aslund, n. 8 above, p. 497; R. Lyle, 'Banking Shake-out Expected to Thin Ranks of Russian Banks' *RFE/RL Weekday Magazine*, 22 August 1996, see <www.rferl.org>; Tompson, n. 4 above, pp.1173–1174.

[22] In the period 1994–1997.

[23] Figures according to *Russian Economic Trends*, Monthly Update, September 1998. Philip Hanson made this point at the BASEES annual conference, Cambridge, England, March 1999.

[24] See below for details on the financial crisis.

[25] *Jamestown Foundation Monitor*, 9 July 1997, see <www.jamestown.org>.

[26] Tompson, n. 4 above, pp.1170–1173; *Segodnya*, 29 November 1996, p. 5.

[27] *OMRI Economic Digest* (an email news service), 5 September 1996.

Vologda region which became known in August 1995. In summer 1994 the region had received nearly 22 billion roubles (at that time about USD4.5 million) from the federal budget for the purchase of grain. The responsible bank, which was partly owned by the brother of the region's governor, did not make the money available for the grain purchase but instead invested it profitably. The parties involved, allegedly, divided the profit, estimated by the State Chamber of Audit to amount to 4.7 billion roubles (at that time nearly one million US dollars).[28]

In the following years the system of authorized banks was repeatedly seen as a major source of corruption and embezzlement. An examination of the Audit Chamber of the State Duma concluded that between October 1995 and June 1996 more than 160 billion roubles (at that time about USD30 million) from state funds had illegally been invested in commercial banks, rather than being allocated to the rightful recipients.[29] In one case, the deputy minister for finance Vladimir Petrov was arrested on charges that he had collaborated with employees of the private Eskado-Bank which had stolen 13 billion roubles (at that time about USD2.5 million) of budget money. Petrov received USD520,000 as his share. The money was paid out in cash by a bank situated in Andorra.[30] On several occasions it has been alleged that authorized banks had embezzled state funds designated for the reconstruction of Chechnya.[31]

In the summer of 1997, the Russian minister for the economy, Yakov Urinson, intimated that profits from arms exports, managed by the state company Rosvooruzhenie, had been seeping out of government control as a result of the system of authorized banks which, he said, had ensured that the company's accounts remained 'convoluted and non-transparent'.[32] More detailed accusations were made by the head of the Russian Central Bank, Sergei Dubinin. He stated that the banks Unikom and MFK had misused more than USD500 million with the help of Vladimir Potanin, former deputy minister for the economy, and Andrei Vavilov, former deputy minister of finance.[33] Vavilov, who had just taken over a position in the management of MFK-Bank, left the bank shortly after the accusations had been published.[34]

In April 1998 the ministry for agriculture accused the bank SBS-Agro of delaying the payment of 2.3 billion roubles (at that time USD4 million) in state credits for agriculture for more than a year.[35] In the following month the State Chamber of Audit accused the bank of not having transferred funds from a development programme for small and medium-sized enterprises to the designated recipients. By illegally keeping the money SBS-Agro had allegedly earned 35 billion roubles (at that time about seven million US dollars) in interest.[36]

---

[28] *Izvestiya*, 15 February 1995, p. 1 and 5.
[29] *OMRI Daily Digest*, 15 November 1996, see <wwww.rferl.org>.
[30] *Kommersant*, 10 September 1998, p. 5.
[31] For a brief summary, see *The St. Petersburg Times*, 1 March 1997, see <www.sptimes.ru/>.
[32] *Jamestown Foundation Monitor*, 26 August 1997, see <www.jamestown.org>.
[33] *Associated Press*, 15 July 1997. See also the interview with Dubinin in *Moskovskie Novosti*, 13–20 July 1997.
[34] *RFE/RL Newsline*, 17 March 1998, see www.rferl.org>.
[35] I. Kirichenko and E. Makovskaya, 'Agrarnaia monopol'ka' (20 April 1998) *Ekspert*, pp. 18–19.
[36] *RIA Novosti Russian Economic News*, 7 May 1998, see <www.ria.ru>.

Mounting public criticism of the system of authorized banks and the possibility to blame this system for the non-payment of wages and pensions, caused the government and the president in 1996 to promise reforms. However, it was only in Spring 1997 when Boris Nemtsov joined the government, that a serious attempt was started to abolish the system.[37] According to a decree signed by president Yeltsin in May 1997 all state budget funds, from 1998 onwards, had to be managed by the Central Bank under the control of the ministry of finance. Until that date banks should get the authorization to manage state funds only as result of a tender.[38]

However, like so many projects in the short history of Russian economic reforms, this important step to put an end to rent-seeking behaviour in the banking sector has been delayed and watered down. Whether this was due to technical problems, as was claimed by the government, or to the influence of the corruption networks, as was alleged in many media reports, is hard to decide. Ultimately, these two aspects may have been mutually reinforcing.

Already in 1997 it was decided that the funds of the Ministry for Defence would continue to be handled by authorized banks.[39] State credits for agriculture were also to be channeled through authorized banks.[40] In early 1998 it was announced that authorized banks would continue to handle funds of the federal budget in regions where the Central Bank does not have a branch.[41] In March 1998 the government decided to transfer bank accounts of the Central Excise Customs Service to Oneksimbank without holding a tender, i.e. again a bank was authorized as result of an administrative decision.[42]

However, the banks were increasingly losing their interest in handling state funds. Budgetary shortfalls meant that the sums of money with which they could operate were declining. In addition, the state treasury system was taking over large parts of the state budget and state control was increasing. In May 1998 leading banks suggested that the state-controlled Sberbank should manage the funds of regional customs authorities.[43]

In August 1998, when many banks had to stop business activities in the wake of the financial crisis, it was no longer possible to maintain the system of authorized banks in the old form. In the aftermath of the crisis, the state-owned Sberbank became responsible for most of the funds handled by authorized banks. The share of other commercial banks was reduced to less than five per cent of all budgetary accounts.[44] However, as if to demonstrate the irrationality of the system, some customs committee

---

[37] *Interfax-AiF*, 26 May 1997, see <wwww.interfax.ru>; *Jamestown Foundation*, 9 July 1997, see <www.jamestown.org>.

[38] Presidential Decree No. 477 (12 May 1997), 'O merakh po usileniyu kontrolia za ispol'zovaniem sredstv federal'nogo byudzheta'. Published in *Sobranie zakonodatel'stva RF*, 20/1997, St. 2235, pp. 3887–3888.

[39] *RFE/RL Newsline*, 6 January 1998, see <www.rferl.org>.

[40] *Ekspert*, 8 December 1997, p. 4.

[41] Stephanie Baker, 'Finance Ministry is Establishing Treasury System' *RFE/RL Weekday Magazine*, 19 January 1998, see <www.rferl.org>.

[42] *RFE/RL Newsline*, 24 March 1998, see <www.rferl.org>.

[43] *RIA Novosti Russian Economic News*, 14 May 1998, see <www.ria.ru>.

[44] *Vremya MN*, 13 April 1999, p. 5.

funds were still being directed to Inkombank in January 1999, even though the bank had lost its license some months earlier due to bankruptcy proceedings. In February 1999, more than a year after the system of authorized banks should have been abolished, the government decided that all banking operations with budget funds have to be performed by state-controlled banks. Included in this group was, for example, the scandalous SBS-Agro, after it had pledged 75 per cent plus one share to the state.[45] SBS-Agro was among the five banks that were chosen to handle state funds for agriculture. In violation of the existing regulation the banks were not determined on the basis of a tender.[46] Moreover, regional budget funds are still being handled by authorized banks. The mayor of Moscow, Yuri Luzhkov, has built his own financial holding around Mosbiznesbank and Bank Moskvy.[47] In late 1998 Alfa Bank became the authorized bank for servicing the St. Petersburg city budget.[48]

VI. PRIVATIZATION AUCTIONS

With the help of the rent-seeking described above, Russia's big commercial banks gained considerable profits between 1992 and 1997. Since banks were normally not interested in providing credits to Russian enterprises or the population, they started to invest in the privatization process. In the first phase of privatization (1992–1994) Russian banks invested, initially, in light and food industries, where relatively small financial means were enough to obtain majority stakes in enterprises. Ownership of industrial enterprises offered the banks tax breaks and provided a guaranteed circle of customers.

In the second phase of privatization which started in 1995 some of the big private banks increased their participation considerably in the process and developed more ambitious investment strategies. These banks, namely Oneksim, Menatep, Alfa Bank and Inkombank, created industrial holdings. Accordingly, the interest of these banks now changed from light industry to the more profitable raw materials sector (mainly oil and metal industries). In order to obtain larger stakes in such enterprises considerable financial means were necessary. As a result, banks increasingly oriented their corruption networks towards participation in the privatization process.[49]

The outcome of this new orientation was the proposal of a group of big banks for the organization of loans-for-shares auctions (*zalogovye auktsiony*). The banks offered the government a credit of about nine billion roubles (at that time about two billion US dollars) for financing the budget deficit. As collateral they demanded shares in a number of enterprises. Control over the shares should be passed to the banks. The

---

[45] *Russia Morning Comment (United Financial Group),* 11 February 1999, p. 3.
[46] *Kommersant,* 2 February 1999, p. 7.
[47] D. Shevelev, 'Zolotaia moia stolitsa' *Novoe vremia,* 27 July 1998, pp. 18–19; *Kommersant Daily,* 11 June 1998, p. 4. See also the interview with A. Borodin, President of Bank Moskvy, in *Moskovskie Novosti,* 18 October 1998.
[48] D. Jensen, 'Rumors Of Oligarch's Demise Greatly Exaggerated' *Johnson's Russia List,* 9 December 1998.
[49] B. Aris, 'Demystifying the Magnificent 7' *Russia Review,* November 1997, pp. 9–10; Johnson, n. 19 above, pp. 344–345.

shares were to be offered in a number of privatization auctions to the banks that had made the highest bid. If the state would not repay the credit, the banks would keep the shares as compensation. In that case, the state would have the right to demand the sale of the shares within three years and would get a part of the selling price.

President Yeltsin accepted the offer and issued a decree regulating the proceedings of the auctions.[50] A list of 136 enterprises whose shares were to be auctioned was drawn up. However, after fierce protest from most of the enterprises included only 29 of them remained on the list in October.[51] The rules for the auctions had three weak spots which offered possibilities for manipulations to the corruption networks of banks. First, all bids were to be collected by one bank which itself was not barred from participating in the auction. This bank could wait with its own bid until it knew all rival offers. Moreover, it had the chance to disqualify its rivals for technical reasons.

Second, foreigners were not allowed to participate in the auctions. As a consequence, the number of potential bidders was rather limited and Russian banks could engage in insider dealings. Two banks, Oneksim and Menatep, were behind more than half of all bids. A further quarter was financed by Rossiiskii Kredit, Imperial and Inkombank.

Third, by setting the minimum bid far below the market value of the shares, the banks involved could obtain these shares at bargain prices. On average the price at which the shares were auctioned off was about 30 per cent below their market value.[52] Lukoil and Bank Imperial, for example, acquired a five per cent stake in the oil company at a price of about one US dollar per share, whereas Lukoil's strategic partner ARCO had only some weeks earlier paid six US dollars per share to obtain a six per cent stake. In the following year Lukoil shares climbed to a high of more than USD12 at the Moscow Stock Exchange.[53]

With such rules the proceeding of the auctions was determined. If the bank responsible for collecting offers was itself interested in acquiring the shares, it made a bid just above the required minimum and disqualified all rival bidders with a higher offer.[54] Accordingly, most auctions were won by the bank participating in the auction's organization. In none of these cases did the loan offered exceed the minimum bid by more than 15 per cent. If the bank responsible for collecting offers was not interested in the shares to be auctioned off, other bidders had a chance. Since the number of potential bidders was rather small, the normal outcome of such a situation was an auction in which only two or more subsidiaries of one and the same bank participated, all offering bids just above the required minimum.

[50] Presidential Decree No. 889 (31 August 1995). 'O poriadke peredachi v 1995 godu v zalog aktsii nakhodiashisia v federal'noi sobstvennosti'. Published in *Sobranie zakonodatel'stva RF*, 36/1995, St. 3527, pp. 6600–6611.
[51] V. Arsen'ev, 'Iskusstvo torgovat'sia s gosudarstvom' *Kommersant*, 14 November 1995, pp. 64–67; E. Siehl, *Privatisierung in Rußland* (FKKS, Mannheim, 1997), pp. 37–43.
[52] *OMRI Economic Digest*, 7 December 1995.
[53] *Pipeline News* (an email news service), 22 November 1996.
[54] I. Gorsts, 'Oil Industry Privatisation, Russian Style' *Petroleum Economist* (February 1996), pp. 3–4; N. Kalininchenko *et al.*, 'Vygodneishaia pokupka stoletiia' *Ekspert*, 11 December 1995, pp. 41–45; A. Privalov and A. Chernakov, 'Chto pokazala vskrytie' *Ekspert*, 28 November 1995, pp. 20–26.

Table 1. Results of the Loans-for-shares Auctions

Stake offered	Date	Bank collecting offers [a]	Required minimum bid [b] [millions USD]	Bidder – offer [millions USD] [Winner of each auction is given in top position]
Surgutneftegaz [c] (40%)	4 Nov. 1995	Oneksim	80	Surgutneftegaz Pension Fund – 89 Rosneft' – disqualified
Noril'skii Nikel [d] (38%)	17 Nov. 1995	Oneksim	150	Oneksim – 170.1 MFK [Oneksim] – 170 Reola [MFK] – 170 Kont [Rossiiskii Kredit] – 355
Chelyabinskii Metal Combine [e] (15%)	17 Nov. 1995	Oneksim	5	Rabikom [management + Imperial] – 13.3 Consortium [Promstroibank] – 10.5 Unikor [Rossiiskii Kredit] – 8 Union [Rossiiskii Kredit] – below minimum bid
Severo-Zapadnoe River Shipping Society [f] (25.5%)	17 Nov. 1995	Oneksim	6	MFK [Oneksim] – 6.05 Oneksim – 6 Karat [MFK] – 6
Sidanko [g] (51%)	7 Dec. 1995	Oneksim	125	MFK [Oneksim] – 130 RTD [Oneksim] – 127 Konsul [Alfa-Bank, Inkombank] – 126 Rossiiskii Kredit – disqualified
Novolipetskii Metal Combine[h] (15%)	7 Dec. 1995	Oneksim	*30*	MFK [Oneksim] – 31 Mashservis [MFK] – 30.5
Murmansk Shipping Society [i] (23.5%)	7 Dec. 1995	Oneksim	4	Strateg [Menatep] – 4.125 Vagant [Menatep] – 4.05
Lukoil [j] (5%)	7 Dec. 1995	Oneksim	35	Lukoil/Imperial Bank – 35.01 Natsional'nyi Rezervnyi Bank [Imperial] – 35
Yukos [k] (45%)	8 Dec. 1995	Menatep	150	Laguna [Menatep/ Stolichny/Tokobank] – 159 Reagent [Menatep/ Stolichny/Tokobank] – 150 Babaevskoe AO [Inkom et.al.] – 350 / disqualified

Stake offered	Date	Bank collecting offers [a]	Required minimum bid [b] [millions USD]	Bidder – offer [millions USD] [Winner of each auction is given in top position]
Novorossiiskii Shipping Society [l] (20%)	13 Dec. 1995	Menatep	15	Novoship [+ Tokobank] – 22 Oneksim – 17 Astarta [Menatep] – 15
Sibneft' [m] (51%)	28 Dec. 1995	Menatep	100	NFK [Berezovsky]/ Stolichny [Menatep] – 100.3 Tonus [Menatep] – 100 Samara Metal Combine [Inkombank] – 177 disqualified Inkombank – 175 disqualified
Nafta Moskva [n] (15%)	28 Dec. 1995	Oneksim	20	Nafta Moskva/ Unibestbank [Oneksim] – 20.01 MFK [Oneksim] – 20

Notes: [a] A government commission under the control of Alfred Kokh, head of the State Committee for State Property, was responsible for the overall organization of the auctions. [b] Kommersant, 14 Nov. 1995, 66. [c] OMRI Daily Digest, 20 Nov. 1995. [d] OMRI Daily Digest, 22 Nov. 1995. [e] Ekspert, 28 Nov. 1995, 20. [f] Ekspert, 28 Nov. 1995, 21. [g] Petroleum Economist, February 1996, 4. [h-j] Ekspert, 11 Dec. 1995, 44. [k] OMRI Daily Digest, 11 Dec. 1995. [l] Ekspert, 18 Dec. 1995, 30. [m-n] Izvestiia, 29 Dec. 1995.

Only two auctions saw real competition and successful offers considerably above the necessary minimum bid. (see Table 1)

The obviously manipulated auctions provoked criticism from many sides. The Duma founded an investigating committee to challenge the legality of the auctions. Banks that had been treated unfairly at the auctions went to court. The banks also used their influence on media outlets to publicize their point of view and accuse their rivals. This so-called war of the banks was not helpful for the election campaign of President Yeltsin, which started in early 1996. As a consequence, no further loans-for-shares auctions were organized in that year. In 1997 this method of privatization was banned by law.[55] The government repeatedly declared its intention to buy back some of the shares. However, that did not happen. By the end of 1998 all stakes had been bought by the banks that had received them as collateral.[56]

In late 1996 large-scale privatization again gained momentum. Stakes in enterprises were now offered in investment tenders. The winner of the tender

---

[55] *RFE/RL Newsline,* 28 July 1997, see <www.rferl.org>.
[56] *Kommersant,* 16 December 1998, p. 7. For more detailed information, see *Russian Economic Trends* 4/1998, p. 44.

undertook to invest a specified amount of money into the company being sold. Since this sum was included in the official selling price, the results of these tenders looked much better than those of the loan-for-share auctions, though the state budget did not benefit much more. Besides, it proved to be very hard to control whether an investor had made the demanded investment and even harder to enforce him to do so.

Furthermore, corruption networks found a way to manipulate the investment tenders too. Especially banks that had not won auctions in 1995 were now being favoured by state officials. For example, a condition for participation in the tender for a 40 per cent stake in the Tyumen Oil Company (TNK) was the provision of refinery equipment owned by Alfa-Bank. Therefore, it came as no surprise that Alfa-Bank won the tender. As in earlier auctions the result was contested by a law-suit and provoked public criticism.[57] When foreign bidders were finally allowed to take part in the large-scale privatization process, the winners of auctions had to pay prices close to the market value of the shares they obtained. In July 1997, 25 per cent in Svyazinvest were sold for nearly USD1.9 billion. In December 1998, a 2.5 per cent stake in Gazprom was sold for USD660 million.

The Svyazinvest auction again produced a scandal, because members of the losing consortium claimed that the government, in particular Anatoly Chubais, had manipulated the auction and determined the outcome in advance. However, with prices having reached market value and with the beginning of the financial crisis, Russian banks were no longer able to participate in privatization auctions. Moreover, the new privatization law which came into effect in late 1997 considerably reduced the potential for manipulations.[58] As a result the Rosneft' auction was cancelled because no offers had been made, and the Gazprom auction was won by Ruhrgas, a German company which obviously had made the only realistic bid.[59]

VII. THE FINANCIAL CRISIS OF 1998–1999:
THE END OF THE GAME OR MERELY NEW PLAYERS?

For a period of time Russia's big commercial banks had always been able to find a new form of rent-seeking when an old one had become less profitable. In the phase of hyperinflation, 1992–1994, they had made profits with the help of cheap Central Bank credits. After macroeconomic stabilization the state offered them new opportunities at the bond market and by authorizing them to handle state budget funds. Moreover, some banks got the chance of 'unbelievable bargains' in the

---

[57] *Nezavisimaya Gazeta*, 22 July 1997, p. 1. On the 'war of the banks' in general, see Johnson, n. 19 above, pp. 355–357.
[58] See *Russian Economic Trends*, 1997, pp. 102–106.
[59] N. Kalinichenko, 'Nordicheskaia stoikost' po-russki' *Itogi*, 21 July 1998, pp. 52–53; N. Kirichenko and A. Privalov, 'To li pravitel'stvo podchiniaet oligarkhov svoei ekonomicheskoi politikoi, to li oligarkhi – pravitel'stvo' *Ekspert*, 15 September 1997, pp. 10–12; *Kommersant Daily*, 25 November 1997, pp. 1–2; *RFE/RL Newsline*, 27 May 1998, see <www.rferl.org>; *Vremia MN*, 21 December 1998, p. 1.

privatization process. However, by 1997 it looked as if the situation was about to change.

The state had less to offer with debts mounting, mass media reporting about scandals in the wake of the 'war of banks' and demands for reform getting louder from all sides including the IMF. Moreover, some banks, for example Oneksim, Alfa and Menatep, were transforming themselves into industrial holdings and adopted a new business strategy, concentrating more on profitable industrial enterprises and less on banking activities. As a result of these developments, Russia's big commercial banks started to increase their lending to industrial enterprises. This change was also promoted by the first signs of macroeconomic growth that appeared in the official statistics in 1997.

However, this reorientation of Russian banks was brought to an abrupt end by the financial crisis that culminated in August 1998. In that month the government announced its default on domestic short-term treasury bills, most notably GKOs, and the Central Bank declared that it would no longer support the rouble corridor, thus allowing for a sharp devaluation of the national currency. The first move deprived the banks of considerable income, since all big banks were still heavily engaged in the GKO-market. At the same time, the second move increased the considerable hard currency debt of Russian banks. In rouble terms this debt rose by more than 300 per cent by the end of 1998. Moreover, the crisis caused many account-holders to withdraw their funds immediately. As a result many private banks became insolvent. Of the 1,500 Russian banks operating in early September, 200 lost their license by Spring 1999, among them four of the big private banks (Tokobank, Bank Imperial, Inkombank and Menatep).[60]

The crisis has changed the relationship between the banks and the state fundamentally. Most of the big commercial banks are now in desperate need of state support in order to survive. Accordingly, the balance in the relationship has changed in favour of the state. Moreover, the relationship is losing importance as the banks have become less powerful, and both – state and banks – have less to offer to each other. Nevertheless, many commercial banks still consider rent-seeking with the help of corruption networks to be the most promising business strategy.

Networks can influence the decision by which banks can get the necessary state support to avoid bankruptcy. The selective support given to favoured banks during the 1995 crisis can serve as an earlier example.[61] In November 1998 Viktor Gerashchenko, the new head of the Central Bank, announced that altogether about 14 billion roubles (at that time about USD800 million) in stabilization credits would be spent to save insolvent commercial banks. He presented a list of 15 banks given priority but did not explain according to which criteria the list had been made.[62] Until March 1999 credits worth USD365 million had actually been granted and the Central Bank had still not publicized any rules regulating its decisions.[63]

---

[60] *RFE/RL Newsline,* 10 February 1999, see <www.rferl.org>.
[61] Tompson, n. 4 above, p. 1175.
[62] *Nezavisimaia Gazeta,* 6 November 1998, p. 4.
[63] *Reuters,* 5 March 1999.

With some of the bigger private banks going bankrupt the government decided to use firstly banks controlled by the state to handle budget funds. In Spring 1999 state-owned Sberbank serviced more than 90 per cent of all budgetary accounts held in commercial banks.[64] At the same time some private banks offered shares as collateral to the state in order to meet the criteria. SBS-Agro and Alfa-bank, which had pledged 75 per cent and 25 per cent of their shares respectively to the state, were among the five banks authorized in February 1999 to handle state money for agriculture.[65] Moreover, SBS-Agro was said to be one of the main recipients of stabilization credits from the Central Bank.[66]

However, SBS-Agro had soon to realize how shaky the ground had become for rent-seeking banks. In late March the agricultural ministry demanded the return of state funds meant to finance the sowing campaign.[67] In early April an arrest warrant was issued for the bank's leader, Aleksandr Smolensky, on charges which had already been suspended once in 1992.[68] Though the warrant was later revoked, it was a clear warning sign to the corruption networks of the banks indicating that their good times were over.

The fact that the Russian state got tougher on banks under the governments of Evgeny Primakov, Sergei Stepashin and Vladimir Putin cannot simply be attributed to the fact that the banks were economically weakened as a consequence of the financial crisis. The attack on the banking sector also illustrates that the new governments were closer to the lobbies of the military industrial complex and heavy industry. These lobbies found a temporary ally in the IMF which was pressing for a restructuring of the banking sector with a view to limiting rent-seeking opportunities. However, two factors complicate the task of cleaning up and consolidating the banking sector. First, the government is still unable to handle the distribution of budget funds without the support of commercial banks. Second, as a result of heavy lobbying from different sides, the government is unable to develop a comprehensive restructuring programme that will find the necessary support.

That means the government still has to cooperate with commercial banks, but is unable to eliminate the corruption networks. The decision to prefer state-controlled banks can be interpreted as a reaction to this dilemma. However, the assumption that state-controlled banks are less prone to corruption is questionable and in the case of self-declared 'state-controlled' banks like SBS-Agro completely wrong. State officials working with the banking sector are used to collaborate with corruption networks that offer them a considerable 'second income'. Moreover, they will extract bribes as long as they have a opportunity to do so. Bank managers, on the other hand, will offer bribes as long as they expect them to ensure preferential treatment. Accordingly, it is not enough to liquidate insolvent banks and to arrest criminal bank managers and corrupt state officials. The important point is to introduce equal

---

[64] *Vremia MN*, 13 April 1999, p. 5.
[65] *Kommersant*, 2 February 1999, p. 7.
[66] G. Winestock and L. Bershidsky, 'The Oligarchs. Who's Up, Who's Down' *Moscow Times*, 12 January 1999.
[67] *Vremia MN*, 31 March 1999, p. 2.
[68] *Kommersant*, 27 April 1999, p. 1.

rules for all banks. As long as banks can avoid bankruptcy proceedings and arrest warrants with the help of informal contacts, corruption networks will continue to operate in the Russian banking sector.

14

Illegal Aspects of Trans-border Capital Flows from the Former Soviet Union

Leonid Fituni

I. INTRODUCTION

The current stage of development of organized crime in Russia is characterized by a pronounced striving of the mafias to legalize their fortunes. On the one hand, criminal syndicates in the Commonwealth of Independent States (CIS) are trying to make their fortunes safe, while on the other, they are trying to legalize the dirty money that they have accumulated. Thus, the country faces a double problem of capital flight and money laundering.

As shown earlier in this book (see the author's paper, chapter 2), the task of criminals was qualitatively facilitated by the introduction of privatization programmes and voucher privatization schemes. Criminal structures were allowed to buy for cash from individuals huge amounts of privatization vouchers, which were later used at tenders and privatization auctions for purchasing controlling stakes in existing state businesses offered for privatization. Needless to say, a significant part of the economy soon fell under criminal control – the financial capabilities of numerous mafias in Russia far exceed even the possibilities of Russian industrial giants. There was no serious resistance or counter-efforts – by Yeltsin's government, or the Soviet-era directors and managers of enterprises. The latter preferred to reach backroom agreements with illegal syndicates by which the 'red directors' preserved their jobs as heads of newly-privatized firms and had some guaranteed share in profits.

For their part, Western mafias found the chaos in legislation, transparent borders, widespread corruption and market *naïveté* which existed in Russia to be an ideal combination of conditions for broad scale money-laundering, including the possibility of investment in respected industries such as oil extraction, high-technology and banking. The laundered capital is not usually reinvested in Russia, but returns to the West, which to some extent explains the enormous size of capital outflow from investment-hungry Russia. Later, when newly rich Russians accumulated significant capital, they joined their western counterparts in smuggling money out of Russia in order to safeguard their assets against investigations or a change of political regime. Therefore, the illegal flows of capital across Russian borders should be viewed not

A. V. Ledeneva and M. Kurkchiyan (eds.), Economic Crime in Russia, 209–221
© 2000 *Kluwer Law International. Printed in Great Britain.*

only as a way of laundering money, but as a 'safety precaution'. When studying them, transfers in both directions should be investigated.

According to the figures provided in January 1998 by the former Russian Minister of the Interior Kulikov, the cumulative volume of capital flight from Russia between 1992 and the beginning of 1997 was about USD600 billion. This figure far exceeded Russia's combined domestic and external debts.[1] This makes an annual figure of outflows of about USD120 billion, while the official statistics put it roughly at USD10–20 billion per year. The gap in Russian International Monetary Fund (IMF) balance of payment projections varies from USD16.7 billion in 1992 to USD27 billion in 1998.[2] The figure gives an idea of the amount of capital that is not repatriated by Russian exporters, but this seems to be only the tip of the iceberg. It does not include sums from those operations that are the main contributors to statistically-exposed capital flight – for example, the funds that stay abroad as a result of the over-invoicing of Russian imports, the under-invoicing of exports, semi-legal bank transfers, and physical monetary outflows from Russia.

Figures from only one very early official investigation were made public in this respect. In May 1992, the Ministry of Foreign Economic Relations (MFER) of Russia made an assessment of capital outflow from Russia based on ministerial statistics. MFER named the following channels of capital outflow from Russia:[3]

- At least 10 per cent of export revenues (about USD4 billion per year) were not remitted to Russia under the pretence that the importer refused to pay for the imported goods. However, because 80 per cent of this money was used for the import of commodities from abroad, real outflow of currency in this form did not exceed USD800 million per year at the time of the review.
- Deliberate over-invoicing of imports and under-invoicing of exports. Companies report to the authorities false prices for commodities they buy or sell abroad, concealing their real profit and pocketing the difference. The latter is deposited in a Russian resident account opened with a western bank. The value of capital outflow in this form was about USD300–500 million per year.
- Advance payments against import contracts which partners 'failed' to fulfil (failed goods deliveries). The sums received by a foreign firm from a Russian partner are deposited in the account of the latter in a western bank. About USD300–400 million per year were accumulated in this form of outflow.
- 150,000–200,000 permanent residents of Russia opened private accounts in the West (not being outright illegal it is, however, normally frowned upon by Russian authorities) and kept there about USD300–600 million.
- Emigrants from Russia sold their apartments, *dachas*, cars, etc. for hard currency, asking to deposit the money in their accounts abroad. The annual outflow in this form is about one billion US dollars. Taking into account interest paid on deposits

[1]   *Sovetskaia Rossia*, 24 January 1998, p. 2.
[2]   Calculated on the basis of IMF, *Yearbook of International Financial Statistics* (Washington D.C., 1992–1999).
[3]   *Ekonomika i zhizn'*, No. 24, 1992, p. 14.

in western banks, the most modest assessment of an annual outflow of hard currency from Russia was about USD4–5 billion at that period. This figure did not include proceeds from smuggling, off-shore assets of corporations, the secret deposits of current rulers kept overseas for a rainy day, and the legal deposits of Russian organizations abroad. Already at that time the Russian Ministry for Foreign Economic Relations warned that without an effective system of state currency and customs control, strong auditing, financial and tax services, the future capital outflows would drastically increase.

In addition, according to the Russian State Property Ministry, in 1999 Russia owned over USD2.6 billion worth of real estate abroad, which included real estate assets of over 2,600 properties covering a total area of more than two million square meters in 120 countries. Russia also owns stock worth a total of USD1.37 billion in 122 foreign companies. Revenue from renting state property abroad came to USD12.7 million, while maintenance costs ran to USD82.3 million in 1997. Revenue from Russian stock in foreign companies came to more than USD200 million, mainly from the activities of the Vietnamese–Russian enterprise 'Vietsovpetro'. The inflows of funds from this property are unsatisfactory (and often disappear before reaching the state budget). There are grounds to believe that at least some of the proceeds from the exploitation of those properties remain abroad and are stashed away, either by the individuals in charge of the use of the property in question, or by the authorities for the purpose of uncontrolled hard currency expenditures (for example, election campaigns, information operations, etc.).[4]

Curiously, at the initial stages of reforms, it was not only outflows of hard currency that drained the Russian treasury. Illegal operations with roubles also proved to be extremely lucrative. The rouble was not and still is not a fully convertible currency. It cannot be freely exported abroad. There is only one legal instrument that allows Russian businesses and citizens to send money abroad without having delivered goods or services – a permit from the Central Bank of Russia. However, according to the bank's press service, no one applied for such a permit until 1997. Yet, over the first two years of Yeltsin's reforms, billions of Russian roubles have been purchased at favourable rates by westerners, who later used the money to buy up Russian industry.

Although non-residents were obliged to use hard currency to purchase Russian companies subject to privatization, foreigners preferred to buy them through Russian proxies or front companies for roubles which, taking into account the existing exchange rate, were much cheaper. Apparently 'business' flourished as hordes of intermediaries from the Former Soviet Union (FSU) flooded Europe, offering Russian currency in any amount. The risk ratio melted as the rouble continued to fall.

There are grounds to believe that the Italian–American mafia has also resolved to enter the 'quiet privatization' scheme. During the investigation of a mafia group headed by Giovanni Le Cassio, Italian police found huge amounts of Russian roubles

---

[4] *Argumenty i fakty*, No. 13, 1999, p. 2.

in Palermo. To understand the situation fully, one should keep in mind that so-called 'clean' and 'black' roubles circulated in Russia. The former were hedged by exchange certificates, but the latter were not – and consequently cost 15–20 per cent less. Both before and after the August 1992 monetary reform, Russian currency was sold off in aircraft containers filled with 1000-rouble and other notes. It is believed that dozens of such containers were flown to Zurich and later delivered to clients by truck.[5]

This kind of transaction has been registered by police in the West since 1991. Back in January 1991, Geneva police detained but then released two business people suspected of smuggling 70 billion roubles into the country. Supposedly, the money was intended for Andreas Bekhrens, a laundering expert of the Columbian Medellin drug cartel. Police officials later explained that they could not fathom why anyone would want to convert drug money into worthless roubles. Strange as it may seem, they were unaware that the rouble became a powerful instrument in the mafia's hands. At that time, an official at Societe des Banques Suisse was quoted as saying that 'the bank management was often approached with 100 million rouble deals'. The proposals could be for both roubles and dollars with offers coming at a monthly rate. Apparently, Western police were unable to break down rouble swindles on their own and in April 1992, Geneva's prosecutor general requested Russia's legal assistance. Journalists pumped up by the atmosphere of secrecy decided that Western police were investigating Communist Party funds, allegedly transferred abroad. Then it turned out that detectives were working to solve a money-laundering mystery that originated in Russia. Jean Louis Crochet, a detective, visited Moscow in September 1992. Upon returning to Geneva, he said police were fairly sure about the true identity of some suspects, adding that they intended to use Switzerland's money markets to dump 140 million roubles.[6]

Russian law-enforcement bodies are also aware that Russian-based representatives of banks from former Soviet republics are instrumental in the flight of billions of dollars and roubles from the country. Baltic banks (particularly Latvian ones) are especially successful in servicing money flows from Russia to the West. Almost all Latvian commercial banks service such flows via Latvia. Many of them sidestep formalities by combining semi-legal 'grey-zone' schemes with black-market practices. The principal advantage Russian clients have in dealing with Latvian banks is that unlike other countries' banks, they freely accept and convert roubles into foreign currency. They also carry on such transactions with the currencies of other CIS countries.

In connection with those services, Latvian banks' profits consist of conversion fees (between 0.5 per cent and 3 per cent, depending on the sum); a commission for accepting cash (the client pays the Russian bank 0.3 per cent to 1 per cent, from which the Latvian bank takes 0.15 per cent to 0.5 per cent); and a commission for paying out cash (from a 1.5 per cent commission the Latvian bank withholds up to 0.7 per cent). On top of this, the Latvian bank can use the client's money for lucrative deals. The average turnover of an typical bank on money-transfer transactions is

[5] L. Violante (ed.), *I soldi della mafia: Rapporto '98* (Laterza, Rome, 1998), p. 249.
[6] Ibid.

currently USD10–15 million a month. In exceptional times it was about USD15 million. Russian businesses may see some other advantages in working with Latvian banks. A legitimate firm can itself manage the funds in an offshore company's accounts, no matter in whose name it is registered. As a rule, Latvian commercial banks open only coded accounts for their clients. Upon opening an account, a client receives code keys, a password, and a telephone code (to obtain information by phone about the movement of funds from account to account). With the help of these code keys, the owner of a real offshore company can manage his account.[7]

Even if the code keys are lost, stolen, or confiscated, the client will not have problems in ensuring the secrecy of their deposits. Without going into detail, there is an original key (a table of letters or symbols) for each financial operation – an outsider cannot possibly make use of the table. On the Latvian side, legislation obliges it to disclose the secrecy and ownership of the deposit only if Latvia's Public Prosecutor's office makes such a request on the grounds of criminal prosecution. Disclosure without legal grounds will entail several years' imprisonment. For the moment, these are the best terms offered for Russian clients who prefer not to transfer funds abroad in a legal way.

II.   THE TECHNIQUES OF THE OPERATIONS

Approximately, until 1994, techniques for transferring money over the border were quite straightforward and unsophisticated. In fact there was not a great need for intricate schemes as the hard currency controls were selective and loose. A *Moscow News* correspondent reported about her friend's experience with such services provided by a foreign bank operating in Russia:

> At the time agreed, his company's employees, carrying cash roubles in sport bags and accompanied by guards, drove to a modest detached house with no special signs. They uttered the password, and were let in. In the corridor inside the house, they joined a long line of people literally holding their money bags. The transfer operation took no more than half an hour. Our heroes were not required to produce any documents (contracts or Central Bank permits) that confirmed the legality of the money to be transferred abroad. The cash was converted into foreign currency and forwarded to the addressee.[8]

Current schemes used for trans-border transfer, though less primitive, are also not very innovative. One of them, known as the 'Offshore Russian Firm' scheme, is the simplest. The offshore firm can be registered anywhere, but it must maintain an account with a foreign bank. (Usually for the sake of proximity and lack of language problems it is a Latvian one. Many of them are run by local Russian speakers who are permanent residents of Latvia.) Under this scheme, a Russian firm transfers roubles via a Russian bank to an off-shore Russian firm on the grounds of, for

---

[7]   *Moscow News,* 3–9 July 1997, p. 9.
[8]   Ibid.

example, a contract to conduct marketing research (used as a justification for the money transfer). The bank converts the roubles into any foreign currency of the client's choice, and then transfers the sum to the address indicated by the client. The weakness of this scheme is that the Russian firm must pay taxes on the results of the year's activity, which is considered to be an affront by many Russian companies.

Another scheme, called 'Two Russian Firms and One Offshore Company,' is more reliable and effective. Two Russian firms are registered: one legitimate and the other a sham. The offshore company is also a sham (for example, one registered with forged documents). The legitimate firm concludes a 'marketing contract' with the offshore company through the agency of the sham firm. The contract gives grounds to send money out of the country. Unlike the first scheme, in this case the legitimate firm will not have any tax problems. Taxes must be paid by the sham firm, which will have been liquidated by the time the tax inspectors come.

More complicated schemes involve the money-laundering element. Such schemes are usually related to foreign trade operations and require the participation of banks at some stage – usually the initial and final ones. Russian launderers predominantly use simple reliable techniques proved by time and experience. A typical one would be as follows:

- A group of people who would like to launder funds set up a company (Firm I), which in its turn would establish two daughter societies (A and B).
- The dirty money (for example, obtained through a bank loan fraud) would be placed in the account of one of the daughter companies – company A.
- The funds are converted through a friendly bank into hard currency and transferred abroad.
- The subsidiary company A is then liquidated.
- In the West, the funds go through a number of financial institutions, usually starting with a Russian owned off-shore company, via companies fully owned by foreigners (e.g. Israeli, Cyprus or other) and finally to 'respectable' banks and financial institutions.
- From the latter, the funds are transferred to the account of Firm II (a company associated with Firm I, or having a privileged agreement with it). The funds are transmitted against a specific contract, e.g. for food or consumer goods imports.
- The commodities are imported by the daughter company B, which resells them to the mother company Firm I and closes soon after the completion of the transaction.
- Firm I sells the commodities on the Russian domestic market and receives 'clean' money, which may be introduced into legal circulation.

As we see, the problem of money-laundering is closely connected to the problem of capital flight. A good example is the use of raw materials exporting firms. They became targets of infiltration and takeovers by criminal capital in 1992–1993. Such companies not only serve to launder illicit proceeds, but also to export the funds safely to the West. Numerous reports covered dramatic scrambles between different mafias over aluminium producers and exporters; the same applies to some oil companies. Russian timber exporters are reported to have concealed 50 per cent of their foreign currency earnings in 1994. According to the Federal Counterintelligence Service, violations by some of the exporters have been acquiring an 'increasingly criminal nature'. About 30 per cent of Russia's timber products was exported at dumping prices in 1994, and some areas (such as the Perm' region) exported timber at prices even below domestic ones. Security services uncovered widespread financial violations, mostly involving barter deals (30 per cent of all deliveries in 1994 were done through barter). Foreign currency earnings were concealed everywhere. The Arkhangelsk pulp and paper mill, for instance, concealed USD7.8 million of export revenues.[9]

A dramatic decline in production, despite a favourable market situation, and widespread violations have made timber producers themselves come out in favor of government regulation of the industry. By the start of 1995 virtually all timber export deals were supervised by the state-owned Roslesprom company, which has been granted the status of a government ministry. In the meantime, major Western financial institutions have been displaying a great interest in Russia's timber industry complex, paying particular attention to investment programmes that are gaining parity in Russian production facilities. Under existing Russian law, a foreign investor could own up to 35 per cent of the stock. However, the Swedish Tetra Laval still managed to acquire absolute control of the Svetogorsk pulp and paper mill, and according to newspaper reports, changes in its production policies have already been creating problems for the mill's traditional consumers inside the country.[10]

III. INTERNATIONAL PERSPECTIVE

Both Russian and foreign organized crime and drug cartels are actively using economic transition and the resulting chaos in Russia for laundering their proceeds. It is not possible to measure precisely the overall volume of the laundered funds. Currently no internationally-accepted methodology for such estimates exists. However, the United Nations (UN) Drug Control Programme[11] directly connects overall figures with the volume of international capital flight.

As far as international connections are concerned, in 1997–1999 there were reported a further sophistication of capital flight and money-laundering mechanisms, geographical expansion, and an increase in the volume of illicit funds laundering. These developments resulted from the increased generation of unlawful profits mainly in two sectors – violations of privatization laws in Russia and the dramatic increase of penetration of US and Colombian drug mafias into Russian and FSU territories. Both areas represent difficult cases for Russian law enforcers due to many factors, including:

---

[9] *Kommersant Daily*, No. 43, 3 October 1995, p. 6.
[10] Ibid.
[11] United Nations (UN) Drugs Control Programme, *Present Status of Knowledge on Illicit Drug Industry* (Vienna, 1994), p. 27.

- Intimate interconnection between the criminal aspect of financial activities and the implementation of free market policies in Russia; redistribution of Russian property is the core element of this course; it is supported by the global political and financial elite.
- Almost total involvement of Russian-based commercial banks in these operations – a factor that leaves practically no place for cooperation with 'honest' financial businesses in the fight against money-laundering.
- The 'Catch 22' situation in Russia: during the last presidential elections, the leading banks had established nearly total control over the mass media (except for marginal right-wing or communist low-circulation publications); in the event of any significant steps by law enforcement, a massive unified anti-police campaign was organized in the press and television, which presented the law enforcement's actions as anti-market, anti-Semitic (measured by the volume of operations, over 85 per cent of Russian banking capital belongs to ethnic Jews), and anti-democratic.
- Many money-laundering links lead to Central Europe, Israel, and the USA where Russian officials and agents have no possibilities to investigate. Cooperation with local law enforcement agencies is also not satisfactory; due to various reasons, the latter are usually reluctant to offer their Russian counterparts access to any serious information, to say nothing about allowing them to act. In the 1990s the general trend in such cooperation has been to take the tip-off from the Russians and then to exclude them from further action.
- The majority of Russian–American money-laundering links are virtually impossible to track in time because of their informal, non-structural nature – over a half of Russian financiers have dual citizenship, many have close relatives who are American citizens, enjoy freedom of movement between both countries, and rarely sign formal agreements or keep written records of their financial transactions. They have physically become the key link in the circulation of financial funds between Russia and the USA – both on the grass root level between small and medium scale business and on the large scale, having occupied the majority of Russian-related positions with big corporations.

The combined effect of the above-mentioned factors brought about a dramatic increase in funds trafficking between Russia and the rest of the world. Consequently, during the last two years, there was a stable increase in reports of individual cases of money-laundering-related movements of capital. The presidential elections of 1996 in both Russia and USA have somewhat reduced the number of such media reports which were harmful to the image of both presidents, but since that time, they have restarted with even higher frequency.

In a bid to halt capital flight from Russia, the government in 1997 set up a special commission headed by the prime minister. Although the law enforcement bodies are well informed about who is taking money out and how, their efforts to stop the outflow of billions of dollars over the last few years have failed.

After the dismissal of Mr. Dubinin as Chairman of the Central Bank of Russia (CBR), when the Audit Chamber of the Parliament had opened an investigation into the CBR's activities following the sharp devaluation of the rouble and the near collapse of the banking system in August 1998, it became known that as an institution, the CBR itself was not without sin in orchestrating capital flight.

The Russian government, at a high level, had permitted the bank to operate without proper control and to speculate on the market ups and downs which it often foresaw. It was allowed to make commercial profit from the game, and to spend on itself any share of the profit. Russia's chief prosecutor revealed that the CBR had diverted some of its reserves into an offshore account with the financial company 'Fimaco'. The CBR alleged that it set up the account to protect the reserves against foreign creditors.

The Prosecutor General's office issued a letter to the State Duma on 1 February 1999, claiming that Fimaco, within a five year period, had received Russian foreign currency assets amounting to USD37.3 billion, DEM9.98 billion, JPY379.9 billion, FRF11.98 million and GBP662.6 million. The CBR was adamant that the funds placed at Fimaco's disposal had been well below the sum stated by the prosecutor's office and that the money had already been repaid to the CBR, with interest. According to the investigation materials, the bank management sanctioned speculative GKO (Russian Treasury Bills) trading with Russia's foreign currency reserves. Back in 1993, the CBR's subsidiary 'Eurobank' and the Fimaco company set up the 'Eurofinance Bank', which became an active player on the GKO market. Thus, Russia's forex reserve funds started circulating on the GKO market. Duma Deputy Nikolai Gonchar estimated that these operations produced a USD38.9 million gain in 1996 alone.

Official data show Fimaco was established in President Gorbachev's times (in 1990) by Eurobank to serve its specific needs (formally established by the USSR in the West to service its foreign trade turnover). It was the period when the power of the Communist Party was dwindling and the farsighted Soviet *apparatchiks* (many of whom later became businessmen, prominent democratic politicians, and heads of independent states) were looking for ways to preserve the financial resources at their disposal for future use. The CBR did not exist then. Having taken over the assets of the former Soviet Gosbank, CBR a few years later turned to Eurobank – allegedly as a customer.

According to Eurobank President Andrei Movchan, 'the commission Fimaco received for managing the Central Bank's assets was below the market rate, constituting 0.062 per cent of the average annual sum of the assets managed'. The CBR's assets were invested in 'either first-rate Western banks or first-rate securities'. Movchan said that all the funds managed by Fimaco grew, peaking in September 1994. By then, the total amount was USD1.4 billion. Then it began to decrease and by 1996, there were no CBR funds under Fimaco's management. The company received less than USD1.7 million throughout the period it was managing the CBR's assets. Due to the company's offshore registration in the Channel Islands, the CBR received larger profits than if it had undertaken fund placement itself through CBR Head Viktor Gerashchenko.[12]

---

[12] *Russkie Zametki*, 9 March 1999.

Strictly speaking, there is currently no evidence that the CBR's relationship with Fimaco was illegal. The Auditing Chamber Chairman Khachim Karmokov restated this at a press conference on 2 March 1999. According to him, the audits performed by the Chamber revealed no serious procedural breaches in the bank's performance. However there are suspicions that some state officials might have gained financially from those operations.

By a strange coincidence, days after the press conference another parliamentarian, Viktor Ilyukhin, Chairman of the of Security Committee of the Russian Parliament, invited Boris Yeltsin to move the President's personal savings from foreign bank accounts to Russian banks. 'There is a way out of the financial blind alley', Ilyukhin said. He alleged that if Yeltsin regards himself as a patriot and is not indifferent to 'the tragedy of the people', he could transfer his personal accounts from foreign banks, 'for example in England', to Russia and 'thus help the people in practice to emerge from the economic crisis'. 'There is money in Russia and abroad', Ilyukhin claimed. According to him, the hundreds of billions of dollars pumped out of Russia during the years of *perestroika* and reform help the West to cope with its own economic difficulties and to continue placing political, economic and military pressure on Russia. If Yeltsin took this step, it would be possible to demand that the business tycoons and 'new Russians' follow his patriotic example, Ilyukhin said. He claimed that the amount of money returned to Russia in this way would be much greater than the sums being negotiated with the IMF and other international financial institutions. Ilyukhin promised to get the ball rolling on amendments to the criminal code that would set criminal responsibility for non-repatriation of capital to Russia. He said his message would be sent to Yeltsin the same day. According to his estimate, Russians keep billions of dollars in bank accounts abroad.[13]

IV. EFFORTS TO REPATRIATE THE MONEY

Even the visible and officially acknowledged illegal flight of capital from Russia is incomparable in volume with the amount of international aid the country received during 1992–1999. In fact it is higher by orders of magnitude. Due to the internal instability and unfavourable foreign currency regulations, Russian companies and individuals stash their currency earnings in foreign bank accounts rather than bringing the money home and investing it in Russia. Money was flowing into Russia as loans and disappeared into thin air.

To get things moving, the government formed a special commission in 1997 to curb illegal import-export and currency-financial operations. It included Prime Minister Viktor Chernomyrdin and the heads of all ministries and departments concerned. For more effect, all commission members were ordered to attend meetings in person, without the right to be replaced. However, in the next two years the situation became even worse than before.

In fact, the top leadership were themselves guilty of directing the money flows abroad. In the summer of 1998, under American pressure, the IMF released USD4.8

---

[13]   Ibid.

billion to Russia, most of it for a futile defence of the rouble. That momentary support for the country's currency allowed members of the Russian pro-Western power structure to convert personal holdings into dollars. In that way, a substantial amount of IMF funds ended up in numbered accounts overseas.[14] A press release of the Security Committee of the Russian Parliament of 23 March 1999 gave the details of those transfers. The document alleged that on 14 August 1998 (three days before devaluation), in accordance with the loan agreement between the IMF and Russia of 24 March 1998, the IMF loan funds were transferred from Account No. 9091 of the Federal Reserve Bank of New York to Account No. 9091 in KreditAnstalt-Bankverein via its Lugano office (Switzerland) as a transit transfer in favour of Ost-West Handelsbank (Frankfurt, Germany). The latter is a subsidiary bank of the CBR. KreditAnstalt-Bankverein credited Account No. 40910 of Ost-West Handelsbank in USD for the whole sum of the IMF tranche (USD4.8 billion) in favour of the CBR.

According to the document, the IMF loan funds allegedly did not reach Russia in full, but were divided among a 'narrow circle of top officials and trusted persons'. It further alleges that on 14 August 1998, USD2.35 billion were directed to the Bank of Sydney (Australia), where USD235 million of the above-mentioned sum were deposited in the bank account of an Australian company, of which the President's daughter allegedly owns 25 per cent of the capital through her Luxembourg based trustee. Of the rest of the sum, USD2.115 billion were converted into pounds sterling and transferred to accounts in the National Westminster Bank.

The document also contains information of multi-million dollar transfers to the Bank of New York, Credit Suisse, and KreditAnstalt-Bankverein, which the Security Committee associates with the name of the then Chairman of the CBR, Mr. Sergei Dubinin.[15] Though there was no independent confirmation of the numbers of the accounts and the exact sums transferred, the fact of funds embezzlement was indirectly acknowledged by the US Secretary of Finance Robert Rubin.[16]

It was only the August 1998 crisis and under the new premier Evgeny Primakov that serious attempts were made to undertake measures against the main perpetrators of the illegal and semi-legal capital outflows. Tax police searched offices of major corporations belonging to the oligarchs, who amassed enormous fortunes in their overseas accounts.

Searches were carried out at individual commercial banks – 'Russian Banking House' commercial bank and its subsidiaries 'Absolut' and 'East Bridge Bank', as well as at the 'Lang' and 'Profodezhda' firms at the beginning of April 1999. According to news sources, searches were carried out on the basis of information that the named organizations had moved large sums of hard currency abroad. During the searches, false contracts and other documents, including financial accounts on whose basis hard currency was transferred abroad, were confiscated. Moreover, the personal files of some staff members were also confiscated. Certain staff members

---

[14]   *The New York Times*, 19 March 1999.
[15]   The full text of the statement of the Chairman of the Security Committee was published in *Zavtra*, No. 13, 1999, p. 1.
[16]   See n. 13 above.

were suspected of involvement in the establishment of front companies through which hard currency was pumped abroad. The sources said that in the first two months of 1999, about USD400 million was transferred abroad. The search and questioning sessions 'have provided serious proof that the managers of some of the said organizations were involved in the establishment of front companies and in transporting large sums of hard currency abroad'. Representatives of the Moscow Prosecutor's Office have told Interfax news agency that 'similar operations will be carried out shortly in relation to some other commercial banks which, through front firms, have transferred "large amounts of hard currency to off-shore zones."' They said that over USD200 million was thus moved abroad.[17]

In its efforts to repatriate the money, the Russian Government tries to combine the stick with a carrot by considering softer ways of legalizing funds smuggled overseas. The Russian Finance Ministry, on 23 February 1999, submitted to the government draft amendments allowing the unrestricted opening of anonymous accounts at commercial banks. It is proposed that anonymous accounts may be opened in all banks operating in Russia, including subsidiaries of foreign banks. The draft envisages that bank accounts will not require personal data, as is the case with numbered accounts. Theoretically, this should attract certain private resources to banking and later to the real sector. While the procedure for servicing anonymous accounts would be developed by the CBR, interest rates would probably be set somewhat lower. Moscow Deputy Tax Chief Mikhail Alexeyev said that the existing system of tax control will guarantee taxation of money in anonymous bank accounts. Moscow Tax Chief Gennady Bukayev said that tax bodies are not interested in the origin of the money: 'We are interested in the taxpayer paying taxes on the income, specifically on interest', he said. At the same time, the idea of 'amnesty on repatriated capital' was discussed in various quarters.[18]

V. CONCLUSION

Illegal cross border monetary transfers remain one of the biggest problems facing Russian society. It is closely connected with the nature of social and economic processes unleashed in Russia after the downfall of the communist regime. The success of the fight with capital flight and money-laundering depends on the attitudes of the authorities, which until recently were not fully interested in curtailing the activity due to political and personal reasons.

Broadly speaking, the problem stems from the revolutionary character of transition in Russia, which is accompanied by numerous outbreaks of political violence and armed confrontation (19–21 August 1991, 23 February 1992, 1 and 9 May 1993, 22 June 1993, September–October 1993, numerous clashes in the provinces, and the war in Chechnya in 1995–1996). Political violence and the liberal revolution have polarized Russian society, while the confiscatory methods of the reforms have eroded their legitimacy. Fundamentally, the transition from communism to capitalism means

---

[17] *Interfax*, Daily Business News Report, 7 April 1999.
[18] *Vek*, No. 11, 1999, p. 6.

a re-introduction of the pre-Soviet (i.e. pre-1917) system of law and the relations of ownership. However, under capitalism and socialism, the same legal terms and notions often have opposite contents. The same economic actions receive opposite legal assessment, i.e. what is absolutely legal in one case is a grave crime in the other. As a result, the current legal space is ambiguous and heterogeneous in Russia.

Judging by election results, in the eyes of at least a half of the Russian population, the current processes in Russia (e.g. privatization, when the former public property is being confiscated from common use and distributed among the chosen few) are illegal. In fact, according to the above-mentioned materials of an independent parliamentary investigation, nearly all significant cases of privatization in Russia involved some kind of violation of laws, even those introduced by the reformers themselves.

The detailed analysis of how well grounded and justifiable those attitudes are lies beyond the aims of this chapter. However, it is disturbing that the transition is seen as nothing more than the process of legalizing illegally-obtained funds and property, which afterwards are illegally smuggled overseas. This makes capital flight, money-laundering, and the legalization of illicit proceeds not merely issues of law, but also political ones. Russian authorities realize that any serious and far-reaching investigation may put under threat the achievements of capitalist restoration of the last decade. The situation is further aggravated by the fact that many outstanding reformers, business and political leaders are concurrently perpetrators of major capital flight and /or money-laundering schemes. International cooperation with Russia in this sphere has its limitations. Elements in the law enforcement bodies in Russia may be genuinely interested in such a cooperation, but their superiors are keen not to allow the investigations to spill over to high political quarters. On the other hand, corruption within the law enforcement agencies also limits the possibilities of cooperation.

Finally, a 'conspiracy of silence' exists both internationally and in Russia about the doubtful legal nature of many privatization projects in the country. On the one hand, it is an open secret that the majority of privatizations were carried out with various violations of law, and therefore that profits generated from those privatized entities may formally be qualified as illegal. However, such acknowledgement immediately makes hundreds of transnational corporations which purchased stakes, or otherwise participated in the activities of privatized businesses, perpetrators of money laundering – a fact that they will never accept.

There is no quick solution to the problem. It is obvious that the phenomenon is likely to persist until a new generation of politicians and business people take over the Russian economy.

15

Russia: Multiple Financial Systems and Implications for Economic Crime

Vladimir Chorniy

I. INTRODUCTION

This paper will demonstrate that the Russian financial system is distorted and that Russia does not have a single financial system but what could be considered a combination of three quasi-independent financial systems, each with its own domestic currency.[1] The existence of this triple financial system with three currencies imposes an additional cost burden on the economy. Attempts by economic agents to reduce this extra cost will inevitably cause an increase in illegal activities and may create a new area of crime. One can draw a parallel with tax evasion that is often excused by the participants on the basis that the tax burden is too high and unfair. Many in the financial system will also consider the burden of this additional cost unfair with obvious criminal consequences.

The reason for the existence of this multiple financial system is that the Russian financial system has been distorted by government regulations. As a result, in many cases, activities that would be considered either near criminal or abnormal by western standards were forced onto the financial and banking system of Russia and other former Soviet republics by the particular features of the legal system. This means that the path of heavy intervention adopted by the state is counterproductive. Consequently, tighter and more detailed regulation of the Russian financial system will have a far smaller effect on reducing economic and financial crimes than might initially be expected.

The intention of this paper is to analyze three financial systems centred on three domestic currencies:

---

[1]   Yulia Latynina distinguishes three types of money in circulation in Russia. They are: dollars issued by the US Federal Reserve System; roubles issued by the Central Bank of the Russian Federation; and surrogate money, including nonpayments issued by enterprises, local administration, banks and individual government department, (*Izvestiya*, January 30, 1997, p. 4). The first type is not considered in this paper. For more information about the dollarization of post-Soviet Russian economy see Edward Feige's contribution in P. Seabright (ed.), *The Vanishing Rouble: Barter Networks and Non-monetary transactions in Post-Soviet Societies* (Cambridge University Press, Cambridge, in press).

A. V. Ledeneva and M. Kurkchiyan (eds.), Economic Crime in Russia, 223–236
© 2000 *Kluwer Law International. Printed in Great Britain.*

- Cash (*nalichnye*) roubles.
- Electronic roubles, i.e. funds deposited in various accounts. We will refer to this as non-cash (*beznalichnye*).
- Barter 'roubles' used in accounting during barter transactions. Although it is acknowledged that barter is also a non-cash transaction, this paper will reserve the term 'non-cash' for electronic money in different accounts.

To make the presentation more convenient this paper will concentrate first on cash and non-cash and then move on to barter.

II. CASH AND NON-CASH FINANCIAL SYSTEMS

In developed economies for the majority of enterprises whose business involves large- and medium-scale monetary transfers, a non-cash system is the most efficient one in which to operate. The non-cash currency functions in the institutional framework of the banking system. In Russia the heavy intervention 'squeezed' the enterprises from the non-cash system into two alternative financial systems: cash and barter. This 'squeezing' is primarily produced by two factors.

The first factor is a strong limitation on the liquidity of money in enterprise accounts. Generally, the state imposes a large number of restrictions on how many and which kind of accounts can be opened, limits on the type of funds that can be transferred between the accounts, and very strong limits on the conversion of the funds in an account to cash. For example in 1994–1995 there were limits of one current account for settlement per company, limits for the transfer between current and long-term deposits, as well as limits on the amount enterprises could take from their accounts.[2]

The second factor is tax pressure. The money in accounts is at risk of extraction by the tax authorities which are allowed to withdraw money from enterprise accounts – in many cases without a court order *and* without the enterprise having the right of appeal.

Both factors create a strong incentive for an enterprise to leave the non-cash financial system. Cash roubles have an ultimate liquidity and tax 'stealth', so it is natural that cash-in-hand is worth more than money in an account. Barter roubles, which will be discussed later, are less liquid and have less 'tax-stealth', but are more suitable for large transactions and thus provide an alternative to the cash route of escape for enterprises. Cash acts as a parallel currency since it is used for high volume (unrecorded) transactions, and is used, stored and transferred outside the banking system, i.e. a separate cash financial system came into existence.

If there are two currencies there will be an exchange rate. At the beginning of the 1990s the ratio of non-cash to cash roubles was as low as 30 per cent; by the end of 1996 it was close to parity.[3] The actual exchange rate can vary depending on the type of enterprise, the amount of non-cash involved, and other details of the deal. Another problem in calculating the exchange rate is that it is heavily

---

[2] See W. Tompson, 'Old Habits Die Hard: Fiscal Imperatives, State Regulation and the Role of Russia's Banks' (1997) 49 *Europe–Asia Studies*, p. 1166.

[3] For example, according to Tompson, ibid, the ratio was 96 per cent.

mixed with charges levied for the transaction. However, even if the exchange rate is at parity, it does not mean that cash and non-cash have become indistinguishable. As long as the dual currency system exists, the market expectations are different for each of them – with typical implications observed in an international currency market. It is common knowledge that even if two currencies happen to have equal value, financial instruments in each currency will behave differently due to different market expectations. In the case of currencies, for example, there would be differing volatility of the spot and forward exchange rates, different yield curves, different associated volatilities and, especially important for Russia, different tax implications. These factors will be incorporated in contracts between all agents in the economy (for example, forward transactions in both currencies), including non-financial organizations (e.g. industrial firms). Although in the case of cash and non-cash both pseudo-currencies are linked to the same economy, our conclusions are not affected since they again carry different market expectations and exist under different circumstances. The effect of the availability of soft credit[4] in 1992–1993 gives a dramatic example of this bifurcation.

Economic operations in two (or more) currencies always incur additional costs (e.g. cross currency transaction cost,[5] cost of hedging of risk, etc.). These costs are passed down to enterprises. This means that the desire of the government to have extra control levers over the financial and monetary system[6] imposes an additional cost on the economy. Naturally, economic agents will attempt to reduce this extra cost by a variety of means, including criminal ones.

If one looks at the legislation as a cause for this multi-currency structure, it will be observed that it has been developed along these lines during the 1990s and is now solidly entrenched in a variety of legal acts. Therefore, the legal system is not underdeveloped – in fact it was developed during the 'capitalist' era. Tompson, who considered the process of separation of cash from non-cash into a dual circuit, listed the major reasons why the authorities prefer such a dual system.[7] He did not, however, consider barter, which forms yet another circuit.[8]

In the Soviet era, money (non-cash roubles) served as an accounting unit to measure the planned flow of goods and services. Any conversion into cash was severely limited, since the only need for cash was for wages and transactions involving private individuals. In other words, there was segregation of a state-planned macro economy involving enterprises that used non-cash and the banking system, and a personal cash economy with its absence of private property, entrepreneurs and a banking system. The two parts were linked through the shadow economy.

---

[4] The term 'soft' refers to credit which is made easily accessible without proper credit check (verification of repaying ability, business plans, current financial conditions of the borrower) and, commonly, on conditions much better that market circumstances would command.

[5] Quite significant resources are involved in converting non-cash into cash. This is also true for barter transactions.

[6] See discussion below.

[7] Tompson, n. 2 above.

[8] The question whether hard currency forms one more circuit will be left open.

Therefore, the separation of cash and non-cash already existed in the Soviet economy and was strongly ingrained in it both economically and psychologically. So an important starting point is that the dual system was not created during market reforms, but was only adapted and retained. The reasons for this retention[9] are several. First, there were the needs of the rouble zone in 1992–1993 (The Central Bank of Russia had a monopoly on the issuance of rouble cash, so central banks of other republics in the rouble zone had freedom only in the non-cash area). Second was the question of income control, i.e. control of inflation through the control of wage growth. Wages are paid in cash, so restricting conversion of non-cash into cash ensured that enterprises would not be able to grant excessive wage increases, which was a worry in the initial stages of reforms. Third, the dual currency circuit detached the cash rouble from the inflationary pressure of soft credit in non-cash in 1992–1993 and, as became clearer later, cash shortages can themselves play an anti-inflationary role. However, the major reason was a fiscal one. The existence of the dual system makes tax collection easier for authorities by limiting the ability of enterprises to conduct unrecorded cash transactions. So the weak administrative capability, and hence tax collecting capability, and the ensuing revenue hunger of the state are the major reasons for retaining the cash/non-cash system after factors such as the rouble zone, soft non-cash credit and fear of excessive wages have disappeared.

Heavy intervention by the authorities to maintain the double circuit resulted in a heavily skewed banking system in which 'banks are not banks'. Generally, all limitations on liquidity in the financial system work strongly against banks. To make the matter worse, the banks are charged with a supervisory role over enterprises in regards to account use and fund transfers, i.e. the banks are forced by law to be the enforcers of these limits on liquidity. A large proportion of these restrictions is the result of the state's attempts to improve tax collection with which, again, the banks, including commercial banks, are charged. In a sense, the banks became the agents of the tax inspectorate. Even apart from the fact that tax legislation is both aggressive[10] and self-contradictory,[11] the fact that the banks are the agents of the tax inspectorate and are the major brakes on the liquidity in the financial system, especially in inter-enterprise markets, puts them in a difficult self-contradictory position as they are forced to act against their own interest and general *raison d'être*. After all, the banking system and banks have a primary purpose and self interest to provide liquidity and flexibility to the financial system.

---

[9] Tompson, n. 2 above.

[10] The banks are required not only to provide information to the tax authorities, but also to assist in 'raids' by authorities on enterprise accounts.

[11] For example, there is ongoing controversy whether taxes have to be charged to the account before wages (generally civil law requires to give priority to payment of wages). In any case, the enterprises have no freedom in choosing payment priorities (this, of course, is well compensated by widespread tax evasion and financial fraud) or even can be blocked completely from managing their own account (if they are in debt arrears – *schyot nedoimshchika*). This of course puts in grave doubt enterprises' ability to escape the debt, which usually requires flexibility in resource management.

Under such circumstances one would expect banks to be unable to make a profit. However, too many tears should not be shed for the banks. To a large extent, the banks in Russia are not 'real' banks. Their business activities can not be considered 'banking' in the western sense – taking deposits from the population and enterprises and lending money for various projects. The general problem is that the majority of assets do not perform and the majority of liabilities are cost free. The major source of Russian banks' income was trading activity (largely foreign exchange operations and investment in GKO (Russian Treasury Bills))[12] or channeling budgetary funds. Moreover, due to the existence of the dual financial system and the necessity for enterprises to deposit money in banks, the banks could offer effectively negative interest rates. As a result, a high percentage (70–80 per cent)[13] of Russian banks' liabilities is free. These free liabilities are not used properly as the money is not reinvested in industry. Only a small proportion is used for normal investment (at the start of 1997 banks' loans to non-financial companies equaled only 10 per cent of gross domestic product (GDP))[14] and even that is poorly performing. In fact, banks often do not have proper facilities to lend; the necessary credit expertise could be severely lacking. Of course, banks follow rational behaviour given the legislative and economic situation in the country, i.e. the possibility of higher profits in capital markets (investments in GKO) and an imperfect legal base.

III.   BARTER AS THIRD FINANCIAL SYSTEM

On one hand, barter stands in opposition to the cash/non-cash phenomenon as the state (at least officially) tries to limit the scope of the barter economy[15] and as the explosion of barter transactions did not derive from state regulation. This differs from the separation of cash and non-cash systems that, as was discussed in the previous section, was a planned (or at least expected) development. On the other hand, it will be seen that barter, as a separate financial system, is a natural result of the heavy intervention from the state and that from an economic point of view, it follows the same logic as the cash/non-cash separation.

The notion of barter as the third financial system in the economy, at least at first glance, appears to contradict the non-monetary nature of the phenomenon. However, this paper will demonstrate that if one accepts a broad barter definition such as that of Seabright and Ledeneva,[16] for example, and considers the complexity and flexibility of the barter economy and the role of the state within it, there is a good

---

12   However, it should be noted that it is normal for a bank in any country to keep a significant proportion of liquid funds in the form of government securities.
13   Tompson, n. 2 above, p. 1165 and pp. 1176–1177.
14   'Russian Banking. Too Much Trouble' *Economist*, 10 January 1998 84.
15   The resilience of the barter economy is the reverse side of the coin of the state support for a cash/ non-cash separation, but this does not cover all peculiarities of barter. For example, the relevance of barter to political independence of local authorities will be ignored. It should be mentioned, however, that this matter relates directly to the interesting point of local pseudo-money.
16   P. Seabright and A. Ledeneva, 'Barter in Post-Socialist Societies: What Does it Look Like and Why Does it Matter?', Ch.4 in P. Seabright, A. Ledeneva (eds.), *The Vanishing Rouble: Barter and Currency Substitution in Post-Soviet Societies* (Cambridge University Press, Cambridge, forthcoming).

case for considering barter as the third financial system with its own 'virtual' currency: 'barter roubles'.

Since this paper will attempt to consider the barter economy as a continuation and escape route from the non-cash rouble economy, it is logical to accept the broadest definition of barter. However, it is important to start with a basic understanding of barter as transactions (exchanges of goods) satisfying matching demands. The commodities are traded directly; this kind of transaction requires a 'double coincidence of wants'. This type of exchange of commodity will not necessarily involve only two parties (and parties in barter can include not only enterprises but also individuals). In fact, the network of parties participating in exchanges can be very complex.[17] In its simplest manifestation it would involve the payment of workers' wages using goods produced in their factory. A more complex variation would involve payment in goods received by the factory from another enterprise as part of a barter transaction. On a more complex scale, this will be part of a chain of exchanges, other links of which might involve surrogate currencies and even the flow of cash and non-cash. It is possible that the entire scheme can be separated into semi-independent sub-schemes, which at first glance appear to be nearly complete (no unfinished flows) and legal, but which exist parallel to an illegal scheme.

The possibility of payment of wages or other obligations by barter makes it logical to include various debt offsets as part of barter transactions. From this the next step is to include in the definition of barter deals which involve what could be called 'commodity currencies'. A commodity currency is a commodity accepted as a payment for services, not for direct consumption, but to be stored and used later in other barter transactions. Seabright and Ledeneva give a number of examples of such commodity currencies[18] and show that it is common for a complex transaction to involve both matched demands and commodity currencies. However, even a moderately complex transaction can include more than that – from commodity currencies there is one logical step to surrogate currencies. Of course, another way to reach surrogate currencies in the step-by-step expansion of the sphere of barter is to use their obvious connection with the issue of debt offsets. In fact, it is often unclear where the simple debt offset instruments stop and where surrogate currency begins. A good example of this is the function of *Katanovka*[19] described in David Anderson's study of surrogate currencies in central Siberia.[20] A surrogate currency issued by a local authority or an individual enterprise is only one step away from a surrogate currency per se, i.e. non-cash roubles. There is a chain of connections

---

[17] See for example A. Ledeneva, 'Shadow Barter: Economic Necessity or Economic Crime?' Ch.11 in P. Seabright, A. Ledeneva (eds.), *The Vanishing Rouble: Barter and Currency Substitution in Post-Soviet Societies* (Cambridge University Press, Cambridge, forthcoming).

[18] Seabright and Ledeneva, n. 16 above. For example, they show how shoes can become a commodity currency for an entire sector which includes cooperative farms which raise cattle, a supplier of animal hides, a leather factory and shoe manufacturers.

[19] *Katanovki* (or *khakassiki*) debt tickets allow pensioners to obtain goods from firms that offset the value of these goods against firms' tax obligations.

[20] D. Anderson, 'Surrogate Currencies and the Wild Market in Central Siberia' paper presented at Conference on Barter in Post-Socialist Societies, University of Cambridge, December 1998. See <www.kings.cam.ac.uk/histecon/barter/anderson.htm>.

between a barter economy (system) and a non-cash economy, which, in turn, is closely linked with the cash economy (both legal and hidden). The extended discussion of various barter arrangements lies outside the scope of this paper. The detailed types of barter transactions ranging from direct barter to mutual offsets to surrogate money are considered by Commander and Mumssen,[21] in a study based on a large scale enterprise survey.

Reports about barter in Russia have recently become popular in the general press, suggesting that barter is a generally accepted phenomenon. However, another suggestion that it is of relatively recent origin is arguable. The 1998 European Bank of Reconstruction and Development (EBRD) Transition Report shows a steady increase of incidence of barter from below 20 per cent of GDP in 1995 to nearly 50 per cent in the first half of 1998. Some authors argue that official figures understate the incidence of barter during the early years of economic reforms (1990–1995). Such an opinion is supported by earlier studies. There is also the following general argument: the very nature of central planning in the Soviet Union would have caused barter to play a significant role in the earlier phases of reform. In the Soviet economy, the planned flows of goods and services had a persistent habit of exceeding the real ones, so that the enterprise managers needed to work energetically to match demand in exactly the same way as is required in barter.[22] Indeed, under the central planning system even the general distinction between barter and monetary transactions was blurred, since the rouble was an accounting unit used to measure flows of goods and services, and consequently, the Soviet economy could be considered one gigantic barter chain.

A brief geographical point will now be added. Barter is widespread not only in Russia but also throughout other countries of the Former Soviet Union (FSU), with the possible exception of the Baltic States. (The particular schemes in other former Soviet republics tend to be less complex). Outside the FSU, barter is not a widespread phenomenon. The geographical distribution of barter in Russia shows it is prevalent outside the centre where most cash (*zhivye den'gi*) and cash investments are concentrated. In provincial areas, the barter economy can reach 80–90 per cent of total trade.[23]

As has already been pointed out, the complexity of a barter economy is such that it can be considered as a separate financial system in its own right or, to be more specific, a 'virtual' financial system. This virtual financial system includes a virtual

---

[21] S. Commander and C. Mumssen, 'Understanding Barter in Russia' paper presented at Conference on Barter in Post-Socialist Societies, University of Cambridge, December 1998. See <www.kings.cam.ac.uk/histecon/barter/ebrd.pdf>.

[22] This argument links to a very interesting phenomenon of networking in the FSU. However the discussion of this area of interpersonal relationships would lead one too far from the focus on the economic and financial system. Of course, a comprehensive study of criminal activities in the economic system would require this anthropological approach as well which seems to address fundamentals as important as economic ones.

[23] The proportion of barter transactions in the economy of Buriat Republic. C. Humphrey, 'How is Barter Done? The Social Relations of Barter in Provincial Russia' paper presented at Conference on Barter in Post-Socialist Societies, University of Cambridge, December 1998. See <www.kings.cam.ac.uk/histecon/barter/humphrey.htm>.

monetary system which operates with the virtual 'barter rouble' mentioned previously. The 'virtual' world is a rough approximation – a concept – since in different sectors of the economy involved in different barter chain networks, the value of the 'barter rouble' could be different. However, this abstraction helps to clarify a number of fundamental interdependencies underpinning the Russian economy.

It has been argued here that the existence of a double financial system (cash/non-cash) in a single country imposes extra cost on the economy, especially on enterprises. This argument can be extended to a triple financial system to include the barter rouble; economic operations in three currencies will include an even larger extra cost of cross-currency transactions, hedging etc. The fact that the barter rouble can have different worth in different sectors/barter chains, thereby giving different exchange rates in the case of our model, does not negate the general applicability of this model. All three currencies will carry different market expectations concerning exchange rates, yield curves, and other associated data. In international markets, operations in different currencies also tend to have different legal implications, for example in the area of taxation. This corresponds well to our three currencies. After all, barter and cash as means of evading taxes are listed as one of the major possible causes of this phenomenon.[24]

Therefore, treating the financial and monetary systems of the barter rouble as separate from cash/non-cash systems allows one to have a different monetary interpretation for a number of phenomena, including some described by the model of virtual economy as proposed by Gaddy and Ickes[25] (the word 'virtual' is used here in a different sense than Gaddy and Ickes, who discuss the role of 'value-subtracting' or 'value-adding' enterprises in an economy where firms collude in over-valuing their output). The issue of sustaining an exchange rate between the cash rouble and the barter rouble will now be considered. As the evidence indicates, in the majority of transactions the value of a commodity (or other product or service) in barter roubles tends to exceed that of the value in cash roubles (in general, the same goes for non-cash). This suggests a non-parity exchange rate, however, in the majority of barter transactions, the barter rouble is treated as if it were the same rouble as cash, thus suggesting a parity exchange rate. What are the implications if the exchange rate is not supported by economic fundamentals (and in this case a barter rouble is overvalued)? In the case of a country, such an exchange rate might be unsustainable in the long run and have a direct implication on economic variables in the short to medium-term.

The interesting question to ask is how the burden of an overvalued currency is distributed between economic agents in this hypothetical economy. This leads to the question of whether or not the economic system is open or closed. The barter financial system will now be considered from this angle. The Russian barter financial system

---

[24] B. W. Ickes, P. Murrel and R. Ryterman, 'End of the Tunnel? The Effects of Financial Stabilisation in Russia' (1997) 13 *Post-Soviet Affairs*, pp. 105–133; Seabright and Ledeneva, n. 16 above.

[25] C. G. Gaddy and B. W. Ickes, 'Beyond a Bailout: Time to Face Reality About Russia's "Virtual Economy"'. See <www.brook.edu/pa/policyupdates/russia/virtualeconomy.htm>; C. G. Gaddy and B. W. Ickes, 'A Simple Four-Sector Model of Russia's "Virtual Economy"'. See <www.brook.edu/pa/policyupdates/russia/virtualeconomy.htm>.

is not closed – leakages in Gaddy and Ickes' terms do occur. Therefore, if the exchange rate is unsustainable (the barter rouble is overvalued) and the system has leaks (is partially open) somebody will have to carry the cost of sustaining an exchange rate that is too high. In the case under discussion, it is very likely to be the agents in the economy who have the most contact with outside cash or even the hard currency world, and the agents who are in most need of cash. This, of course, means that it will be the workforce on the one hand, and utilities and natural resource exporters/producers (e.g. Gazprom) on the other hand, which will have to support and finance an overvalued barter rouble exchange rate[26].

The question of the role of utilities actually relates to another interesting matter. So far this paper has proposed that the barter economy can be considered in practical terms as a complete virtual financial system with its own currency. Logically, therefore, this financial system should also have a market and banks. After all, as stated earlier, the behaviour of different currencies (cash, non-cash and barter) will be different due to different market expectations. If there are market expectations, there should be a market; if there is a market (at least a developed one), there should be 'banks'. Therefore, if the huge networks involving barter transactions can be considered to be an unorganized 'wild' market, what entities could be viewed as 'banks' in the barter financial system? It is proposed here that it is the utilities.[27]

First of all, utilities (especially large companies such as Gazprom) have fairly large networks and facilities to handle barter, particularly in commodity currencies. This is supported by research findings that transactions with public utilities are more likely to involve barter than other transactions of equivalent size and complexity. Considering utilities as 'banks' in the barter world also addresses the matter of collateral and the suggestion that barter can serve as a means of increasing the enforceability of private contracts in the absence of a credible system of civil law. Indeed, the utilities are well placed to treat collateral as part of the firm's barter transactions, including the difficult cases of illiquid commodity currencies or bulky and untransferable goods. For example, it could raise a smile if one imagines one of Moscow's large commercial banks (even before the crisis when they were healthier) accepting a shipment of tanks (or any bulky goods) as collateral from a defence enterprise. If the enterprise were to default, it is rather hard to imagine the Moscow bank claiming the collateral and storing it in its central office in the middle of Moscow. However, arranging the storage and later realization of such goods, although difficult, is feasible for a large utility company which, not only has a larger network, but also the storage facilities, land and workforce to handle such activities. So the conclusion stands and this paper can model the barter world as a financial system with its virtual currencies, virtual markets, and virtual banks (the utilities).

---

[26] The fact that enterprises producing the most illiquid goods tend to lose out during barter (they have to offer the most discounted barter price) has different origin: these enterprises are forced to contribute a larger share to the operational cost of the barter chain in order to participate in it. This cost is different from the cost of subsidizing of the exchange rate.

[27] Banks in a role of liquidity providers, rather than providers of retail banking.

IV. MULTIPLE FINANCIAL SYSTEMS AS A REALM OF INFORMAL ECONOMY:
     IMPLICATIONS FOR ECONOMIC CRIME

Therefore, as a result of limitations on liquidity and tax pressure, at least three parallel financial systems exist in a single country.[28] This duplication is forced on enterprises that are forced to support it, since, unlike private persons, enterprises cannot completely withdraw from the non-cash system as they have to maintain a respectable flow of transactions to be above suspicion (at least officially) of various government agencies, in particular tax authorities. However, since this non-cash financial system works against enterprises' interests, they have a strong incentive to minimize participation. Therefore, it is not surprising that a large number of transactions are unrecorded and conducted either in cash or in barter.[29] The volume of unrecorded transactions is very difficult to estimate. For example, according to the estimate of the Russian state statistics committee, about 500 billion roubles (EUR18.8 billion, USD22 billion) of Russia's 2.7 trillion-rouble GDP last year was not reported to authorities.[30] The exact ratio of cash, non-cash and barter economies is difficult to estimate. However, it must be emphasised that barter transactions, especially in provincial areas, dwarf both cash and electronic (account) money transactions. As, already mentioned earlier, there the barter economy can reach 80–90 per cent of total trade.[31]

The existence and burden of a triple financial system, argued in the introduction, has a direct relation to informal activities either criminal or near criminal. Indeed, it should be expected that a number of criminal and near criminal activities are (at least partially) a direct result of the attempts to reduce the cost of the triple financial system.[32] Therefore, it could be argued that the behaviour of agents is rational and

---

[28] The role of hard currency has been excluded from the considerations contained in this paper.

[29] Naturally, barter and cash also have their shortcomings and in an economy that is not skewed, they tend to be less efficient. The former is too inflexible and latter is badly suited to large and frequent transactions. This is of course obvious, otherwise a developed world would not have developed a modern banking system.

[30] *Russia Today*, 16 February 1999, *Agence France Presse*.

[31] Humphrey, n. 25 above.

[32] A detailed account of what makes enterprises chose to operate in one of the three available financial systems lies outside of the scope of this paper. Some of these issues were addressed in the discussion of the development of a legislative base, which forces a triple financial system. Generally the problem is quite complex and one can identify not only economic and financial, but also psychological reasons: the inertia of Soviet mentality becomes intertwined with new economic incentives of a barter chain, such as, for example, a defence against market uncertainty. Participation in the barter chain reduces the probability of bankruptcy in each of the links, since it links the probability of the bankruptcy to the profitability of the chain rather than profitability of an individual firm. However, the pure model of barter as a third financial and monetary system relates well to the causes of barter's appearance and continuous existence. Seabright and Ledeneva, n. 16 above list 8 reasons: 1) Flight from money due to hyperinflation; 2) A response to the high cost of working capital; 3) Lack of trust in the banking systems; 4) A response to inter-enterprise arrears; 5) Means of evading taxes; 6) Means of firms to collude in over-valuing their output to soften budget constraints (virtual economy hypothesis); 7) Means of increasing the enforceability of private contracts in the absence of a credible system of civil law; 8) A more general breakdown of trust in those economic institutions that depend on collective confidence about the functioning of the market economy. It can be seen that the model of barter as a virtual complete financial system contains practically all of the above. A small comment for the less obvious cases: 1) The barter rouble is outside the control of the central bank and government; 6) Virtual economy hypothesis, which, in the interpretation of this paper, translates as the means of

aims to improve the efficiency of the system. However, this argument is akin to the argument that corruption is not necessarily bad for the economy and society since in some form it improves the efficiency and flexibility of the system by removing the inefficiencies and constraints imposed by bureaucracy and stringent laws. This proposition is the subject of much discussion by economists.[33] The discussion of whether or not it is possible to have 'good' corruption is certainly not ended. For example, some evidence[34] suggests that although corruption smoothes the existing bureaucratic barriers, it gives an incentive to keep them and create new ones (in the form of unreformed laws and larger bureaucracy), thus defeating the initial reasons for helping the economic system.

At this point, a return to the 'distortive' legislative base will now be undertaken. It has been illustrated that this is a direct cause of the triple financial system. The separation of cash and non-cash is an immediate result, followed by the slower but solid growth of barter, which always takes a significant time to arrange. By limiting the available liquidity and the possibility of managing enterprises' liquidity, the state squeezes the enterprise into cash and barter systems that allow them to increase their liquidity, and their control and management capability. Therefore, a large proportion of the current financial system and its peculiarities has arisen as a result (perhaps expected by the government for cash/non-cash and unexpected for barter) of the *planned* development of the legislative base, and not as a consequence of the underdeveloped base falling behind market economy developments. Following the Tompson analysis,[35] it can be concluded that this is the result of the authorities' revenue hunger, their desire to have additional (somewhat 'Soviet') means of control of the economy, and a continuation of certain 'Soviet' policies in new 'capitalist' circumstances. The existing system was designed primarily to suit the immediate needs of the government.[36] In the short-term, at least, the current system benefits banks (or rather, benefited them before the crisis) as it allows them 'easy' profits, but from a very narrow and sensitive list of sources (which until August 1998 were also considered by many as risk-free). Of course, in the medium and long-term it makes normal banking far more difficult, thus making their future unstable.

This point is well-illustrated by developments after the latest crisis. The regional banks (for example in St. Petersburg) which were less involved in speculative activities and engaged more in lending to the real economy, on average survived in much better shape; some even posted a moderate profit last year (1998). It is unclear, however, whether this crisis can serve as an evolutionary event pushing financial power to the regions and encouraging the survival of 'real' banks (banks which do 'bank'). After all, the distorted financial and legal system that encouraged Moscow

---

transferring the burden of the unsustainable exchange between the barter rouble and the real rouble onto particular agents in the economy, i.e. getting subsidies through abnormal exchange rate from utilities and labour; 7) See the discussion of collateral.

[33] 'A Global War Against Bribery' *Economist*, 16 January 1999, p. 27.

[34] Ibid.

[35] Tompson, n. 2 above.

[36] Of course, in the long-term the legal strait-jacket depresses the Russian economy and does not benefit anybody, including the government.

banks to enter a short-termist and destructive path of profiteering is still in place.[37] Finally, the largest losers are non-financial enterprises and organizations, since they have to operate in a market environment without any financial flexibility or other 'free market' benefits.

Since changes in legislation are largely driven by government (both the legislative and executive branches) and only to a smaller extent by business, and because government is the biggest beneficiary of the distorted system, one can assume that distortion will continue and will be further supported by legislative changes in the near and medium term future. This situation will persist until banks start to prioritise long-term over short-term considerations when determining what is in their interests. Likewise, it will continue until non-financial organizations (industry, including SMEs[38] which currently have very little representation in Russian politics) acquire a stronger voice in the political and legislative process and a clear understanding of the importance of liquidity and the proper operation of the financial system for their own prosperity.

This investigation into the triple financial system should now be linked with the analysis of tendencies in crime development in Russia. If one looks at financial and economic crime patterns in Russia and the former Soviet Union, two broad areas emerge at the beginning of the 1990s. In a broad sense, criminal activities can be put into two categories. The first category is criminal activities per se, i.e. acts by which the law is clearly broken. The second category is much broader and it covers actions that could be considered 'criminal'[39] only from a general point of view (for example, they would be considered criminal or completely unacceptable in the majority of western societies). However, they are not criminal in the strict sense of the word, as the existing law is either not broken or is broken only in minor aspects. This is usually presumed to be possible because of the inadequacy of the legal system that has arisen due to very fast changes in the economic and financial environment of the CIS since the beginning of 'capitalist' reforms. Thus, the second category is defined as criminal activity that arises due to loopholes/underdevelopment of the legal base.

As an example of the first ('real crime') category, the Chechen *avizos* affair and related frauds should be mentioned (these have been described in a documentary novel).[40] As an example of the second category, one can list fraudulent loan guarantees issued by a branch of a commercial bank. The fraud became possible due to problems with the definition of a legal entity (a person) of a bank vs. its branch. The problem is whether the branch is a legal entity and can offer guarantees, for example loan

---

[37] This of course does not mean that this distortion is the only problem with Russian banks. There are quite a variety of issues to be addressed. See, for example, T. T. Azarchs, 'Search for Solvency: Russian Banks in Dire Straits' (3 February 1999) *Standard & Poor's Credit Week*, p. 9. However, the analysis of the banking system is not complete without consideration of the issues that have been discussed in this paper.

[38] Small and Medium Enterprises.

[39] From this point on the term criminal will be used with an extended meaning including 'abnormal' activities of the second category.

[40] S. Byvalov, *Afera:Chechenkie avizo* (Olimp, Moscow, 1997). *Avizo* is a money transfer mechanism in the inter-banking system that was designed to speed up payments. The fraud was based on the fact that outgoing funds could not be verified in quasi-independent areas of FSU/Russia.

guarantees, in the course of normal business. As a result, a branch of the commercial bank may give a guarantee for a loan. However, in the case of borrower default, the guarantee will not be fulfilled. Frequently, a guarantee is deliberately given as part of a fraud when the borrower has no intention of repaying the loan. The confusion was created by legal definitions inherited from Soviet times when the problem of independent loan/investment policies by local branches of commercial banks clearly did not apply. This muddle continued for a long time and was actively discussed as recently as 1995.[41] A later example of 'near' criminal activities due to imperfections of the legal system is the phenomenon of pyramid schemes. There were, of course, some irregularities in registration and some illegal activities in terms of investment and operations, as well as many political reasons for the ability of pyramids to operate freely. However, one of the major reasons for the endurance of pyramids was the inadequacy of the law, which did not prohibit this type of scheme directly.

The second category of criminal activity is very broad. It emerged, in its present form, in the 1990s as the rate of change in the economic and financial system outstripped the speed with which the legal base was changing. Consequently, either existing laws were not amended in time or mistakes were made while amending them.

Looking at this situation an observer might be inclined to predict that as capitalism develops in Russia, the situation will improve. Only the first category of criminal activities will remain while the legal base will catch up with 'capitalist' development and close loopholes available for 'near' criminal activities of the second category.

However, it is maintained here that this prediction is overly optimistic and thus, there is a need to alter the scheme initially suggested. Initially this paper proposed two categories of criminal activities (breaking the law and using loopholes). The analysis of the triple financial system demonstrates that a third category of crime covering the consequences of the financial and banking system being distorted should be introduced (such distortion is hardly a loophole), consequences which led to the creation of such a triple financial system. According to the arguments contained in previous sections, the third category will continue to be very significant in the near and medium-term future.

To have a complete picture of crime it should be noted that there is an extra factor affecting criminal activities which was relatively minor in the beginning of 1990s, but has certainly grown in significance (however it does not constitute a separate category by itself). This factor is political influence: the merging of financial/criminal activities with political power. This covers all categories and goes well beyond mere corruption. Of course, some criminal activity was initiated due to the corruption

---

[41] A customer could not assume that a guarantee given by the branch in the course of normal business was valid but had to verify that the particular branch had proper *doverennost'* from the bank itself since only a bank is a proper and registered legal entity. Hence, there exists the situation when the responsibility to monitor the bank's compliance lies with the customer! See V. V. Hahulin, 'Organizatsionno-strukturnye (pravosub'eknye) predposilki ekonomicheskikh prestuplenii' in V. K. Mamutov (ed.), *Khoziastvenno-pravovye sredstva predotvrashcheniia ekonomicheskikh prestuplenii'* (Economic and Legal Research Institute of the Ukrainian National Academy of Sciences, Donetsk, 1996), pp. 14–17. A number of similar issues are also discussed in this volume.

process (first category), and some loopholes can be exploited with the help of political power (second category), again often involving corruption, but importantly, the factor also affects the third category – the distortion of the system. In this case, the distortion is supported not by the economic reasons that have been considered previously, but for political convenience and profit to the ruling elite. As examples, election campaign financing, privatization (especially the first period), distribution and placement of budget funds can be listed.

To summarize these findings, in the current political and economic climate it can neither be hoped for significant reduction of the 'pure' crime of the first category, nor for the reduction of criminal and near criminal activities of the third category. These activities will continue to remain strong together with the triple financial system that caused them. This leads to the unhappy conclusion that only the second (and least significant) of three categories of criminal activity in Russia[42] shows any reasonable hope of subsiding in the near term.

---

[42] This analysis also applies to various extents to a number of other republics of FSU.

16

Money-Laundering Control and The Rule of Law in Russia

Frédérique Dahan

I. INTRODUCTION

There is growing concern throughout the international community about the incidence of economic and organized crime in Eastern Europe as a whole, but especially in Russia. Whilst organized criminal groups can be found in all countries, the fall of the iron curtain in 1989, the demise of the Soviet Union in 1991 and the dramatic changes in the former socialist countries of Central and Eastern Europe have created a unique environment for them to flourish in these regions. Despite fundamental reforms such as the establishment of democracy and the development of a market economy together with the support of the West, the political vacuum in Eastern Europe left by these changes has favoured the development of a new generation of criminals and criminal organizations. Furthermore, the emergence of free-market reform in particular has led to these countries experiencing the sorts of problems associated with all periods of substantial transition – problems which themselves constitute impediments to the development of a civil society and the market economy – such as increased economic crime, money-laundering, narcotics trafficking and corruption.

The *rule of law* is now seen by many as a key element of a successful transition. Experience has shown that for markets to work effectively, adequate substantive laws, a complex web of effective institutions, well-run legal substantive and procedural systems and effective, uncorrupted bureaucracies are necessary. Democracy ensures that there is agreement between the State and society with regard to these laws. However, merely creating or reformulating laws to meet the needs of the market economy is not sufficient. Underlying the actual content of the law is the fundamental concept of the *rule of law* as an element of social cohesion:

> Under central planning, law was first and foremost an instrument of state control. Law in market economies is fundamentally different: it defines the rules of the game and gives individuals the rights and tools to enforce them. Where the rule of law is in force, laws are applied fairly, transparently and evenhandedly to all; individuals can assert and defend their rights and the state's powers are defined and limited by law. People in countries with a well

237

A. V. Ledeneva and M. Kurkchiyan (eds.), Economic Crime in Russia, 237–256
© 2000 *Kluwer Law International. Printed in Great Britain.*

established rule of law rarely stop to wonder where it comes from. But transition economies need to start over, to replace arbitrary rule by powerful individuals or institutions with a rule of law that inspires the public trust and respect that will enable it to endure.[1]

Due to the threat that organized crime represents, not only to the development of a market economy in Central and Eastern Europe, but also to the establishment of a functional democracy, it is, therefore, particularly important to examine *whether* the law can help control the spread of economic crime and if so, *how* this will be done. Specifically, the discussion in this paper will focus on the legal measures that have been taken to control the practice of money-laundering. Money-laundering, as it is well known, arises as the consequence of previous criminal activity. As a result, the fight against money-laundering cannot be separated from the general fight against organized and economic crime since the latter is what generates the flow of dirty money in the first place. Moreover, money-laundering takes place at least partly in an institutional context, usually the financial sector, since the ultimate purpose is to make the laundered funds reappear as 'clean' and legal for injection into the legitimate economy. Therefore, the attempt to combat money-laundering must itself take place within an institutional framework.

Given its role in support of economic crime, money-laundering constitutes a serious threat to countries in transition: it can lead to reduced tax revenues through underground economies, unfair competition with legitimate businesses, damage to the financial system, and general disruption of economic development. In consequence, governments have shown determination to eradicate money-laundering on their territory.[2] These responses have not taken place in isolation. International conventions have been signed and model laws drafted which provide a framework for individual countries' legislative reforms. Thus, on the one hand, countries in transition who are parties to these treaties have undertaken to adopt certain sets of measures. On the other hand, they have found it hard to strike the right balance between measures which will neither impose too stringent a degree of regulation – thus inhibiting commercial development and potential foreign investment – nor allow the emerging market to become infiltrated by criminal groups through deliberate failure to take the required measures. Such nations have found that some of the inherent characteristics of the free-market economy, such as competition or the open banking system, can be rapidly exploited by criminal organizations. It then becomes increasingly difficult to differentiate between legitimate entrepreneurial activity and the business activities of organized crime.

---

[1]   The World Bank, *From Plan to Market: World Development Report 1996* (Oxford University Press, Oxford, 1996), p. 87.
[2]   An example is provided by the so-called *Riga Declaration* of 14 November 1996, made on behalf of the European Commission, the UN International Drug Control Programme and the FATF and the respective governments of the Baltic States, Estonia, Lithuania and Latvia. See <www.oecd.org/fatf/Riga.htm>.

Progress in money-laundering control has been extremely variable from country to country. It is interesting to take a close look at some of the domestic reforms and to compare the choices made by the respective legislatures. This paper will focus on the example of Russia, examining its situation and progress and comparing it with a number of neighbouring countries such as Slovenia, Hungary, Poland, Bulgaria, Czech Republic, etc., so as to highlight their differences. It will then be contended that such differences in progress and approach in fact reveal the general approach of the country to the *rule of law* in the fight against economic crime, which may have serious consequences on the general development of the country as a functional democracy with a free market economy.

II. MONEY-LAUNDERING CONTROL IN RUSSIA

A striking feature of the current money-laundering situation in Central and Eastern European countries is its diversity. Their attractiveness to criminal organizations, vulnerability and (perhaps most importantly) their determination to fight the problem all vary significantly. Nevertheless, no country has been left untouched. According to the *1996–97 FATF Report on Money-laundering Typologies*, the sources of illegal proceeds in Central and Eastern Europe can be categorized into four broad areas:[3]

1. the illegal sale of natural resources such as oil, natural gas, metals, etc.
2. the smuggling of alcohol, tobacco, arms and drugs
3. proceeds from traditional organized crime activity such as extortion, prostitution, theft, fraud, motor vehicle theft, etc.
4. white-collar crimes such as embezzlement of state property and funds, income and profit declaration evasion, tax fraud, tax evasion, and illegal capital flight

The most commonly cited method of laundering is the opening by individuals of accounts at financial institutions into which are deposited large amounts of cash which are then transferred out of the country to, for example, offshore shell companies, trading companies and other overseas institutions. Extensive investments in real estate, hotels, restaurants and other businesses in Western European countries, especially on the French and Spanish coasts, are also common. As well as transfers, other laundering methods used are false invoicing schemes (particularly for wiring the funds), keeping a double set of books, and contract fraud. Once laundered abroad, the money may come back to the country of origin via participation in privatization or foreign investment.[4] The types of institutions used to launder include banks, currency exchanges, casinos, and real estate companies. Banks are a particularly favoured target and it remains true that 'the best method of both stealing and

---

[3] Financial Action Task Force on Money Laundering, *1996–97 Report on Money Laundering Typologies*, FATF VIII, February 1997.

[4] V. Dobrev, 'Money Laundering in Countries in Transition' paper presented at the Council of Europe Conference on Money Laundering in States in Transition, Strasbourg, France, 29 November – 1 December 1994, cited in W. Gilmore, *Dirty Money – The Evolution of Money Laundering Counter-measures*, 1st edition (Council of Europe, 1995), p. 198.

laundering money is to own a bank'.[5] Generally, the financial systems are still vulnerable to this sort of practice and the judicial and regulatory systems are not yet equipped to cope with the complexity of the cases.

Russia constitutes a perfect large-scale example of this laundering system. The laundered funds consist mostly of illegal proceeds derived from domestic sources going through domestic financial and commercial institutions for eventual transfer and investment abroad.[6] Businesses operating in Russia routinely make use of a variety of offshore locations such as Ireland and United Kingdom dependencies in Europe, parts of the Caribbean, and most recently the South Pacific, taking advantage of bilateral tax treaties in place between these jurisdictions. Once the proceeds have been transferred through such a series of offshore business transactions, they become extremely difficult for the Russian authorities to trace. Another avenue providing opportunities to launder illegal proceeds is the so-called gray economy. Many service firms, brokers, retailers and small businesses do not file tax returns, making fiscal oversight difficult.[7]

1. International cooperation and assistance to Russia

Obviously, given the dimension of the problem and Russia's importance on the international stage, many governmental and intergovernmental bodies have been very active and willing to collaborate with the Russian government in order to address the question of money-laundering control. The most active bodies so far have been the United Nations (UN), the Financial Action Task Force on Money-laundering (FATF), the Council of Europe and the USA.

Through its specialized agency (the United Nations Office for Drug Control and Crime Prevention, based in Vienna) and its implementing programme, the United Nations International Drug Control Programme (UNDCP), the UN plays a very active role in Russia with several assistance programmes taking place in the country.[8] An International Conference on Drug Control Cooperation was organized in April 1997 by the UNDCP and the Government of the Russian Federation.[9] The UNDCP also drafted in November 1995 a *Model Law on Money-laundering, Confiscation and International Cooperation in Relation to Drugs*.[10] The Model Law provides several variants to its sections with the intention of facilitating the work of those States which wish to adopt or update their legislation on drug money-laundering, including Russia.

---

[5] M. Gold and M. Levi, *Money Laundering in the UK: An Appraisal of Suspicion Based Reporting* (London, 1994), p. 2, cited in Gilmore, ibid, p. 198.
[6] Bureau for International Narcotics and Law Enforcement Affairs, *International Narcotics Control Strategy Report 1998*, (US Department of State, Washington DC, 1999), section on 'Russia', <www.state.gov/www/global/narcotics_law/>.
[7] Various official estimates place the Russian gray economy at 25–45 per cent of the gross domestic product (GDP) with the service industries accounting for 50–75 per cent.
[8] See <www.undcp.org/undcp/activ/ob/c-europe>.
[9] See *International Conference on Drug Control Cooperation*, Proceeds of the Conference.
[10] See <www.undcp.org/model_legislation.html>.

Another body involved in advising Russia is the FATF. This was established at the G-7 Economic Summit in Paris in 1989 under the auspices of the Organisation for Economic Cooperation and Development (OECD). It is an inter-governmental body whose objective is the development and promotion of policies to combat money-laundering within its members (currently numbering 26 jurisdictions and two international organizations). The FATF has drafted 40 recommendations for a sound anti-money-laundering system, addressing four general themes – the overall context, the legal framework, the role of the financial system and the strengthening of international cooperation.

Naturally, these recommendations have no binding force as such. Moreover, no Eastern European country is yet a FATF member although the Czech Republic has recently applied to join. Nonetheless, the FATF recommendations have had an impact and many non-members have adopted them or referred to them when drafting their own money-laundering legislation. In particular, the first draft of the Russian law on money-laundering was positively reviewed by FATF. Moreover, the FATF provides expertise, particularly to countries in Central and Eastern Europe. A joint FATF/ Central Bank of Russia Money-laundering Conference took place in October 1997 in St. Petersburg as a follow-up to the FATF high-level mission to Moscow in 1996.[11]

A third international forum of particular interest to Russia is the Council of Europe. It is the only truly pan-European inter-governmental organization as its members are both Western and Eastern European States, including Russia which has recently been admitted. From the outset, the Council has shown great concern for economic crime and money-laundering. Under its auspices, a Convention on Laundering, Search, Seizure and Confiscation of the Proceeds from Crime (hereafter the Council of Europe Convention) was signed on 8 November 1990 and entered into force on 1 September 1993. As at March 1999, it had been signed by 34 States and was in force in 25 of them.[12] Russia, however, has not signed it yet. In 1993, a Presidential Decree 'On Additional Measures of Enforcement of Law and Order in the Russian Federation' instructed the Ministry of Foreign Affairs to complete the preparations for accession to the Council of Europe Convention, but this did not actually take place. Nonetheless, Russia agreed to participate in the work of the Select Committee of Experts on the Evaluation of Anti-Money-laundering Measures (PC-R-EV) which the Council of Europe launched in 1997 to assess the anti-money-laundering measures of its non-FATF member States. The PC-R-EV conducts self and mutual assessment of the anti-money-laundering measures in place in a country. Evaluation is done by local experts and external evaluators according to a defined calendar and reports are drafted and adopted by the committee. Despite being a latecomer to the work of the PC-R-EV, Russia has agreed to be evaluated in the year 2000.[13]

---

[11] Financial Action Task Force on Money Laundering, *Annual Report 1997-1998*, FATF IX, June 1998, p. 29.

[12] In particular, Bulgaria, Croatia, Czech Republic, Hungary, Poland, Romania, Slovenia, and Ukraine have signed the Convention.

[13] See CDPC and PC-R-EV, *Annual Report 1997–98*, Council of Europe and PHARE-EU, p. 4.

Finally, the USA has also developed privileged relationships with Russia in this field. In the 1997 and 1998, the *International Narcotics Control Strategy Annual Report* (INCS Report) drawn up by the Bureau for International Narcotics and Law Enforcement Affairs of the Department of State classified Russia as a country of primary concern with regard to money-laundering. To support Russia's efforts, the Drug Enforcement Agency (DEA) office in Moscow was expanded in 1997. More than 3,300 officials from the police forces, customs, border service and procuracy were trained throughout the year, with an emphasis on organized crime, narcotics trafficking and money-laundering.[14] The 1998 INCS Report noted that despite the lack of specific anti-money-laundering law, Russia is making some progress in detecting and prosecuting the practice. However, such progress remains desperately slow.

The developments reviewed above demonstrate that the money-laundering issue is a serious matter in Russia, about which the international community has expressed great concern. It is now appropriate to examine the domestic legal measures so far adopted and assess their content.

2.   Domestic money-laundering legislation

The development of specific money-laundering control legislation in Russia was anticipated as early as 1995.[15] That year, William Gilmore wrote:

> Public statements by officials indicate that in a number of important jurisdictions, such as the Russian Federation, the recommendations of the FATF are under active consideration and that draft money-laundering legislation is in preparation. Only time will tell to what extent such statements reflect reality rather than the rhetoric of diplomacy.[16]

Four years on, it must be said that Russia's achievements have been limited. In July 1997, the report of the 6th International Banking Congress held in St. Petersburg with the participation of the Russian Central Bank urged the Duma (Parliament's lower chamber) to accelerate the adoption of the laws on money-laundering.[17] Indeed, a Bill on 'Countering Legalization [Laundering] of Illegally Gained Incomes' was drafted by the government and placed before the Duma in October of the same year.[18] The Bill passed its first reading in mid-November and the two subsequent requisite readings were scheduled for December, where the bill failed. A new draft

---

[14] The training took place in Russia, the USA, and at the International Law Enforcement Academy (ILEA) in Budapest.

[15] Resolution No. 439 of the Russian Government of 28 April 1995 envisaged the adoption of a special law devoted to money laundering. See M. Gray, 'Russia Fights Crime and Corruption' (November-December 1995) 6 *Transition-The World Bank*, p. 7.

[16] W. Gilmore, n. 4 above, p. 201.

[17] See Y. Borisova, 'Central Bank Weeds Weak Performers' *The St Petersburg Times*, 16–22 June 1997: <www.sptimes.ru/>.

[18] Previous legislation had been defeated in 1996, falling short by 20 votes of the number needed for approval.

was then presented and approved by the Duma on 21 October 1998, but again voted down in the Federation Council (upper chamber) on 12 November, and sent back to the drafting committee. A joint Duma-Federation Council commission negotiated a compromise which was approved in June 1999, but this time, the law was vetoed by President Yeltsin because of its scope. In October 1999, following the Bank of New York scandal, the Russian government gave new assurance of its commitment for the introduction of the legislation. But this will have to be, once more, put to test.

The failure to pass legislation may be attributed to a lack of genuine commitment on the part of the legislature, with the attempts to pass the above-mentioned Act being motivated more by the 'rhetoric of diplomacy' than any real intent. Also, the issues involved are difficult and the severe economic problems that Russia has experienced, in particular since mid-1998, have considerably slowed down the process of reform. Nonetheless, the August 1998 crisis, according to the Central Bank, only confirmed the need for money-laundering legislation:

> As for the factors that influence the pace of reform in foreign currency relations, many of them resulted from the absence of legislation protecting the banking system from being infiltrated by illegal capital. The Bank of Russia believes that the most efficient way to prevent the infiltration of the Russian banking system by criminal capital is to complement the applicable foreign exchange legislation with a number of fundamental enactment, such as the draft federal law 'On Amending the Russian Federation Law on Foreign Exchange Regulation and Foreign Exchange Control' and 'On Countering the Legalisation (Laundering) of Illegally Obtained Incomes'.[19]

At present, the only legal provision effectively in force is found in the Criminal Code.

3. Criminal law

The new Criminal Code, adopted in 1996, deals with money-laundering in Chapter 22 on 'Crimes in the Sphere of Economic Activity'. Article 174 condemns 'the legalisation (laundering) of monetary assets or other property obtained by illegal means'. It reads as follows:

> (1) The performance of financial operations and other transactions with monetary funds or property knowing that they were illegally obtained, and the use of such funds or property for performing entrepreneurial or any other economic activity shall be punished by a fine of between 500 and 700 minimum monthly wage or the amount of the wage or incomes of the convict for a period of 5 to 7 months, or by imprisonment up to 4 years with or without a fine of a minimum of 100 minimum monthly wage or of the amount of wage or incomes of the convict for a period of 1 month.[20]

---

[19] See <www.cbr.ru/eng/banktoday/reg.html>.
[20] The current minimum wage is approximately equal to 80 roubles. As of March 1999, the exchange rate of the Russian rouble with the US dollar was 24 to 1.

(2) The same acts as in paragraph (1) committed:
   a) by a group of people in conspiracy [preliminary agreement]
   b) repeatedly [more than once]
   c) by a person using of his official position
shall be punished by imprisonment for 4 to 8 years with or without confiscation of property.
(3) The same acts specified in paragraphs (1) and (2) committed by a criminal organised group or in large scale shall be punished by imprisonment of 7 to 10 years with or without confiscation of property.

The Russian legislature has taken the view that, as far as criminal law is concerned, the offence of money-laundering should not be limited to drug money but to 'monetary funds or property knowing that they were illegally obtained'. Other countries in the region have taken a different view. Croatia, for example, has chosen to limit the offence to funds emanating from previous criminal activity punished by five years of more of imprisonment, and criminal activity committed as part of a criminal group.[21] Similarly, under the Hungarian Criminal Code, Article 303, the predicate offence must be a crime punishable with imprisonment of more than five years, the smuggling of people, the misuse of narcotic drugs, or the infringement of an obligation of international law. The new Polish Article 299 of the Criminal Code lists some predicate offences (such as drug trafficking, drug dealing, fraud, counterfeit) but this list is not exhaustive. Romania has also adopted a new Act which, in its Article 23, gives a comprehensive list of predicate offences. The Slovakian Criminal Code, Article 252, on the other hand, makes only reference to the income of a crime, with no restriction as to the nature of this crime. Slovenia has made the same choice, excluding only cases of passive tax evasion although a current reform may eliminate this exception (Article 252, Criminal Code). Finally, in Ukraine, no general offense of money-laundering has yet been adopted and only money-laundering connected to drug offenses is punished by Article 229, Paragraph 12 of the Criminal Code.

As far as Russia is concerned, there is evidence that a lot of dirty money in fact originates from criminal activities other than drug trafficking.[22] It is therefore important that Article 174 can encompass the laundering of proceeds from all types of crime. However, there have as yet been no successful prosecutions. Approximately 70 cases have been investigated in the last two years, among which two or three have reached the courts, but between September 1997 and September 1998 there were no convictions. The sticking point seems to be the gathering of evidence, the burden of which rests on the prosecution. Another problem may be the *detection* itself of the money-laundering cases in the first place, which is a further reason to push for the adoption of a special Act.

---

[21] Criminal Code, Article 279.
[22] 'The Problems of Laundering Proceeds from the Drug Business', Conference Paper No 2, 'International Conference on Drug Control Cooperation – Drug Threat in the Russian Federation and its International Implications', United Nations International Drug Control Programme and the Government of the Russian Federation, 16–17 April 1997, v.97-21465.

4. Why is a specific law on money-laundering control needed?

As explained above, the UN Convention only requires criminalization of the laundering of drug money. However, this measure alone is not sufficient if a state is serious about eradicating money-laundering on its territory. The FATF, as previously shown, recommends a very comprehensive set of measures that only a specific Act can provide. An adequate approach for money-laundering control must comprise two separate but complementary parts: an offensive part and a defensive part.[23]

The *offensive* part consists of increasing the risk of being detected by law enforcement at all stages of the laundering process. The complete laundering of funds usually comprises three stages, beginning with the deposit of currency into a financial services institution ('placement'), continuing with the movement of funds from institution to institution to hide the source and ownership of the funds ('layering'), and concluding with the reinvestment of those funds in an ostensibly legitimate business ('integration').[24] The available evidence suggests that detection is more successful when it takes place at the placement stage. To use an analogy, if layering can be thought of as a stone gradually dropping to the bottom of a pond, 'the money in flight will be most noticeable when it splashed first into the pool'.[25] This is why international regulatory and law enforcement efforts have concentrated on the report of suspicious transactions or suspicious funds deposited in financial institutions, the cross-border monetary declaration requirements and the 'know your customer' rules for those accepting cash deposits.

Once the layering stage has been reached, the most serious impediment to detection is bank or professional secrecy and lack of transparency. Here, the focus will be on the lifting of these barriers by law. Finally, at the integration stage, strengthening asset forfeiture laws and organizing asset freezing could allow the prosecution to seize some proceeds of criminal activities even when these proceeds have been reinvested in ostensibly legitimate enterprises. This must be done in harmony with the general legal framework of the country in terms of tracing, confiscation and forfeiture.

Despite the adoption of these measures, the small overall number of successful prosecutions demonstrates that the offensive approach is limited in its effect. This suggests that a second strategy for the prevention and control of money-laundering is needed – the *defensive approach,* which aims to establish a deterrent to the activities of money-laundering. Firstly, the collection of data on crimes and offenders must be organized such that it is readily accessible for training, investigation and prosecution at the national level and can be effectively used and exchanged at the international level. This role must be undertaken by a specialized governmental agency or 'financial intelligence unit' (FIU). Secondly, the defensive approach prescribes greater transparency in the financial market, the banking sector and the privatization

---

[23] *U.N. Crime Prevention and Criminal Justice Newsletter*, p. 5.
[24] International Narcotics Control Strategy Report (INCS) 1997 (US Department of State, Washington DC, 1998).
[25] B. A. K. Rider, 'The Practical and Legal Aspects of Interdicting the Flow of Dirty Money' (1995) 3 *Journal of Financial Crime*, p. 239.

programmes, promoting competition and fairness. Thirdly, public awareness of the dangers of these activities must be improved. It is thus important that society in general is aware of the phenomenon and supports the government's offensive action. In conclusion, both defensive and offensive approaches require the country in question to make important policy choices, taking into consideration its domestic legal, social and economic situation, and to adopt the appropriate legal provisions.

5. The Russian draft law on countering the legalization (laundering) of illegally obtained incomes

As explained above, despite many attempts, no provisions of this nature have yet been adopted in Russia. However, several drafts have been presented and discussed before the Parliament. It is thus of interest to examine the latest draft, as published by the Ministry of Interior.[26] With 32 articles, this is a comprehensive piece of legislation dealing with 'the discovery, prevention and termination of actions that legalize proceeds of criminal activities and their confiscation'.[27] It draws substantially on the existing laws in other jurisdictions and general international trends. However, a close study reveals some unique features that raise questions as to the approach envisaged by the Russian legislature. This section first examines the measures for the prevention of money-laundering, second, the detection of crimes, third, the relevant sanctions to be applied, and fourthly and finally the competent authorities.

a) Prevention. According to the Russian draft bill, the targeted 'financial institutions' are banks and their branches, stock exchanges, investment funds, trust companies, dealers and brokers and other institutions that provide, obtain, pay out, transfer (either by cash, or wire), exchange or keep funds, and institutions that give notification and registration of property rights (Article 3, Para. 4). Financial activities are defined as the activities of the financial institutions, plus those of the post-office, telegraphs, casinos and other gambling institutions, bookmakers, lotteries, and pawns (Article 3, Para. 3). Pursuant to Article 4, all institutions which undertake financial activities must:

- Identify their customers;
- Report by means of a form filed in every month on every transaction in cash or wire transfer of a sum equal or superior to 200 monthly wage in the case of a

---

[26] My warmest thanks to Mr. Valery Ananyev, General Prosecutor's Office, Moscow, for providing me with a copy of the draft and very valuable comments.

[27] A major obstacle for the adoption of the draft has been said to be the scope of the law. The law refers to the acquisition, ownership, use and management of financial means and property rights obtained by illegal means (Article 2). The term 'illegal means' was considered by many as too broad since it could include proceeds from civil and administrative violations and not just proceeds from criminal predicate offenses. This difficulty is compounded by Article 3, Para. 1 which defines 'illegal proceeds' as cash, letter of credit, bonds and shares, movable and immovable property, property rights and generally any profit obtained by *criminal* activity (emphasis added). In this case, the definition refers to the criminal sphere only.

physical person, and 5,000 monthly wage in the case of a legal person. The same applies when this amount is reached by the addition of separate but related operations;

- Send the form to the tax authority every month;
- Inform the tax authority within 24 hours of any suspicious, illegal or economically unjustified operation;
- Suspend the operation until the tax authority has expressed a view on the operation. In the case where preliminary notification was impossible before the performance of the operation, the report must be made as soon as possible afterwards;
- Hold only personal accounts (as opposed to anonymous);
- Provide all information for investigation purpose to criminal investigation authorities, prosecutors and courts as requested;
- Keep customers' register, accounts and transactions data for ten years;
- Not inform the customer that information about him or his operation(s) has been released.

The list of potentially suspicious operations is given in Article 5 and covers cash operations, operations on bank accounts, operations on bonds and shares, foreign transactions and credit operations. Determination of the suspicious character of the operation, however, is the responsibility of the institution.

The law also sets up a number of prescriptive rules for financial institutions. In particular, investments made by non-residents must be made exclusively through non-resident banking institutions (Article 7). Article 8 provides that the source of incomes must be declared by citizens when:

a) the transaction is superior or equal to 200 monthly wage (or the sum of linked operations amounts for as much) in the case of deposit in banks, property auctions, acquisition of property rights, shares and bonds, creation of enterprises and exchange of currency.

b) The transaction is superior or equal to USD300 in the case of currency exchange transactions and import or export operations.

Finally, cash transactions are to be limited: according to Article 10, transactions between physical persons superior or equal to 500 monthly wage must not be made in cash but through bank transfers. The maximum amount of cash transactions between legal entities or between physical and legal persons is to be fixed subsequently by the government.

If adopted, these provisions would represent a major change in the way banking and non-banking financial institutions operate in Russia. At the time of writing, they are allowed to keep nominee and numbered accounts and are not required either to maintain records of their client or to develop formalized programmes against money-laundering.[28] With the adoption of the law, stringent identification requirements will

---

[28] Conference Paper No. 2, n. 22 above.

become mandatory, putting an end to anonymous accounts. It will be noted that these provisions do comply with the recommendations expressed in the UN Model Law 1995 regarding the list of financial institutions and customers' identification. Where the Russian provisions differ, and thereby raise important questions, is with regard to the reporting obligations, which are very wide-ranging. Not only banks, but also non-banking financial organizations such as casinos or notaries, will be required automatically to report on transactions above or equal to a certain threshold. This threshold at present corresponds to any transaction superior or equal to approximately USD650 for a physical person, and USD6,400 for a legal entity. In comparison, the Slovenian 1994 Law on the Prevention of Money-laundering requires the report of transactions in cash, securities, precious metals and stones of 2,200,000 tolar, that is about USD12,572 (Article 4). In Hungary, according to the 1994 Law on the Prevention and Impeding of Money-laundering, the performance of transactions involving the receipt or delivery of cash in local or foreign currency superior or equal to 2,000,000 forints, that is USD8,610 (Article 2) requires the bank to obtain the client's identity. Finally, the 1991 European Council Directive on Prevention of the Use of the Financial System for the Purpose of Money-laundering (91/308/EEC) requires a report when a single transaction or linked transactions exceed €15,000. Concern has been expressed that the Russian law will give overly broad access to financial records by regulatory and enforcement agencies. Apart from the privacy issue, whether the Russian tax authorities would actually be able to monitor the sheer volume of reports that they would undoubtedly receive is also open to question. Somehow, this concern undermines the law itself. In fact, the draft law is generally resented by the public as a threat to small tax evaders – especially small businesses.[29] This confusion of purpose – money-laundering and tax evasion – is particularly regrettable since (as a recent study demonstrates clearly) although sometimes sharing elements of *modus operandi*, they are diametrically opposed operations in intent:

> In general tax evasion involves taking legally earned income and either hiding its very existence (if, for example, it is skimmed in cash) or disguising its nature (by making it appear to fall into a non-taxable category). In either event it turns legal income into illegal. Money-laundering does the opposite. It takes illegally earned income and gives it the appearance of being legally earned. In terms of their impact on the fiscal position of the state, evasion and laundering also have quite opposite effects ... The point is that, contrary to the stereotype that sees criminal activity as an off-the-books, unrecorded and untaxed activity (with its existence hidden from the authorities), once the money is laundered it becomes at least in part on-the-books, recorded and taxed, albeit with its precise nature disguised.[30]

---

[29] In June 1997, the Central Bank felt necessary to reassure people that the law was not directed against 'small-time tax dodgers' such as the many Russians who earn revenues 'by working as gypsy cab drivers – technically a misdemeanor'. See Y. Borisova, 'Central Bank to Help Kulikov Fight Crime' *The St. Petersburg Times*, 9–15 June 9–15 1997: <www.sptimes.ru/>.

[30] J. A. Blum, *et. al.*, 'Financial Havens Banking Secrecy and Money-laundering' UNDCP Technical Series No 8 (United Nations, New York, 1998), pp. 9–10.

This demonstrates a key problem with the draft bill, and one that will arise again when discussing the competent authorities issue – the confusion of objectives. As indicated in the UN Model Law, a money-laundering law cannot be too all-encompassing as it is 'an invasive legislation, in that it places a duty on a citizen to report suspected criminal conduct' and it is also important that the authority to whom the report of transactions is made 'does not become an adjunct of the tax authorities'. Clearly, the Russian legislature has not followed this approach and appears to be willing to become involved in tax evasion rather than money-laundering as such.

b) Detection. With regard to the detection stage, the most important point is to ensure that bank and professional secrecy will not prevent the conduct of investigations. Article 9 of the draft law tackles the question of bank and commercial secrecy. Pursuant to this article, the transfer of information by banks or other financial institutions to controlling bodies, judicial institutions, prosecution or courts does not constitute a breach of secrecy. Moreover, bank and commercial secrecy cannot be invoked as a justification for refusing to pass on information about entities suspected of money-laundering and employees would be held liable by doing so.

Similar provisions have been adopted across the region. For example, the Bulgarian Banking Act 1997, Article 52 provides that banks could, pursuant to a court ruling, disclose information on their customers. The prosecutor in particular could make a demand to the court if there is any reason to believe that a crime has been committed. In Slovakia, Section 8 of the 1994 Anti-Money-laundering Act has expressly provided that duties to inform and to report cannot be limited by legal secrecy, except in the case of lawyers. Moreover, pursuant to the Banking Act 1991, Article 37, reports on matters subject to confidentiality can be submitted by a bank without the customer's consent upon request made by an authority engaged in criminal proceedings. The UN Model Law also recommends provision for the disallowance of bank secrecy in connection with drug money-laundering, which could be extended to professional secrecy for lawyers, judicial officers etc, when acting as financial intermediaries.

Unfortunately, the Russian law is mute on the practicalities of this detection principle, such as the investigative measures and the conditions under which investigating bodies could have access to information on customers' accounts without the customers' knowledge. International instruments – such as the UN Model Law – recommend the use of special investigative techniques such as the monitoring of bank accounts, phone tapping, access to computer systems, etc. only when ordered by a judicial authority, and only when there are strong grounds for believing that money-laundering is taking place. The Russian bill contains no such provision, leaving a gap that needs to be addressed either within this law or through a separate Act.

c) Sanctions. The draft law covers, respectively, criminal, administrative and civil responsibilities. As far as criminal liability is concerned, the legalization of criminal income (that is, proceeds) which consists of providing legal form, cover-up or distortion of the source, nature, location, form, movement or actual ownership of financial means or property rights obtained through criminal activities, is punishable by up to three years imprisonment, with or without confiscation of the proceeds

(Article 11). Aggravated circumstances cause the penalties to be increased: if the legalization was part of a repeated set of activities, concerted in group or if it involved officials, then the penalties would increase to five years imprisonment with confiscation of the proceeds plus the infringement of the right to perform certain activities for three years. If the crime was committed in large volume[31] or by an organized group of criminals or through the creation of legal entities, again the penalties are aggravated to five to 10 years imprisonment, confiscation of the proceeds, and infringement of certain activities for five years.[32] However, it is not clear how these provisions are to be coordinated with Article 174 of the Criminal Code which defines and prosecutes money-laundering in different terms. This would need to be resolved in order for the law enforcement agencies to proceed with criminal prosecution in confidence.

Articles 13 and 14 also sanction criminally the violation of the preventive measures listed in Article 4. In particular, the failure to inform tax authorities or other controlling bodies that a suspicious transaction had taken place or has been ordered, or releasing the information to the client is punished by up to three years of imprisonment, a fine of 100 to 500 monthly wage and the infringement of certain rights for five years. This sanction is in direct opposition to the view adopted by one of the variants of the Model Law. Here, the drafters took the view that failure to comply with the duty to report on unusual or complex transaction should not be criminally sanctioned unless it is deliberate, as these transactions cannot be objectively defined. Such breaches should be dealt only by disciplinary sanctions. The Russian legislature has ignored this recommendation, enacting a stringent criminal penalty against the non-reporting institutions.[33]

d) Data Collection and the Role of a Financial Intelligence Unit. As illustrated earlier, a very important aspect of money-laundering control is the collection and centralization of data to allow exchange of information and a better understanding of the money-laundering trends in the jurisdiction. This role should be assumed by a special central body, usually referred to as a Financial Intelligence Unit (FIU). The definition of an FIU as established by the Egmont Group in November 1996 is

> a central, national agency responsible for receiving (and, as permitted, requesting), analyzing and disseminating to the competent authorities, disclosures of financial information: (i) concerning suspected proceeds of crime, or (ii) required by national legislation or regulation, in order to counter money-laundering.[34]

---

[31] A note explains that 'large volume' is to be understood as a sum of money or property value superior or equal to 200 monthly wages.

[32] However, no criminal condemnation would be pronounced if the person voluntarily reported the crime.

[33] Administrative responsibility can also be pronounced for the same wrongs. Finally, civil liability is provided in articles 19 to 21: it mainly consists in the nullity of the transactions on criminal proceeds, the invalidity of the transfer of property rights and the impossibilty of acquiring them by time.

[34] The Egmont Group is an informal structure that serves as the principal forum for FIUs to network with one another and to work to identify and solve common problems.

The advantage of an FIU playing the role of a 'buffer' between the private financial sector and law enforcement and judicial and prosecutorial authorities is that it fosters a greater amount of trust in the anti-money-laundering system. In practice, however, despite the specialized nature of such unit, there is often some confusion with other official entities. Police units established for the purpose of investigating financial and white-collar crime – including money-laundering – have often been referred to as 'financial investigative units' with the acronym 'FIU'. However, they do not fulfil the definition adopted by the Egmont Group.

Again, the models across the region vary considerably. For instance, the Office for Money-laundering Prevention in Slovenia was established on 3 December 1994 within the Ministry of Finance. Its role and tasks are defined by the Law on the Prevention of Money-laundering. It collects and analyses data received from reporting organizations, and passes the relevant information to the law enforcement authorities. The Office is also charged with issuing recommendations and engaging in awareness and training programmes. In the Czech Republic, a Decree of the Ministry of Finance of 24 June 1996 on 'The Notification Obligation to be Fulfilled by Financial Institutions' created the Financial Analytical Unit within the said Ministry. Reports of unusual and suspicious transactions must be made to the Unit. On the other hand, in Poland, there is no FIU as such. In November 1998, two national-level police agencies were created to combat organized crime and drug trafficking which report directly to the Polish National Police Headquarters and work in close collaboration with tax, customs and border patrol authorities. However, they do not constitute a FIU as defined above. In Russia, pursuant to Article 22 of the draft bill, the State bodies controlling the financial activities previously defined are:

- the State tax office and its regional branches, plus the Federal Tax Police,
- the Ministry of Finance and State Privatization Funds,
- the Central Bank,
- the Federal Currency and Export Control Agency,
- the Customs Service,
- other Ministries in their respective competence.

These bodies must check financial institutions' compliance with the requirements set up in the present law; develop and maintain mechanisms for internal audit and investigations of these institutions; provide judicial bodies with information and facilitate their investigation and provide methodological leadership in this area for the financial institutions. Should a breach of their obligations be established, the controlling bodies must initiate administrative proceedings against the wrongdoer and refer the case to the judiciary for criminal investigation (Article 23). As far as the judicial system is concerned, investigation and prosecution are of the competence of the General Prosecutor's office, the Police, the Russian Secret Service, the Federal Tax Police and Customs. Finally, pursuant to Article 28, coordination of the State bodies is ensured by an Intra-Body Committee of the Security Council of Russia on Anti-Criminal and Anti-Corruption Activities. Clearly, the Bill has not opted for the creation of a FIU and instead reports will be sent to each law enforcement body which will then be able to set up its own inquiry department, in particular the tax offices. The lack of an FIU was already a concern raised by the FATF mission in Russia in November 1996.[35] The reason for its absence may well be that, as seen above, the law aims not only at detecting transactions of money-laundering but also tax evasion transactions and other violations of prescriptive regulation. This would also explain the wide spectrum of bodies involved. Moreover, there is evidence that at present these bodies do not intend to collaborate and cooperate. In July 1997, the Central Bank of Russia took the initiative to set up a national system of preventive measures aimed at safeguarding the banking community against dirty money.[36] It issued a Resolution No. 479 to prevent illegal funds passing through banks and credit institutions, and an Order No. 02-378 of August 1997 instructing banks and credit institutions that participate in financial markets how to organize internal controls. However, when the Bank published its recommendations, it complained that law enforcement agencies were not willing to cooperate.[37] However, the draft law has not resolved this problem of competence by creating a FIU. It is naturally difficult to condemn this approach *prima facie* without any practical test of how it would function. However, the lack of a centralized agency makes exchange and cross-reference of information within the country more difficult, as well as hampering international cooperation – there would be no single Russian body able to liaise with the various FIUs around the world. This could undermine the success of money-laundering control.

Naturally, it is too early to draw firm conclusions on the approach Russia has adopted. It remains to be seen whether the draft as it now stands will be adopted in any form, although this seems very doubtful. Furthermore, even if adopted, its implementation will raise difficulties and the draft's provisions already raise a number of serious concerns. The main objection clearly is the use of criminal law as a deterrent under very strict terms, with no stated defenses or remedies. A second problem is the key role allocated to the tax authorities and the lack of any centralized authority specifically devoted to money-laundering. Finally, the overly broad access by regulatory and enforcement agencies to financial records, through the compulsory and systematic report of all transactions above what is actually a very low threshold, raises questions as to the general objective of this piece of legislation and the place of the rule of law in combating economic crime.

III.   THE RESPONSE OF THE RULE OF LAW TO ECONOMIC CRIME

At this stage, we need to step back from the specific provisions of a money-laundering law, whether in Russia or elsewhere, and consider how best the rule of law as a

---

[35]   As reported in Conference Paper No. 2, n. 22 above.

[36]   Yasina, 'Dubinin Acting to Fill Legal Vacuum.' *The St. Petersburg Times*, 28 July–3 August, 1997. <www.times.spb.ru>.

[37]   Alexander Khandruyev, the Central Bank Deputy Chairman was reported to have declared: 'Of course, the Central Bank is not an arm of law enforcement, but cooperation with these forces is what we need to make our banking system healthy.' See Borisova, n. 29 above.

general concept can address the problem. In particular, we should ask whether the law needs to be mainly punitive in order to succeed as a deterrent. Experience has shown that criminal legal provisions are not the most efficient means of preventing crime and they leave unsolved more fundamental problems, such as the condition of the banking and financial system. Consequently, where criminal law is the main weapon used by the legislature, the question is whether this actually reveals some important features as to the role of the rule of law in this jurisdiction.

1. Is criminal law an appropriate tool for money-laundering control?

The key question is whether or not criminal enforcement constitutes a strong enough deterrent to inhibit money-laundering activities from taking place. The Russian legislature is fully aware that money-laundering is not only a criminal law issue. Indeed, the preamble to the draft law on money-laundering states that its objectives are not solely to act as deterrent and punishment but also to promote and ensure the normal formation and development of market relations based on the recognition of the economic liberty of business activity entities.[38] Nonetheless, the draft law gives priority to criminal provisions and criminal sanctions although many authors argue that criminal prosecution can give only limited results.[39]

The application of civil law in this area could be appropriate and useful. Firstly, an action on civil liability brought by the victims of money-laundering crimes could give excellent results and would usually be less cumbersome with regard to the rules of evidence. Moreover, civil law has other weapons it could use to inhibit money-laundering. In particular, the English law of Equity has developed the concept of tracing which, in the case of misappropriated funds laundered through a series of bank accounts and, therefore, mixed with other funds, will still grant to the victim a remedy against the recipient, namely the banks.[40] Generally, civil measures can be taken in areas that are usually not necessarily related: administrative law, tax law, banking law, civil and commercial law, competition law, etc. In other words, '[a] truly integrated, multisectorial, multidisciplinary and balanced approach should be ensured'.[41]

What is missing in the Russian law, crucially, are actions to remedy the *structural conditions* which provide the fertile ground for money-laundering activities. As early

---

[38] Conference Paper No. 2, n. 22 above.

[39] See B. A. K. Rider, n. 25 above, p. 246. It is revealing that in many countries said to be "in transition", the topic usually described by Western scholars as "economic crime", is denoted by the term "economic *crimes*" (in plural). This is not a minor difference. The Western approach deals with the phenomenon as a global one not only through criminal law but also civil and regulatory law. In countries in transition, the approach adopted is to address each illegal activity through separate specific offences. See China-Europe Legal Seminar, *The Effect of the Rule of Law on Economic Growth*, Proceedings of the Workshop on Economic Crime, Beijing, 13-14 November 1997, unpublished.

[40] Stephen Moriarty, "Tracing, Mixing and Laundering", in P. Birks (ed.), *Laundering and Tracing* (Clarendon Press, Oxford, 1995) p.73.

[41] *U.N. Crime Prevention and Criminal Justice Newsletter*, p. 15.

as 1994, Rowan Bosworth-Davies and Graham Saltmarch denounced the close link that existed in Russia between organized crime and the banking and financial sector.[42] The die-hard habits of soft lending and political influence over banks, and what was in fact loose regulation and supervision had facilitated criminal organizations' infiltration of banks.[43] Moreover, financial liberalization coupled with an inefficient financial market meant that borrowers in need suffered the consequences of untenable transaction costs or reduced lending volumes.[44] The three options open to them were to seek government support, to reduce operations, or seek informal credit. Clearly, what is needed to address these issues are profound reforms of the banking and securities sectors. Laws and enforcement policies which are fashioned to address money-laundering through conventional banking systems are at present of little relevance if these systems are themselves rotten.[45]

2.   What the use of criminal law reveals as to the role of the rule of law

The reason why Russia is opting for a coercive approach to the problem rests on the general attitude towards business activities and the understanding of how the rule of law should govern business. As noted before, it is important to ensure that society understands the importance of the fight against money-laundering and supports the means adopted to control it. The difficulty here is that:

> [i]n essence, the rule in successful money-laundering is always to approximate as closely as possible legal transactions. As a result the actual devices used are themselves minor variations on methods employed routinely by legitimate businesses ... On the surface it may be impossible to differentiate the legal and illegal variants – the distinction becomes clear only once a particular criminal act has been targeted and the authorities subsequently begun to unravel the money trail.[46]

To this inherent general difficulty is added the specific problem that in the mind of the Russian people, business is generally linked with criminality as the early entrepreneurs were in effect outlaws under the Soviet system. Johan Bäckman shows elsewhere in this volume that the mafia threat has been used in Russia by the State-government to legitimize a return to centralized power. Similarly, a study on the legal models in post-communist societies has shown that the major events of legal change in Russia have so far been concentrated in the areas of the *prohibitive* function

---

[42]   R. Bosworth-Davies and G. Saltmarch, 'International Overview', in J. Reuvid (ed.), *The Regulation and Prevention of Economic Crime Internationally* (Kogan Page, London, 1995), p. 91.

[43]   Y. Gilinskiy, 'Economic Crime in Contemporary Russia' (March–April 1998) 5 *European Financial Services Law*, p. 60.

[44]   D. I. Keh, 'Drug Money in a Changing World: Economic Reform and Criminal Finance' UNDCP Technical Series, Paper No. 4. See <www.undcp.org/publications/index>.

[45]   See B. A. K. Rider, n. 25 above, p. 241.

[46]   Blum *et. al.*, n. 30 above, p. 20.

(criminal law) and the *ideological* function (constitutional reform and human rights) of the legal system.[47] Privatization, market economy and democratization as the major drives for transformation have not been sufficiently supported by legal practice: a systematic, comprehensive and consistent legal reform in the areas of commercial and company law has still not been achieved. Rather, the reform process has been accompanied by a traditional – and restrictive – suspicion of unregulated free enterprise and free trade. This suspicion is reflected in the prohibitive measures in criminal law to protect individuals from the fall-out of economic liberalization and privatization, especially in the fight against white-collar crime and organized crime, as the preceding review of the current draft law has shown. Generally speaking, the Russian legislature has found it difficult to deal with the freedom unleashed by the collapse of communism. Unlike in countries with advanced market economies, the 1960 Criminal Code did not provide for economic crimes. Following the economic changes of the 1990s, a thorough reform was undertaken with the adoption of the new Criminal Code in 1996. Two chapters are devoted to economic crimes, namely Chapter 22 'Crimes in the Sphere of Economic Activity' and Chapter 23 'Crimes against the Interests of a Service in Commercial and other Organizations'. The main difficulties with the reforms were in deciding whether certain harmful activities should be deterred by civil damages or criminal penalties. The adoption of the new Criminal Code should have been seen as '[a major effort] to discard a lawless and repressive Soviet legacy and join the mainstream of progressive penological cultures'.[48] Indeed, the Code recognizes the supremacy of the rights of individuals and makes their protection central, above government interests. However, typically, a repressive attitude is still very present in the Russian society.[49]

This touches on the core of the problem, namely the role of the rule of law in Russia at present. The former Soviet approach was to emphasize law as a tool for social control and render it a coercive and effective instrument of the state for imposing its policy goals. As such, the law never really *mattered*, that is, it never served as

a means of constraining official power, vindicating citizens' grievances, and facilitating private transactions. That is, we can speak of 'law' mattering in a consciously reciprocal sense that acknowledges the existence of both state and society as participants in the creation and maintenance of a legal regime.[50]

---

[47] K. Ziegert, 'A Theory Design for the Assessment of Legal Change – The Cultural Differentiation of Post-Communist Societies and their Law' (1996) *Political Regulation of Modern Industrial Societies*, p. 42.

[48] S. Pomorski, 'Reflections on the First Criminal Code of Post-Communist Russia' (1998) 46 *American Journal of Criminal* Law, p. 375.

[49] Ibid, p. 392.

[50] K. Hendley, *Trying to Make Law Matter – Legal Reform and Labor Law in the Soviet Union* (University of Michigan Press, Ann Arbor, MI, 1996), p. 3.

Despite the reforms, there are signs that things have not really changed. The legislature is still using law as a coercive tool when addressing the question of money-laundering and economic crime. More than tough laws on economic crime – that is, criminal law sanctions and intrusive legislation – what is needed in Russia is the adoption of legislative measures compatible with respect for human rights and the protection of individual freedoms. Without this major safeguard, the measures taken could attract criticism and fail to obtain legitimacy. Whilst it is true that the models offered by the West put a strong emphasis on the repressive role of the law – the offensive approach of criminalizing money-laundering, introducing identifying and reporting obligations and generally easing prosecution – this offensive approach is nevertheless balanced by adequate remedies. The countries of Central and Eastern Europe are finding it harder to achieve this balance as they are pressed on the one hand to reach standards of human rights (in particular when signing the European Convention on Human Rights) and on the other hand efficiently to fight organized crime. The fight against economic crime and money-laundering control must work hand in hand with human rights and the protection of individual freedoms. One thing is certain: the simple adoption of international instruments into domestic law, such as Russian law, will not be sufficient if Russian law is not embraced by Russian society (especially the business community) as a reciprocal instrument, protecting values on which a social agreement has been reached. This must be the ultimate aim of every international body advising on the issue, if such advice is to bear fruit in the future.

17

The Hyperbola of Russian Crime and the Police Culture

*Johan Bäckman**

I. INTRODUCTION

After the fall of the iron curtain a new threat entered the public focus in the Western countries. Communism was substituted by so-called transnational organized crime, originating in the former East block countries and targeting their Western neighbours. This threat brought the police of various nation states together, leading to intergovernmental agreements in crime prevention, a proliferation of liaison officers, and finally to close cooperation in crime intelligence and investigation. Organized crime, particularly Russian, is acting as a central reference point of this 'law enforcement adventurism'.[1]

Since 1995, several interviews have been undertaken by the author with the Russian, Estonian and Finnish police about the crime trends in Russia and Estonia and their influence on Finland.[2] Of course one can isolate various kinds of influences, but in the author's opinion the influence of Russian crime is more evident in the Finnish criminal policy and the activities of the Finnish police, than in the Finnish crime situation. During this research it was realized that the extent to which the Russian police culture was influencing the Finnish police by causing them pressures

---

* The author would like to thank Alena V. Ledeneva and Robert Reiner for their critical and useful comments while preparing this article. Thanks also go to Zelda Dalling, who edited the language.

1 M. den Boer, 'The EU and Organised Crime: Fighting a New Enemy with Many Tentacles' *Organised Crime in Baltic Region* (Criminological Research Centre, Riga, 1997).

2 Since 1995, the author has collected over 100 unstructured thematic interviews with Russian, Finnish and Estonian police. About a half of the interviews have been collected with Finnish police officials from various agencies, such as the national bureau of investigation (KRP), the security police (SUPO), the local police agencies, and the Finnish liaison officers operating in Russia and Estonia. Moreover, in Estonia 24 interviews were collected with the Estonian police officials from the central criminal police (KKP), the security police (KAPO), and the local police prefectures. In addition, interviews were collected with various departments of the organized crime combat agency (RUOP) in St. Petersburg, and since 1999, interviews with the tax police service (FSNP) and economic crime combat agency (UBEP) in St. Petersburg have also been collected. Access to the agencies has been gained by means of special negotiations and agreements between the Finnish police, the liaison officers, the National Research Institute of Legal Policy and the Russian and Estonian agencies. The majority of the interviews have been recorded and transcribed. In addition, the police have given confidential and other materials for research purposes. More information about the author's studies can be found at: <http://personal.inet.fi?tiede/johan.bachman>.

A. V. Ledeneva and M. Kurkchiyan (eds.), Economic Crime in Russia, 257–273
© 2000 *Kluwer Law International. Printed in Great Britain.*

and changing their way of thinking and acting. This development is exceptional. The main reason is that the relations between Finnish and Russian police are very close and active in terms of cooperation in crime prevention.

The above-mentioned disclosures were influential in going against the general stream of thought among the students of the East European crime problem and speak about the inflation of crime,[3] as rooted mainly in the Russian police culture, in that the inflated picture of crime in Russia reflects more the collective thinking of the Russian police than actual crime. The main hypothesis in this paper is that the proliferation of the Russian police culture is more problematic than the proliferation of Russian crime, because in the face of the inflated threats, constructed within the framework of a police culture shaped by totalitarian rule, the Finnish police is obtaining features of the Russian-style policing. The problem is in the strength of the principal reference point of this activity – the threat of organized crime originating in Russia.

Although transnational crime has been widely covered by contemporary students of crime, the parallel internationalization of police practices and way of thinking has rarely been studied. Therefore, it is the intention of this paper to study the interactions, collisions and changes caused by the cooperation between Estonian, Russian and Finnish police cultures. The theme of this research is the dynamics of interacting and colliding police cultures which utilize 'organized crime' as their reference point, and in particular the pressure this point puts on the Finnish police.

This hypothesis can be linked with the postmodern view on social development, which is characterized by a diffusion that makes the police function vague and transforms the police from centralized control over nation states toward specialized international units.[4] Although nation states seek centralization in their control functions, the basic nature of the international system can be described as anarchic, because the international cooperation lacks strict and centralized control.

II.   THE POLICE CULTURE

The unstructured interviews with Russian, Estonian and Finnish police consist of depictions of crime cases, crime trends, attitudes of the police toward foreign and domestic police agencies, and descriptions of problems of legislation and the trends in criminal policy. Therefore, the interviews reflect various characteristics often attributed to the police culture. Such elements include the different ways of thinking, values, norms, perspectives, common prejudiced stereotypes, stories, aphorisms and other references, 'the vehicles for analogous thinking'. They transmit the underlying culture, guide the actions of the police, and instruct the officers on how to see the

---

[3]   J. Bäckman, *The Inflation of Crime in Russia. The Social Danger of the Emerging Markets.* National Research Institute of Legal Policy. Publication Series No. 150. (National Research Institute of Legal Policy, Helsinki, 1998).

[4]   R. Reiner, 'Policing and the Police' in M. Maguire, R. Morgan, and R. Reiner (eds), *The Oxford Handbook of Criminology* (Clarendon Press, Oxford, 1994), pp. 755–757.

world and act in it. Particularly, the interviews reflect the various kinds of pressure to which the police are subjected, and what helps them cope.[5]

It is the intention of this paper to illustrate how the Russian police culture is transforming the Finnish police through international cooperation. In a broader sense the goal is to show how the Russian police culture is constituting the principal conceptual universe[6] in which the features of Russian crime are rather uncritically constructed, not only by the Finnish police, but by most Western students of Russian or East European crime.

The police culture studies are often concentrated on the rank-and-file officers. In this case, most of the informants represent managerial positions of elite agencies. However, this clear distinction can only be made in the Russian case, due to their developed system of education, whereas in Finland the police force is so small that such categorization is more difficult to make, especially due to the comparatively limited differentiation in education.

III. THE RUSSIAN DISCRETION

After the collapse of the Soviet Union, the various police agencies of Russia did not collapse, but continued their activities, and even new agencies were established. The ministry of the interior (MVD) is responsible for the main police function. The estimated 80,000 police officials under the main administration of internal affairs (GUVD) of St. Petersburg (a city of five million) work for various agencies.[7] In addition to GUVD, several other federal agencies operate in the city, such as the organized crime combat agency (RUOP) with the special fast reaction troop (SOBR), founded in 1992 and 1993 as a part of MVD. However, it is not just the MVD that is responsible for the police system. St. Petersburg has two federal services of the tax police (FSNP) founded in 1993, and the successors of the state security committee (KGB), such as the federal security service (FSB). In addition, there are hundreds of private security companies.

In terms of organization, education and laws regulating the activities, I believe, the Russian police system is modern and developed. However, the totalitarian legacy has given the Russian police exceptional powers for discretion, strongly embedded in the criminal law and informal practices that developed during the Soviet rule.

The term 'militia' does not now have ideological flavour. Although militia (the MVD structures) and police (the tax police) are nowadays parallel organizations, in

5   R. Reiner, *The Politics of the Police.* 2nd edtn. (Harvester Wheatsheaf, London, 1992); R. Reiner, n. 4 above; C. D. Shearing and R. V. Ericson, 'Culture as Figurative Action' (1991) 42 *British Journal of Sociology*, pp. 481–506; J. Skolnick, *Justice Without Trial* (John Wiley, New York, 1966).

6   P. L. Berger and T. Luckmann, *The Social Construction of Reality. A Treatise in the Sociology of Knowledge* (Penguin Books, London, 1991).

7   The agencies operating under GUVD are e.g. the militia of societal security (MOB), the special-purpose militia detachment (OMON), the drug trade combat agency (UBNON), the special service of the militia (USSM) which investigates criminality committed by or against foreign citizens, the economic crime combat agency (UBEP), the extra-departmental guard (UVO) which provides contract security for private businesses, about a hundred local militia stations, and various other agencies.

the following all of the Russian law enforcement agencies carrying out operative investigation and other duties (as defined by the federal law) will be referred to as the Russian police.

Louise Shelley has distinguished several formal elements of Russian police culture in her study of Soviet policing,[8] such as defending an exceptionally broad range of state interests, with wide tasks in social control and maintenance of social order, and technically and methodologically advanced practices (covert techniques, crime intelligence and the use of informants) particularly in the framework of totalitarian, militaristic and colonial traditions. According to Shelley, citizens were defenceless against police abuse, and the police was highly effective in reaching its objectives.

Culminating from the author's studies into crime, the police and the culture of criminal justice in Russia[9] has enabled this paper to isolate eight core elements of the Russian police culture. While informal in nature, they still reflect the strong legacy of formal elements, some of which are rooted in the early years of Soviet rule.

The Russian Police

1. Are an instrument of political rule and influence;
2. Merely secures the state interest than protects the public ;
3. Exaggerates and inflates the crime problem out of all proportion ;
4. Applies criminal law rather according to analogy than legality principle;
5. Considers penetration into all aspects of privacy as a duty;
6. Targets activity considered as 'socially dangerous';
7. Suppresses all private enterprises, particularly private businesses;
8. Concentrates on stigmatization, filing and repression of the dangerous elements.

IV.   SOCIAL DANGER AND THE ANALOGY OF LAW

In Russia, the criminal code has a much wider role in social control than in the Western countries. Therefore, the police have much wider tasks in social control, often placing them above the law. The role of the police is underlined by the fact that the individuals suspected of crimes suffer more than the individuals convicted of crimes, which is a traditional feature in the Russian administration of criminal justice.

This paper will illustrate how the culture of criminal justice practically dissolves the border between actual crime and any activities contradicting state interests. Due to this vague border, the line between political resistance and actual crime is

---

[8]   L. I. Shelley, *Policing Soviet Society: The Evolution of State Control* (Routledge, London, 1996).

[9]   J. Bäckman, *Venäjän organisoitu rikollisuus.*(English summary: Russian organized crime) Oikeuspoliittisen tutkimuslaitoksen julkaisuja No.135. (Oikeuspoliittinen tutkimuslaitos, Helsinki, 1996); Bäckman, n. 3 above; J. Bäckman, '*Sudella on sata tietä...*'. *Pietarin organisoitu rikollisuus Venäjän rikosoikeuskulttuurin kehyksessä* (English summary: 'The wolf has a hundred paths...'. Organized crime of St. Petersburg in the framework of Russian culture of criminal justice). Oikeuspoliittisen tutkimuslaitoksen julkaisuja No. 166 (Oikeuspoliittinen tutkimuslaitos, Helsinki, 1999).

impossible to define. Since the culture of criminal justice, created during the early decades of Soviet rule, is still influencing the police work, a deeper historical backdrop is needed here.

The Russian state has always been active in defining ultimate foes as objects of stigmatization and repression. After the revolution in 1917, the protection of the 'revolutionary state and society' took precedence over protecting the rights of the individual. The principal foe was the 'class enemy'. The social element of crime ('social danger') and the analogy principle, defined by the criminal code, were the legal basis for the repression carried out by the state organs.

What does 'social danger' mean? During 1922–1960 the criminal code of Russia defined *all* acts or neglects representing 'social danger' as offences. The concept of crime accentuates the 'socially dangerous' *consequences* of an act (consequences which contradict the state interests), not the guilt of the suspect. Based on the positivistic school of criminology and causal interpretations on the societal reasons of crime, the concept of guilt was replaced with the danger of personality.

What does the analogy of law mean? Since the legislators found it difficult to compile a comprehensive list of offences to protect the state from the 'class enemies' in the 1920s, they applied the analogy principle, found in many criminal codes of the 19th century European autocracies. The analogy principle opened possibilities for terror, because it empowered the judges to place themselves above the law and to convict persons they judged to have committed 'socially dangerous' acts not defined as crimes, by applying an article *most similar* in kind to the offence.[10] The vague definitions of the criminal code contributed to this practice. Analogy was often abused as an instrument for convicting an offender of a crime more serious than the one that they had actually committed, and in the 1930s analogy was applied more frequently. The main point was that many dangerous offenders would go unpunished unless the law remained flexible.[11]

Analogy was the corner stone of the political programme of the radical legal theorists during 1929–1936. Believing that crime would disappear, the radicals, Pashukanis and Krylenko, demanded a simplified criminal code in which definitions of crimes and punishments were omitted as features of 'bourgeois pricing'. This would have enabled the judges to analogize in every case, according to the 'social danger' of the act. The legality principle – *nullum crimen sine lege* – was considered a 'bourgeois principle' that only served the interests of the ruling exploiters in the Western countries. However, this proposal by Pashukanis and Krylenko was never implemented.

Analogy was finally excluded by the criminal code of 1960, which defined an offence as a 'socially dangerous act stipulated by the criminal code'. While the

---

[10] This was legitimized, for example, by a Marx slogan, 'The law is general, but the case is unique' (*zakon vseobshch, a sluchai edinichen*).

[11] The analogy was indeed such a drastic feature that it divided the community of legal scholars. Surprisingly enough, the chairman of the USSR Supreme Court stated *publicly* in 1939 that 'the court often uses analogy to violate the law' see P. H. Solomon, Jr., *Soviet Criminologists and Criminal Policy: Specialists in Policy-Making* (Columbia University Press, New York, 1978), p. 24. The elimination of the principle was strongly advocated.

criminal code of 1996 was drafted, the theorists argued for the exclusion of 'social danger' because of the controversy in its history, however, it was retained as well to the code of 1996, which defines an offence as 'guilty committed socially dangerous act provided for by the criminal code'. Although guilt was introduced in the code of 1996, the danger of personality has remained as an informal element of the police culture, very much present in the constant stigmatization, surveillance and filing of individuals defined as 'socially dangerous'.

As Solomon[12] has shown, the removal of analogy has had only a small effect in the administration of criminal justice since the 1960s. Due to the vague nature of the definitions of crimes in the criminal code, and the existence of the social element of crime, the analogy principle is still influencing the administration of criminal justice in Russia, particularly as an informal legacy in the police culture.

How is all this reflected in the police work in Russia? Today, organized crime, the main reference point of police work in Russia, is defined by the Russian criminologists according to the principles explained above.[13] Given that the mainstream of criminological research in Russia is carried out by specialized police officers, the Russian criminology constitutes merely a reproductive system rather than an independent and critical scientific tradition. As Solomon[14] has noticed, the Soviet criminological expert tradition was not critical but lenient due to a limited influence on policy-making.

In the criminal policy rhetoric, 'organized crime' has gained an analogous position with 'class enemies' (often labeled as 'thieves'), the previous principal foes of the Russian state. Another interesting analogy is the official rhetoric about 'transition'; earlier the discretion was legitimized by 'the transition from socialism to communism', nowadays the analogous rhetoric is clearly visible concerning 'the transition from socialism to the market relations'.

The contemporary Russian criminologists, often high-ranking police officers, exaggerate the 'social danger' of organized crime out of any proportion, as if it would represent a new class enemy. The core idea is that organized crime poses a pronounced social danger for individual, state and society. The actual 'creator' or inventor of organized crime is the leading Russian criminologist and general of the militia Aleksandr Gurov, who in the late 1980s demanded severe combat measures against organized crime, the introduction of organized crime in the criminal code,

---

12 Solomon, ibid, p. 26.
13 In fact the early definitions of 'organized crime' were serving terror. In summer 1947, a repression was sought for punishing 'thieves of state, social and personal property'. See Solomon, n. 11 above, p. 31. Harsher punishments were sought by defining a theft committed by 'organized group' or 'gang' more socially dangerous. However, as usual, the laws left 'organized group' practically undefined. According to critics, 'organized group (gang)' should refer to a *stable* organized criminal group, and loose criminal partnerships should be excluded. Stability should have meant that the group had engaged in criminal activities prior to the offences in question. In 1948, a definition was issued stipulating 'organized group' as being a group of two or more persons organized in advance to commit one or more thefts after some preliminary agreement among the members of this group, organized for this purpose. Finally, criticism that ran counter to the extreme repression failed and a vague definition of 'organized group' served discretion. The contemporary definitions in the criminal code are analogous.
14 Solomon, n. 11 above.

and the establishment of federal organized crime combat agencies (nowadays known as the RUOPs). Although the critics said that the existing categories of 'group crime' would be enough, as a term, organized crime got official acceptance, as demanded by Gurov. Several other leading criminologists (and high-ranking police officers) have emphasized the way in which individual, spiritual and material values, as well as the constitutional structure, sovereignty and regional unity of the state can become the objects of the 'pronounced social danger of organized crime'.[15] The Russian state could hardly have a more fundamental threat.

The exaggeration and inflation of crime out of all proportion is well-communicated in an official criminal policy programme of Russia, titled *Foundations of State Policy in Combating Crime in Russia – A Theoretical Model*, compiled by the research institute of the general prosecutor.[16] This programme clearly reflects the nature of a totalitarian police state. According to the programme, the society is undergoing 'total criminalization' due to weakened legal control, because 'immoral, anti-societal, and socially dangerous behaviour' is spreading and 'the state has created an administrational vacuum in combating crime and other violations of the law'. The problem is that many 'socially dangerous acts' have been 'decriminalized'. According to polls, more than half of the population thinks that 'criminal structures and the mafia' are the real governors of the country. The programme says that the influence of organized crime is growing in official structures, while organized crime controls a remarkable part of the economy, penetrates everywhere, and tries to take under its control the law enforcement, other state organs and the media. According to the programme, to gain ideological support in combating crime, the state should control the media because 'freedom of the mass media cannot lead to permission of everything'. Finally, the book says that criminal policy should encourage 'a more objective image' of Russia's crime in foreign countries![17] The increase in the combat of crime, legitimized by this rhetoric, is visible in the growth of the massive statistical evidence the law enforcement has produced e.g. about organized crime during the 1990s.[18]

---

[15] V. S. Ovchinsky, *Strategiia borby s mafiei* (Sims, Moscow, 1993); V. S. Ovchinsky, V. E. Eminov, and N. P. Jablokov (eds), *Osnovy borby s organizovannoi prestupnostiu* (Infra-M, Moscow, 1996); .A. I. Gurov, 'Organizovannaia prestupnost' i mery borby s nei''in V. N. Kudriavtsev and V. E. Eminov (eds), *Kriminologiia* (Iurist, Moscow, 1995), pp. 263–265; A. I. Gurov, *Organizovannaia prestupnost' i mery borby s nei. Stenogramma lektsii* (Znanie, Moscow, 1989), p. 10.

[16] A. I. Sukharev, A. I. Alekseev, and M. P. Zhuravlev, *Osnovy gosudarstvennoi politiki borby s prestupnostiu v Rossii. Teoreticheskaia model'*. Nauchno-issledovatelskii institut problem ukrepleniia zakonnosti i pravoporiadka pri generalnoi prokurature Rossiiskoi Federatsii. (Izdatelstvo NORMA, Moscow, 1997).

[17] Frequently, the Russian sources stated that the image of Russian crime is exaggerated in Western countries. However, in this case it is possible that the report thinks that crime in Russia is underestimated in foreign countries.

[18] Since the battle against organized crime began, the police has been actively recording various elements of this phenomena. The number of suppressed elements of organized crime has multiplied during 1990s, reaching the number of 8,000 organized criminal formations and 21,000 prosecuted criminal leaders in 1996. According to the estimate, the number of crimes committed by organized groups and criminal communities will increase 2.5–2.7 times by 2005, reaching 60,000. Sukharev *et al.*, n. 16 above, p. 20.

The exaggerated rhetoric about crime shows how the state is returning towards a totalitarian police state. The hyperbola of crime in Russia rises from the strong totalitarian legacy that contradicts the democratic reforms. This puts severe pressure on the Russian police, and their Western counterparts as well as via international cooperation.[19]

V.   STIGMATIZATION FOR DISCRETION

Extra-judicial discretion is the core element of the Russian police culture. The Soviet militia was controlling a wide range of individuals labeled as deviant or 'socially dangerous'; these groups were severely stigmatized and officials maintained detailed files on them. A strict conceptual system, based on criminal law and criminological studies, acted as the principal instrument of this discretion. The stigmatized elements included various subcultures (dissidents, intellectuals, homosexuals, youth cultures), and individuals who made their living outside the state structures, labeled as 'parasites'. Since profit-making was criminalized as speculation, the militia controlled a wide range of shady businessmen, speculators and gamblers. The recidivists were targeted with the most severe stigmatization. All this was widely reproduced by criminological studies.

A traditional category of victims of discretion were women labeled as prostitutes for an 'anti-societal and a parasitic' way of behaviour. Today the inflated discussion of prostitution in Russia is indeed an interesting field of study; many Russians say that prostitution is wide-spread, and that many young women dream of becoming prostitutes. However the anti-marketism stipulates that capitalism is driving most Russian women to become prostitutes (such as housewives or lovers of rich businessmen) or simply proliferating other forms of bourgeois immorality (such as pre-marital relationships) all being labeled as prostitution. Today, the way of thinking of the Russian police is mainly reflecting these old moral principles, for example most of my informants said that the markets are only beneficial to 'anti-societal parasites', and that the state should carry out 'ideological propaganda' to hinder the youth in becoming 'bandits and prostitutes'.

Nowadays, the principal targets of the police are the various elements of so-called organized crime, such as leaders and active participants. The police often refer to these people as 'bandits' or 'apes', often with racist stigmatization of the nationalities of Caucasus as 'blacks'. The members of the fast reaction troop (SOBR) of the organized crime combat agency (RUOP) maintain that they prefer staff with combat experience in war and employ veterans of the war in Afghanistan. The St. Petersburg SOBR also took part in the Chechnya war.

---

[19]   While the hyperbola of Russian crime is being uncritically constructed in the Russian framework of culture of criminal justice and the police culture, one can say that several Western students of Russian crime are actually shaking hands with Stalin and his principal legal theorists, Pashukanis and Krylenko, whose main principles of criminal justice and police work, founded in the 1920s, are still influencing the image of crime. Indeed, it would be interesting to study the analogies between combat against class enemies in the 1920s and 1930s and combat against organized crime in the 1990s.

The most traditional target of stigmatization are individuals described as 'acknowledged thieves' (*vory v zakone*), very often translated as 'thieves-in-law'. However, the translation 'thief-in-law' is misleading, since here *v zakone* does not refer to law (*zakon*) but to something as generally acknowledged (*priznannyi*) by the underworld. Although 'thieves professing the code' is a good suggestion,[20] simple 'acknowledged thief' is better.

This concept allegedly refers to leaders of the traditional underworld originating in the early decades of this century, as rooted in a wider stigma of 'thief' (*vor*), meaning the general mass of the underworld. Both Western and Russian criminologists have spent considerable efforts in describing the dimensions of 'acknowledged thieves' as the major Russian criminal tradition. Several scholars, most of them Russians, share the view that the tradition was spontaneously created in the underworld in the early 1930s and has existed ever since.[21]

However, maybe this category has practically nothing to do with the actual underworld, but is invented and reinforced by the Russian police? Could it be possible that the 'acknowledged thief' is a pure police term and one of the stigmas serving the discretion of the Russian police culture?

Some Russian authors have indeed claimed that this stigma was in fact an early invention of the Russian police, and propaganda about the danger of 'acknowledged thieves' has been widely proliferated since the 1930s. Andrei Konstantinov has mentioned the possibility that the concept is *a police term*, introduced in the 1920s, and rarely used by criminals themselves.[22] The fact that this tradition is often described as a 'movement' (*dvizhenie*) speaks for the assumption that political resistance is also in question. The racist element of the stigma is communicated by the fact that many Russian experts claim that Georgians constitute the majority of 'acknowledged thieves'. Equally, instead of an underworld tradition, the stigma of 'thief' (*vor*) is an invention of the Russian police in the 1920s, serving the repression of individuals labeled as class enemies, especially 'thieves of the socialist property'.

Aleksandr Gurov has explained how a decree in 1956 stipulated that the 'criminal tradition' of 'acknowledged thieves' was to be eliminated by using harsh propaganda (including public confessions and memoirs of alleged 'acknowledged thieves'), and

---

[20] S. Adamoli *et al.*, *Organised Crime around the World*, European Institute of Crime Prevention and Control, affiliated with the United Nations. Publication Series No. 31. (HEUNI, Helsinki, 1998), p. 54.

[21] A. I. Gurov, *Organizovannaia prestupnost' — ne mif, a realnost'. Sotsialnye, pravovye i kriminologicheskie aspekty borby s organizovannoi prestupnostiu* (Znanie, Moscow, 1992); A. I. Gurov, *Professional'naia prestupnost'. Proshloe i sovremennost'* (Iuridicheskaia Literatura, Moscow, 1990); V. G. Grib *et al.*, (eds), *Problemy borby s organizovannoi prestupnostiu i korruptsiei: Sbornik nauchnykh trudov* (NII MVD Rossii, Moscow, 1993); V. S. Afanasiev, *Organizovannaia prestupnost' v sovremennoi Rossii: opyt sotsiologicheskogo analiza. Trudy Sankt-Peterburgskogo filiala instituta sotsiologii RAN. Seriia I. Nauchnye doklady i soobshcheniia. No. 2.* (Institute of Sociology, St. Petersburg, 1994); A. I. Gurov and V. Riabinin (eds), *Praviteli prestupnogo mira* (Zelenyi parus, Moscow, 1992); A. Konstantinov, *Banditskii Peterburg: Dokumentalnyi ocherk* (Bibliopolis, St. Petersburg, 1995); J. D. Serio and V. S. Razinkin, 'Thieves Professing the Code: The Traditional Role of Vory v Zakone in Russia's Criminal World and Adaptions to a New Social Reality' (1996) 5 *OICJ Online*; see <www.acsp.uic.edu/oicj/pubs/cje/050405.htm>.

[22] Konstantinov, ibid, p. 11.

by collecting all the individuals with this stigma in a special camp, this 'criminal tradition' and those who follow it, would be virtually eradicated.[23] However, according to Gurov, the combat against 'the community of the acknowledged thieves' was not effective enough, and the tradition 'has survived until the present'.[24]

Several studies provide strict statistical information about the people with this stigma (both in and out of the forced labour camps). This is evidence of the filing practices based on the harsh stigmatization. The number of filed 'acknowledged thieves' grew to tens of thousands in the 1930s and 1940s. According to a confidential report compiled by the MVD, in 1992 there were still 179 acknowledged thieves filed in Russia, of which 46 were in penitentiary facilities and 19 were prosecuted.[25]

There were actual attempts to institutionalize this stigma in the criminal code during the 1950s, for example by criminalizing membership in this community.[26] However, this became successful only in 1958 when the legal stigma of 'especially dangerous recidivist' was introduced. The stigma increased the punishment for offenders posing a great social danger and excluded all parole privileges.[27] One informant stated to the author that the stigma of the recidivist made discretion possible, because even petty crimes led to stigmatization, and that the institution was removed from the criminal code of 1996 because it was a severe violation of human rights. However, the label of 'acknowledged thief' is still widely proliferated by Russian criminologists and their Western followers, and most Russians believe it to be the major Russian underworld tradition.

Therefore, it appears evident that the origins of these terms are not in the underworld, but in the repressive stigmatization of the Russian police. Interestingly enough, the author's informants both from St. Petersburg and Estonia stated that 'acknowledged thieves' are no longer present in their territories, and that this tradition has lost its role. A possible reason is that active stigmatization and propaganda are no longer carried out by the police. However, the tradition of stigmatizing a number of individuals and social elements defined as socially dangerous has survived as a crucial part of the Russian police culture.

VI.   THE SOCIAL DANGER OF PRIVATE POLICING

Traditionally, in the USSR there was no private sphere in which the police could not penetrate, and the suppression of private businesses or any other non-governmental activities was a crucial part of the police work. Hence the contemporary privatization of all spheres of life causes severe pressures and frustration for the police. For example, in Russian context the word illegal (*nelegalnyi*) can still be used as referring to all spontaneous activities without the initiative of the state. The frustration of the

---

[23]   Gurov (1990), n. 21 above, pp. 119–120.
[24]   Gurov (1990), n. 21 above, p 122.
[25]   S. A. Seliverstov, *Izpol'zovanie spetsial'nykh podrazdelenii bystrogo reagirovaniia v borbe s organizovannoi prestupnostiu. Uchebno-metodicheskoe posobie.* MVD Rossii. Glavnoe upravlenie kadrov. (Uchebno-metodicheskii Tsentr, Moscow, 1994), p. 5.
[26]   Gurov and Ryabinin, *Praviteli prestupnogo mira*, n. 21 above, p. 89.
[27]   Solomon, n. 11 above, pp. 91–92.

police is well-communicated in the claims that all business is criminal, all businessmen are 'bandits' (or cooperating with the bandits) and, particularly, that all means for securing economic interests without state intervention are 'organized crime'. Profit-making was described as 'dirty ideology' by my informants in the Russian police. One of the author's informants from the tax police maintains that although the business activities indeed might be on legal basis *de jure*, they are *de facto* 'criminal' because they contradict state interests.

While the provision of security has become increasingly privatized since the late 1980s, the attitude toward private security businesses (contract security) has become extremely hostile. It is a strongly held belief that security companies are covers of 'organized crime.' The private protection of economic interests is often considered a criminal activity and described with the stigma of 'roof' (*krysha*), one of the most popular pejorative stereotypes used by the Russian police and most students of Russian crime.

Although private security activities were legalized with a federal law in 1992, the police officers interviewed for this paper said that this only gave the 'bandits' and 'apes' easier ways to legalize their 'roofs'. The state has applied exceptional means in controlling the contract security markets, since the extra-departmental guard administrations (UVO) are providing equal contract security according to a decree from 1992.

The concept of 'roof' is a prejudiced stereotype of the Russian police culture, stipulating that all contract security is criminal, and making it easier for the police to cope with the growing pressures and collapse of power caused by the emergence of private policing. However, it is true that there is a criminal element in the security industry, but this is not adequate evidence that all contract security is involved in 'organized crime'.

Moreover, in the interviews with the Russian police they were not able to define clearly enough what 'roof' means. The definitions were controversial; some of the police stated that roofs are extortion-oriented criminal organizations; others maintained that nowadays most licensed security companies ('roofs') only guard and do not extort anything; whilst others said that licensed security companies are covers for organized crime that carry out all possible crimes, including murder. Most of the police could hardly conceal their anger and frustration about the legalization of private security companies.

In these interviews the hostile attitude was also targeted at defence advocates, defined as 'collaborators of organized crime' who have learned the 'dirty ideology' of the 'bandits'. One informant said that the 'rule of law' gives actual possibilities for the 'bandits' to develop their organized criminal activities with the assistance of clever lawyers. In general, all means of protecting economic interests, solving disputes or developing business ideas without intervention (control) of the state can be stigmatized as 'roof'.

Most Western students of Russian crime apply the fashionable stereotype of 'roof' as a starting point for their research, claiming that a specific Russian-style organized crime is in question. Thus, many studies unintentionally reflect the cynicism and hostile anti-marketism embedded in the Russian police culture, particularly in relation to the newly emerged private policing. There are no studies that would see these attitudes as reflections of the inertia in the thinking of the police, or compare the hostile attitude towards privatization of all spheres of life to how the private-public distinction has been used and developed in histories of policing. Most of the studies about 'roofs' deny analogous developments of privatization of the criminal justice in the Western countries since 1940s, claiming that 'roof' is a peculiarity of Russia's organized crime. Therefore, one can say that they also agree with a totalitarian criminal policy that demands an ultimate state monopoly in law enforcement and intrusion into all aspects of privacy. Such studies can even be seen as part of the Russian legitimization campaign toward the re-establishment of a totalitarian police state. The problem is that the existence of 'roofs' as a socially dangerous organized crime is so well communicated in the Russian and Western press reports, criminological studies and statements of officials and other people, that the stereotypes criticized here are easily present in almost every commentary as self-evident facts of social reality.

Why are the earlier findings of Western criminology about the privatization of police or criminal justice in general not applied in this context? The possible reason is that the students of the 'roofs' *a priori* deny the modern nature of the police function in Russia and emphasize the exceptional nature of Russianness (spontaneous communal spirit versus Western rationalism), which is a traditional feature of Slavophilia or Russian nationalism.[28] As no Western theories can be applied in the Russian context, students of crime to accept as fact everything Russian police officers or specialists say or write.

The interviewees both from the Russian and Estonian police were equally skeptical about the security firms, and both said that 'roofs' exist in their territories. There were some differences in the definitions; mostly it seemed that the Estonians defined 'roofs' analogous with the criminal groupings, while Russian definitions included all private means for protecting economic interests, particularly the security companies. The smaller size of Estonia, the police reform and the stronger democratic development make it easier for the police to cope. It also diminishes the pressure on the police, making their opinions on contract security or business in general not so hostile.

The Russian police culture is attempting to monopolize law enforcement at any cost, categorizing most democratic phenomena as infested with deviancy and social danger. Suspicion, a typical element for any police culture, has grown out of all proportion. To put it simply, for the Russian police everything in contradiction with the former monolithic state control represents a threatening deviancy and a social danger (which means the same as crime according to the legacy of the Soviet criminal justice). The democratization processes have thus made the Russian police culture subject to severe pressure and tension between the communist values of state control and due process that should be based on the democratic values.

The main problem is that also in Western countries, the principal image of crime in Russia is being constructed in the framework of the Russian police culture; the

---

[28] R. Pipes, *Russia under the Old Regime* (Penguin Books, London, 1995), pp. 166–167.

way of thinking of the Russian police is spreading. In the author's opinion, it is not acceptable that Western criminologists uncritically apply this framework in their studies, bringing them to the same exaggerated conclusions as their Russian counterparts. Moreover, Western students of Russian crime also campaign for a return to ultimate state monopoly in law enforcement at any cost, stipulating that social danger is embedded in all businesses or non-governmental activities and all contract security is organized crime. This view gives full acceptance, or even encourages, the continuum of the legacy of a totalitarian police culture and the discretion embedded in it, very much present in Russia's criminal policy of the 1990s.

In the following I intend to show how close cooperation between Finnish and Russian police has brought questionable elements into the Finnish police culture.

VII.   THE FINLANDIZATION OF THE FINNISH POLICE

The collapse of the Soviet Union caused an increasing flow of people, goods and capital over the 1,300 kilometre-long Finnish-Russian border. As a consequence of the alarming information about crime in Russia during the early 1990s, the Finnish police decided to develop cooperation with Russia and the Baltic states. In 1991, the first liaison officer was placed in St. Petersburg, and an intergovernmental crime prevention agreement was signed in 1993 with Russia and in 1994 with the Baltic states. Presently, there are about ten Finnish liaison officers working in Russia and the Baltic States, and nearly 20 have liaison experience. The primary task of the liaison officers is to investigate the crime situation in general, develop cooperation with the local police, and to act as specialists in combating international crime. However, the problem is that the Russian-style discretion and exaggeration of crime is becoming a part of the Finnish police culture.

While interviewing the Finnish police, they were asked their opinions about the efficiency and professionalism of their Russian and Estonian colleagues. Almost all of the Finnish police, particularly the liaison officers, admire the Russian police. The Russian police gained admiration for professionalism and efficiency, while the Estonian police was mocked as non-experienced amateurs. One liaison officer informant nicknamed the Russian police 'caterpillar officers', while the 'non-experienced and young idealists' of the Estonian police were described as 'boy scouts'.

The positive attitude toward the Russian police resembles some sort of administrational loyalty, a possible legacy of the period of 1809–1917 when Finland was a Grand Duchy of the Russian Empire. Critics have claimed that a similar kind of loyalty emerged after the Second World War when Finland was under the influence of the Soviet Union[29] Since the 1950s, the Soviet Union's political influence in the

---

[29] Whilst interviewing the former head of the Finnish security police (SUPO), the author was able to glean some hints about the influence of the Soviet criminal policy in Finland in the 1980s. When the head of the KGB, Yuri Andropov, launched his harsh anti-corruption campaign, SUPO organized parallel information campaigns targeted at Finnish businessmen involved in the Soviet-Finnish barter trade. As some of the Finns had been arrested in Soviet Union for bribery, SUPO informed the Finnish businessmen not to give valuable presents, such as 'money, gold, diamonds or furs' to the Soviet officials responsible of barter decisions.

domestic policy of Finland (and Finland's soft and uncritical attitude towards the Soviet Union) has been labeled as 'Finlandization' by some foreign and domestic critics. Therefore, the transformation of the Finnish police culture towards the Russian model can be described as the Finlandization of the Finnish police. However, it is argued here that this problem (the influence of the Russian police culture) is international, as was the problem of Finlandization.

In reality, Finlandization means that the Finnish police, particularly the liaison officers, are not able to analyze critically information about crime in the Russian context, but rather adopt the conduct and way of thinking of the Russian police, which causes interesting tensions, conflicts and changes for the Finnish police. In the following, it is intended to describe this development by means of analyzing the consequences of Finnish-Russian police cooperation in combating organized prostitution.

VIII. THE SOCIAL DANGER OF RUSSIAN WOMEN

The introduction of Russian prostitutes in the early 1990s in a limited number of restaurants and streets of Finland led to a spectacular publicity in the press. The general argument was that this might be the gateway for 'Russian organized crime' to infiltrate the country. The activated liaison networks approached the Russian police and asked about the possible danger of this phenomena. Naturally, the Russian officials reported to the Finns that this prostitution was extremely dangerous and fully under the control of 'strong criminal groups' involving the drug trade and money-laundering. Consequently, the Finnish police considered Russian prostitution to be organized, while Finnish prostitution was seen as harmless individual activities. Therefore, the police demanded extraordinary measures to hinder the 'strong criminal groups' infiltrating the country through Russian prostitutes.

However, there was practically no legal basis for the activities of the officials in this case. The only real reference point was the opinion of the Russian police about 'strong organized criminal groups' in the background. According to Finnish legislation, prostitution is not illegal while procuring is a crime (although difficult to prosecute). In addition, Finnish legislation provides no definitions for organized crime. In Russia the legislation has been much more developed; prostitution is a violation of the code of administrational violations of law, and the criminal code provides for a wide range of definitions for organized crime and crimes in connection with prostitution. However, as a result of the debates, the Finnish Parliament passed an amendment that made prostitution illegal, however, (in practice) *only* if committed by Russian women! According to the law, the selling of 'sexual services' became violation of law only if carried out by individuals who are not citizens of the European Union (EU). In practice the law targets only Russian (and some Estonian) women.

The prostitution problem was publicized in a sensational television documentary in the Autumn of 1997 titled 'Red Houses', which showed evidence of dozens of Russian women arriving by bus from St. Petersburg to two motels in small Finnish towns. The main informants for the programme were the Finnish liaison officer in St. Petersburg (an experienced former security police officer) and a Russian police officer, who said that 'organized crime' and external 'strong criminal groups' were involved. The documentary also alleged that the travel agency organizing the trip had 'a strong KGB-background'.

The highest police chief of the area, Jorma Ahonen was asked in the documentary why the police do not stop an activity that involves 'Russian organized crime'. Mr. Ahonen responded that prostitution is not a crime in Finland and his people had been trying to produce evidence of procuring. However, journalists had produced evidence of Mr. Ahonen's link with the motel where the prostitutes were working, as he was the director of the board of the local bank that rented the motel. Although such links might be typical in the Finnish countryside, this was enough for a public witch-hunt. The ombudsman of the Finnish parliament Lauri Lehtimaja reacted and demanded the immediate exposure of all procuring in Finland, especially because of the 'well-known' involvement of prostitution with organized crime. The public outcry against Mr. Ahonen (concerning his position in the bank) was primarily initiated by Mr. Lehtimaja, who is very skilful in utilizing the media, and whose behaviour closely resembled the activities of an influential Russian prosecutor.

IX.   THE ANALOGY OF LAW IN FINLAND

Finally, and rather surprisingly, Mr. Ahonen was very publicly prosecuted for procuring. The process was long and painful, but the court decided that Mr. Ahonen could not be sentenced for procuring, because he did not intentionally procure the women. According to the court, sentencing Mr. Ahonen for procuring would require *the analogy of law* (sic) which the Finnish penal code does not provide, but which the public, the ombudsman, the Finnish liaisons and finally the prosecutor demanded, by vague references to the danger of prostitution, claimed of being controlled by 'Russian organized crime'. Meanwhile, the activities of Finnish prostitutes were not especially targeted, because this activity was not considered as involving 'organized crime'. Targeting only Russian women resembles the Russian-style stigmatization of 'socially dangerous' persons.

Ahonen's case is an example of the drastic influence of the Russian police culture in Finland. Given that prostitution originating in Russia was considered as 'socially dangerous,' partly as described by the Russian police, the Finnish prosecutor took freedom to apply analogy of law in Ahonen's case. Although the rule of law did not actually suffer, as the court decision pointed out, the application of the analogy of law is impossible in Finland, the case illustrates that the influence of the Russian police culture causes real danger for the Finnish democracy and rule of law. In particular, Ahonen's case demonstrates the drastic pressures to which the Finnish police are subject to due to the influence of the Russian police culture. In general, the people suspected of crimes were suffering more than people convicted of crimes, which in this case, includes the women suspected of prostitution, which is not at all a crime nor a violation of law in Finland (before the amendment of the alien law).

From access to police material, the author conducted a small analysis that testified that the claims of 'Russian organized criminals' in the background was exaggerated. According to the analysis of about 30 procuring cases investigated by the police in

1996–1998, and the interviews collected by the Finnish police, the typical organizers of procuring in Finland were not Russian organized criminals but Finnish men, who recruited prostitutes abroad or in Finland (of course there were also a few Russian organizers). Crime connected with prostitution was of minor significance, although there were e.g. a couple of extortion cases. Most of the problems were linked with illegal trade of alcohol and cigarettes, but on a small scale. Following the interviews with liaison officers, they were unable to define how an external criminal group in Russia could control such activities, although they actively claimed this to be true.

X.   THE ACTIVE STIGMATIZATION OF RUSSIAN WOMEN

Following the scandals, the Finnish liaison officers continued to demand the total elimination of prostitution originating from Russia, and control measures were targeted at Russian women suspected of prostitution. The Minister of the Interior at that time, Mr. Jan-Erik Enestam demanded a list of the names of the Russian women accused of prostitution (which is not a violation of law) for deportation and visa denial. The alien law provided the measures for deportation if the person is 'making his/her living by dishonest means'. As a consequence, in Autumn 1997 the police began to deport alleged Russian prostitutes claiming that they were making their living by 'dishonest means'. A number of court decisions about alleged illegal deportations exist. According to one decision, the deportation of a Russian woman was 'against the law' because the Russian woman was not committing crimes nor violating the law (which were the 'dishonest means' the law refers to). The woman, however, admitted that she had entered Finland 11 times for prostitution. In addition, she said of being threatened by two violent Finnish men. In another case, the court decided the deportation was legal, although the Russian woman denied prostitution and was married to a Finnish man. The woman claimed that the evidence about her prostitution was fake and that after the arrest the police would not let her call her husband.

Soon the alien law was reformed so that a foreigner who is 'evidently suspected of selling sexual services' can be deported from Finland. The term 'prostitution' was not used because the law-makers wanted a single act of selling sexual services to be enough for deportation. However, it is not clearly known how the police produced the evidence of 'selling of sexual services'.

Since suspected Finnish prostitutes are not controlled by the police, but suspected foreign prostitutes can be deported on the discretion of the police (even if married to Finnish men), it would appear that the foreign women in Finland have become victims of police discretion originating in the Russian police culture. The problem is that after the scandals, the public opinion in Finland labeled all Russian women as prostitutes. For, in general, it is the public opinion that defines what is 'socially dangerous', in principle any foreign woman, particularly Russian, can be deported by the police on the basis of more or less weak evidence. The problem is evident, because the Russian-speakers are the biggest foreign minority group in Finland.

In addition, the liaison officers in St. Petersburg began to compile so-called 'whore lists' of Russian women alleged to be prostitutes. The first version of this list included 632 names, but the liaisons said that the list would expand to 2,000 names on information obtained from the Russian police. A confidential letter compiled by the police department for other police agencies states that: 'Concerning suspected prostitution, information provided by foreign officials can be considered as trustworthy'. The fact that the intelligence tactics of the Russian police are serving discretion for repressing and stigmatizing 'socially dangerous' individuals does not appear to be problematic for the Finnish police. The 'whore list' is compiled by one single Finnish liaison officer in the consulate of St. Petersburg. It is not known on what evidence a person is put on this list, and it is not known how a person misleadingly categorized as prostitute can be removed from this list. Another problem occurs, if such lists are exchanged with other countries of Europe.

This problem has caused some tension inside the police. The head of the information service of the national bureau of investigation (KRP) insisted that the police cannot collect information about individuals who are not suspected of crimes or other violations of law. Although most of the prostitution of foreign women in Finland is organized by Finnish men, the liaisons insisted that it is organized by 'foreign criminals' and 'strong criminal groups' of St. Petersburg. Therefore, the police try to find legal ways for deporting all Russian women suspected of prostitution, while the prostitution of Finnish women remains legal.

XI. CONCLUSIONS

Given that young foreign women are the most vulnerable group of any society, the activities of the Finnish police are problematic. The deportation of suspected foreign prostitutes is not a solution, since masses of new prostitutes can always be found, and once deported could enter the country again with fake documents. Although the aim of the police is to protect the human rights of prostitutes, one may ask whether the deportation of foreign women on unclear evidence and the collection of the 'whore lists', carried out by the police alone, are not also human right violations.

The reason for these activities is the pressure caused by the proliferation of the Russian police culture into Finland. In this case at least the following elements, typical for the Russian police culture, have been introduced to the way of thinking and acting of the Finnish police.

The Finnish Police

1. Exaggerates the crime problem, more so in relation to the Russian crime;
2. Uses 'organized crime' as one of the central reference points;
3. Gains more discretion due to the 'social danger' of prostitution;
4. Is ought to stigmatize 'socially dangerous' individuals ('the whore lists');
5. Has the main role in the combat measures against prostitution (deportation);
6. May cause more suffering for the stigmatized ones than for the convicted ones;
7. Has been able to make the police work more flexible.

18

The Development of Appropriate Responses to Organized Crime in Post-Communist Societies

William Tupman

I. INTRODUCTION

This paper argues that fashionable anti-crime strategies based on counter-terrorism fail to understand the totality of roles played by organized crime networks in Western societies, let alone post-communist societies. It is argued that wittingly or unwittingly ideas drawn from revolutionary theories are already embodied in policies against organized crime employed in the USA and Western Europe. Although these approaches have their advantages, piecemeal borrowing can lead to inappropriate policy transfer.

The nature of civil society in post-communist states in Eastern and Central Europe is considered together with the position of organized crime within that civil society. Gramsci argued that the nature of civil society in Russia is qualitatively different to that of Western Europe.[1] A theory and practice of countering organized crime that does not recognize that civil society and the state are less complex in the post-communist states than in Western Europe, or the USA, is unlikely to be successful because it is more likely to strengthen the state at the expense of civil society. Techniques and strategies developed in Western societies may be totally inappropriate in the post-communist Eastern European context for this and other reasons. A thoroughgoing reexamination of strategists of revolution in general, and Gramsci in particular, is required to create an appropriate strategy for countering organized crime in Eastern Europe without undermining the growth of a developed civil society essential for the underpinning of a successful transition to democracy. So post-communist East European social scientists who argue for the creation or recreation of civil society need to address the limits of permissible citizen behaviour and the power of the state to enforce law at the same time as addressing the need to establish non-State networks. It must also be recognized that reducing centralized state power may simply create a vacuum into which organized crime and associated networks are equally, if not more, likely to move as is a developed civil society to be spontaneously created.

---

[1] A. Gramsci, *Selections from the Prison Notebooks* (Lawrence and Wishart, London, 1982), pp. 235–237.

A. V. Ledeneva and M. Kurkchiyan (eds.), Economic Crime in Russia, 275–287
© 2000 *Kluwer Law International. Printed in Great Britain.*

There are general problems, non-specific to Eastern Europe, in creating a strategy against organized crime. Arresting and prosecuting individual criminals has no effect on the criminal network as a whole. No individual is indispensable and all are easily replaced, which is why 'zero-tolerance' policing is little more than political rhetoric. Even identifying 'leaders' and targeting them has little effect.[2] Both the structure of the organization and the reasons for its existence have to be addressed. Traditional police investigation and prosecution are only partially successful because of the problems involved in getting people to give evidence and widespread interference with witnesses. The move towards proactive investigation is likely to bring police legitimacy into question, which is not helpful to the police in post-communist societies.[3] In Eastern Europe there are particular problems in that both the present and previous government and bureaucracy interpenetrate organized crime.

Counter-insurgency and counter-terrorist strategies have become sources for policies to combat organized crime because there has been a perception that national security is threatened and that criminal justice policies are an inappropriate response.[4] The paramilitary professionals brought into policy-making characterize the investigation of contemporary organized crime as presenting problems similar to those encountered in combating Lenin-style Communist parties and cellular-based 'terrorist' structures. The response is disproportionate, because organized crime in the 1990s makes economic elites feel threatened in the same way that terrorism impacted upon political elites in the 1960s and 1970s.[5]

There are competing theories as to why there is a problem with organized crime in Eastern and Central Europe. Without attempting to be exhaustive, there are those who argue that organized crime was inherent within the communist state before it fell;[6] or, as reviewed later in the paper, that organized crime is market-driven and a response to globalization; or that the fundamental problem for Eastern and Central European states is their proximity to the European Union (EU).

II.   CONTEMPORARY STRATEGIES TO DEAL WITH ORGANIZED CRIME

As Matti Joutsen pointed out in 1993, 'organised crime control in the West has lagged behind organised crime; both East and West have a long way to go'.[7] There are very few policies available for Eastern and Central European governments to choose between when trying to counter organized crime. Traditionally there are legislative tools, mostly based on the US anti-racketeering model. In the long-term,

---

2   R. Trojanowicz and B. Bucqueroux, *Community Policing: A Contemporary Perspective* (Anderson, Cincinatti, 1990), pp. 282–283.
3   W. A. Tupman and A. J. Tupman, *Policing in Europe: Diversity in Uniform* (Intellect, Exeter, 1999).
4   National Security Council, 'A National Security Strategy for a New Century' (Washington DC, 1997) Preface, Point 5; see <whitehouse.gov/WH/EOP/NSC/strategy>.
5   W. A. Tupman, 'Where Has All the Money Gone? The IRA as a Profit-making Concern' (April 1998) 1 *Journal of Money-Laundering Control*, pp. 303–311.
6   W. A. Tupman, 'East Meets West' (July 1996) 2 *Policing Today*, pp. 30–36; R. Lotspeich, 'Crime in the Transition Economies' (1995) 47 *Europe–Asia Studies*, pp. 555–589.
7   M. Joutsen, 'The Potential for the Growth of Organised Crime in Central and Eastern Europe' (1993) 1 *European Journal on Criminal Policy and Research*, p. 86.

policies based upon justice being done, and being seen to be done, are those most likely to assist in the development of democracy. In the medium-term, however, most Eastern and Central European states are only beginning to develop appropriate experience and have a long way to go before their criminal justice systems develop the level of legitimacy that will give citizens confidence to come forward as witnesses and give evidence in court.

The competing police-related fashions of the moment which are discussed below are:

- 'Zero tolerance' policing
- 'Problem oriented' policing
- 'National defense' policing

There are also economic-related strategies. In former Communist states the hard-line free-marketeer analysis is that organized crime exists because many of these governments have failed to privatize properly. The problem will disappear once privatization is in place. Lotspeich's analysis of crime trends demonstrates the lunacy of this approach.[8]

1. Zero tolerance policing

This is fashionable amongst right-wingers because it involves law-enforcement. Any strategy in which offenders are not punished is seen as 'giving in' to criminals and, therefore, cannot possibly work. A crude view is that deterrence is an essential aspect of crime control and that deterrence depends upon punishment. Zero tolerance advocates argue that, if petty offences are punished then more serious offences will not take place. In its crudest form this is based upon the idea that drug addicts commit offences in order to obtain money for drugs. In its more sophisticated version it is founded upon 'broken windows' style analysis. A further argument current among United Kingdom (UK) CID officers is that burglars on bail commit on average 55 further offences before imprisonment. The argument has already been made that removing individual offenders does nothing to affect the criminal network as a whole. Zero tolerance is good rhetoric, but little more.

2. Problem oriented policing

Problem Oriented Policing is normally presented as a way of implementing a Community Policing strategy.[9] Most such strategies depend upon the existence of a community that can be developed into a partnership with the police. There are communities, however, that Alderson calls 'poisoned soil'[10] where such a strategy is difficult because survival by legal means only is problematic for the inhabitants.

---

[8] Lotspeich, n. 6 above.
[9] Trojanowicz and Bucqueroux, n. 2 above, pp. 8–11.
[10] J. Alderson, *Policing Freedom* (Macdonald and Evans, London, 1979).

Trojanowicz and Bucqueroux distinguish three levels of community on a class basis. The type of community that presents a problem for community policing is associated with the underclass as a group.[11] For these a special strategy is required.

'Poisoned soil' is now referred to in the UK as 'High Crime Districts'. These are characterized by multiple victimization (residents are both victims of the same crime on more than one occasion, and victims of more than one type of crime), higher than average levels of crime (which may or may not be reported), high levels of drug misuse – and often multiple deprivation.[12] In other words, markets for exploitation by organized crime related businesses.

Problem oriented policing is intended to be a research driven strategy properly monitored before, during and after implementation.[13] In 'High Crime Districts' it consists of the following stages.[14]

- The first step is to remove the drug dealers from the area. This will involve a major deployment of police manpower in raids on houses, and street stop and searches.
- The second step is the institution of regular foot and vehicle patrols to make it quite clear that the police have come to stay.
- The implementation of public relations campaigns and consultation campaigns, building up to an Alderson-style Community Policing strategy of foot patrol, inter-agency cooperation and community involvement.
- When research such as questionnaires shows that support for the police is the same as elsewhere. (It will as easily be monitored by experienced officers in terms of witnesses being prepared to give evidence and a rise in the rate of convictions).

This is a territorially-based strategy which confronts effects rather than causes, rather than one aimed against organizations. Problem oriented and Community Policing are excellent strategies to follow where civil society is already developed, but are

---

[11] Trojanowicz and Bucqueroux, n. 2 above, pp. 89–90.

[12] G. Farrell and K. Pease, 'Once Bitten Twice Bitten: Repeat Victimisation and its Implications for Crime Prevention' *Police Research Group*. Crime Prevention Unit. Paper 46. (London, 1993).

[13] H. Goldstein, 'Improving Policing: A Problem-Oriented Approach' (1979) 25 *Crime and Delinquency*, pp. 236–258; H. Goldstein and C. Susmilch, 'Experimenting with the Problem-Oriented Approach to Improving Police Service: A Report and Some Reflections on Two Case Studies' (University of Wisconsin Law School, Madison, WI, 1982); H. Goldstein, *Problem Oriented Policing* (McGraw Hill, New York, 1991); J. E. Eck and W. Spelman, *Problem Solving: Problem-Oriented Policing in Newport News* (Police Executive Research Forum and the National Institute of Justice, Washington DC, 1987).

[14] D. Stephens, 'Policing in Urban America' in *Policing in the 21st Century: Interfaces with the Social, Cultural and Private Security Services.* Proceedings of the XIIIth Higher Police Course (Intercentre, Messina, Italy, 1989), pp. 96–128; Farrell and Pease, n. 12 above; Trojanowicz and Bucqueroux, n. 2 above, pp. 283–285. Problem-oriented policy may owe a great deal to counter insurgency theories derived (whether consciously or unconsciously), from the British experience of the Malaysian insurgency of the 1950s. The evident similarity between the four stages presented here and the four stages of Thompson's counter-insurgency strategy – CLEARING, HOLDING, WINNING, WON – illustrate how closely the two are related. See R. G. K. Thompson, *Defeating Communist Insurgency: Experiences from Malaya and Vietnam* (Chatto and Windus, London, 1974).

indistinguishable from more militaristic strategies when applied to areas where civil society is weak or even different to the norm. Like Maoism, they will create the illusion of a developed civil society, but such civil society is directed from above rather than genuinely independent and capable of self-development.

3.   *National defence policing: globalized crime as imperialism*

There is a danger of distortion creeping 'Chinese Whisper'-style into a strategy against organized crime that has been borrowed from counter-insurgency theorists, who in turn created their strategy by inverting the strategy of their communist opponents. It cannot be appropriate to persuade the former Communist states to adopt strategies derived from an imperfectly understood theory, that was itself originally developed to create revolution in a primarily rural society.

Revolutionary theory is an appropriate source of strategies to counter organized crime in either or both of two ways: directly, from its analysis of the nature and weaknesses of urban society and indirectly, through what has been learned in the West from the experience of countering Leninist clandestine hierarchical conspiracies as they have been applied in the urban setting. It also may be the case that Leninist analysis of state behaviour and his consequent revolutionary strategy is descriptive of and applicable to contemporary organized crime group behaviour.

In returning to the source and speculating as to how Lenin's Bolsheviks would have combated contemporary organized crime it should be born in mind that analysis of crime is not absent from early Communist strategy. Lenin, for example opposed 'partisan actions', because it 'lowers the consciousness of revolutionaries to that of drunkards and bums'.[15] Mao Tse Tung's Chinese Communist Party had the good fortune to be handed control of the Elder Brother Society when Ho Lung inherited its leadership from his father.[16] Today this would be considered one of the Triads. Subversion and seizure of crime networks was also successfully achieved, although only temporarily, in the Chingkangshan when Mao began his campaign in the countryside.[17]

According to 'Armed Insurrection',[18] a section of the Bolshevik Party organized by Piatakov, between the 1905 Revolution and 1917, attempted with some success to built cells within the organizations of the Tsarist state – particularly the army and the police. Though the essence of Leninism was to built cells in factories and work places, Piatakov's work was essential in that the intent was to have a hierarchy in place that could seize control of the levers of coercion if and when the State itself lost control of those levers.

In 1916, Lenin added to his proposals on how a revolutionary party should be organized[19] an analysis of the circumstances under which the State could be expected

---

[15] V. I. Lenin, 'On Partisan Warfare' (1906) Translated in F. M. Osanka, *Modern Guerilla Warfare: Fighting Communist Insurgency 1941–1961* (Free Press, New York, 1962).

[16] E. Snow, *Red Star Over China* (Gollancz, London, 1937).

[17] Snow, ibid.

[18] A. Neuberg, *Armed Insurrection* (London, New Left Books, 1971). First published in 1928 as *Der bewafnette Aufstand*.

[19] V. I. Lenin, *What is to be Done?* 1902. (Lawrence and Wishart, London). Various editions.

to lose control.[20] Lenin's argument, which is in many ways different from that of Marx, was that the world was in the final stages of capitalism which he characterized as imperialism. The existence of States with territorial boundaries means that capitalists try to get their governments to exclude foreign capitalists. Foreign capitalists will persuade their governments to go to war in order to redistribute markets, as enterprises in each country improve their technology, become more competitive, and strove to penetrate the existing markets of enterprises of other states to break down the territorial barriers to their growth and expansion. Such wars, Lenin argues, will lead to defeat for somebody. A State in the process of defeat is a State that loses control of its own coercive mechanisms and is vulnerable to take-over by whoever could seize the levers of coercion. A cellular hierarchically-based organization like the Bolshevik party would be in a good position to do so.

Certain types of organized crime are akin to these warring States. Drug dealers seek markets as do the purveyors of the various illegal pleasures. New vendors who wish to penetrate established markets have to do so by means of violence: the Colombians (Medellin and Cali cartels), the Jamaicans (Yardies), and the Chechens are examples in recent times. These battles for turf have thus far simply been seen by the security forces as ways to get criminals to eliminate each other. This is mistaken. Under the prevailing conditions of globalization this process benefits the larger crime groups that can deploy high levels of violence. Local groups thus fall into the network of international groups. Were these organizations, however, infiltrated on a more coherent basis than the incursion of the occasional individual undercover agent, these turf wars might provide opportunities for state organizations to seize control of criminal organizations and change their direction.

There is a second track to this strategy. Marxist-Leninists also built cells in the workplace, as this is where people develop their world-view and learn their collective power and the degree to which they are collectively exploited. In the conditions of breakdown as described above, these cells are in a position to control economic activity. 'Turf wars' between organized crime groups should provide opportunities to change the position of workers in the illegal businesses – and even to change the nature of those businesses.

To put it in Maoist rather than Leninist terms: analyze the contradictions of organized crime, break the coercive machine, build a parallel hierarchy to battle for possession of the hearts and minds of the underclass and others active in criminal enterprises, finally mobilize the illegal workforce into those aspects of illegal business that could be brought in from the cold.

Against this, it is argued that organized crime is now organized in a more complex fashion than a series of Mafia-style top-down hierarchies.[21] To capture the top of any one of the remaining hierarchies by a Leninist coup would not guarantee control

---

[20] V. I. Lenin, *Imperialism – Highest Stage of Capitalism* 1915–1916. (Lawrence and Wishart, London,). Various editions.

[21] Tupman, n. 5 above, pp. 303–311; W. A. Tupman, 'Violent Business? Networking, Terrorism and Organised Crime' in I. McKenzie (ed.), *Law, Power and Justice in England and Wales* (Praeger, London and Westport, CT, 1998); P. Van Duyne, 'Organised Crime Markets in a Turbulent Europe' (1993) 1 *European Journal on Criminal Policy and Research*, pp. 10–30.

of the business of crime. Within that business there is still in place, however, an apparatus of coercion that rivals the supposed monopoly of coercive force held by the state. Violence is one of the services for sale. Extortion is characteristic of criminal enterprise in post-communist societies. The subversion and capture of this apparatus would undermine the whole system, since by the nature of their business, criminals cannot take each other to court for failure to deliver goods or services promised. Crime's territorial markets and the movement of goods without seizure by other crime groups, payment of debts and obedience to directives are all preserved by the threat of violence. A limited strategy, based on infiltration and takeover, could be derived from a Leninist analysis, despite the changing nature of organized crime.

Implementation of such a strategy would be controversial. Revolutionaries and counter-insurgency specialists operating outside the industrial democracies can use violence in ways that state agencies under democratic and legal controls cannot and should not. Principles of 'due process' are essential to protect ordinary citizens from abuses of power. There are serious ethical and legal problems already encountered by undercover operatives and organizers of 'stings' when suspects are brought to trial in Western democracies.

The first problem with adopting such a strategy is that it threatens democracy itself and the development of a healthy civil society. If the state and its organizations were able to engage in such subversion, how long would they be able to prevent themselves from using such methods against their political opponents? This is almost Maoist in its contradiction. Mao argued that China was fertile ground for Communism because it was divided between various colonial powers, none of whom would allow any of the others to become strong enough to stamp out Communism because they would be afraid that such a strong colonial power would expel the others; nor would any of the colonial powers allow the domestic government to become strong enough to stamp out Communism because such a domestic government could also expel the colonial powers.[22] Similarly, groups in modern society are unlikely to permit the State to become strong enough to take the necessary measures against the organized crime networks because such a state could then take measures against any organization within society, and presumably move towards a form of totalitarianism. This will be especially so in post-communist Eastern Europe, where such a strategy will be perceived as a step backwards.

The second problem has to do with the State, violence and legitimacy. Under what conditions can a state legitimately employ violence against sections of its own citizenry? It was argued above that violence is central to organized crime. The threat of violence preserves organized crime's territorial markets and it permits the movement of its goods without seizure by other organized crime groups. Similarly, it ensures that debts are paid and that orders from the bosses are obeyed. Any attempt to subvert organized crime will involve the subverters in the utilization of violence, on occasion, on behalf of organized crime as well as against organized crime. Seizing control of organizations in periods of violent conflict will also involve the use of

---

[22]   Mao Tse-Tung, 'Why Is It That Red Political Power Can Exist in China?' in *Selected Works of Mao Tse-Tung. Vol. 1* (Foreign Languages Press, Peking, 1967), pp. 63–72.

violence. Without legal sanction such violence is itself no more or no less than criminality. Legal measures have been established in the past that legitimize such action against the agents of foreign governments. Intelligence Agencies have been involved in their operationalization.[23] The introduction of Intelligence Agencies to the area of organized crime reflects a perception that policies against drug traffickers especially are as much a part of national security policy as of criminal justice policy.[24] This also opens the door to the possibility that agents of this policy may be tempted to use lethal force to remove a suspect from circulation.

All this will be disastrous if it undermines the legitimacy of the criminal justice system, itself a fragile thing. A policy is succeeding when citizens are prepared to report crime and give evidence in court. A purely instrumental policy against criminals that involves counter-violence and does not take into account the rule of law may ultimately do as much damage to the working of the criminal justice system as the failure of the present system successfully to prosecute the perpetrators of organized crime.

The third problem is a familiar one for all undercover agents, namely that of themselves having to get involved in criminal activities to maintain their credibility within an organization. Are they to be immune from prosecution? Problems of provocation and entrapment are also related here. 'Breaking the law to prevent the law being broken' has never been seen as a sensible policy slogan for the law enforcers. Its apologists use the phrase 'noble cause corruption' to excuse it, but it is still morally wrong and politically damaging.

If such a strategy were to be followed, which organization would be appropriate to carry out such infiltration and subversion? Police officers have the advantage of being a disciplined organization used to exercising discretion and checking with superiors as to appropriate courses of action. They are accountable both to superiors and to the law, and have some understanding of the principles that govern their activities. They are thus accustomed to the importance of the idea that justice needs to be seen to be done, that evidence needs to be gathered and due process followed. On the other hand, they are already involved in a number of other roles and to add yet one more form of behaviour for them to engage in is likely to create conditions of cognitive dissonance. It is difficult enough to convert a police officer's mind-set from public order role to public service role. They should not be required to involve themselves in the moral dilemmas implicit in tactical disruption and harassment of criminal conspiracies. The aftermath of the Miners' Strike demonstrated the dangers involved in expecting officers to behave in a paramilitary fashion one moment and be friendly service providers the next. It would be even more difficult to maintain good police-public relations if one added this subversive role to their responsibilities. In post-communist Eastern Europe, there are also severe problems with their financial

---

[23] Statewatch, 'Turf War: MI5 Bids for Policing Role' *Statewatch Bulletin* 4 (November–December 1994); Statewatch, 'MI5 and Police Carve Out New Roles' *Statewatch Bulletin* 5 (September–October 1995); Statewatch, 'MI5: New Head, New Powers' *Statewatch Bulletin* 5 (November–December 1995); Statewatch, 'MI5 and Organised Crime' *Statewatch Bulletin* 6 (January–February 1996). All Statewatch sources available through searchable database at <www.statewatch.org>

[24] National Security Council, n. 4 above; Trojanowicz and Bucqueroux, n. 2 above.

rewards. They are easy to corrupt, given the sums of money available to organized crime.

The Peace Dividend in Western Europe has produced under-employed Intelligence Services desperate for new responsibilities and partly able to justify taking on organized crime.[25] MI5's website now includes the combating of serious crime as one of its main functions.[26] In the aftermath of the Cold War they claim the skills outlined above and add to them the additional skills of electronic surveillance and technologically sophisticated intelligence-gathering. If the struggle against organized crime can be correctly characterized as similar to a war against an enemy state or an occupying power, then they may be appropriate for carrying out such a strategy. They have a tradition of operating out of the country, are skilled in communications interception, have experience of recruitment of agent networks and have been known to engage efficiently in violence. Unfortunately their track record against terrorism does not suggest that they will be successful. They are not good at distinguishing between 'the fish and the sea' in the Maoist phrase. They also have a tendency to get involved in the playing of the game for its own sake and the gathering and hoarding of information for its own sake. They also have an alarming tendency to turn out, on occasion, to have been recruited by the other side!

Insofar as organized crime operates from outside a country, there may be a role for the intelligence services to play, especially where internationally organized crime is operating from bases within countries where government is weak or corrupt. Any in-country operation can only occur after they have received training in the rules of evidence and are under proper judicial supervision. *The Sunday Telegraph* report of 3 December 1995, suggesting that Chief Constables should authorize technological surveillance and that there should be judicial oversight, is a step in the right direction.

There are contradictions within organized crime that can be exploited, but infiltration should be for far more than just intelligence gathering. It should be for the purpose of hijacking the organization when opportunity inevitably presents itself. To do this, the workers at the coal face have to be subverted into legal rather than criminal careers by legitimizing those parts of the businesses that can be legalized. Ex-insiders of organized crime might be available to engage in this sort of activity. British counter-subversion specialists have long stressed the importance of 'turning' captured insurgents and making them counter-guerrillas. There are usually two types of ex-insider, those bought over and those ideologically won over. Again, success and failure here has been mixed in the counter-terrorist field. There were many successes in the counter-insurgency field where the colonial relationship was involved and a highly rural population. The urban equivalent does not demonstrate major successes with this form of organization, although the modern institution of the detective began with Vidocq and his team of former criminals in Paris, so there is a precedent.

A major problem in the Eastern European context is that this inexorably leads back to a strong centralized state rather than to the development of autonomous

---

25   Statewatch, 1994, 1995, 1996, n. 23 above.
26   The Security Service [MI5] Official Web Site. 1999; <www.mi5.gov.uk>

social and economic sectors comprising civil society. In particular, business is going to be frightened of such a situation, as what can be used against organized crime will also be used against the money-launderer and fraudster, who are all part of the same nexus.

In a globalized economy, if governments cannot overcome the problems already enumerated and find ways of mobilizing the police and intelligence services into a proactive multi-agency approach, the initiative will inevitably pass to the private sector. Ethical, moral and legal objections to a policy are not safeguards against its implementation by a globalized private sector. As nation states are no longer sovereign in the nineteenth century sense, the most likely organization to engage in this form of activity, if indeed they are not already engaged in it, are the transnational corporations themselves and their security divisions or the security companies they hire. Their goal is often going to involve taking over the businesses and markets created by organized crime. It is arguable that the people most interested in hi-jacking the drug culture are the alcohol and tobacco barons. It has long been rumoured that a number of American cigarette companies have already patented or copyrighted the names of some of the famous brands of marijuana in order to be able to sell them as packets of 'joints' when legalization takes place. Similarly, the sex industry of legal clubs and publications is most interested in hijacking the illegal prostitution business. The producers of designer products are most interested in preventing product counterfeiting. Although these organizations are opposed to allowing the police to become strong enough to deal with their enemies, they are themselves interested in creating at least the level of counter-organization that can disrupt the illegal businesses and perhaps negotiate agreements with them. Leninist strategies of subversion would thus be of great interest to these people and to private security organizations who might wish to sell these skills to the multi-nationals.

Nevertheless, strategies based on counter-terrorism undermine the growth of civil society, as a network of autonomous organizations independent of the state. It may be acceptable for mature democracies to take steps backward, temporarily, from the rule of law. It is not going to assist the development of a democratic culture in post-communist societies.

III.   GRAMSCI, ORGANIZED CRIME AS/AND CIVIL SOCIETY. IN LIEU OF A CONCLUSION.

This final section proposes that a Gramscian critique of existing policies can lead to the development of policies more appropriate to the actual structure of civil society in the country or area concerned. Empirical research is required as to how far and in what direction civil society has developed in different countries in post-communist Eastern Europe. A classificatory system is required to categorize the nature of civil society within Eastern and Western Europe. A theory needs to be developed by applying these and related propositions to high crime areas in Western Europe and the USA, to see if the nature of civil society in such areas is qualitatively different to the norm. From such comparative analysis a strategy for dismantling organized crime needs to be deduced, including the complex problem of challenging the hegemony of organized crime in areas where it can be said to be the dominant ideology.

There are a number of civil-society-related lines of analysis that would repay study. 'Civil society' means quite different things to different academic schools.[27] Szacki criticizes its East European incarnation as weak in its understanding of economic activity which at first sight implies difficulties in using it as a tool for the development of strategies against organized crime.[28] This is a reason for developing an economic strand to civil society analysis, not a reason for abandoning it in this and other areas. A strategy to counter criminality that fails to include provisions for strengthening civil society is doomed to fail. It is citizens, not police officers who report crime, give evidence and identify offenders. The police cannot deal with all crimes on their own.

Organized crime plays both social and political roles in the process of transition similar to that played by Lenin's Bolsheviks in October 1917. For a period, it is the only national, rational organization able to enforce its instructions. It thus follows Weber's definition of a state in possessing the monopoly of force over a population on a given territory. It might even lay claim to legitimacy. These proto-states imitate Lenin's imperialist capitalist states in warring over territory in order to gain access to new markets. This in turn relates to Angell's view of organized crime as 'governments in waiting'.[29] Eastern and Central Europe are experiencing the criminogenic consequences of globalization ahead of Western societies. There needs to be empirical analysis of the argument that 'organized crime' has simply substituted itself for both civil society and the state in parts of post-communist Eastern Europe. Where it is true that, with the dismantling of the Party, there was no civil society to emerge, organized crime may have become an important mechanism structuring the relationships necessary for the economy and society to function.

Organized crime may thus be the most developed area of post-communist civil society, in the sense that the variety of structures and functions it exercises are more complex than other social groups. It is assisted in this by the underdevelopment of a cash economy, and the continuing existence of barter relationships among significant sectors of society. Organized crime has grown out of specific peculiarities of the Communist system. Mechanisms had to be created 'on the left' to ensure that a market mechanism actually delivered goods to those sectors of society that were demanding them and to those factories and geographical areas that had no officially sanctioned ways of obtaining them.[30] This was a consequence of the absence of a cash economy in many sectors of Soviet life, and thus, either produced a different form of civil society to that in the West or what can be characterized as an underdeveloped civil society.

---

[27] D. Castiglione, 'Civil Society,' entry in P. Newman (ed.), *The New Palgrave Dictionary of Economics and Law* (Macmillan, London, 1998).

[28] J. Szacki, *Liberalism after Communism* (Central European University Press, Budapest, 1995), p. 102.

[29] I. Angell, 'Economic Crime: Beyond Good and Evil' (1996) 4 *Journal of Financial Regulation and Compliance*, p. 14.

[30] Lotspeich, n. 6 above, p. 576; Tupman, n. 6 above.

Some of the authors discussed in Lotspeich's superb overview,[31] argue that organized crime is simply what would be legitimate business elsewhere, made illegal by irrational taxation laws and a refusal by successive Russian and other East European Governments to confront the need for full and genuine economic reform. To take this analysis to its logical extreme, 'extortion' is simply taxation by other means, payment for contract enforcement and security. For this to be true, it needs to be demonstrated that those governments such as Poland, that have carried out the most profound economic reform, suffer least from organized crime. It should be possible to place post-communist states on a continuum, relating crime to reform.

Modern criminologists[32] would argue that organized crime in Western Europe is increasingly market-driven and is no longer, even if it ever was, a simple pyramidical structure, but a set of functional networks. Organized crime in post-communist societies partially reflects this development but also involves a complex set of relationships that interpenetrates legal society and perform a number of state-replacing roles like providing employment, services, access to goods not available for roubles or other local currencies and, indeed, replaces legal businesses because it is the sector most involved in the global economy. Its structures are thus more a response to world market forces rather than local, regional or national ones.

The present structure of civil society and its relation to organized crime reflects the juxtaposition of the former Communist states and the EU. The latter's huge wall of protective tariffs and the soft currencies of the former result in a situation where there is no legal way of satisfying a high proportion of consumer demand in the former Communist countries.[33] With no hard currency the choice is either to steal the goods required or get somebody else to steal it and set up a trade relationship such as exchanging prostitutes for stolen cars.

Comparison is required with Italian and US cities with major organized crime problems. It may be that there is a city, rather than a national basis for this phenomenon. There may be areas of cities, earlier referred to as 'high-crime districts' which have a different structure of civil society to that prevailing in the society as a whole. This may relate to a refusal by central government to encourage the development of autonomous local government structures or to a refusal of the middle classes and commercial undertakings to pay the taxation required to fund local services adequately. Analysis of this area is vital before implementation of Community Policing and Problem Oriented Policing Strategies. Any such strategy has to be integrated into an overall framework of policies aimed at the development of civil society itself.

Borrowing a final concept from Gramsci, there will be no successful policy against organized crime that does not confront the question of establishing the hegemony of an ideology based upon the rule of law and the acceptance of the right of the state to

---

[31] Lotspeich, n. 6 above.
[32] Van Duyne, n. 21 above; D. Gambetta, 'Inscrutable Markets' (1994) 6 *Rationality and Society*, pp. 353–368; Tupman, n. 5 above; Tupman, n. 21 above.
[33] W. A. Tupman, 'Supranational Investigation after Amsterdam. The *Corpus Juris* and Agenda 2000' (1998) 7 *Information & Communications Technology Law*, pp. 85–102.

tax the citizen in return for the provision of services.[34] It may be that the ideology of organized crime is the ideology of the future and that organized crime has an important role to play in creating opportunities for profit that will become legal businesses. It may also be the case that organized crime has a fundamental role to play in destroying the nation state and moving capitalism on to a total world market. Crime changes its nature constantly. Strategies will be developed by multi-nationals, police services etc., to cope with these rapidly changing situations. There will be constant attempts to disrupt criminal organizations and these strategies will also be used to disrupt political organizations critical of governments and multi-national corporations.

The relationship between organized crime and society is increasingly complex. Individuals move between legality and illegality hourly in their daily lives. Free-marketeers argue that this is an inevitable consequence of state interference with the free operation of the market. Such socialists as still raise their heads above the parapet argue that capitalism is only legalized crime. There are no quick fixes. Yet hegemony and civil society are concepts whose time has come to assist in the creation of a more complex strategy to deal with organized crime and the communities it controls. A strategy that does not develop civil society as part of the struggle against criminality is a short-term strategy doomed to failure.

---

[34] S. Hall *et al.*, *Policing the Crisis: Mugging, the State, and Law and Order* (Macmillan, London, 1978), p. 208 et seq.

Index